WORKING
WITH
WINSTON

The Unsung Women
Behind Britain's Greatest Statesman

CITA STELZER

Foreword by Randolph Churchill

HEAD
of ZEUS

First published in the UK in 2019 by Head of Zeus Ltd

Copyright © Cita Stelzer, 2019

The moral right of Cita Stelzer to be identified as the author
of this work has been asserted in accordance with the
Copyright, Designs and Patents Act of 1988.

9 7 5 3 1 2 4 6 8

A catalogue record for this book is available from
the British Library.

ISBN (HB): 9781786695864
ISBN (E): 9781786695857

Typeset by Adrian McLaughlin

Printed and bound in Great Britain by
CPI Group (UK) Ltd, Croydon CR0 4YY

Head of Zeus Ltd
First Floor East
5–8 Hardwick Street
London EC1R 4RG

WWW.HEADOFZEUS.COM

For Irwin, once again, and always

'Every biographer of a public figure who depends on secretarial help, can only benefit by tracking down those often silent witnesses who sat at the receiving end of their subject's voice, and were witness to the aspirations, short-comings and strivings of public life.'

Martin Gilbert, In Search of Churchill.[1]

'Throughout my work I was conscious of how Churchill's extraordinary productivity depended in such large measure upon those unsung labourers [the secretary shorthand typists] in the Churchill vineyard.'

Martin Gilbert, In Search of Churchill.[2]

'It took a nineteenth-century man – traditional in habit, rational in thought, conservative in temper – to save the twentieth century from itself... Totalitarianism... came and went... And who is the hero of that story? Who slew the dragon?... Above all, victory required one man without whom the fight would have been lost at the beginning. It required Winston Churchill.'

Charles Krauthammer[3]

'Like many others in all parts of the globe, I regard you as the greatest Englishman in your country's history and the greatest statesman of our time, as the man whose courage, wisdom and foresight saved his country and the free world from Nazi servitude.'

David Ben-Gurion[4]

'His genius often outranged lesser mortals, to his cost. This was his fatal flaw.'

Barry Gough[5]

CONTENTS

Foreword by Randolph Churchill   *xi*

Preface by Cita Stelzer   *xv*

1	Violet Pearman	1
2	Grace Hamblin	15
3	Kathleen Hill	47
4	Patrick Kinna	65
5	Jo Sturdee	95
6	Marian Holmes	133
7	Elizabeth Gilliatt	165
8	Lettice Marston	181
9	Cecily 'Chips' Gemmell	195
10	Jane Portal	221
11	Doreen Pugh	259
12	Catherine Snelling	283

Epilogue   299

Appendix 1: Operation Desperate   307

Appendix 2: The black mollies   311

Sources   317

Acknowledgements   319

Notes   323

Bibliography   347

Image credits   357

Index   361

FOREWORD

Randolph Churchill

MUCH HAS BEEN written about my great-grandfather and of the important world leaders, politicians and high-ranking military officers with whom he worked. But to maintain the pace at which he worked as an historian, painter, parliamentarian, cabinet minister and war leader, he required a vast staff. When Churchill strode the world stage, the secretarial and typing staff positions were inevitably filled by women, because during the most notable part of his career most men were in the military or in war service. Many of these female secretaries and shorthand typists, although extraordinarily talented and invaluable to Churchill in enabling him to live and work a full life with as little friction and annoyance as possible, remain unheralded.

Helping Churchill to persevere was a small army of hard-working, skilled women whose stories have come to light in a series of oral histories stored in the wonderful archives at Churchill College, Cambridge. Cita Stelzer has mined this source, giving us a view of my great-grandfather only hinted at in scattered journals until now. This is not a report on how Churchill behaved under the glare of publicity, nor when on his best behaviour dealing with his generals and allies. This is Churchill at work, as seen, day-to-day, under severe stress from outside events and self-imposed deadlines to produce the vast volume of histories that he somehow managed to compose during his Wilderness Years, as prime minister during the war, as Leader of the Opposition, and once again as prime minister. Here also is Churchill at play, usually painting – and all beautifully described by Stelzer.

That his work habits were eccentric there is no doubt. Stelzer describes the start of every day: a meeting in his bedroom promptly at 8 a.m. to read the papers and dictate his famous 'Action This Day' memoranda on everything from the conduct of the war to the bricks he would need for his next construction project. Secretaries scribbling, military officers talking, a budgie flying about and landing on any available head, including his own, cigar lit, cats being petted, telephone ringing – a veritable circus. All managed with calm precision over the years by a succession of women whose talents Stelzer so well describes.

These women somehow managed to have a complete office set up for Churchill wherever he travelled. Work never stopped and these exceptional women never stopped 'taking down', as it was called, keeping him in control of the government. Churchill was demanding; everything had to be ready whenever he arrived, things organized just as they had been at his beloved Chartwell and in Downing Street. And at home, fish had to be fed, dogs walked, financial records kept, appointments made and unmade, travel plans set and re-set.

And he could be impatient at times. But because any flashes of impatience were immediately followed by a smile and a soft word, these women adored him. Years after their employment ended they would come back to help their replacements in moments when the work became unmanageable.

I was really touched to be asked to write this foreword. The Churchill family can never repay the debt that we owe those remarkable ladies that supported my great-grandfather. It has been wonderful to know some of them as friends.

I had the particular privilege to know from a young age the wonderful Grace Hamblin. Grace worked with my great-grandfather and Clementine Churchill from the 1930s to the 1960s, thereafter becoming the first administrator at Chartwell. She often recounted to me how, after taking dictation late at night, she would walk through the darkness back to her home in Crockham Hill on unlit paths and return in the morning with the proofs from the night before. It is fair to say that Grace and many others dedicated their lives to Churchill. I asked Grace why she did the remarkable work she did and the impossible hours. She said: 'We all knew that what Winston was doing was so important we felt compelled to give him that support.' Lady Williams – Jane Portal as she was then – and others still provide a great link with Churchill. In 2016 at the Sir Winston Churchill Award Dinner in London the late, great Robert Hardy recited Churchill's eightieth birthday speech in Westminster Great Hall. Jane, who attended the dinner, was completely taken aback as she had typed that speech and gone through all the proofing with Churchill.

This dedication to the Churchill family continues to this day. In 1964 Nonie Chapman came to help Lady Churchill. She continued working for Clementine until her death in 1977, whereupon Nonie worked for Lord and Lady Soames until Mary died in 2014. Not being one to retire, Nonie is now found volunteering at Chartwell on a regular basis. She had helped Clementine set up Chartwell for the public opening and now joins the 400 volunteers who lovingly care for Churchill's legacy and make every visit to Chartwell so special.

I am thrilled that the spotlight is being put on these remarkable women who played their full part in preserving our freedom by ensuring the lion's roar was heard.

PREFACE

———

E VERY HISTORIAN IS obliged to explain why still another book about Winston Churchill, adding to the thousands already published, can contribute to our knowledge and understanding of this great man. My answer is that this book captures the man as seen by a group from whom we have heard very little – the women who worked for him and made his life and work so productive and important. From other studies we know, as historian Geoffrey Elton has said, that Churchill was quite simply a great man; or as Pulitzer Prize-winning columnist Charles Krauthammer put it, the indispensable man; or as Churchill himself put it, a glow-worm among the more ordinary worms. We know, too, what the famous thought of him: a man with whom it was fun to share the same decade, according to Franklin D. Roosevelt; a man who could be good to work with if he avoided hooey, according to Harry S. Truman; the greatest Englishman of our time, according to Clement Attlee, the leader of the party committed to defeating him at the polls; the true victor of the Second World War, according to Charles de Gaulle.

These are examples of the three broad sources on which we rely for our opinion of Winston Churchill. The first of these was, of course, Churchill himself, a prodigious recorder of his deeds during a long life that led him from cavalry charges to reckoning with the atom bomb, and of political battles that included just about everything – abdication, India's status, Irish home rule and all of the events in which he participated in his long life. The second source of information is provided by professional historians, most notably Sir Martin Gilbert in his eight-volume biography and associated documents, and now, Andrew Roberts's monumental biography. Third, we have the diaries and recollections of men – and some exceptional women – whom Churchill regarded either as equals or, more often, as people important to him to impress, or at least before whom displays of unpremeditated bad behaviour would not be in his interest.

That has left largely unaccounted for the experiences and views of the many women who worked for him, who were far from his equals. That gap is what this book intends to fill.

During the course of his career Churchill was served by changing teams of secretaries and shorthand typists who devoted their lives and careers to managing the 'torrent of dictated notes... comments, questions and requests'[1] and the vast volume of his private correspondence, the production of and contractual arrangements for his multi-volume histories that sold more copies than any other twentieth-century historian, according to biographer Andrew Roberts, and his houses, horses, pets, record-keeping and finances, and arrangements for hundreds of thousands of miles of travel.

I call these women (and one man) 'secretaries' only to use the job titles of their time. Today, women of equal talent and willingness to work would have grander titles in recognition of the work they were doing. Kathleen Hill's granddaughter, Georgina Hill, who vividly recalls conversations with her grandmother, tells me that 'Even though her job title was "secretary", it is clear that the job involved much more than just typing. Some of her functions included what we would understand in the modern political world as "chief of staff", "press secretary", "advisor" and "researcher".'[2]

But 'secretaries' or shorthand typists is what they were called in Churchill's day, and so I use that term, even though among other things they had major administrative roles, not least among them organizing major international summits that brought together in often-inaccessible places not only the principal players, but hundreds of military advisors in need of thousands of documents, secure communications facilities, food and, inevitably in those days, alcoholic refreshment.

A very few, most notably Joan Bright Astley and Elizabeth Nel (née Layton), left records of their own experiences in informative and important books. But until the prescient Churchill Archives intervened and arranged for many of these women to provide oral histories of their days with Churchill, we had no record of the daily experiences of many of these women in the service of a great, impatient, multi-tasking (to use a word not in currency during Churchill's years) man. Churchill wanted what he wanted when and where he wanted it and was unembarrassed to make unusual requests. A stewardess on a BOAC flight reports that 'Sir Winston handed me a pair of velvet-monogrammed slippers and asked me to warm them up... The head steward... put them in the oven... Twenty minutes later he returned the slippers cracked and curling up at the toes, on a silver tray... Churchill looked up with a wry smile and said that was rather a silly idea.'[3]

The women whose oral histories are on deposit in the Archives[4] served him through his Wilderness Years, long before the Second World War, during the triumphs and tragedies of his years in government, during his country's darkest and finest hours, and during his long search for lasting peace in the years of the Cold War. They saw him when he woke in the morning and went to bed the following morning. And all hours in between, since he was determined never to be without a secretary in case he wanted to commit his thoughts and commands to paper – immediately. They were with him, pad, pencil and at times typewriters at hand when he was building a wall at his beloved Chartwell, at the races cheering his horses to victory, facing off against an angry Stalin, negotiating a truce in the Greek civil war with shells flying around them, and with him travelling to Fulton, Missouri, to work on his speech warning of the descent of an Iron Curtain across Europe. In short, they are supremely qualified to provide insight into how Churchill was able to accomplish as much as he did, and what Churchill revealed of himself to his subordinates when in full work flow, a subject to which I return in the Epilogue.

The women (and one man) whose stories are told here quite literally made Churchill's achievements if not possible, at least far easier to achieve than they would have been in their absence. Listening to these first-hand accounts of working with Winston makes one realize how much can be missed when restricted to mere pieces of paper. These women had perfect, rather posh English accents, as that phrase was understood years ago. One secretary thought she had been hired because of her 'convent-learned accent'. All were highly intelligent and superbly organized, and, somehow, in an age when educational opportunities were not widely available to women, well educated, several at high-level secretarial colleges. All knew how to spell all the words in Churchill's enormous vocabulary, or at least most of the time. All were capable of coping with dictation from a man who often insisted they do so under trying conditions. And they all had excellent memories, helpful in coping with his myriad and varied requests. All jumped at the opportunity to trot off to the library to fetch books he requested or to find special paints. Listening to their tales of working with Churchill, one could hear their command of the language, both its range and its 'music', as one of them, Kathleen Hill, called it when describing Churchill's speeches. What they did not have was Churchill's command of history, and they knew nothing of the speeches he had delivered before many of them were born or became adults – something their boss at times found truly incredible, and rather annoying when this gap in their knowledge interfered with their ability to take down his dictation.

You can hear in their voices the self-confidence that allowed them to serve without being servile, to approach Mrs Churchill when her husband was being most unreasonable, to prepare a jokey request for nylons and cosmetics during rationing, to remain poised and able to work when confronted with a boss in his bed or his bath, military officers in the room or on the phone, dogs and cats roaming around, a budgie perching on their heads, cigar smoke billowing, telephones ringing. It was that self-confidence that permitted them to endure a rather unnerving initiation into what Churchill called his 'Secret Circle'.

When they were first introduced to their new boss, he looked them over and immediately began dictating. If the result was not to his liking, a mini-explosion resulted, perhaps a result of genuine frustration, perhaps contrived as a trial by fire. It took more than a little self-confidence and a great deal of resilience to pass that test.

I was also impressed by the shrewdness of their observations of their taskmaster and enchanted by the good nature with which they told their tales, chuckling at the recollection of amusing events; their sweetness of tone when calling him, as they almost all did – but not to his face, of course – 'The Old Man'. Notable, too, is the lack of animosity when describing how Churchill's driving ambition and work habits often made their personal lives difficult. Or of the times when his behaviour reflected his work-first, worker-second priorities. The usual response to rebukes was to blame themselves and avoid the great man's presence until the storm blew over, as it inevitably and quickly would, the glower or criticism replaced with a smile or a bit of praise of some later work well done. All left Churchill's service still loyal, available to their successors for advice, and willing to show up to lend a hand on occasions such as birthdays, when the volume of correspondence was overwhelming. All take satisfaction from looking back on a career that enabled Winston Churchill to live and work so successfully with as little friction and annoyance as possible.

These women lived in a time very different from our own. They understood and accepted the social and class distinctions characteristic of the employer–employee relationship – late-night work did not often result in an invitation to dine with the family or Churchill's guests, even though they had to wait until dinner and the inevitable round of brandy, cigars and films concluded so that they could resume work with him. Unanticipated demands were to be met without discussion, no matter the resulting personal inconvenience. No line was drawn between taking dictation and walking the dogs or feeding the fish or helping Churchill to prepare for bed. It is a marked contrast with today's sharp demarcation between secretarial chores and fetching coffee.

They were acculturated. They knew most of the names of the rich and famous with whom Churchill corresponded; they knew that seating at a dinner was guided by rules not to be treated lightly; that rank had its privileges; they knew whom to call if they needed information not readily to hand. When they did not know the answer to one of Churchill's questions, they knew the correct response was 'I don't know, but will find out.' They understood when to allow the Churchill family its privacy and when to fade into the background if photographers were present. They understood the need for discretion, and not only in wartime when the importance of absolute secrecy was made clear to them; they, who were privy to all the great secrets of the war, including all the details of the planning and date for D-Day. They knew the sort of dress appropriate to an office: no need to make a dress code explicit, except for a warning that white gloves were in order when meeting royalty. And, of course, they were top-notch stenographers and typists, crucial when working for a man who 'could talk a book better than write one and he often got through three or four thousand words a day'.[5]

And they were drawn from a work pool of women with similar values and expectations. Yes, some of these women were brought up overseas, some came from homes on the upper end of the middle class, some were less fortunate. But all seemed to feel comfortable working with each other – no back-biting, no begging off assignments deemed unpleasant. In such cases trades could easily be worked out with colleagues with different preferences, in order that Churchill's work could be accomplished seamlessly. Indeed, cooperation was so smooth that to Churchill these women were almost interchangeable parts. He cared very little which secretary responded to the call 'Miss', so long as it was a familiar face. Over the years he maintained his work habits and schedule unchanged – it was his staff, not Churchill, that did the adapting.

Of course, we cannot ignore the fact that Churchill's secretaries lived at a time and in a country in which opportunities available to men were not available to them. Few had the financial or social resources to obtain a university education, although all clearly had the intellectual equipment to complete successfully degree-granting programmes. For a good many of the years before the Second World War jobs were scarce, good jobs scarcer still, as at least a few of Churchill's secretaries discovered when they occasionally became overwhelmed by his demands and sought other positions. Many women under the pressure of wartime labour shortages came to realize that they were quite capable of 'manning' factories, flying aeroplanes and surviving the rigours of dangerous cross-Atlantic journeys.

As early as 1941 the deeds of some of these shorthand typists/ secretaries were recognized when they received MBEs. Others later received various honours for sacrificing the normal lives of other women to the cause of supporting Churchill in his multiple endeavours, especially during the war. And in many cases, as we will see, an impish grin or a 'beatific' smile was thanks enough.

There is another reason to study the experiences of these extraordinary women. In telling us what it was like to work for Churchill, they also tell us much about the man that we could not learn from his self-descriptions or from reports of those colleagues to whom he had reason to defer, to charm or to heed. We see here, through the eyes of these women – who worked with him in peace and war, in and out of office – what Churchill, a consummate actor, revealed of himself when not on stage, when not performing, when not under the glare of a public spotlight. Or not in a setting in which his behaviour could shape what historians might say about his exploits, his histories. These witnesses tell us how he treated subordinates, women he had no reason to please. It is to their tales to which we now turn.

It is not surprising that many of these attractive and talented women married, during or after their work with Churchill. I have chosen to use the names by which he knew them.

1

Violet Pearman

'I have watched this famous island descending
incontinently, fecklessly, the stairway
which leads to a dark gulf.'

Winston Churchill, 24 March 1938

'Thank God, our navy has you with your heart of gold
to lead "our hearts of oak and jolly tars."'*

Violet Pearman, 28 February 1940

---

* Words from the official march of the Royal Navy.

VIOLET PEARMAN SERVED as Winston Churchill's personal secretary from 1929 until 1938, when she was forced by illness to retire.* She continued to work for Churchill on a part-time basis at her home near Chartwell until her death in 1941, from the effects of a stroke. Grace Hamblin, one of those who worked under Pearman, later reflected in a letter to Sir Martin Gilbert:

> In appearance she was tall and striking. She seemed to me to work like a Trojan – fast and furious, without stopping. I have never come across anyone who typed so fast! She was always surrounded by papers – a pile of 'work to do' on one side and a pile of 'work done' on the other. She ran up and down stairs. Sir Winston referred to her as Mrs P. She was devoted to him, and very loyal. She seemed to be in charge of every single thing – not anything special – just <u>everything</u>![1]

Pearman's service came at a difficult time in Churchill's life, his so-called 'Wilderness Years', during which he pined for but did not receive a cabinet post. This was also a time in which, like other investors caught up in the Great Depression, he lost a great part of the wealth he had acquired not by inheritance, but by hard work. To make matters worse, during the Pearman years Churchill suffered several serious illnesses, and was hit by a taxi in New York, a serious accident requiring hospitalization.

The relationship between Pearman and her boss was at times a rocky one. At one point she wrote to a Miss Neal, who worked at a firm of secretarial agents (an employment agency) in Bedford Street, London, in search of alternative employment: 'We are all fed up with the hours of work here. In spite of the fact that we arrange matters as we think satisfactorily, and they are approved by Mr

---

* Because Violet Pearman died long before the Churchill Archives existed, we have no oral history. Fortunately, other sources provided sufficient material to allow me to include her in this book.

Churchill, he always breaks them.'[2] This was no overstatement. Churchill's main Private Secretary Jock Colville describes the chaos that surrounded Churchill's movements, 'Trains and aeroplanes would be ordered, but not used. Cabinets and Chiefs of Staff meetings would be summoned at short notice and at inconvenient times… There was a lot of rhyme, especially at meals, but very little reason. Yet the machine worked.'[3] So Pearman had it right, at least in part. It does not seem to have been true that 'We are all fed up.' *She* clearly was. But *others* caught up in the Churchill whirlwind 'loved Churchill as much as they respected his energy and his abilities'.[4]

This would not be the last time that Pearman decided to seek other work with another boss. Several years later, recovering from a serious injury (of which more in a moment), Pearman decided to contact Sir James Hawkey, an important figure in Churchill's constituency. Eight years as Churchill's 'loyal, devoted secretary' was enough, Pearman wrote, and she implored Sir James to find her a post among his 'large circle of friends and acquaintances'. For our purpose, to understand how Churchill was viewed by those who worked for him, Pearman's characterizations are important: thoughtless and self-centred are the most damning, unwilling to allow 'me to live a more human life… I must have a change or something will snap'.[5]

There are several reasons for these occasional outbursts. The first was the workload, created by Churchill's unrelenting drive to publish more, correspond more, speak more, and in effect take time off only when he had so loaded his secretary with work that he was forced to wait for his dictation to be transcribed. Churchill would dictate all morning, then go to lunch, while the secretary transcribed the morning's work. He would then edit it. Then off to dinner, expecting the secretary to be available after dinner and into the early hours of the morning. That might reasonably be considered unreasonable, especially at a time when Churchill did not have the large staff made available to him later in his career. In 1936 Pearman told an interviewer from the *Sunday Express*, 'No hours, no time for hobbies. Believes a secretary's chief value lies in taking burdens from her employer's shoulders.' Pearman was surely correct in believing that her life was not her own. In some part, of course, the problem might have been due to the fact that it is not uncommon for workaholics like Pearman to hoard work, and then become overwhelmed by what lies ahead.

The second cause of Pearman's occasional inability to cope with the stress of her job was outside pressure that at times became difficult for her to bear. She was trapped in an unhappy marriage with a man who had lost both legs in the First World War and was severely shell-shocked, but refused to grant her a divorce. At the same time as she worked for Churchill, she was raising two young children in an age in which personal considerations were no excuse for a refusal to work overtime.

Finally, Pearman's options were limited. The unemployment rate hit 20 per cent in those years, and women who refused to accept domestic work were not eligible for the benefits that employers often conferred on household staff. Not a happy circumstance. As Pearman pointed out in her letter to Sir James, 'posts are difficult to get, especially when one is 42'.[6] As another talented secretary put it, 'there were more secretaries than jobs in those days'.[7]

Fortunately, these eruptions always proved temporary, in the latter case perhaps because shortly after she wrote to Sir James her workload must have been eased by the hiring of Kathleen Hill, who began work in mid-1937 as the first secretary to take up residence at Chartwell.[8] Pearman's decision to let the storms pass was to the benefit of both parties. She found an exciting employer, who provided steady work during a time when stable jobs were scarce, and Churchill found an indispensable employee, described by Roy Jenkins as 'for a decade, beginning in 1929... Churchill's principal and dedicated dictating and literary secretary... ever accompanying'.[9] Churchill was well aware of Pearman's competence and did not hesitate to recognize it publicly. 'I ought not forget to add,' he wrote in a newspaper column, 'that since I have looked into my dispatch box and I have found that my far-seeing private secretary in England, Mrs Pearman, had furnished me with a travelling address book of people I might want to communicate with in the United States, and in this I read "Baruch, 1055 Fifth Avenue", with the private telephone number duly set out.'[10]

Pearman performed two very distinct functions for Churchill. The first were what he, but few others, viewed as ordinary secretarial chores, the tasks that kept his life in order and his output at an astonishingly high level, both in quality and quantity. Pearman worked mostly at Morpeth Mansions, the Churchills' London penthouse,[11] and at Chartwell. Churchill, no longer a member of the cabinet, was eager to make up for the ministerial salary he would no longer be getting and embarked on what for anyone else would be called a writing frenzy, making up for the lost salary many times over.

The time shuttling between Morpeth Mansions and Chartwell was put to good use. Pearman took dictation from him and often typed in the car between the two houses, a Churchillian habit of a lifetime that proved a considerable problem for Mrs Pearman and her successors, especially since Churchill often urged his driver to make good time between destinations. As his driver from 1928 to 1936 reports, 'We had close calls on the road. The kind of driving he demanded made this inevitable.'[12]

Pearman not only had to attend to Churchill's secretarial needs when he was in Britain, she also had to arrange for those needs to be met when he was travelling alone without her. She knew that on his tour of the United States and Canada it would be important to arrange for secretarial assistance. It is not clear that she initiated the arrangements, but that is likely the case. In any event, the private railway cars made available by the Canadian Pacific Railway for the Canadian leg, and by Charles Schwab for the US portion of the trip, came equipped with the loan of secretaries in both countries.[13] As Churchill wrote to Mrs Churchill: 'This is a gt [sic] boon as I don't know how I shd [sic] dictate correspondence, telegrams etc. without this help.'[14]

There seems to be no systematic list of the variety of chores Pearman performed for Churchill. We do know that she was among the earliest to attempt to curb his expenses. In the mid-1930s she 'suggested losing three of the servants to save wages of £240 a year; reducing the swimming pool temperature to halve heating costs; pruning the £240 annual laundry bill, and, boldest of all, recommended that the expenditures on wine and cigars should be "investigated"'.[15] Perhaps the best summary is provided by Martin Gilbert: 'His personal, political, literary and financial correspondence was all within her compass. Her discretion was absolute.'[16]

Pearman performed another and more delicate role for Churchill. If Churchill had allowed the various difficulties Pearman encountered to result in her resignation, he undoubtedly could have found a skilled secretary to replace her, although finding one with her range of talents would not have been easy. But he would be unlikely to have found one who could help him in his efforts to awaken Britain to the threat posed by Nazi Germany.

Pearman's belief in Churchill's lonely drive to inform the nation of Britain's lack of preparedness for the inevitable conflict with Germany took her far beyond the role one would normally ascribe to a secretary. She became the trusted intermediary between Churchill and insider sources of information – 'leakers' in today's jargon – providing Churchill with information and data about the diminished state of the nation's armed forces.

That role began in the spring of 1936, when Pearman had a bad fall at Chartwell, while, as was her habit, she was rushing to do a chore for Churchill. She slipped on a polished floor, caught her heel on a rug and fell against a stone fireplace, hitting her head on the metal fender. She broke a bone at the base of her spine and was ordered to rest.[17] Churchill's letters of 23 and 30 March reveal two sides of the man. He compassionately ordered her to stay in bed, generously told Hamblin, her assistant, to send Pearman salary cheques 'as required', and offered to pay for any 'extra treatment you may require'.[18] But in one he writes, 'Let me know when you are able to do any typing', and in the other he tells her 'Do not worry about typing for the present', which might remind her to do just that, worry – Churchill's 'for the present' perhaps meaning that at some point she should indeed start worrying.[19]

Pearman was not idle while recuperating. In May she set in train a series of events of great importance to Churchill. Before returning to work after her fall and travelling to the south of France with him in September of 1936, Pearman met Torr Anderson, who at the age of forty had had a long and distinguished military career and was then a squadron leader (and later group captain) in the air arm of the military. Sir Martin Gilbert describes Anderson as an 'able, anguished soul'.[20] Pearman, who Gilbert notes was 'attracted by' Anderson, knew that his concerns were identical to Churchill's, and that Churchill did not have good information on the condition of the air arm. So she wrote a note to her boss:

> A serving Air Force officer would like a talk with you very soon... as a serving officer you would appreciate his position. He did not wish to write but thought a talk was better. Would you speak to him tomorrow, if possible? He would come to the Flat or the House.* He would confidently say you would be much interested in what he has to say. When can he come and see you?

Pearman then added the officer's name and contact details.[21] The meeting was held and Anderson, like others in the military and government, provided Churchill with valuable data, memos and other information about the state of Britain's air arm and of the German build-up. It is probable that Pearman 'encouraged Anderson to do what he had done'.[22] We do know that many of Anderson's memos, in which he referred to Churchill as 'Papa', were dictated to Pearman.[23] She understood the work Churchill was involved in, shared his goals, and was confident and able enough to step in when she thought it useful or necessary to help Churchill pursue them.

And she had the complete confidence of Anderson and others

---

* The 'Flat' was Morpeth Mansions, the 'House' was Chartwell.

who were passing on to Churchill the data and information he needed for his campaign to awaken the nation to an impending threat. These officers provided that information via back channels – meaning Pearman – who was a hugely important conduit between Churchill and those willing to jeopardize their jobs and careers by leaking data to support his then-unpopular position that Britain was unready for a war and that it would eventually have to face German military might. 'By the autumn of 1937 Churchill's sources of information on defence had become widespread, regular and of high quality.'[24]

That confidence in Pearman's discretion and loyalty was essential to this clandestine operation, in which the sources of information always feared discovery. Pearman warned Churchill that Anderson and several others providing data were worried that the leaks might be traced back to them. She wrote to Churchill: 'Commander [sic] Anderson told me very seriously that he had never been frightened in his life before... He does not know whether they are suspicious of him and may try to trace him. The figures are accurate and so accurate and staggering, that he thinks this is the reason those who know are frightened of facts coming out.'[25] The 'revelation of British weakness in the air was known only to a handful of senior Air Force officers, and now, thanks to Anderson, it was known to Churchill'.[26] And their source was known to Pearman.

Pearman was more of a participant in the operation than a mere conduit of information. Fearful of being discovered, Anderson telephoned Pearman, and she related the call to Churchill, writing

> please do not <u>use</u> what he gave you on Sunday. Bear the facts in mind and say if you like that it had come to your ears but do not show the copies to anyone... He said <u>himself</u> that you were not to think he was not 'balanced', because he was so pessimistic. I explained that I had said this was because he brooded too much owing to his lonely life, therefore being thrown back into his thoughts and worries, and he agreed this was so.[27]

This is more than a robotic stenographer or keeper of the diary at work; it is a trusted co-conspirator providing her own interpretation of events, and soothing words for a very nervous source.

Anderson feared not only discovery, but that he might be ignoring his loyalty to his service. In typically sensitive fashion, Churchill understood his dilemma. One day, still lying in his bed, Churchill told Anderson: 'I know what is troubling you. It is loyalty to the Service and loyalty to the State. You must realize that loyalty to the State must come before loyalty to the Service.' Anderson explained that 'Churchill brought me into the family life at Chartwell. He did it to protect me. He could then say – he is a member of the family.'[28]

Recovered from the effects of her fall, and while the covert operations remained in full swing, Pearman returned to work in August of 1936, writing letters under her own name to Churchill's proof-reading editor Charles C. Wood regarding delivery of the third volume of *Marlborough: His Life and Times*. Wood was not popular with the secretaries[29] and was famous for picky editing and disagreeing with Churchill on the use of commas, rather like Churchill's friendly, ongoing disagreement over the use of commas with his secretary and friend, Sir Edward Marsh. Because Wood was a superb proof-reader, Churchill had him apply that talent to *A History of the English-Speaking Peoples*, *The Second World War* and *Marlborough*. From then on, Churchill used the phrase 'wooding' 'for the process of proof-reading'[30] and Wood's 'green pen' became famous among the teams working with Churchill.[31]

No account of Pearman's responsibilities would be complete without reference to the several trips on which she accompanied Churchill, so that work could continue at its relentless pace, even on those billed as vacations.

Pearman accompanied Churchill on his trips to France – where vacations included an astonishing output. Her chores included handling requests that originated with Mrs Churchill, who, while en route by ship to America to visit her son Randolph, wrote one of the detailed letters the couple exchanged when apart, concluding with a request that he 'let Mrs Pearman copy suitable portions & send them to [their daughters] Sarah at Broadstairs & Diana in London.'[32] When they were in the same house such letters were marked 'via House Post'.[33]

With Mrs Churchill home from America, the Churchill family decided to decamp to France in August of 1931 for a month-long vacation, as they called the working holidays of which Winston was fond. Then, and indeed until the end of his life, he needed a secretary (or two) along to facilitate his work, which at this time included 'final proofs of the Eastern Front [a chapter in *The World Crisis*] and further chapters on Marlborough',[34] the latter a project that was in the process of ballooning from its planned two-volume, 90,000 words to be completed in five years,[35] into four volumes containing almost 800,000 words, which took ten years to complete,[36] at which time Pearman was still working for Churchill, although at home, from where she organized the final research teams and editing of Volume 4.

And we do have another glimpse of the varied nature of her chores from reports of Pearman's trip with Churchill to France and on the extensive tour of the Middle East that followed in the summer of 1934. This was only a few months after the letter in which she complained about her working conditions and appealed to Miss Neal to find alternative employment for her. Pearman travelled with Churchill to Chateau de l'Horizon, the home of Maxine Elliott,[37] an American actress famous for establishing and funding a Belgian relief barge that fed thousands of Belgians after the First World War. The house 'was beautifully proportioned, an exquisite white art-deco villa on the French Riviera which acted as a collecting point for a group of people who were often world-famous celebrities, many of whom were able to enjoy a life-time of unrelenting pleasure'.[38] Pearman was in charge of 'a large collection of boxes and suitcases', although she undoubtedly had help from Churchill's ever-present valet Sawyers,[39] also along to smooth the way for Churchill, who rarely let the details of every-day life interfere with his work. Or his painting, the pleasure to which he had been introduced by his sister-in-law Gwendoline Churchill in 1915 and which made 'all his cares and frustrations appear to vanish'.[40]

As always, Churchill dictated from around 8 a.m. until noon, in this case working on Volume 3 of his life of Marlborough,[41] then dressed and went down to lunch, while Pearman transcribed the morning's output, the correspondence ready for signature, the memos ready for editing at an opportune time later in the day.

On Christmas Day 1935 Pearman accompanied Churchill to La Mamounia in Marrakesh, Morocco, one of his favourite places – 'The Paris of the Sahara', as he called it – and to which he would return a mere eight years later with Franklin D. Roosevelt in tow as they took a break from the wartime Casablanca Conference. But in 1935 the burdens to be dealt with at Casablanca were not yet worrying Churchill.[42] That left him free to dictate to Pearman 'three draft chapters of Marlborough, sent back to England with Lindemann [Professor Sir Frederick Lindemann, Churchill's scientific advisor], seven paintings completed, much brilliant sunshine, translucent air'.[43] A letter from Churchill to his wife mentions six paintings '[sent] home tomorrow or next day by Mrs P, but do not unpack them till I come; for I want to do the honours with them for yr benefit myself'.[44] Presumably the indefatigable Pearman not only had to transcribe and coordinate the delivery of the chapters, along with several newspaper articles, but to arrange the packing crates for the paintings and their transport, plus all the paraphernalia she needed for her office while abroad. Churchill expected a fully functioning office wherever he went, ready the minute he arrived.

Churchill was still in Marrakesh on 20 January 1936 when he received word that King George V had died at Sandringham. That event would test Pearman's organizational skills. The News of the World, at the time a broadsheet, included 'prominent political and public figures' among its contributors. The editor regarded Churchill as 'the brightest light in a galaxy of star contributors'. He telegraphed, asking for an article on the king for the Sunday, 26 January edition.[45] Churchill, whose relations with the king had often been strained,[46] immediately began to dictate it, while he and Pearman were en route by train to Tangier for the flight home.[47] She typed the article on the Moroccan train and arranged to have it telegraphed from Tangier through Paris to London, where it arrived four days ahead of the deadline. Churchill's powers of concentration triumphed over the hectic nature of the trip from Marrakesh to London by car, train and plane, and Pearman's secretarial skills enabled him to meet the deadlines set for him by several media. The editor of the paper wrote to Churchill 'all Fleet Street… considered it to be the best written on that solemn occasion'.[48]

Pearman, of course, not only had to handle the chore of taking dictation and transcribing the eulogy; she also somehow had to find time when Churchill did not need her at his side to make arrangements for shipping all the personal and work materials from Tangier to England. No easy task given the inevitable language and customs problems.

In September 1936 Churchill spent several days in Paris meeting with top French military leaders and politicians en route once again to Chateau de l'Horizon. From there he wrote to his wife that 'I have been painting every day and all day'.[49] Pearman was well enough to accompany him. As usual, Churchill was doing more than painting. He also dictated three articles (out of thirteen commissioned) on 'Great Events of Our Time' for the News of the World, and an article for the Evening Standard entitled 'A Testing Time for France', while finding time to review French military manoeuvres and tour battlefields.

In January 1938 Churchill returned to Chateau de l'Horizon for a month's rest, at least as Churchill defined that term. 'The comfort and convenience of this house are perfect,' he wrote to Mrs Churchill.[50] Pearman arrived one week later, on 9 January, to his immense relief. 'Mrs P arrives here tomorrow so I shall feel less helpless than [when] I am alone.'[51] Being without Pearman for an entire week was almost more than Churchill could tolerate, even though he had spent part of that week at the British embassy in Paris,[52] where secretarial help was certainly made available. For Pearman, by now accustomed to the routine at Maxine Elliott's house, the usual workload began at once: 'letters, forwarded regularly to France from Chartwell and Morpeth Mansions, continued'.[53] She reports in a letter to Lindemann:

> Mr Churchill looks better even for this short change... but the sunshine he expected has, alas, sadly disappointed him... He is working very very hard on his book, *Marlborough*, which he hoped to finish the following month, 'come what may'[54] and has not had time to paint. I am so glad he has come away at last because I think he would have tired himself out at Chartwell. Contrary to our expectations he has not lost a single thing on his journeyings alone and is very pleased'.[55]

This was to be Pearman's last trip abroad with Churchill.

In early 1940, now a part-time employee, she wrote to Churchill:

> If I wrote to you every time to praise and bless you it would be very often, but I refrain except on special occasions from doing so because your mail is already burdened by such letters. But you know that here in Edenbridge [the village, near Chartwell, where she lived] one humble person follows your joys and griefs with a very full heart.[56]

Later that year, at the age of only forty, she suffered a stroke, and was told by her doctor to take several months off.[57] She did remain at home, but continued to work for Churchill from her cottage. He had her doctor come by Chartwell to give him a full report, and Churchill visited Pearman whenever he could manage it. 'Do not overdo the homework,' he advised in a letter in May of 1938. 'I will try to come and see you again either next week or the week after.'[58] Whether Churchill did find the time, we do not know. In 1941 Violet Pearman died. But not before congratulating her former employer on a speech revealing the government's 'appalling lethargy over defence preparations'.[59]

Churchill, who had assured Pearman early on in her illness that she would be paid for the entire year they both anticipated would be required for the full recovery that never came, arranged for her monthly salary of £12 (about £580 in today's money) to be paid to her eleven-year-old daughter Rosemary, presumably for a year, although that is not clear from available reports. And for a further seven years beginning in 1943 he paid £100 annually (over £4,000 in today's money) towards her education,[60] a posthumous recognition of Pearman's efforts on his behalf, perhaps tinged with guilt. In a letter to Pearman, preserved by her daughters and eventually turned over to Sir Martin Gilbert, he said her stroke was 'due I fear largely to yr devotion to my interests & fortune'.[61]*

A new secretary, Mary Penman, was brought in and she now 'did a large share of the night work when *A History of the English-Speaking Peoples* was being dictated. I made many journeys with Mr Churchill in the brown Daimler, taking dictation as we travelled,'[62] continuing the tradition started with Violet Pearman.

---

* Pearman's daughter was not the only individual whom Churchill cared for throughout his life. His former servant in Bangalore, Munuswamy received £5 a year from 1945 onwards, and, after he died, Churchill sent a final £5 to his widow along with a sympathy letter.

2

Grace Hamblin

'a dynamic but gentle character.'

Grace Hamblin, oral history

'[if] his public personality was aggressively masculine;
[there] was a softer, more feminine side.'

A. L. Rowse[1]

'A T THE AGE of twelve, I decided that I would become
private secretary to the Queen,' Grace Hamblin told the
Churchill Archives interviewer. While she understood that
she would be a working woman, she was sufficiently ambitious to
make that working life a successful one by the standards of her
time.[2]

Born in a village near Chartwell on 1 January 1908, Hamblin was
the daughter of a head gardener on a nearby estate.[3] She attended
Crockham Hill Church of England School and graduated from a
secretarial training college. Because she had to care for an ailing
parent, her job search was limited to an area close to home. In
October 1932 she replied to an ad in the local paper for an assistant
for literary work and, to her surprise, got the job, although she had
no literary training and was only twenty-four years old. She was
thrilled to learn that her new place of employment was Chartwell,
which she had known as a child. It had been empty for years before
the Churchills bought it and she and her friends roamed its grounds
and the house, making the place a sort of private playground.

When Hamblin was hired, Churchill had just returned from a
sanatorium where he had recovered from what was diagnosed as
paratyphoid, which he described in a letter to the Duke of Marlborough as 'an English bug which I took abroad with me, and no
blame rests upon the otherwise misguided continent of Europe'.[4]
The hiring process was identical to that used with all of the women
whose careers are related here. Hamblin was interviewed by an
existing staff member – in this case at Chartwell by Mrs Pearman
– and then, as with all the other secretaries, she was sent to see
Churchill, who merely said, '"You're coming to us," and that was it'.

Although Churchill-style interviews were perfunctory, he had
a way of making new employees feel at once part of 'the Secret
Circle', as Churchill called his staff.[5] That, along with the intrinsic
importance of what they were doing, explains at least in part why
they felt such loyalty to him and to his work; and were so willing to extend themselves on his behalf, even when his demands
were what might be considered unreasonable. As Elizabeth Nel

(née Layton), one of Churchill's secretaries during the war, puts it in her wonderfully detailed memoir *Winston Churchill by His Personal Secretary*, 'We of the personal staff were called upon to put forth the maximum effort of which our frames, nerves and minds were capable. I do not think this was only because it was wartime. I believe he has always been a fairly exacting employer.'[6] As we shall see, she was right.

Hamblin recounts a time when Pearman became ill, and she stepped in to cover the work of both of them. 'I got awfully tired so I thought I would ask him if I could have Sunday off and he said yes, of course, my dear. You must be very tired. Do get someone down [meaning hire a temporary secretary]', which she did and spent a day training and working alongside her. On saying good-night to him on Saturday night, she reminded Churchill that she '[would not] be there tomorrow. Miss So and So will look after you, and he was horrified. He said, "oh no". I said yes, you said I might have the day off. "Oh no [he repeated], I thought I would give you the work and Miss would take it from you".' She thinks she had the day off anyway. Hamblin asked for her regular daily wage, 10 shillings (about £1 today), for the extra Sunday work, and Churchill agreed. But he undoubtedly regretted granting that day off. He did not like adjusting to new faces, which Hamblin found odd in a man 'of his calibre' who had held so many political offices and responsibilities. Churchill considered new faces as 'intruders' into his work/family circle. She surmised that 'he did not want to expand his horizons', meaning the inner circle on which he relied to get his work done. That preference for familiar faces would remain with Churchill his entire life, but would have to be sub-ordinated for his need to expand that circle as his workload grew to include the management of a global war.

Holidays were sudden and 'very erratic, [Churchill would say] "you can take a fortnight's holiday as I shan't be here". But we didn't seem to mind.' Hamblin makes no mention of whether she was paid for the time off, or if she ever actually took time off. And of course, during the war, whether working at Downing Street or

Chequers, the prime minister's country house, she had virtually no time off at all, like everyone else. Occasionally, if Mrs Churchill was at Chequers, Hamblin might get a few hours off to go home, which was quite close to Chartwell. In fact, Mrs Churchill was the secretaries' court of appeal when the workload and hours became intolerable. At such times the secretaries felt they could complain to Mrs Churchill, who might 'sometimes say to him you keep the girls too late, or don't be so rude to Hambone.... but we couldn't [say anything directly to him]'. 'Hambone' was the nickname the Churchill children invented for Hamblin, and Churchill, who generally called her 'Miss', as he did the other female secretaries, used that nickname at times, much to Hamblin's disgust: 'From quite an early stage... he would say that awful name.'

Nicknames were common, as Vanda Salmon, another of Churchill's secretaries, explains:

> Either we would hear the cry of 'Miss' from the hall or the telephone would ring and a gruff voice would say 'Come'. The term Miss puzzled me at first because we were known by our Christian names (unusual perhaps then, though all the Royal staff were called by their Christian names.) One day Jo Sturdee [see Chapter 5] said to Mr Churchill, 'You know all our names why do you always call Miss?' Mr Churchill looked over his gold rimmed glasses at her and replied, 'If I call Jo or Lettice or 'Chips' and you are not there no one will come, but if I call Miss then someone will come.' He gave a satisfied smile and returned to business. He had christened me Vanda the Wandering Salmon. He felt that Vanda should be spelt with a W; he also held that I had wandered into his life – hence Vanda the Wandering Salmon.[7]

Hamblin had taken a job with an employer who was not entering the best years of his life. Churchill had been ill, which never improved his temper. And there were what Hamblin calls his 'doom and gloom days' when he acted like a 'bear' to everyone, including family. She attributes this to his worry over the rise of

Germany and his inability to influence or make policy, a period we now call his Wilderness Years. He fought losing battles over policies towards India and Nazi Germany, and, according to Hamblin, the 1936 Abdication Crisis was also of grave concern. She adds that Churchill was very 'tense during that time'. Although he could not see it then, those years he 'spent in the political wilderness meant that he had been spared the physical strains of office. They meant, too, that he had escaped the need to compromise, to which he would have been subject if he had been a member of the cabinet.'[8] But according to Beaverbrook, Churchill also 'suffered tortures when he thought that lesser men were mismanaging the business'.[9]

Hamblin might have added that the world was entering a long Depression, which put pressure on Churchill's always fraught finances, characterized by a constant race for his income from his writing to keep up with his rather lavish lifestyle,[10] which Hamblin tells us included a household staff of some ten or eleven servants at one time.* The value of his investments was not immune to the effects of the Depression, which put him in what one visitor described as 'a very grim mood',[11] and caused his brokers at one point to attempt to curb his stock-market activities with the advice that 'your policy should be... one of masterly inaction.'[12]

That instruction notwithstanding, Churchill continued his lifelong practice of following the prices of his shares on almost a minute-by-minute basis. Hamblin kept track of his share prices, developing a graph form to show movements in the prices of shares he owned. He took to calling for his 'Hamblin Graph', which she took as a compliment. 'He liked to know where they were every hour... we kept a... graph of the prices as they went up and down.'[13] She had to take this graph to him even when he was painting or 'doing something on the lake, [walking] through the

---

* 'I mean there was a butler, and a head house maid, and an under-house maid, and a tweeny, and a footman. And then in the kitchen I think there was a cook and a kitchen maid and a scullery maid, and then there was someone else in the pantry – oh, that would have been a parlour maid... And Sir Winston's valet and a parlour maid and Lady Churchill's lady's maid.'

mud to take him the prices wherever he was. It was very amusing.'
That procedure – giving him notes on his share prices – applied
as well to other information. Everything had to be written down
for him, 'you never told him a thing. He had his news in notes.'*
And of course he always asked for news, so she would hand him
a written note of the news, or a letter or a newspaper, and he was
disappointed if there weren't any.

At least at the beginning of her working life with Churchill
Hamblin had two advantages. The first was that with Churchill
still recovering from his illness, she had a few weeks in which he
was not doing much dictation, perhaps only an hour or so each
day, highly unusual for so prolific an author. As a result – and
unlike those women who joined Churchill's secretarial staff in the
run-up to and during and even after the Second World War – she
could ease into her job. Second, Violet Pearman had been working
for Churchill for four or five years, knew the ropes and was willing
to train Hamblin.

But some things just can't be taught to fill the gaps in the knowledge of a twenty-four-year-old moving into the high-pressure
world of a senior politician born in Blenheim, and moving easily in
the highest reaches of British and international society. Hamblin's
lack of knowledge and experience of the wider world beyond the
narrow confines of her childhood and education resulted in some
moments of embarrassment, and in some not very understanding responses from Churchill. On one occasion, Churchill asked
her to 'get Emerald on the telephone'. But she had no idea who
Emerald was, so Churchill told her: 'Good God, don't you know
who Emerald Cunard is? She was the greatest hostess of the day.'
It is a testimony to the British class system that this young, ten-
shilling-per-day secretary, telling this tale in 1985, still attributed
the episode to her own youth and limited education and experience:
'I ought to have known this. And I was terribly ignorant of politics.'

---

* A boon for historians, as all these notes have been perfectly filed, restored
if need be, and are available at the Churchill Archives.

On another occasion, when Churchill asked her to ring up his dentist, she didn't know who that was. When she asked, he replied, 'It's Mr. Fish who died.' Kathleen Hill tells a similar story, her version involving a request that she dial the number of a doctor whose name she did not know and which Churchill could not remember. Both tales might be accurate, or the two secretaries might have shared favourite anecdotes. Memories conflate after decades have passed. No matter: these retellings present a true picture of Churchill, who, as Hamblin describes him, could be unreasonable and harsh at times.

Although no amount of training could bridge the gap between Hamblin's and Churchill's backgrounds, Mrs Pearman could teach Hamblin lessons that she hadn't learned in secretarial school. First there was the very important matter of the new girl's responsibility for the Churchill menagerie. Hamblin had to help him in what came to be called his Butterfly House, constructed from an old larder: laying out the chrysalises so he could watch as the adult butterflies emerged. He instructed her to leave the door of the Butterfly House open, with a cheesecloth curtain, so the adult butterflies could escape into his Chartwell gardens, saying, 'I am tired of all this captivity.' Churchill's knowledge and appreciation of butterflies began as a child and developed further when he was serving in India, and later on tour in Uganda, where he called them 'flying fairies… with splendid liveries'.[14] To Churchill, his butterflies were just as important as his other creatures: he left specific instructions to the National Trust* for the care of them after he and his wife died. 'I hope the National Trust will grow plenty of buddleia for my butterflies,' he said. Butterflies thrive today at Chartwell on the buddleia-bordered walkway leading to Churchill's Butterfly House.

---

* The National Trust acquired Chartwell in 1946. The necessary funds were provided by a group of Churchill's friends, on the understanding that the Churchills were to be given life tenancy of the property. Lady Churchill surrendered her lease on Churchill's death in 1965 and Chartwell was opened to the public in 1966.

Butterflies were not the only 'pets' for which Hamblin had responsibility. She recalls that in 1931 Churchill developed a device to protect the black swans given to him by the Australians. It was 'a light… to protect them at night. It was a very amateur thing on a bicycle [wheel]. It went round and round and round all night. It was supposed to keep the foxes away but the foxes didn't take much notice and they still burrowed underneath and came up in the water and killed the black swans.' There were the dogs, as well. As early as his teenage years, Churchill had sold a bike in order to buy a bulldog, which he named Dodo. Hamblin describes 'a funny little pug and a Blenheim spaniel, and later of course, Rufus', the black-brown poodle that Churchill loved especially.* As Hamblin was the one taking care of Rufus, especially during long periods when Churchill was away from Chartwell, Rufus became fond of her. When Churchill returned from a trip, he noticed that Rufus went to Hamblin first. He became 'quite cross, [saying] you've stolen my dog's affection'. 'Thereafter,' reports Howells, 'he paid little attention to Rufus; with Sir Winston it was a case of all or nothing.'[15]

When Rufus I died in 1947, Hamblin called Mrs Churchill for advice about how to tell her husband. Mrs Churchill suggested that Hamblin write a note, which she would then hand him. 'When he read it, the tears ran down his face… because he was very emotional… and he said, "poor Miss, she must have a puppy".' This is the compassionate Churchill, saddened at the loss of his favourite pet, but also recognizing that Rufus's death had deeply affected Hamblin as well. So much so that he gave her a puppy, which took up residence on Churchill's bed.

When Rufus's death became known, Mr H. F. Parmiter, the owner of an export/import firm who had no prior connection with Churchill, sent Churchill 300 mixed crocus bulbs with the wish that they be planted on the poodle's grave. Hamblin received the package at Chartwell and minuted Elizabeth Gilliatt (see Chapter 7) that 'as Mrs C saw them and thought that in view of this Mr C

---

*   This was Rufus I. There would later be a Rufus II (see Chapter 9).

ought perhaps to sign a letter of thanks'. Mr Parmiter's 1947 letter adds, 'Further there will be a quantity of May flowering tulips and from the colours thereof – you can have no possible doubt as to how I voted in the last election.'[16]

Then there were the goats. Churchill mourned the loss of

the brown nanny goat named 'Sarah' [who] died by misadventure… [A gardener] scattered some nitrate of ammonia on the grass. She ate it and expired. [But] the white horned nanny goat named 'Mary' survived thanks to a timely dose of castor oil. She is expecting a family… I think it is very important to have animals, flowers and plants in one's life while it lasts.[17]

Alongside butterflies, goats and dogs, cats – a particular Churchill favourite – were another of Hamblin's responsibilities. To this day a yellow marmalade cat named Jock VI* (the descendant of an earlier 'Jock' who was named after Jock Colville) lives at Chartwell. 'Ginger was the favoured colour', Hamblin remembers. The original marmalade cat was called Tango and Colville describes a lunch with the prime minister at which Tango sat on a chair to Churchill's 'right-hand side and attracted most of his attentions. He [Churchill] was meditating deeply on the Middle East'.[18]

Hamblin recalls an unamiable cat that would not respond to Churchill's 'Good morning, Cat', so Churchill threw some papers at him. The cat ran off, as cats will. Churchill predictably became very upset and fretful, blaming himself and Hamblin for the runaway. One night, after the cat had been gone for some ten days, Sarah Churchill came down from dinner and told Hamblin that her father had finished working, and that she could go home, but only after she 'put a card in the window to say that if Cat cares to come home, all [will be] forgiven'. Cat did return, a bit wounded, but very much alive, and was rewarded with 'cream and the best salmon'.[19]

---

* The present-day Jock is a frequent blogger on the Chartwell page on Facebook.

Pets were not the only animals requiring Churchill's and his staff's attention. There was a commercial aspect as well. He farmed lands adjoining Chartwell, raising pigs[20] and Belted Galloway cattle, the latter distinguished by the white stripe around their bellies. Churchill built a pigsty with his own hands, and involved Hamblin's father in the pigs' care. Mr Hamblin 'fixed a wire brush to a long stick and presented it to [Churchill] as a back scratcher for his pig', a gift which delighted Churchill and, no doubt, the pig.[21] When Hamblin's father was ill, Churchill sent him some port.[22] An example of Churchill's 'loving heart', to use Elizabeth Layton's description.[23]

Zookeeping was only one of Hamblin's many responsibilities. Churchill was a builder, a bricklayer, never satisfied with the facilities at Chartwell. Hamblin was charged with the responsibility for ordering the bricks for each project – the number and type – and making certain they were ordered sufficiently in advance of their use, so as not to delay construction. She also had to help with the bookkeeping. Unlike animal care and brick supply, this was a chore for which she had been hired. And with the help of Churchill's accountant Mr Wood* she set up the household accounting system that would remain in use throughout the war years, making Hamblin Churchill's principal in-house bookkeeper from 1932 until his death in 1965, overseeing and managing all the accounts: household salaries and expenses, books and 'pot-boiler' income, and financial and banking records.

The problem was that 'he could not bear to pay bills'.[24] She recounts his unusual but 'lovely delay in action' routine: she would present the household bills for approval and payment. He would then go down the list saying:

'yes, we'll pay that one… we'll pay twenty pounds off that one…

---

* He was called 'Mr Accounts Wood' to distinguish him from C. C. Wood, Churchill's very skilled and truculent proofreader, who was called 'Mr Literary Wood'.

and we'll pay so much off that one'. Then he came to the electricity and said 'that's impossible. It can't be eighty pounds... Look up the same one eight years ago.' Before the war, you see he was not a rich man at all.

In 1956, decades after Hamblin left Churchill's employ, he was still scrambling to pay his bills. According to Sir Martin Gilbert, 'There are three that he [Churchill] had queried, one for wines and spirits (£115, about £8,000 today), one for the wiring of special lighting for paintings in the first-floor corridor (£96, about £6,000 today), and one for clothes and repair of clothes from Turnbull & Asser of Jermyn Street (£105, about £7,000 today).'[25]

Hamblin, always a good manager, did her best to contain Churchill's profligacy, an attempt that was not always rewarded with his approval. She realized that it was impractical to ship his champagne from London to the South of France when he visited there. So she arranged for his champagne to be sent directly to him in France from local suppliers. But when he saw the bill from a French wine supplier he was upset and asked her why he was being billed by a new supplier. She recalled: 'I ought to have said because it is cheaper, but I said... it was the easiest way. He then said: Since when have I asked you do things the easiest way?'[26]

Zookeeping and financial management, important as they were, were not Grace Hamblin's main job. That was to take dictation – 'taking down', as it was called – often until two or three in the morning, from which she was expected to produce flawlessly typed copies of letters and memoranda; and what he called his 'pot boilers', such as a series he wrote for the *Strand Magazine*,[27] which she says he wrote for the money as well as 'for the pleasure of [writing] something down about whatever was going on'. 'He worked like a tiger', she later recalled.[28] More troublesome from her point of view was his biography of his great ancestor, the first Duke of Marlborough, which she found 'dreary and dim', with long unfamiliar names, complicated by Churchill's tendency to skip back and forth in the historical narrative, making it more difficult to follow. The research assistants working on *Marlborough* were often in the room while he dictated, and later added to or corrected the draft. She would then consolidate all these and type them up for Churchill 'to mull over'.

Hamblin's problems were not confined to the times when Churchill was working on his biography of the Duke of Marlborough. Churchill's special dictating style, which remained unchanged throughout his long career, reflected the intensity with which he worked to get his speeches and memoranda to mean precisely what he intended them to mean, and left little room for concern for any difficulties he imposed upon his secretaries. Recalling his dictating habits, Hamblin says he paced up and down while dictating to her shorthand:

> when he got to the end of the room and out of your little circle, his voice would drop very often so that part was not easy... Suddenly he would quote something from a book... and I could never take that down in shorthand... [I'd] try to get a hold of the book [but] you'd find he had taken the book to lunch or something like that. It didn't go smoothly... It was all being turned over in his mind. He went over and over and over sentences and it was for you to decide which was the final one.

Things were even worse when Churchill was on the move. Churchill's secretaries would be driven down from London to Chartwell in the car, with the dog, cigar smoke, typewriters, shorthand pads and pencils, detectives such as Walter Thompson,* rugs and papers and work boxes.† In the late 1940s, this collection in the already crowded car was augmented by a 'beautiful

---

* Churchill's bodyguard Walter Thompson has told his tales of protecting Churchill in several books and television programmes. He married Mary Shearburn, one of Churchill's secretaries. Edmund Murray, who took over the job of protecting Churchill many years later, has also written his autobiography.
† In addition to flowers and vegetables, suitcases and painting equipment.

amaryllis lily', which he insisted be regularly transported between Chartwell and London. The potted plant was given to him by Princess Marina, Duchess of Kent, when Churchill was Leader of the Opposition.[29]

In the car Churchill would dictate just as he would in the quiet of his bedroom. Hamblin and Pearman agreed that Hamblin would make local trips in the car and Pearman would go on the longer trips with Churchill. If the trips for speeches and meetings were near Chartwell, Hamblin would drive her own 'little car'. And of course, if she were driving, Churchill could not dictate to her. As she recalled: '[O]ne could escape that. I think the dictation in the car was a nightmare really.' She often drove him to Blenheim, a place she did not much enjoy. Her recollection of working there was that it was 'bleak and cold and one spent hours and hours in a huge room getting frozen. It seemed to be winter to me. And one was treated by the staff as rather a nuisance.'

To compound Hamblin's difficulties, Churchill did not warn her when he wanted her to go up to London to work. On one such surprise trip from Chartwell she had 'no hat' or anything else. She worked until midnight and then went to a hotel, as the Churchills were staying in Morpeth Mansions, where there was clearly no room for her. He was, she says, a mixture of

kindness and harshness... He didn't like us to leave the house... he didn't like you to just go off. And you would go up to say good night, Mr Churchill, and if it had been a particularly bad day he would say 'good night, my dear, it wasn't your fault.' But of course, it was... There was kindness. He didn't want the sun to go down on harsh words.

She goes on: 'I met... a girl who was working for him a little while before me... when she came to him she was eighteen, pretty, young, fair and dainty... so when he'd seen her, he said to Mrs Pearman "I mustn't be rude to her because she was too gentle and wouldn't take it."'

Not only the working conditions, but the working hours remained unchanged for most of Churchill's life, with an understandable increase during the war. Hamblin usually worked six days a week, at times seven. On some days she took dictation until about 2 a.m., had a short sleep and returned early enough to transcribe her shorthand notes for his review when he woke up. On other days, she would leave around 7 p.m., waiting until her counterpart arrived for night duty. She explains: 'His work was his pleasure... and his hobbies were all part of his life... We had to take part in them all... Sunday was like any other day. We had to be on duty all the time... He liked the world to be busy and something happening all the time.' Hamblin, speaking decades after her work with Churchill, can be forgiven if she recalls both a six-day working week and Sunday labour, which might or might not have been a regular feature of her job.

The peacetime routine that Hamblin describes would continue throughout the war, during which time there were more secretaries to shoulder the burden, working in relays to keep up with the prime minister's massive output as he added direction of the war to his already crowded schedule. But almost everything else changed, abruptly. Churchill's Wilderness Years came to a close on 3 September 1939. He was offered the Admiralty, a post from which he had been removed almost a quarter of a century before, leaving 'in pain and sorrow'.[30] Consistent with what was to become his famous 'Action This Day' policy, learned from Jackie Fisher,*[31] Churchill immediately took up his position as First Lord even before kissing hands two days later. The Board of Admiralty immediately sent its now famous signal to the fleet: 'Winston is Back.'[32]

---

* Admiral Sir John Fisher (known as 'Jackie'), a reformer of the Royal Navy, served from 1911 to 1915 as First Sea Lord when Churchill was First Lord of the Admiralty.

The Churchills moved into the flat at Admiralty House. Weekends at Chartwell would be rare, which had different effects on the Churchills. Hamblin was certain that Mrs Churchill was relieved when Chartwell was eventually put 'to sleep' for the duration of the war as

> it wasn't the sort of house she liked. I always sympathized with her as it was a terribly difficult house to run. Piled up high… she would have liked a lovely low perhaps old-fashioned house… so that you could step out into the garden easily. But in Chartwell you had to come right down the stairs before you were anywhere near the garden. And it was awfully difficult for staff… off the bus route. Nothing to interest them at all.

For Churchill closing up Chartwell was more difficult, but 'he accepted it… his mind was on other things… his great love of Chartwell had to go into the background for a bit.'

Not only was Hamblin to move her work from Chartwell to the Admiralty, she also was to get a new boss. Miss Whyte, a cousin of Mrs Churchill's, brought a message to Hamblin informing her that Mrs Churchill wanted her to work as her secretary, a job in which Hamblin remained until after Churchill's death. Hamblin was, writes Mrs Churchill's biographer, 'beautiful, funny and astonishingly efficient, and she had a knack of knowing what Clementine wanted even before Clementine herself'.[33] Lady Soames, Churchill's daughter, would later describe Hamblin as 'a built-in part of my mother's private and official life, and her devotion, tact, efficiency and charm soon became a byword among all those with whom she had dealings'.[34]

Hamblin recalls that Mrs Churchill loved living in the Admiralty flat and that she 'immediately made it look homey [sic] and pretty… as she could anywhere… [Their] elegant office there was very strange… sort of a round room… lit by pictures which intrigued me a lot. The pictures had lights and there were lights all around the room. Quite the smartest office I'd ever, ever been in.'

Hamblin was not quite so fortunate, at least initially. She moved to London, took a 'poor little room in Pimlico' and lived there until the building was destroyed by German bombs.

In May of 1940, when Churchill moved to Number 10 Downing Street, Hamblin's living conditions improved markedly. She and Kathleen Hill (see Chapter 3) were sharing an office when they heard they were both going to Number 10. 'They formed a ring of roses around the office and gave three cheers.' They moved into 'lovely rooms at the top of the house' at Number 10, a dangerous spot: with the exception of the ground floor, the building was for the most part closed after Number 11 was hit by a bomb, weakening the structure of its neighbour.[35] But the two women 'decided we would rather die straightforwardly than be smothered... we slept happily at the top of No. 10 like two birds nesting.'* She felt no danger because

> you're in very good company and looked after... and it was all so interesting. We were allowed to go into the Map Room if we'd like, to see after a night's bombing... I remember once it had been very very near my home... a matter of yards away. And I felt very worried so I asked Lady Churchill if I might go down to see... if my parents were all right... I think that was the only time.

As usual, Mrs Churchill made Downing Street and the upstairs apartments, their 'nest',

> immediately warm and liveable... instead of stately and unliveable... [using] some of her own furniture... Doing the flowers there was always a great thing, she always had flowers, as you would in your own house... She had the pictures lighted... and had a lot of Sir Winston's own paintings there to brighten it, and always flowers... [She] really had a great flair.

---

*   So close were Hill and Hamblin that Hamblin was asked to be godmother to Kathleen Hill's granddaughter, Georgina Hill.

No complaints from Hamblin, who had to add to her secretarial chores for Mrs Churchill the added jobs of organizing the moves and redecoration, a melding of secretarial and personal chores to which she had become accustomed working for the man who was now the prime minister of a country at war.

When the Churchills moved to the safer Annexe[36] to avoid German bombs, the 'two birds' had their Downing Street nest virtually to themselves, the only other person living there being Winston's brother Jack.

One of Grace Hamblin's important new chores was to help Mrs Churchill hire domestic staff. Hamblin didn't see much of the domestic staff until she went to work for Mrs Churchill, who was ultimately responsible for interviewing and hiring all the domestic staff. Unlike her husband, who simply looked over secretarial candidates who had been recommended to him before having them join his staff, Mrs Churchill and Hamblin wrote descriptions of the household positions available, typed them and had them printed in (presumably) *The Lady*, checking references for each, a chore later taken on by Kathleen Hill, who found that task among the least agreeable of those she undertook. Many of the maids came from Wales and Hamblin felt they were

> quite raw in their first post... poor little things... Chartwell was their home so one had to try to make them feel that it was home and that there were some pleasures in life as well as work. I remember I used to [take] them into dances in Westerham... and sometimes they got back very late and had to climb through a window... I remember taking part in that sort of naughtiness.

Hamblin could not have been much older than those girls, for whom she felt considerable empathy, and whom she treated with kindness.

The domestic staff served meals to the secretaries before their number increased beyond the original two. Nothing elaborate: bites between typing. Later, when there were more than two, Mrs

Churchill set up a separate dining room for their own privacy, a few minutes rest and the possibility of making a cup of tea.

Of course, Hamblin was not completely removed from her former boss, who shared every detail of his work with his beloved wife, from whom he kept no secrets. Hamblin often had to interact with the prime minister's staff on diary items, social and official functions and tours, such as those to bomb sites, which both Churchills toured frequently, with Mrs Churchill taking a special interest in the problem of the shelters.

Once ensconced at the Admiralty and then at Number 10, Mrs Churchill began her war work. She concentrated at first on the shelters provided as protection from the German bombing raids. She and Hamblin toured shelters when raids were in progress, because Mrs Churchill was 'very worried about the conditions there… hundreds of people underground and the toilets weren't adequate'. Mrs Churchill spent a good deal of time at different shelters, talking to people and making notes for improvements. Whatever she did, she 'didn't do lightly'.

Mrs Churchill also took on the chairmanship of the Young Women's Christian Association and worked very hard to ensure that hostels for young women were set up all over the country and were properly run, as so many young women had either been bombed out, or were working in factories unable to go home, or, like the Land Girls and Lumberjills, working far from home. Mrs Churchill worked harder and more skilfully than she ever had and 'became much much more active'. During the First World War, she had undertaken volunteer work organizing canteens for munitions workers, 'opening, staffing and running nine canteens, each feeding 500 workers', and ensuring that female workers would also have access to smoking areas on an equal basis with their male co-workers.[37] She read all the letters addressed to her, dictating her responses after discussing the nature of that reply with Hamblin, and then dictated a response.[38]

But Hamblin's position within Number 10 was odd: she was told by a civil servant that she would not have any official status and 'to more or less keep her place'. She took satisfaction from Mrs Churchill's decision to employ her, since Mrs Chamberlain had offered Mrs Churchill her own secretary who knew the Number 10 ropes. But Mrs Churchill: 'with her usual frankness and niceness [replied] thank you very much, but I have a perfectly good secretary of my own'.

There were significant changes in Hamblin's position. She recalls that Mrs Churchill was easier to work for and the hours not quite as long. More important, and of enduring significance, were the changes in her standing within the Churchill family. Hamblin notes that the war changed everything:

> With the war, came an <u>acceptance</u> of people. I can remember that line quite distinctly. Before the war, secretaries were just secretaries. They were there to work and not ever included in the family circle... Perhaps not <u>unkindly</u>, but it just happened that way. But when the war came, you were all more of family... And you were all pulling together.

They were also establishing far less formal relationships. Mrs Roosevelt visited London in late 1942, bringing along her secretary, whom, records Hamblin, 'she called by her Christian name and Lady Churchill was obviously quite knocked out by this, because in those days we didn't use Christian names. I was always Miss Hamblin. Lady Churchill said to me one day: "Mrs Roosevelt calls her secretary Della or whatever it was. I think I shall call you Grace."' With this wartime relaxation of some of the formality, it was only natural that Hamblin and her boss should become friendlier, or as close as anyone could get to Mrs Churchill. Churchill never called Hamblin anything but 'Miss', or rarely 'Miss Hamblin', although he inscribed a photo 'to Grace from Winston', but he never said it.

Class barriers were breaking down across Britain. In late 1940 Churchill commented on 'the disappearance of the aristocracy from the stage and their replacement by the excellent sons of the lower middle class. [And] referring to the RAF pilots, he noted 70% of them came from Elementary Schools and professional classes. "They have saved this country, they have the right to rule the country."[39]

A more exciting change for Hamblin was the opportunity to accompany Mrs Churchill on several overseas trips. When working with Churchill, Hamblin almost had an opportunity to take her first trip out of Britain.

> He was very very tired and he was going to rest... going for a holiday in South America and he was going to take me... he wasn't going to take a valet. He said if I could look after his socks he'd be quite happy. He was going to paint and would I just look after his pallet. No serious work.

Hamblin, still new at her job, probably did not realize the sheer implausibility of that latter statement. Churchill gave her £10 (about £650 today) to buy appropriate dresses – she called it her trousseau – for a trip 'first class on one of the big liners'. She was then making £3 a week (about £198 today). Alas, it was not to be. The trip was cancelled twenty-four hours before they were set to sail, because of the Abdication Crisis and his work in the House of Commons. But she did keep the £10.

And later she did get to the South of France. Once, in the early days of her working for Churchill, she stayed behind at Chartwell while he vacationed in the Midi. Quite unexpectedly he cabled her: 'Bring me the papers on India and some cobalt blue.' She noted: 'Bring – not send – and I who had never been out of the country had to obey.'[40] That is what it was like working for Churchill.

Hamblin's experience with Mrs Churchill was entirely different. In August 1943, when Mrs Churchill joined her husband on a trip to attend the first Quebec Conference (codenamed Quadrant), Hamblin was 'lucky enough' to accompany Mrs Churchill aboard the *Queen Mary*. It was Hamblin's first time crossing the Atlantic, and 'lovely, lovely to go on the sea, zigzag all the way to avoid anything that might be lurking there'. Her enthusiasm was not dulled by the fact that the great liner, built to carry 2,000 passengers in the height of luxury, had been remodelled to handle 15,000 troops: the Grand Salon had been turned into a mess hall to feed the troops in twenty-minute shifts, and the Art Deco pool had been drained to accommodate bunks.[41] Her work for Mrs Churchill was not too onerous, although 'masses of letters to her... telling her to tell the prime minister so-and-so... and all the letters wanted acknowledging... I went sightseeing when other people did and so it was great fun.' These journeys abroad were 'breaks... [from] the bombing and the monotony of war'. We know that Marian Holmes (see Chapter 6), who was also there working for Churchill while Hamblin tended to Mrs Churchill, managed to find some time to shop for nylons, clothes and to go dancing one night. It is not unreasonable to suppose that Hamblin joined in a bit of the fun.

It must be remembered that the women were coming from a Britain in which rationing of just about everything was common. Nevertheless, they maintained their senses of humour. In a famous memo marked 'Most Secret – Burn Before Reading' (see Appendix 1) addressed to the War Cabinet and labelled 'Operation Desperate', the Joint Planning typing pool laid out its requirements for 'vital commodities'. To avoid 'extreme embarrassment' US Resources should be tapped to supply silk stockings (size 10½, Mist Beige), chocolates (large), and cosmetics (powder, lipstick, creams). If those demands are not met, one of the signatories intends 'to remove all my normal clothing and substitute for it a complete covering of silk stockings'.[42]

The shortages to which Mrs Churchill addressed her efforts, before and after the Quebec trip, were of a more serious nature. Her war work began with such efforts as organizing the knitting, collecting and distribution of 'sea boot stockings',* a task at which she excelled and would repeat, with greater political complications,

---

* Long woollen socks meant to be worn under boots, and not just at sea.

when she took over the British Red Cross Aid to Russia Fund in October 1941. But the tasks quickly expanded, which resulted in an expansion of her staff; this made it a bit easier to work at Downing Street and to interact with Number 10 staff.

After Hamblin and Mrs Churchill returned from the Quebec trip in 1943, Mrs Churchill was assigned her own Number 10 staff and Hamblin quickly learned which 'particular [male private] secretary to go for answers that Mrs Churchill required in order to respond to the thousands of letters she received, championing many causes'.[43] But before the year ended she was off again with Mrs Churchill, this time flying to 'Carthage in 1943 when Sir [sic] Winston was so ill', and then on to Marrakesh for his convalescence. Hamblin recalls, 'I was not in his [and Mrs Churchill's] plane but in the one that the door fell off in the middle of the desert which was a terrifying experience'. Hamblin did manage to have 'three lovely weeks in Marrakesh, never to be forgotten' while the prime minister convalesced.

Perhaps the most memorable of all the trips occurred in 1945, when she accompanied Mrs Churchill to Moscow. When Hitler violated the Molotov–Ribbentrop Pact in June of 1941 by invading the Soviet Union, Churchill famously said of his former Bolshevik bête noire, 'If Hitler invaded hell I would make at least a favourable reference to the devil in the House of Commons.' Mrs Churchill threw herself into work supporting Britain's new ally. In October 1941 the Red Cross established an Aid to Russia Fund with Mrs Churchill as its chairman[44] and began raising funds for Britain's newest ally. By 'Christmas that year she had already raised £1 million pounds, [recruiting] factory workers, millionaires and widows, she organized auctions, flag days and galas and per-suaded celebrity musicians to give concerts'.[45] Hamblin was Mrs Churchill's principal aide, secretary and organizer for all these endeavours. By 1945 the Appeal had raised some £8 million pounds (about £300 million today) and the Russian Red Cross invited her 'to go and see the hospitals her fund had equipped… and she said she could take me,' added Hamblin, 'which was lovely!'* Of course, the Soviets had to approve her travelling with Mrs Churchill. As the prime minister saw them off in his own 'beautiful' Skymaster plane, he 'kissed Hamblin and said to her: "You will take good care of her?"', surprising Hamblin with that show of emotion.

En route to Moscow, the pair flew south to Cairo to avoid enemy planes, where they stayed with the minister resident in the Middle East, Sir Edward Grigg, whose 'lovely home and spontaneous welcome… felt like falling into a downy bird's nest and being fed on peaches and cream'.[46] They were grounded by weather and had to spend four days in Cairo, where Mrs Churchill visited local YWCA chapters and Red Cross installations and celebrated her sixtieth birthday with 'a beautiful diamond-encrusted heart-shaped brooch' as a gift from her husband. Churchill might have secretly given this gift to Hamblin when they flew out and asked her to give to her boss on the day.

Many surprises were in store for Hamblin during these travels. In a Corps of Royal Electrical and Mechanical Engineers (REME) camp in the African desert, outside Cairo, she and Mrs Churchill toured a large vegetable and flower garden, flourishing in the desert sands of North Africa.

> Here, the Colonel had decided to make a garden for the boys. He had found a man who had had a market garden in Surrey, so he gave him a plot of desert, some seeds and eight natives and made him a Corporal… He had made his own potting shed and green-house… a really beautiful garden full of vegetables and flowers.

At lunch, after an Easter service in Cairo's cathedral, Hamblin 'sat between the Soviet Minister here [in Cairo] and our own Wing Commander: bliss.'[47]

---

* Clementine Churchill and Hamblin went alone, without a Foreign Office official, only a British Red Cross representative, Miss Mabel Johnson, who later became a close friend of Clementine's.

Hamblin and Mrs Churchill flew on to Moscow, arriving on 2 April 1945. They settled into their own State Guest House with their own butler, chef and maids. 'Lady Churchill could entertain as she pleased, and on our first day we had... our own pilot to lunch. Saying goodbye to him was quite emotional... It would be five long weeks before the Skymaster met us once more in Moscow.'[48] Joseph Stalin had asked to meet Mrs Churchill in order to thank her in person. Unlike her husband, who rarely if ever introduced his secretaries to the famous people he met (although he expressed regret at having failed to introduce Kathleen Hill to Franklin D. Roosevelt during the Hyde Park meetings; and later introduced Jo Sturdee to President Truman), Mrs Churchill invited Hamblin to join her to meet Stalin in the Kremlin. Unfortunately for Hamblin, she got only as far as the door to Stalin's office before she was stopped by 'members of the Red Army Guard, [who] indicated in no light terms by placing their guns across the entrance so that I could go no further'.[49] She recalled 'bayonets across the door'. From then on as they toured the country, 'we were allocated a train which was equal, I suppose to a Royal train. We had our own bedrooms and sitting room to work in and have our meals... we were [also] allocated a butler and a doctor.' And, of course, they each had their own interpreter throughout the six-week tour of the Soviet Union, an interpreter who left them only when they went to bed, when he temporarily suspended his work as the spy he undoubtedly was.

While in the Soviet Union, Hamblin attended a performance of *Swan Lake* at the Bolshoi, performed in honour of Mrs Churchill's visit. Sitting in the equivalent of a royal box, Hamblin watched 'as the ballerina was taking her bow, she raised her hand in a gesture to Lady Churchill... and the whole audience turned around and cheered.' That experience was repeated at every stop on their long train tour across the Soviet Union: the Russian people cheered their British visitors. But it was not all a series of wonderful, heartwarming experiences. Hamblin remembers the terrible devastation and suffering she saw as they visited hospitals, sanatoria, orphanages and children's homes in all the large cities and small towns in which their private train stopped.

Towards the end of their trip, news arrived that Germany had surrendered. Because VE day was celebrated a day earlier in the United Kingdom (8 May) than in the Soviet Union (9 May), Mrs Churchill and Hamblin went that night to celebrate at the British embassy, where they 'made quite merry'. The following day, when the Soviets celebrated their VE day, Hamblin celebrated in Red Square, where she was surprised to be 'thrown up into the air. Apparently, it is quite an honour. If you're light, you are thrown high up. It's terrifying in a way.' Either Mrs Churchill was simply too grand to be tossed around in that manner or she was not out among the Russian people in Red Square. Whatever the reason, this was one of the rare instances in which Mrs Churchill and Hamblin were separated. It was a joyful day, but both women missed being in their own country on such a momentous occasion.

Both viewed the trip as a success – 'wonderful' is the word Hamblin uses to describe it. Mrs Churchill reassured the Soviets that Britain was doing all it could to relieve their pain, and Hamblin contributed by keeping all of the schedules and other aspects of the long journey in perfect order. Despite the hectic pace, Hamblin managed to keep up with all of Mrs Churchill's enormous correspondence, including the almost daily letters between her boss and the prime minister, who attached great importance to her visit at a time when relations between the Soviet Union and the West were worsening, just as the Allies were winning the war. Mrs Churchill sent telegrams, Churchill dictated long newsy letters to her, both in code and *en clair*, sometimes sent through the diplomatic pouch. Churchill had instructed his Foreign Office and the British Embassy to share all cables with his wife, so that she continued to be as knowledgeable as he. Hamblin was probably as up-to-date as her boss, and helped relieve the burden the possession of secret information placed on Mrs Churchill by serving as 'a constant, steady and "padlock" companion'.[50] And we can assume that as her last chore in relation to the trip, Hamblin

submitted to a grilling by the prime minister, his usual procedure
with all returning travellers. She would have related what she saw
and heard, and her impressions, feeding them into the flow of
information the prime minister so valued.

In 2016 a memorial plaque to Lady Churchill was unveiled in
the building in Rostov-on-Don where she stayed on her visit to
the Soviet Union. She called that city 'the highlight of her whole
trip for it is there that the Aid to Russia fund is re-equipping two
great hospitals'. The Foreign Office official at the unveiling of
the plaque reminded the invited guests of the great work Lady
Churchill had done and said that the plaque was 'a very visible
reminder of our shared history as we prepare to commemorate
the 71st anniversary of the end of World War Two'.

Hamblin was in those years remarkably happy, or 'as happy as
one [could be] in the war and after'. She was working hard and
appreciated by her boss and those around her. When asked by the
Churchill Archives interviewer if she were happy, she answered
'[T]here are so many degrees of happiness, aren't there? I don't
think that I was <u>consciously</u> happy, but I think that I was. I mean,
these days I'm very consciously happy, but I think in those days I
wasn't conscious of it, but yes, I <u>think</u> I was happy. As far as one
was in the war and after.'

That happiness must have been reduced, at least temporarily,
when the voters in the July 1945 general election entrusted their
post-war future to the Labour Party rather than Churchill's Tories.
Although Churchill retained his seat in parliament, Labour won
a convincing victory, taking 393 seats to the Conservatives' 210,
and polling some two million more popular votes. Churchill
declared himself 'deeply distressed at the prospect of sinking
from a national to a party leader',[51] but 'the instinct for change
was understandable and doubtless wholesome'.[52] Hamblin very
quickly adapted to the changes in the work and office structure of
Churchill's new role as Leader of the Opposition.

As with the move to the Admiralty in 1939, and the subsequent
move to Number 10 in 1940, so with the move *out* of Number 10,

once again Hamblin assisted him and Mrs Churchill in organizing their living and working quarters. The Churchills bought 28 Hyde Park Gate, because as Leader of the Opposition Churchill needed a London base from which to attend the House of Commons. As Number 28 did not have enough room for an office, the Churchills bought Number 27 next door, part of which was let out, and part turned into offices for the secretaries, including Hamblin. She organized this move, calling it 'very household', perhaps because she viewed it from Mrs Churchill's perspective; in fact, the move was much more complicated than the usual household move. She was helping to convert a former prime minister into the Leader of the Opposition, and arranged things so that he could resume work on his multi-volume *A History of the English-Speaking Peoples*, while at the same time beginning to consider writing his war memoirs. In fact, Hamblin worked between both households, doing whatever was required, as did all the other secretaries.

The good news, for Churchill if not for his wife, was that with war over, Chartwell was accessible again. It took a good deal of rehabilitation, with Hamblin helping with the scrubbing and polishing.[53] She had always 'helped Clementine to grapple with the ups and downs of Chartwell life',[54] so this was nothing new for her. She loved working there, as did so many of the other secretaries, and as, of course, did Churchill. When they were driving down from London and

we entered the precincts of Chartwell... he would say 'Ah, Chartwell' and he'd throw all the things to one side. I loved it so much that I always said, 'oh, yes, Chartwell' and I felt that once we were here everything would be all right.... It has been said, and this is very true, that he built Chartwell not only with his hands but with his heart... There was [always] a great deal going on. It was like a little Factory... It was very much a home but there was never a dull moment. It was terrific.... Everything is made to feel very important. He had his way of making one feel that everything you did was of great importance... [a] wonderful quality that one rarely finds in an employer… although he could knock you down and be really rude and beastly but he made you feel that whatever you did was of importance.[55]

He worried about Chartwell when he was away. Just before sailing to America in 1949 he wrote to the head gardener ordering new rhododendrons and reminded him to 'Report to Miss Hamblin at once any signs of trouble with the goldfish. The most serious need was more logs. For these a fallen beech tree should be cut.'[56]

In October 1951 Churchill, at the age of seventy-six, was returned to Downing Street as prime minister, the Tories having won the general election. Hamblin was still working for Mrs Churchill, and once again found herself helping to organize the move into Number 10, this time from Hyde Park Gate rather than from the Admiralty. It was during Churchill's 'Indian Summer' that Hamblin was to be treated to an unexpected and delightful trip by Mrs Churchill, a trip not quite as fraught as their wartime travels. In the hope of curing a painful case of neuritis, Mrs Churchill went to a spa in Aix-les-Bains in Savoie, and took Hamblin, who was suffering from what she later described as tension-induced shoulder pains.

Lady Churchill was very kind and she said [as]… she was seeing the best man in Europe and… I might see him too. And when he saw me he said, 'Oh yes, you're _very_ tense so I'll give you the works,' and I had three weeks of – I've never had anything like it in my _life_. I had mud baths and underwater massage and the lot.

In the likely event that Hamblin was interrupting her 'cure' to handle Lady Churchill's correspondence, she would have known that the prime minister inquired as to not only his wife's progress, but Hamblin's as well. In a letter to Mrs Churchill he asked, 'How is the Hambling [sic] getting on? Is she having a stronger or weaker dose than you?'[57]

The 30 November 1954 celebration of Churchill's eightieth birthday started well enough. Hamblin describes 'the greatest party at

No. 10... a large family dinner and then after dinner a real old-fashioned evening party at 10 p.m.... with masses and masses of people... He had two wonderful cakes with 80 candles on them... it was fantastic.'

Hamblin goes into great detail about one of the cakes, made as usual by Madame Floris, who baked him one specially every year. Hamblin describes the cake Madame Floris made for his eighty-fifth birthday:

> she decided she would write to countries all over the world and get whatever they produced which could go into a cake... Carrots from the country which produce carrots, dates and wheat and so on... the response was terrific and she had masses... we had them in a pile in the corner of one of the State Rooms for the party. I think they went to some good cause afterwards.

So far, so good. But earlier in his eightieth birthday year, parliament had decided that a portrait of Churchill would be an appropriate gift for his upcoming eightieth birthday celebration. Members of the House of Commons and the House of Lords donated 1,000 guineas and commissioned Graham Sutherland to paint it. Instrumental in that selection was Jennie Lee MP, who was a friend of the artist and wife of Aneurin Bevan, godfather of the National Health Service. Churchill agreed to sit for Sutherland about three times, a process more fully described by Elizabeth Gilliatt and Jane Portal. No one in the family saw the final version until it was publicly unveiled in Westminster Hall, recalls Hamblin. But Jane Portal remembers something slightly different: Lady Churchill (she had become so in 1953, when Churchill was knighted) was invited to see the portrait at the house where the painter was staying. She came back from that visit 'shaken'. There was a photograph, of unknown origin, which Churchill showed Portal and to which he reacted with distaste.

Both Churchills hated Sutherland's portrait and Hamblin says that Lady Churchill 'didn't want it to go down to posterity because she felt it didn't do him justice... [he was] much stronger than that. After all, it was a gift to them... and they could do what they liked with it.' And so Lady Churchill decided to have it destroyed and asked Hamblin for ideas. Hamblin confesses:

> I destroyed it myself... I could not do it alone because it was a huge thing... [So I said to Lady Churchill] I think my brother would help us... So [in] the dead of night, in the dark, we took it away in the van and we took it to his house and burned it in his garden... a few miles away [from Chartwell.] But of course it was a deadly secret... Lady Churchill and I decided we would not tell anyone... [when] a thing like that comes out, it would make life impossible for me.

Later, Mary Soames told the press that the portrait in fact had been destroyed, but revealed nothing about how it had been done or by whom. Hamblin goes on to recount: 'Mary thought she had better come out in the clear... She made me go and see her solicitor and swear an affidavit about how it was done... because it might come up again in fifty or a hundred-years' time.' Sutherland called the destruction of the portrait 'an act of vandalism'.[58] Portal was among those glad to see the end of what she considered an unfair representation of a great man.

In April 1955, only six months after what Hamblin called 'the greatest party', Churchill felt compelled by his failing health, and pressure from a no-longer patient successor, Anthony Eden, and others, to resign as prime minister. The Churchills, and of course Hamblin, returned to Chartwell. Because Winston remained in the House of Commons, to which he was re-elected in 1959, and attended the House as often as he could manage, and continued to dine at The Other Club (his dining society at the Savoy) almost until the end of his life, the Churchills maintained their London residence at Hyde Park Gate.

Hamblin was there throughout these final years, and, less frequently, at Chartwell. As we have seen, the usual guests arrived to visit and Mrs Churchill would 'feed him people... She would think all the time and get him people who would entertain him and be good with him'. Anthony Montague Browne had become Churchill's Principal Private Secretary and 'was a great companion to him', and added 'a great deal to his life in the end'. Hamblin arranged all these visits with some help from other more junior secretaries.

Following Churchill's death on 24 January 1965, Hamblin was one of the very few non-family members invited to attend his burial service at the churchyard of St Martin's Church, Bladon, in Oxfordshire. In his will, Churchill left Hamblin £500, about £10,000 today.

Later that year, Lady Churchill moved out of Chartwell and into Hyde Park Gate. That same year Grace Hamblin was awarded an OBE and was appointed the first curator/administrator at Chartwell when it was turned over to the National Trust in 1966. The Trust assigned Hamblin 'the arduous task of putting Churchill's vast archive back into order'.[59] She ran it until 1973. No one knew Chartwell as well as she did – possibly only Churchill himself. Cecily 'Chips' Gemmell says that Hamblin 'ran [every aspect of] the house beautifully [and] that everyone depended on her'.

Having retired from running Chartwell, Hamblin 'dreaded this [not working] more than anything... and the blank it would leave... suddenly out of the blue, came this bomb of a job'.[60] In 1974 she was appointed secretary to the Churchill centenary exhibition in London's Somerset House and travelled with it to Australia in 1975.

Grace Hamblin died in 2002, aged ninety-four. She had spent seventy of those years working with the Churchills and strengthening and promoting their memory, the longest-serving member of Churchill's secretarial staff.

3

Kathleen Hill

'I had never been in a house like that before. It was alive, restless. When he was away it was still as a mouse. When he was there it was vibrating.'

Kathleen Hill describing Chartwell in 1936[1]

'… the ruthless partition of the day, the planning of things all to come. There was never a wasted moment. He had intense control.'

Bill Deakin describing Chartwell in 1936[2]

BORN IN AUGUST 1900, Kathleen Hill trained as a professional shorthand typist, and began her secretarial career in Portsmouth working for several insurance companies. She was also a solo violinist and was first violin in the Portsmouth Philharmonic Society.[3] After her marriage to an Indian Army officer in Calcutta, Hill 'worked for the girl Guides' in Bengal.[4] In India the Girl Guides movement had started in 1911 and by 1928 Hill had become senior secretary to the Chief Commissioner of Girl Guides for All India. As a violinist, too, while she lived there, her performances were broadcast on the radio in Calcutta, Bombay and Delhi. In India, she 'had that late-Raj life-style... masses of Indian servants', according to her granddaughter Georgina Hill.[5]

While in India Kathleen Hill borrowed from the club library and read several of Churchill's books, little thinking that a few years later she would be working for him in London. She later said that when she returned from India she 'had hoped to find a post in a school combining school work with music supervision, and I remember thinking when he [Churchill] was in good dictational form – well, I have lost the music, but I have got the music of words'.[6]

In 1936 she divorced her husband and moved back to England, where she applied for a job with an employment agency, but was considered too old to be a secretary. She was asked if she played bridge – perhaps they thought she might be hired as a companion. In any event she 'was sent down to Westerham... and had an interview'. Hill waited patiently in the drawing room until Mrs Churchill arrived to ask her if she were willing to work at night. Hill agreed. Then Churchill

came down in a boiler suit and looking all very pink and white. I was struck by the fairness of his skin, very white... he stared glaring at me sitting down... I didn't really know if I got the job or not. But Mrs Pearman, already working there, wrote to me and said you've got the job and will you start next week.

Churchill asked her only if she could do shorthand and typing.

In July 1937, as the political situation in Europe worsened, and his political and literary work grew, Churchill decided that he needed a resident secretary in addition to Violet Pearman and Grace Hamblin, both of whom came each day from their homes nearby. That would permit him to dictate into the early hours of the morning 'without a taxi having to be summoned to take a wilting secretary home'.[7] His choice was Kathleen Hill. As the first 'resident secretary' at Chartwell she lived in that house, and when she travelled with Churchill to London to work at Morpeth Mansions,* she returned every night to sleep at Chartwell. Mrs Pearman divided up the job, keeping for herself the personal work, while assigning to Hill all the literary work. Over the years, Hill set up and managed some of the accounting procedures and kept the minutes of all the meetings on book publications, due dates and delays, as well as income payments.[8] She also set up systems to track the salaries of the staff and the amounts they would owe in income tax.[9] In January 1943, acting as rather more than a typist, she 'suggested an early deal on a third volume of war speeches while military victories were fresh in the public mind', and recommended that tax advice be sought from Lloyds Bank. She straightened out complex problems with film rights for *A History of the English-Speaking Peoples*.[10]

The original plan had been that she would also work for Mrs Churchill, who was an early riser and wanted a secretary to come into her bedroom at 8.30 in the morning to help with her own correspondence and with managing the household. We had 'trouble getting servants and that sort of thing'. Hill would work for Mrs Churchill in the mornings, rest during the afternoon, and then work for Churchill at nights, sometimes until 2 or 3 a.m.

---

* The Churchill penthouse had once been occupied by David Lloyd George (British prime minister 1916–22). Hill recalls that she still received letters there addressed to Miss Frances Stevenson, long-time mistress, personal secretary and confidante of the Welsh politician. She became his second wife in 1943, becoming Frances Lloyd George, Countess Lloyd George of Dwyfor.

She seldom had a break, for there was simply too much work and the travel between Morpeth Mansions and Chartwell disrupted the hours she might have taken off. One reason why Hill preferred working at Chartwell to working at the London flat was 'the very good telephone service. Even at three o'clock in the morning. At the end of our working session... he used to ring up... the *Daily Mail*... [to] know the latest news. He always had to be on the spot, the latest news before he went to bed.' And every morning while still in bed, as all secretaries attested, Churchill read nine or more daily newspapers, before, during and after the war. In 1947, according to Denis Kelly, Churchill 'took sixteen newspapers [on his bed in the mornings], from *The Times* to the *Daily Worker*'.[11]

Hill recalled the excitement of Chartwell when Churchill was in residence.

> I had never been in a house like that before. It was alive, restless. When he was away it was still as a mouse. When he was there it was vibrating. So much happened... that I was bewildered by it all. He could be very ruthless. He used to get impatient with delays. He was a disappointed man waiting for the call to serve his country.[12]

Another reason for preferring Chartwell might have been 'For the first time, they had a little dining room in the sort of base-ment... a nice little dining room... [for me and] whoever was on duty.' There was also quite an extensive domestic staff at Chartwell: butler, head parlourmaid, housemaids, Lady Churchill's maid and the much-loved cook, Mrs Landemare, who often provided an early breakfast for the young ladies who worked into the early hours of the morning.

Hill had the job of ringing the employment agencies and doing the first interviews for any openings in the domestic staff – a task she hated. She must also have hated turning down requests for interviews and/or jobs from unqualified applicants – a task she took on herself. Keeping track of expenses was another chore. For example, in June 1939 she spent £1.10/4 (about £68 in today's money) on advertising for a new secretary, to be charged to Churchill's literary account.[13] In July of 1939 she bought, on approval, three maps of Switzerland, to be delivered to Morpeth Mansions, from Edward Stanford, cartographer to the king. Perhaps Churchill was considering the boundaries of neutral states, for he could hardly have been planning a trip there. Hill arranged for an account to be set up for a regular messenger service – something Churchill used constantly. Her schedule was often changed without much notice – 'every day was different... We had to play it as it came.' An added problem was Churchill's constant tardiness: his friend Sir Edward Marsh observed: 'Winston's disregard of time when there is anything he wants to do is sublime – he firmly believes it waits for him.'[14] A Foreign Office official, Alexander Cadogan, reviewing a speech in the prime ministerial bedroom, said: '[Churchill is] due to make it at 11, and did not upheave himself out of bed until 10:40.'[15] Throughout his life, all the secretaries – and Churchill's valet Sawyers, as well as Mrs Churchill – struggled with Churchill's last-minute demands and his lateness for meals and meetings.

In those days, she said, the valet would bring up all the mail for Churchill, while he was still in bed eating his breakfast. That system would change as the volume of mail increased. Churchill would then decide what to answer or what could simply be acknowledged. If Mrs Churchill had finished her own work or if she were away, Hill sometimes helped Churchill in the mornings. 'I had to do everything,' she recalls, especially after Mrs Pearman had a stroke. They had tried to bring in some temporary help, but that didn't last – either for financial reasons, as the Churchills were always trying to cut their administrative costs, or because the new 'girls' were unwilling to work the required hours, or to put up with an often-difficult boss. Churchill could be irritable and moody, but one 'just took it in one's stride. I mean everything as it came', and then waited for the inevitable remorse and a sign from Churchill that all was forgiven. As Jane Portal put it many years later, when Churchill had a fit of temper, 'just get out of the room' for a while, and all will be forgiven when you return.[16]

In one incident General Hastings Ismay found Hill outside the cabinet room 'in obvious distress'. He asked Churchill if he had been bullying her and a puzzled prime minister replied, 'Oh, dear! I must put that right.' He rang for Hill and very gently said, 'Please take this letter,' which he dictated slowly and more clearly than was his custom. 'My dear Mr Ambassador, I fully agree with you.' That was it. He asked Hill to type it immediately and when she returned he studied it carefully and said, 'That is a very good piece of typing. It is beautifully done. Thank you very much!' When an astonished Hill left the room, 'He turned to Ismay with the air of a conjurer demonstrating just how easily a difficult feat could be accomplished!'[17]

If Hill were working at night, it was mostly taking dictation on *Marlborough*, which Churchill was rushing to finish so that he could start work on *A History of the English-Speaking Peoples* – he needed the money that both books would produce.

In general, Hill accompanied Churchill on his travels, but with one notable exception, of which he was exceptionally proud. In 1938, travelling as a private citizen before he was called back into government, Churchill decided to visit Château de l'Horizon in the south of France. He announced to Maxine Elliott, one of his favourite hostesses, 'My dear Maxine, do you realize I have come all the way from London without my man?' Elliott replied, 'Winston, how terribly brave of you.'[18]

Hill often travelled with him to London for his appearances in the House, making sure her portable typewriter was in the 'old Daimler' with her (as did Mrs Pearman when it was her turn to go up to London). Hill would type speeches in the car, trying not to make herself sick; cars were unheated in those days, so her fingers were frozen. Another time, she handed Churchill the pages of his speech in the House of Commons a matter of minutes before he strode into the chamber to deliver it. These were tense moments.

One night, her first night as she recalls, Hill was summoned to the Chartwell dining room where Churchill asked her to 'Fetch me klop.' She had seen in his study some volumes by the German historian Onno Klopp, so she brought those fourteen volumes of the professor's *Der Fall des Hauses Stuart und die Succession des Hauses Hannover* (1875–88) down two flights of steps, as she puts it, 'clutching them up to my chin' to the dining room. 'God Almighty!' Churchill roared. '[He] looked at me in amazement… good try, very well done but not what I wanted,' he said.[19] What he wanted was his 'klop', a word he had invented 'for reasons of onomatopoeia', which was a metal paper-piercer that would allow a tag (often called a Treasury tag) to be used to tie pages together. 'He detested staples and paper clips,' because, as he told one secretary, 'they are very dangerous as they pick up and hold together <u>wrong</u> papers.'[20] It was another Churchillian invented word. 'Once Churchill realized that he had hurt Mrs Hill's feelings, however, he complimented her on her handwriting.'[21]

Churchill continued to develop his own rules of language and punctuation: 'aircraft' rather than 'aeroplane'; seasons and points of the compass to be spelled with a capital. He also used words such as 'pray' as in 'Pray let me have a report.'[22] 'Churchill used it deliberately and anachronistically even though it was almost as old-fashioned as "prithee"… Attempting to persuade the British people to look back hundreds of years to similar moments of national peril, Churchill found it helpful to adopt anachronistic language.'[23]

When at Chartwell, if Churchill were laying bricks for a cottage or a wall, Hill would have to run outside, climb up the ladders and give him any messages that had come in. He would dictate an answer, which she would take down, then she would run back inside to type it up. She estimates each of these running trips may have been as much as a quarter of a mile, several times a day. When she accompanied Churchill to Blenheim, she again had to race around the palace as there was only one telephone then and that was in the gun room, some considerable distance from where Churchill was working. She said: 'so I had to go quite a long way and down long passages to do any telephoning and it wasn't very pleasant'. Running up and down ladders and along the back corridors of the palace must have been strenuous – and cold, as Hamblin describes – in addition to the actual typing.

Churchill used the telephone extensively. In what he called his Factory, the ground-floor office where the secretaries worked, he would ask to be connected to one of his many colleagues – he was in 'constant contact' with many people, Hill recalls. One day, early in her time with him, he 'flopped down in the office and said: "Call the doctor, I don't feel very well." "Who's your doctor?" I asked. He answered "Dr Scott, he died"' – a different recollection from Hamblin's of a dentist named Fish (see Chapter 2). So she looked in the address book under Scott and found the name of his successor. And Churchill could be less than explicit in his demands. One day he asked Hill to place a call to someone named Ian who lived in Sussex. She asked herself who might know this man and called Brendan Bracken, Churchill's lifelong friend and Parliamentary Private Secretary (PPS)* from 1940 to 1941, for the answer – apparently, a man called Ian had been at a dinner with Churchill and he wanted to follow up on a conversation they had.

There were, of course, times when secretarial ingenuity could not suffice, and then Churchill had to be consulted. On one such occasion a secretary was directed to discover whether or not Churchill had greeted the ninth Duke of Marlborough and his new wife when they returned to London from their honeymoon. When 'find out' proved an insufficient instruction, Churchill directed the secretary to his *Story of the Malakand Field Force*. 'If you find out I was out with the Field Force at the time the happy couple were returning to London,' he said, 'I could not have been there to meet them. I have never enjoyed the ability to be in more than one place at a time.'[24]

---

* A Parliamentary Private Secretary is a member of parliament appointed by a minister as an assistant, to be their 'eyes and ears' in the House of Commons. PPSs are selected from the ranks of backbench MPs.

The secretaries had to be ready for everything. One of Churchill's Private Secretaries recorded that one lesson he learned from Churchill, 'which all my career has helped to emphasize: never be surprised by anything; always be ready to deal with the unexpected by unorthodox or improvised methods, and, above all, notice and care'.[25] In September 1939, when Churchill was again First Lord of the Admiralty, Hill had accompanied Churchill to a meeting at the Admiralty. Surrounded by the Sea Lords, Churchill was signing documents with his traditional red ink with an old-fashioned stylo pen. In those days, the pens had to be filled 'with a rubber top... they were beastly. They were always going out of order.' But when Churchill 'got the red pen out of his pocket and it got blocked up or something... I quickly handed him... his pen that I had newly filled up. He said, "see how well I trained her."' In fact, no one had trained Hill to be prepared for this. She had thought ahead and wanted to be ready for any eventuality – a valuable trait if you were working for Churchill. He expected everything to be done for his convenience and the secretaries had to anticipate his every need. They also had to adapt to changing circumstances, as the dictating load increased. Hill 'in order to accelerate the work... instead of taking shorthand notes and then typing them out, typed directly onto Admiralty notepaper as Churchill was dictating... [later] she did the same directly onto 10 Downing Street paper'.[26]

In early 1939 Churchill had his two shotguns examined by the gunmaker James Woodward & Sons. The firm recommended several repairs, including 're-joint 2 pairs of barrels (At present the barrels are very loose in the action due to fair wear and tear).' It was Hill who sent off the guns and, at Churchill's instructions, paid the repair bill in full, keeping track of both the estimate and the money paid.[27] Was Churchill beginning to worry about his personal safety or was he thinking of a shooting break after the war ended? Or perhaps they had belonged to his father.

Churchill's secretaries had to remain discreet and out of sight, regardless of whatever important work they were doing. When Churchill left his London home to return to the Admiralty, Hill was photographed on the doorstep waiting just behind him. 'But when the photo was published in the newspapers the next morning, she was not there: she had been airbrushed out.'[28] She was probably neither surprised nor disappointed.

There were some adventures. One of the trips was to Sir Philip Sassoon's house at Port Lympne in Kent. Sassoon was a politician, art collector and flamboyant society host, and his house was known for its luxurious style and celebrity guests.* Hill was there working for Churchill when she 'looked through and saw – [them] having dinner and there seemed to be a flunkey behind everybody's chair'. She dined with the Churchill family only once or twice after the war, but at the Sassoons' she was served pineapple cocktails by a butler, although not at the formal dinner table.

Much later, when Churchill was prime minister, Hill wrote under her own name to the Duchess of Marlborough about a dinner seating plan the duchess had sent to Churchill for his approval. Hill wrote that Churchill 'very much hopes that he may sit next to yourself [the duchess] at dinner'.[29] There was no division between his personal and public lives, and the secretaries had a role in both. Hill managed Churchill's private dinner invitations too, as can be seen from her note to him on 5 August 1945 asking whom he would like to invite.

A varied job indeed. In early June 1941, the month in which Hill received an MBE,[30] Lord Beaverbrook sent Churchill five dozen bottles of Deidesheimer Hofstück, 1937 vintage, a German Riesling wine. Hill suggested the thank-you telegram, which was to read: 'Thank you so much for your exhilarating gift.'[31] Churchill accepted her draft and the telegram was sent.

During the war, the Churchills and their entourage moved at weekends to stay at Ditchley Park, a country house in Oxfordshire, instead of Chequers, because it was feared that the German bombers would be able more easily to find the prime minister's

---

*   Today the house is a hotel with many of the luxurious features and rooms intact.

house, especially when the moon was full and could illuminate the driveway. The owners of Ditchley, Nancy and Ronald Tree, had some trouble feeding all their invited guests because of rationing restrictions, so Hill asked Churchill 'if it would be in order to grant extra rations to Nancy Tree's chef'.[32]

Chequers was a favourite family venue. Churchill's daughter Mary Soames fondly recalls the four Christmases the family spent at Chequers: 'the great rather gloomy house truly seemed to come to life and glow on those occasions, with blazing log fires, miraculous decorations made by Hill, a towering Christmas tree in the Great Hall'.[33]

In January 1939 Bill Deakin, one of Churchill's most important researchers, wrote to Hill to ask for help in getting temporary resident visas for two Jewish shopkeepers in Bad Gastein, Austria. Mrs Churchill had skied there decades before and 'bought some hats and clothes' at their shop. Deakin suggested Hill send the letter to the German-Jewish Aid Committee, stating that Mrs Churchill 'would like the matter attended to'.[34] We do not know if they got their visas.

Hill recalls that while sometimes dictation came easily to Churchill, at other times it was tentative as he re-thought paragraphs or policies. One night he told her: 'leave me, I'll finish it in the morning'. When she arrived the next day, Churchill said to her, 'I've laid an egg' – that is, he had successfully written it.* This was unusual, for 'He didn't [hand]write a script very often.' Churchill liked egg references. As he once said: 'I shall live on this history [*A History of the English-Speaking Peoples*]. I shall lay an egg a year – a volume every twelve months should not mean much work.'[35] Thanks to Hill and his 'prodigious memory', he was able to do that. Cassell's copies of the 1939 proofs were destroyed when the company's premises were bombed later in the war. But Hill

---

* An example of the language gap separating the United Kingdom and the United States. To 'lay an egg' in America is to fail badly. In Britain it can mean to bring forth a successful result, as it does in this instance.

had the foresight to retain Churchill's less polished drafts, from which he could recreate the destroyed versions when he returned to the research and writing after a hectic wartime premiership.[36]

Unlike the other secretaries, Churchill called her 'Mrs Hill', perhaps because she was a bit older and married. Or perhaps later when he had more secretaries he was less apt to depend on – and call for – one specific person. He wanted to be called 'Mr Churchill', saying 'I was born Mr Churchill and I'll die Mr Churchill. He would not be called sir by us. With the servants, perhaps.'

Since almost every paper was kept,* files and the filing systems were a problem. At first, there were simple wooden slats, 'no real proper cupboard', and tin boxes; later there was a filing system for letters, organized by Mrs Pearman, and considered 'nothing short of a miracle'.[37] This system worked well from 1929 until 1939. The papers used in his book *The World Crisis*, Churchill's six-volume history of the First World War, were stored in a black tin box, as were his personal financial papers. Hill enlarged and maintained this filing system.

Hill served as Churchill's bookkeeper, in addition to performing her other duties. She was responsible for writing cheques for the domestic staff, and also for the workers at Chartwell such as architects, builders and repairmen. 'There always seemed to be some building work going on… there was so much going on that it was hard to keep a record of what was going on.' Hill was also responsible for keeping track of staff members' salaries, so that they could pay their income tax.[38]

Hill mentions the same female visitors that other secretaries noted, including the aristocratic socialites Venetia Stanley Montagu, Violet Bonham Carter and Sylvia Henley, as well as family members. The officer and government official Desmond Morton was a regular dinner guest at Chartwell. Other visitors included Charles Wilson (later Lord Moran), who became Churchill's doctor

---

* Except when Lady Churchill decided to 'have a tearing-up session of old photographs, etc., which I rather regretted'. And so do we all regret this.

and frequently accompanied Churchill on foreign tours. Wilson was first introduced to Churchill by Brendan Bracken, two weeks after his patient became prime minister, but Churchill wanted no doctor fluttering and fretting around him, so he issued an order, Hill recalls: 'keep that old fool away from me.' However, some sources suggest that the government assigned Wilson to monitor the newly installed prime minister, others say that Beaverbrook suggested Wilson. In any case, Wilson would become a familiar presence in Churchill's life (once he became familiar with his face), and he would become well-known to all the secretaries, although these intrepid women earn few mentions in his published diaries.

In September 1939 Churchill joined the Chamberlain government and became First Lord of the Admiralty once again. Hill, 'who accompanied him, later recalled how he rushed up to the First Lord's Room and went up to a cupboard in the panelling. I held my breath. He flung the door open with a dramatic gesture – there, behind the panelling was a large map showing the disposition of the German ships on the day he had left the Admiralty in 1915 – twenty-four years before'.[39]

She later remembered that 'When Winston was at the Admiralty, the place was buzzing with atmosphere, with electricity. When he was away, on tour, it was dead, dead, dead.' She said, 'Chartwell was vibrating – you never knew what was going to happen next when he was there. It came to life.' Several other secretaries noticed the excitement Churchill brought to any office, any task, any room or indeed any dinner table.

Hill 'had to sort through the flood of letters that reached Churchill from the public after his appointment to the Admiralty, and to decide which ones to put before him. One of these letters was from a young Conservative, apologizing for having tried to oust Churchill from his constituency earlier that year'. Hill sent the letter to Churchill with her note attached, saying: 'Please read this.' He did, and this was the response he dictated to her: 'I certainly think that Englishmen ought to start fair with one another from the outset in so grievous a struggle and so far as I am concerned the past is dead.'[40] He had great powers of forgiveness. Bracken said about him: 'Hard fighter as he is in debate, he is a man almost devoid of rancour. A defeat does not sour him.'[41]

In early November 1939, as First Lord and with the added responsibility of a seat on the special War Cabinet Committee, Churchill took a destroyer to Boulogne and then the train to Paris to meet with the French military command. Admiral Darlan had provided his own train to bring Churchill to Paris. 'It was his [Churchill's] first war time visit across the channel, his hundredth trip to France since he had first gone there, as a boy, with his father, more than fifty years before. His love of France was profound.'[42] With him at the Ritz Hotel was Hill, who recalled that 'Paris didn't seem like a place that was under the cloud of war. The war was on, but life seemed to be going on as normal in Paris then.' Of course, the Paris that she and Churchill were seeing was not the Paris of ordinary Parisians. On arrival, he met with his French naval counterparts, promising British help and cooperation, as he did at a later meeting with the French prime minister, Daladier. That night he gave a dinner in a private room at the Ritz and the next morning, 'using his room at the Ritz as an office, he dictated a number of departmental minutes' to Hill.

As the workload increased, a new secretary, Mary Shearburn, was brought in. She had been working for a few months at Chartwell and was now brought up to London to help with dictation at the Admiralty.* Shearburn proved as loyal and inventive as her predecessors and successors. When Churchill entrusted her with some papers to carry from the Orkney Islands, back to London, on a night train and in a sleeping compartment by herself, he asked what she would do if someone attacked her to get the box of papers. 'I would scream at the top of my voice,' Shearburn said. 'You know it is the best way of discouraging unwelcome attentions

---

* Shearburn would later marry Detective Inspector Walter Thompson, Churchill's principal bodyguard, and she would later type his memoirs, since made into a TV documentary.

of any sort. It attracts so much publicity.' Her husband Detective Inspector Thompson tells us, 'Winston then grinned and nodded his head, adding: 'You may well be right. I should never [have] thought of it."'[43]

Churchill took an incidental decision at this time. He 'agreed to the department store Harrods' request to transfer twenty-two varieties of rare fish into [his] lakes; in return he could keep as many fish as he chose at the war's end.'[44] Hill and the other secretaries would have managed this intriguing piscatorial manoeuvre.

After Churchill became prime minister in May 1940 he knew that the Germans intended to invade Britain. Plans were made to evacuate the government, codenamed Black Move. The prime minister, his private office and his family would be moved to the house in Spetchley Park's 4,500 acres, near Worcester, and Hill was included on the list of those to be evacuated with the PM. One morning in late June 1940 Churchill was in bed, at Chequers, dressed in 'a red dressing gown, smoking a cigar',[45] dictating minutes to Hill requesting information from the Admiralty about possible landing areas the Germans might use, and how the weather and tides might affect the choice of landing spots. It is not reported whether, as was the case a few days earlier, Hill, taking dictation, was seated

> at the foot of his bed with a typewriter. His box, half full of papers, stood open on his bed and by his side a vast chromium-plated cuspidor[46] to throw his cigars into [and] demanding the candle to light his cigar. His black cat Nelson, who had quite replaced our old Number 10 black cat, sprawled at the end of the bed and every now and then Winston would gaze at it affectionately and say, 'Cat, darling.'[47]

Churchill said that 'Nelson was doing [a lot] for the war effort since Nelson served as the prime ministerial hot water bottle'.[48] Churchill's Private Secretary Jock Colville, and perhaps others, were also in the room.

Churchill could at times show consideration for his secretaries, as we have seen. In early January 1940 Churchill was aboard HMS *Codrington*, once again on his way to France. Churchill was on the bridge with the captain and halfway across the channel, when he said: 'I know it is not usual for ladies to be on the bridge of a destroyer in wartime, but I would be glad if you would give my secretary a cup of tea. I am going down to your cabin to work.'[49] Hill got her cup of tea aboard the British destroyer. Hill also notes that Churchill 'would never let us carry things… or run up and down stairs quickly. He was afraid we would get a heart attack.'[50] When flying at high altitudes, he constantly warned his staff to 'blow out their ears on landing and take-offs'.[51]

On another occasion, in November 1940, Colville describes the scene as Hill takes dictation in Churchill's bedroom at Chequers:

> He lay there in his four-post bed with its flowery chintz hangings, his bed table by his side. Hill sat patiently opposite while he chewed his cigar, drunk frequent sips of ice water, fidgeted his toes beneath the bed clothes and murmured stertorously* under his breath what he contemplated saying… to watch him compose some telegram or minute for dictation is to make one feel that one is present at the birth of a child, so tense is his expression, so restless his turnings from side to side, so curious the noises he emits under his breath.[52]

The unflappable secretary took all this for granted and steadily took down his words.

Secretaries were often present on important occasions, important to the nation, but also to the family. There were no divisions between Churchill's work and life. Hill was there in late 1941 when the dreadful news came through to Churchill that both warships HMS *Repulse* and HMS *Prince of Wales* had been sunk in the Pacific. She later recalled: 'I sat in the corner of the room

---

*   A descriptive adjective also used by Lieutenant General Sir Ian Jacob.

silently and unobtrusively... when he was upset I used to try to be invisible. When the two ships went down I was there. That was a terrible moment.' Churchill recalls being 'thankful to be alone. In all the war I never received a more direct shock.'[53]

She also joined Grace Hamblin and Elizabeth Layton during the latter part of Churchill's recuperation in Marrakesh, a period sufficiently extended to require that quite a large contingent be brought from London, so that Churchill could continue to manage affairs of state. 'It was almost as if the centre of British government had been moved from Whitehall to Marrakesh.'[54]

Oddly, Hill does not mention travelling to Quebec with Churchill for the Octagon meeting in September 1944, as one of the four secretaries who went with him.

After the war, when the family reopened Chartwell, which had been closed for the duration of the war, Churchill set about rearranging his books. The beautifully bound leather editions of the translations of his own works – into Norwegian and Swedish, for example – he called his 'Snobs Library', his best books. He also had a gramophone there and loved to play Boer War songs, such as 'Soldiers of the Queen'. In preparation for the move out of the prime ministerial limelight, Churchill asked Hill to establish 'a secretarial schedule for his life as Leader of the Opposition'. Her memo to him and Lady Churchill says: 'I cannot conceive a plan whereby we could manage with less than three secretaries plus the assistance of Miss Hamblin at Chartwell on alternate weekends.' She continued: 'at Chartwell, the off-duty secretary... would answer telephones, prepare meals, wash dishes, make beds etc.'[55]

Kathleen Hill received an MBE in 1941. After the election defeat in 1945, she was appointed Curator of Chequers in 1946, where she worked until 1969. On Boxing Day 1952 she and her son Richard, who 'succeeded to a baronetcy, becoming the 10th Baronet, were luncheon guests of Churchill at Chequers'.[56] Kathleen Hill officially retired in 1970 and died aged ninety-two in 1992.

4

Patrick Kinna

'No females – good heavens, no.'

Elizabeth Layton[1]

'Here she [Kathleen Hill] was slaving away… in the Annexe and had slaved away before the war in the Admiralty with him and yet these exciting trips, she wasn't having those. I thought she deserved them… I used to get so tired because we had so many trips abroad – and generally in those days no girls went.'

Patrick Kinna, oral history

N O CHRONICLE OF what it was like working with Winston would be complete without mention of the role played by Patrick Kinna, the only male shorthand typist in Churchill's world. Kinna occupied that undefined middle ground between Churchill's Private Secretaries (high-level civil servants operating out of Number 10) and the personal secretaries whose stories are told in this book. For reasons at which we can only guess, including social status, Kinna was never offered the title and civil service standing of a Private Secretary, although he eventually came to do many of the chores traditionally reserved for that group. But neither was he treated as just another secretary. The reason for that distinction is not difficult to determine: he was a man. During many of the years covered by this book the distinction between men and women was stark and meaningful, although increasingly blurred as the war wore on. Its final erasure can be attributed to Ernest Bevin's introduction of registration for women, when, 'on 18 December 1941, the National Service (No. 2) Act was passed, making conscription for women legal'.[2] Single women and childless widows between twenty and thirty now had a wide range of choices for service. The Women's Royal Naval Service (WRNS) was the choice of service for many, and at their peak in 1944 numbered over 74,000. Even before registration 'twelve female cypher officers, ten Chief WRNS special operators and a naval nursing sister were killed instantly when their ship, SS *Aguila*, was torpedoed on 19 August 1941 en route from Liverpool to Gibraltar.'[3] Nevertheless, WRNS continued to serve on naval ships throughout the war. Robert Meiklejohn, the American diplomat Averell Harriman's only private secretary, notes in his diary that on the 1943 voyage to America, passengers included 'thirty WRNS code clerks to handle incoming messages for the PM', who could receive but not send messages lest enemy submarines home in on the signal. Commander 'Tommy' Thompson, Churchill's principal aide-de-camp, who travelled on all of Churchill's trips, said this 'drives the PM nuts'.[4]

Men were allowed to travel with the prime minister, but

non-military, civilian women could not be exposed to the hazards of wartime travel. That, of course, changed during the war, and by its end it was considered acceptable for female secretaries to bear the risks of dangerous travel, at least on non-military ships. But for Churchill gender distinctions survived the end of hostilities in Europe. In July 1945 he issued a cabinet minute laying out plans for demobilization of the armed forces: 'Women ought not to be treated the same as men.' If the men are not brought home quickly they might become rebellious. 'But women are an entirely different category. They do not mutiny or cause disturbances, and the sooner they are back at their homes the better.'[5]

Kinna, who could and did travel with Churchill on dangerous voyages, was not to be exposed to all the chores often assigned to the female personal secretaries, whose work is recorded in this book. In addition to taking down and transcribing Churchill's massive output of speeches, memoranda and correspondence, often under trying conditions, the women who worked with Churchill were charged with feeding the fish at Chartwell, making certain that flowers and foodstuffs moved efficiently between Number 10 and the Churchills' other residences, and performing personal and household tasks, none of which are so much as mentioned by Kinna in his extensive interview for the Churchill Archives.

Kinna, born in September 1913, was described by Meiklejohn as 'the PM's very meek and Casper Milquetoastish stenographer',[6] which unfairly minimized his role. Jo Sturdee describes Kinna as

> very much twixt-in-between, not a member of the 'serfs club' because he wasn't with us so much... he would have qualified because he was such a darling... When Churchill went on these trips abroad... to the desert... where he would be behind enemy lines, where he would be with the fighting forces, Churchill said that women could not go there so that's when Kinna was brought in to go as a shorthand typist. I [was] never so fast as he. He was marvellous. [But] we didn't see much of him. He was so damn

good and invaluable and so jolly that he then joined the No. 10
staff... doing confidential filing.

It is reported that Kinna's typing was so fast that the keys stuck,
so a 'special portable typewriter with the keys shaved' was ordered
for his use. No other secretary mentions this special typewriter.[7]

Kinna was a key member of the team that worked with Churchill, his ill-defined job description reaching into the world of
the Private Secretaries (senior civil servants), although not into
the personal areas of Churchill's life, which was reserved for the
personal secretaries. When Kathleen Hill was taken ill and had to
take an extended leave after removal of her appendix, Kinna was
'brought along' to help an overworked Elizabeth Layton. He disliked shorthand and typing, at which he was extraordinarily good,
and between trips with the prime minister 'he minded official
documents and filing, arranged transport and so forth.'[8] He must
be included in this book not only to contrast his experience with
that of the women who worked with Churchill, but also because
his long service and revealing oral history tells us much about
Churchill the man. Kinna's experiences working with the prime
minister provide both support for the observations of Churchill's
secretarial staff, and reveal characteristics not recorded by the
women, who generally adopted an attitude more of staff and less
of an equal. Kinna felt free to ask for favours, such as transport to
visit his brother in Italy, which even the most self-confident of the
secretaries (who even needed support from Mrs Churchill to plead
for some time off at Christmas) would not consider requesting. So
in Kinna's history we benefit from the different perspective of a
man who worked with Churchill neither as Private Secretary nor
merely as a personal secretary. And someone for whom Churchill
had great respect, so great that he included him in events to which
only a small handful of people were invited.

Kinna was born into a family with a long tradition of army
service. His father, Captain Thomas Kinna, had been decorated
for his part in the relief of Ladysmith (28 February 1900) during

the Boer War, a battle in which Churchill, then an armed correspondent for the *Morning Post*, had also played a role.[9] Kinna hoped to become a parliamentary reporter, and after school learned shorthand and typing. He took shorthand at a phenomenal 150 words per minute and typed at 90 words per minute on the clunky machines of that era,[10] the latter matching the speed at which Churchill dictated.[11]

Kinna won the All-England Championship award for secretarial skills. When war with Germany seemed almost certain, one of his brothers told him to enlist, which he did, joining the reserves. In early 1939, having been called up, he was promoted to Lance Corporal, assigned to the Intelligence Corps, because the company needed a skilled secretary, and asked to sign the Official Secrets Act. Kinna was then sent to Paris to work for the war cabinet secretariat, presumably meeting Churchill there, when the new prime minister travelled several times to France to meet with French officials to, according to Kinna, 'urge them to carry on the struggle'. Kinna then worked at the British Embassy in Paris as clerk to the Duke of Windsor, who had settled there with his new wife, the former Wallis Simpson. One of the chores he performed for the duke was burning some of the embassy files as the Germans neared Paris. Shortly before the Germans entered Paris, the duke was spirited away to safety in Spain, abandoning his newly recruited secretary. When the Germans occupied Paris, Kinna fled, hitchhiking to the coast, and then catching a ride on a cruiser bound for Britain.

So good was his reputation that Kinna was ordered by Downing Street to Washington aboard the battleship *King George V* to work with the American, British and Canadian staffs, who were secretly 'setting up the joint staff mission', the so-called ABC-1 meetings. These meetings between January and March 1941 were convened to plan for the possible entry of the United States into the Second World War. After Washington, Kinna returned to Britain, unsure of what to do next. When Churchill's Private Secretaries were planning what was to be the first meeting between President Roosevelt and the prime minister in August 1941, in Placentia Bay, Newfoundland,

John Martin, Churchill's Principal Private Secretary, sent for Kinna. He told Kinna: 'This is very secret. The prime minister is going on an important trip and we want you to come and do the best you can with all the correspondence and dictation and all that.'

It was assumed that a female secretary – it would have been Kathleen Hill – should not go on such a trip. The feeling was 'No females – good heavens, no.'[12] For one thing, at this early stage in the war, with U-boats prowling the Atlantic, it was considered inappropriate to expose a non-military, civilian woman to so dangerous a journey. Perhaps more important were the traditions of the British navy, 'generations of men of the British Navy who had guarded their ships as jealously as they had guarded our shores'.[13] That inhibition faded as the war progressed and women proved quite up to managing among male sailors, as did Churchill's secretaries, often to their and the sailors' delight. Women could also handle dangerous assignments: Christine Granville spied on Germany and became known as 'Churchill's favourite spy', [14] while Josephine Butler's exploits behind enemy lines are detailed in her book, *Cyanide in My Shoe*.

In at least one particular, the British proved more adaptable to the introduction of women on battleships and at conferences than did the Americans. By the time of the Churchill–Roosevelt Conference in Cairo, prelude to the Teheran Conference with Stalin, 'The Chiefs of Staff found it was not necessary to have only uniformed staff, as the Americans did, and General Eisenhower was once overheard remarking to [General Sir Leslie] Hollis: "You don't put your girls in uniform then?" Hollis replied: "It wouldn't make them any more reliable if we did."'[15]

It was also thought that accommodations 'in war time on a battle ship' would cause problems were a woman to be on board. Kinna reports that he was always assigned 'a nice cabin, [one of] the officers' cabins… delightful and well furbished', but it was certainly not feasible for the female secretaries to live alongside the male officers aboard a battleship with shared bathing and toilet facilities. That problem was later solved in part by assigning to the women 'their own batman', but one woman noted that 'it seemed strange sending off all their clothes, even their underwear, on a mainly male battleship'. And stranger still when one of the women 'lost one of her "smalls" so there was some embarrassment when a seaman was assigned to tracking it down'.[16]

Kinna also thought that 'sailors would have loved to have a few of the girls on board to break the monotony but it wasn't possible really'. But Kathleen Hill, by then accustomed to the prime minister's work habits, might not have found it as annoying as did Kinna to be awakened early with the sailors, especially after taking dictation until two or three in the morning.

What was true of the space on battleships was also true of the space on many trains. When Churchill met with Turkey's President İnönü in January 1943 (in a failed effort to persuade him to bring Turkey into the war on the side of the Allies) the chosen site was a train in the middle of the most barren part of the country. Kinna found himself 'living in a train' with the British officials – no female secretary would have been included in this intimate – and unusual – meeting, during which Kinna met President İnönü.

Finally, there was one insurmountable barrier to women working with Churchill: he 'loved dictating… in his bath which obviously he could not do with his ladies'. In a letter to his mother, a fourteen-year-old Churchill wrote about a fellow student at Harrow: 'Milbanke* is writing this for me as I am having a bath.' It was a habit he kept for the rest of his life, to great advantage.[17] Male staff noted that he would submerge himself in the tub and come up spitting, pretending to be a fountain, or blowing bubbles or using the sponges to show the positions of battleships, much like he did at dinner tables with salt-and-pepper shakers and cutlery. As we shall see, as the war wore on, Churchill's female secretaries found a way of dealing with his bath times, perching outside the bathroom and taking dictation as best they could.

---

* Sir John Milbanke won a Victoria Cross in the Boer War and was killed at Gallipoli.

Despite all of these very compelling reasons for replacing Kathleen Hill with Kinna, he was nevertheless uneasy about accepting. There was such a strong sense of staff cohesion that he felt badly that he was asked on this trip rather than his co-worker. 'Here she was slaving away [Kinna often likened anyone working for Churchill to slaves] in the Annexe and had slaved away before the war in the Admiralty with him and yet these exciting trips she wasn't having those. I thought she deserved them. I didn't. I didn't see any reason why she couldn't go.' Nevertheless, Hill's time to join her boss on these trips would soon come.

Before sailing, Hill briefed Kinna, telling him how to use the famous klop or hole punch through which string was run to bind multi-page memoranda, how to 'clean his pens frequently, fill his inkwells, [making] sure he never runs out of ink', probably with blue and/or red ink, which Churchill used on occasion. Also 'his little mask if he wants a cat nap, his little black mask that goes over his eyes'.

The trip to Washington began when the train left Marylebone Station, stopping near Chequers to pick up the prime minister. 'Train' might be a misnomer. 'In fact, Churchill's train was a mobile hotel, office and communications centre.' Also wartime rationing rules did not apply either on the train or on the HMS *Prince of Wales*.[18]

Well-briefed and ready, Kinna was summoned to Churchill's cabin aboard the *Prince of Wales* and remembers 'his first words to me were "this is a melancholy story."' Not realizing that Churchill (as was his habit with new staff) had ignored any greeting to get straight on with work, and had begun dictating a memorandum, Kinna responded, 'Oh yes, sir. He [Churchill] said, "take it down!!" But everything went well on the trip.' As with the female secretaries, after an initial kerfuffle, either out of impatience to get on with work or deliberately to give a newcomer 'a fairly taxing time' (initiation by fire) or a bit of both, the way was smooth. 'Once you were in, you were in totally and unconditionally,'[19] and all early errors were forgiven.[20]

Kinna's first impressions of Churchill were of his 'greatness and power... not as tall as I expected. He used to walk round with great deliberate footsteps with this sort of pensive look and quite frankly he terrified me because I felt I was near this tremendous man and who am I to be here.' Kinna reported that the sailors aboard the *Prince of Wales* asked him for Churchill's old cigar butts, whether for smoking later or for selling at some future date is unclear, although those sailors could never have imagined how much an old Churchill cigar butt would one day be worth.

While on the trip, Kinna carried the personal letter from King George VI that Churchill was charged with handing to President Roosevelt when they met face to face. He found the work constant: '[I] had to be on call always on all these trips during the war. One was never sort of a tourist... Never had a moment.' Although there was one notable exception in Italy later in the war, as we shall see.

In addition to the letter from the king, Kinna was responsible for far bulkier items, such as

> a large standard typewriter, silent one, with large type... [like] the ones used in the Annexe and No. 10. It would have been much easier to have taken a portable but the prime minister would have objected to the noise and wouldn't like the small type... The only way to transport these standard noiseless typewriters was to have made huge cases [so] the machines could just slide in and wouldn't be damaged and [could] be kept locked... [when we arrived] without any delay, the first thing to unpack would be the typewriter because almost certainly the PM immediately would want some dictation or even some typewriting done straight away.

And certainly, there never was a dull moment. 'One morning' he recalls

> I was taking dictation from WSC in his cabin feeling none too well because of the very rough seas, my feelings being aggravated

by the PM's cigar smoke, I could hear some matelots whistling
and I knew only too well from experience that the PM could not
bear whistling at any time. I hoped he would not hear it – but
he did! Suddenly, he angrily told me to... tell those sailors to
stop... I had a shrewd idea what they would say to me! However...
I hastily left his cabin, not knowing quite what to do, I think I said
a few hurried prayers (two quick Hail Marys) and the whistling
miraculously stopped. The prime minister obviously believing
that I had quieted the ship's company![21]

Later, he recalled the incident: 'I thought this was the end of my
career at sea because I knew exactly what the sailors would tell me
to do if I asked them please would you mind stop whistling.' But
Kinna 'was very proud of himself when he got home'.

No one had any time off. On the trip to Placentia Bay, Churchill's
Principal Private Secretary John Martin, and Sawyers, his valet,
worked very long hours together. 'One of the most remarkable
characters on the PM's staff,' wrote the Conservative politician
Charles Mott-Radclyffe, 'was his shorthand-writer, Patrick Kinna,
who shadowed him everywhere, taking down almost every sentence uttered from some discreet place of vantage, within hearing
but out of sight. He would then disappear and type the memorandum or the draft telegram.'[22]

Kinna's recollections, like those of so many other wartime visitors to America, was of 'fantastic' food.

> One could not believe such lovely food existed. Steaks were about
> four times the size of anything I had ever seen for many many
> years. All the lovely fresh fruits... whenever I was coming home
> by sea or air, I would cram my cases and perhaps some of the
> document cases with tin fruits and... stockings for my sisters,
> and perfumes. Very unfair but after all rather human.

Kinna was not the only one to benefit from access to American
food. The WRNS, who 'had not seen an orange for almost four

▲ 1. Winston at 9 a.m., 1920.

▼ 2. Passports to success, 1922.

Give Me the Tools

► 3. WSC working at Chartwell, with some of his prodigious daily output, 1947.

▼ 4. Jock VI and the Remington, equally indispensable.

▼ 5. WSC and his editors at Chartwell: Denis Kelly, centre, Commodore Gordon Allen, left, and Rufus II, 1953.

The P.M. is represented as having saved us
from horrors of war, which glared upon
us in such a hideous form.

There was never any danger of Gt. Britain
or France being involved in war w G.
at this juncture,
if they were ready to sacrifice
CZ.

The terms which P.M. brought back fr Munich
cd hv bn easily agreed thro ordinary
channels of diplomacy, at any time
during the summer.
There was no need for all this tremendous
perturbation.

There was never any danger of a fight
if all the time one side meant to
give way completely.

When one reads the Munich terms,
& sees what is happening from hour to hour
in CZ.,
when one is assured tt Parliament
supports it all,
it is impossible not to ask –
what was all this fuss about?

resolve taken, & the course followed
may hv bn wise or unwise,
prudent or short-sighted,
but there was certainly no reason
to call all this formidable
apparatus into play, if
in hearts you were
ready to abandon the whole
contention,

◄ 6. A draft page from WSC's Munich Speech, 1938, in psalm format. Edited at 2 a.m., to be retyped by 10 a.m.

▼ 8. WSC with his Sound Scriber, 1946. No substitute for the ever-ready 'Misses' on call.

▼ 7. WSC's Chartwell desk with 'klops' and a drawing of Jan Smuts, alongside other memorabilia.

▶ 9. Young WSC at work. The chair and desk are his father's and the black coat is identical to the one that his father wore. Painting by Arthur Ward *c.*1900. In 1949, LIFE Magazine photographed WSC seated at this chair.

▲ 10. Grace Hamblin at Chartwell's 'Factory' in front of a portrait of WSC, painted in 1942 by Sir Frank O. Salisbury. This photo was taken in 1966 when Chartwell was opened to the public and Hamblin became the house's first curator.

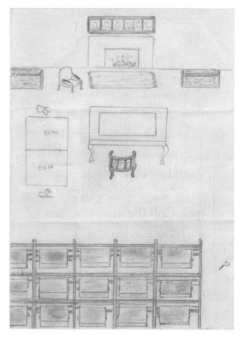

▲ 11. Grace Hamblin's sketch of the files and archival boxes at WSC's Chartwell 'Factory'.

years', were exposed to orangeade and quickly ordered additional rounds, some with maraschino cherries.[23]

Churchill must have agreed with Mott-Radclyffe's assessment. When the British team returned to Downing Street from the Churchill–Roosevelt meeting in late August 1941 John Martin wrote to Kinna saying the prime minister was very pleased with his work and

> thought it a wise thing if I joined the staff at No. 10 particularly to be available for these trips. Martin obviously thought I was going to be delighted over this but I wasn't because then strangely enough I was young and thought I ought to do something outside Whitehall. To John Martin's surprise, I said, could I have a week to think about this? When Martin recovered his breath [he agreed to the week's delay].

After considering the offer, Kinna returned to Martin's office and said

> I'm very honoured and flattered but I've decide not to come. When [Martin] had recovered his strength and breath again, he said this is as near a royal command as you are likely to get, young man, and I think you are going to join us at No. 10. We are going to take you out of the army and put you on the staff of the Treasury and we hope you will start on a certain date. I then saw the point.

Jock Colville notes: 'When Winston Churchill wanted something and chose to exercise his persuasive gift, there were few who found it possible to refuse.'[24] Churchill had his way.

Kinna was based in the Annexe and sat and worked alongside the several Private Secretaries – not with the female secretaries. He recalls that

> I would deal with all the messages to the PM from the theatres of war and President Roosevelt... and receiving the C boxes which

were the secret service boxes… making sure they went into one
of the PPS's boxes for transmission to the PM… I was almost a
Private Secretary. I wasn't called a Private Secretary. [They] were
very high-grade permanent civil servants and I was a back entrant.
Very interesting because the PM always referred to the Private
Secretaries as young gentlemen but I was always referred to as Mr
Kinna so I didn't reach the higher level. They were all very friendly.

However, Kinna says he 'was not one of the young gentlemen. I was
there to work and work I did. But he [Churchill] was always very
nice but we were not on a social level.'

Staff relations were friendly at all levels. Kinna records glowing
memories of the several female typists with whom he worked. So,
too, with the Private Secretaries. During the long hours of wartime
work Churchill 'occasionally had a little sort of pleasant evening
in the Private Secretary's mess in the Annexe. We had a very good
cook there, Brendan Bracken's [Swedish] cook, she used to produce lovely meals and Jack Churchill, Winston's brother, often
would invite very interesting characters along… one was able to
relax and laugh.' No females were invited to these gatherings. He
continues: 'There was a nice rapport with… everybody and I was
very happy there. I loved it. My only complaint was that I used to
get so tired because we had so many trips abroad – and generally
in those days no girls went.'

The 'young gentlemen' had direct access to the prime minister's
office; Kinna and the other shorthand typists did not. They had to
wait to be summoned. At the start of his secondment to Number 10,
Kinna was held in special reserve for foreign trips. But gradually,
as the other staff grew to rely on him, he did 'the 8 o'clock duty in
the morning… [especially if the Private Secretaries] probably had
a very busy day the previous day and night'. One early morning, he
was asked to ring Anthony Eden, who

was living at the Foreign Office… it seemed to ring when he was
in the bath so he wasn't very pleased about that and I would put

him through to the PM… We were not supposed to listen in to these calls early in the morning but it was understood that we should in case the PM decided to arrange a meeting and not tell his Private Secretaries that he had arranged it.

As Kinna began to have closer contact with Churchill, he realized that there were certain problems. Churchill was a 'very difficult' man to work for, as we have seen with the female secretaries. 'At times, an exacting and somewhat exasperating master to serve. He was apt to take little account of the difficulties under which people might be working.'[25] On the return trip from Moscow in August 1942, the group stopped in Cairo where the heat was unbearable in those pre-air conditioning days. 'At the hottest part of the day'[26] Churchill wanted to dictate a letter to Mrs Churchill, but in his bedroom Kinna saw only a fairly low table, on which he

plunked down his heavy typewriter… Churchill… started dictating very quickly because he was in rather angry mood having been with Stalin which was understandable… the legs of the table kept shaking… nothing was making sense that was coming out of the typewriter. I had to stop him which made him even more angry… finished up by putting it on a chest of drawers and trying to reach the keyboard but we got by and nothing more was said.

That is not the only instance in which Churchill's obsession with work led him to pay no attention to the plight of those working for him. Kinna once had malaria:

I was very yellow looking… I felt terribly ill and Winston sent Sawyers along. 'Tell Mr Kinna I want to dictate.' I said: tell the PM I am too ill. [Churchill] never did… enquire are you feeling better today. I think he thought [it a] jolly dreadful nuisance… he wanted to dictate and [I] wasn't well enough… [H]e wanted to get on. He didn't want to be delayed.

As with the young lady who sprained her ankle in North Africa and Hill, who was out with an appendix attack, Churchill always asked if they could still take down dictation. A point made graphically by Cecily Gemmell in Chapter 7.

So, too, again, for Kinna:

> I remember in particular in Cairo one day I was working very hard, in the mid-day sun… Typing itself is very exhausting. In the hot weather, it is even twice as exhausting especially with these old manual hand machines, not electric… General Smuts… a humanitarian who always seemed to be a little concerned about me because when we generally met in hot climates he said to Winston: 'You're going to kill this chap. Making him work in the heat of the day.' And I remember the PM saying 'yes, I am very sorry but we have got a lot of work to do.' So we carried on working to near faint.

In addition to his lack of sensitivity to the circumstances of others when in full work mode, Churchill 'could not really accept a mistake. Particularly if one were typing… he very much liked dictating to me… at No. 10 and the Annexe straight onto machine. I think he rather thought it was fun dictating onto a machine and there was this slave pounding away like mad.' He wasn't always clear, but very much disliked being interrupted. 'If you had the temerity to ask him to repeat a word, he nearly killed you with words. It upset his train of thought. He never paused.' Or slowed down, which created still another problem for Kinna and anyone taking dictation and typing up memoranda and minutes for Churchill.

Still another problem was the speed at which Churchill preferred to dictate. Kinna complains that he had no time to insert carbon between the paper when changing pages, so he had to 'always have sets of paper with carbon paper in it so [I] probably had just enough time to put the new one in while he was still dictating. That was very tricky and exhausting because of one's tension all the time. But it worked.' Protocol usually required an original plus two carbon sets. And there was a problem of another sort for those who took Churchill's dictation: fascination with his remarks. 'Sometimes I just wanted to listen and not take it down,'[27] Kinna told Sir Martin Gilbert in 1982. Kinna and the women who worked for Churchill were not mere mechanical typists: they understood the substance of what they were hearing and transcribing, knew these memoranda and letters were a crucial part of the prime minister's effort to win the war, and had to discipline themselves not to merely listen, but to take down and type, often at 3 a.m., often in a car travelling at high speeds on bumpy roads, often against unreasonable deadlines. The lucky ones then got to attend the House of Commons to take down the speech as delivered.

Fortunately, there were times when the difficulties Churchill's work habits created for Kinna took on comic, madcap proportions, more akin to a scene in a Marx Brothers film than to one in which the war to save the world from Nazism was being conducted. He travelled with two groups, one led by 'Air Commodore Frankland', the other by 'Don Quixote', the code names adopted by, respectively, Churchill and Roosevelt. FDR assigned the code name 'Sancho Panza' to his trusty advisor Harry Hopkins.[28]

'Madcap' also describes a post-conference work session attended by Kinna. In January 1943, after the Casablanca Conference, Churchill was in bed dictating and breakfasting at the same time, as usual. Brigadier Ian Jacob reports:

> Sawyers brings the breakfast, Kinna is sent for to take something down, meanwhile the bell is rung for the Private Secretary on duty who is asked for news, and told to summon someone, then it is the candle for lighting cigars that is wanted. Then someone must get Hopkins on the phone... the PM... half sitting, half lying, in his bed surrounded by papers.[29]

All of this at 9 a.m. The PM was working on a joint communiqué to be issued by him and the president. Churchill wrote 'wigs by

Clarkson, his expression for what he wanted filled in and checked'.
'Wigs by Clarkson' was a uniquely Churchillian phrase from

> the early part of the century. At the theatre, Clarkson's seemed
> to have a monopoly of headdresses, wigs, etc., and in every
> programme the line always appeared 'Wigs by Clarkson', so
> when Churchill had approved the text of the communiqué
> at Casablanca, all he had to say was 'wigs by Clarkson', and I
> knew... he wanted the text... cleaned up and the necessary
> ancillary remarks included.[30]

Kinna's second big trip, after Placentia Bay, was with Churchill
to Washington DC, just after the attack on Pearl Harbor. Arriving
in the United States with Churchill in late December 1941, he
recalls 'frequently we stayed in the White House which was always
very nice... The one thing that pleased me was on Christmas
morning the valet brought in my breakfast tray and with it was an
outsize photograph of President and Mrs Roosevelt which they had
signed.' He and the staff worried about the possible heart attack
that Churchill suffered on Boxing Day night. However, Churchill
'was very resilient and he had a doctor* there, but we were more
worried than anyone else at this critical stage of the war... without
him then, what would have happened?' Kinna is recollecting this
many years later, as it is most likely that the staff did not know at
the time of his possible heart attack.

At the White House one morning Kinna was taking down, while
Churchill

> was in his lovely bath and kept submerging and coming up rather
> like a lovely fish... saying a few more words and then submerging
> and coming up... [H]e wanted to get out of the tub, so the valet
> had these outsized bathrobes all twisted around him... walking
> back to his adjoining bedroom... I was trailing behind listening

---

*   Charles Wilson, later Lord Moran.

and taking down like mad... walking up and down this huge bedroom [chosen by Churchill for its proximity to the President's],...
eventually the bathrobe fell off and he was completely nude...
quite unconcerned, he continued pacing the room and dictating
all the time... there was a rat-ta-ta-ta on the door, the door
opened and there was President Roosevelt in his wheelchair. And
Winston never being lost for words as we all know said, 'You see,
Mr President, I have nothing to hide from you.' And I think that
was very funny.[31]

That story has been told and retold and is so amusing that its points
are often lost. First, in the bath or striding around in the nude,
for Churchill all that mattered was the work and having someone
there to ensure it got done. If that meant pacing naked in front of
staff while dictating, so be it. (No young ladies would have been
present!) Second, the speed at which Churchill could convert a
possible embarrassment into a winning moment was amazing: in
the nude, in a surprise confrontation with the most powerful man
in the world, Churchill continued his wooing of Roosevelt. One
wonders whether the alliance would have survived had the person
on the other side of the door been Mrs Roosevelt, who had little
use for a fully clothed Winston Churchill and the British Empire
he represented – and she resented his ability to keep her husband
from bed until the early hours of many mornings.

There were, of course, advantages that more than offset the
frustrations of working with Churchill. There was the opportunity
'to have a place in the thrice-blessed crowd who went on trips! –
to eat American food!!... to wander around the shops... buying
little reminders of better times for those at home,'[32] noted Layton,
who accompanied Kinna on one of the prime minister's trips to
Washington aboard the *Queen Mary* to confer with President
Roosevelt. Churchill also delivered another address to Congress,
which he dictated from 9.30 a.m. until 4.30 p.m. without a stop,
then resumed from midnight until 2.30 a.m., according to Layton.[33]
One had to work hard to earn the right to feast on American food.

In January 1942 Churchill and his entourage took time off from planning the strategy that would eventually win the war. For a few days he stayed at 'a very nice villa' near Miami. Time off meant Churchill could swim in the ocean a few times a day – in the nude, as 'it was very much an all-male party... the staff took this opportunity for a little bit of rest but we were more proper, we put on swim suits'. As was to prove true during the rest of the war and thereafter, a Churchill vacation included more than a bit of work: couriers went back and forth daily from both the prime minister and the president's office in Washington.

In August 1942 Churchill went to Moscow, avoiding flying over the area near where the Battle of Stalingrad was still raging. The prime minister's purpose was to tell Stalin that there would be no second front in 1942, but that the Atlantic convoys would continue to get through with supplies for the Red Army, and convince the Soviet leader that the upcoming Operation Torch in North Africa would provide great relief for the Red Army. Kinna was assigned a 'lovely bedroom and beautiful bathroom but it was lacking in one thing, it did not have a bath. It had a wash basin and enormous bottles of perfumes and things but no bath.' Churchill's accommodations must have had a bath, because as he later wrote of State Villa No. 7, where he stayed:

> The hot and cold water gushed. I longed for a hot bath after the length and heat of the journey. All was instantly prepared. I noticed that the basins were not fed by separate hot and cold water taps and that they had no plugs. Hot and cold turned on at once through a single spout, mingled to exactly the temperature one desired... In a modest way, I have adopted this system at home [at Chartwell]. If there is no scarcity of water it is far the best.[34]

Presumably at Chartwell he could afford plugs. This recollection of what for many would have been a forgettable minor experience immediately before a first face-to-face meeting with Stalin, shows the importance Churchill attached to his bathing rituals, to his personal comforts, and to even minor innovations.

While the prime minister was meeting Stalin, Kinna asked if he might tour Moscow with General Sir Ian Jacob, assistant military secretary to the war cabinet under General Ismay. A car and driver were provided, as well as the usual security people. He found Moscow 'stark... evacuated, roads lined with soldiers... miles-long queues trying to get food'. Certainly no female secretary would have imposed on a general with a request of this or of any kind.

Soon Churchill was back from his meeting with Stalin and Kinna went to work taking down a telegram to deputy prime minister Clement Attlee

> talking about this rude dreadful man Stalin who has no appreciation for what we were sending him, all the men we were losing... harping on why we have not started the Second Front?... Suddenly [Ambassador] Clark Kerr said prime minister I must remind you that this will be [bugged] like all the rooms in Moscow so I think you'd better be careful. This had the opposite effect and Winston became more vitriolic against Stalin... I'm not going to stay here!

It is conceivable that Churchill was well aware that he was being spied upon and intended his remarks for Stalin's ears. Churchill's willingness to make such seemingly indiscreet remarks in the presence of Kinna shows his confidence in his secretary's discretion. As with all other secretaries, at all levels, confidentiality was essential – there were never any leaks from Churchill's private office.

That may be the reason, as Kinna reports, that

> next day there was a meeting with Stalin all charm... The last night we were in Moscow, the small British party was invited to the farewell banquet at the Kremlin.... We were received by

Molotov which was a disappointment... I would like to [have
been] received by this ghastly man Stalin. Winston was in his
siren suit... Stalin was in what I call his boiler suit and the evening became very convivial... The meal went on, course after
course, the waiters all looked terrified in their eyes and almost
starving. And I felt like saying, look, you sit down, you have
this... it was terrible to see these poor obviously hungry men
seeing this wonderful czarist-type banquet in war time. At the
end of the evening we were taken to the door by Stalin... and
[he] shook our hands.

Certainly no females, military or civilian, would have been included at this dinner.

The 'siren suit' that Kinna mentions was a 1940 invention of
Churchill's, 'a garment based on his bricklaying boiler suit...
with a full-length zip up the front'.[35] Much like a pilot's flying
suit today. It is sometimes also called his 'zip suit' or ridiculed
as his 'rompers'. The colours and fabrics varied, with velvet the
favourite material, and Royal Air Force blue among his favourite
colours. Ben Macintyre describes the siren suit as 'a military-style
one-piece boiler suit that would not become fashionable again for
another seventy years until the invention of the "onesie".'[36]

Kinna's next trip was to Quebec in August 1943 for the meeting
with Roosevelt and the Canadians (known as Quadrant) to begin
planning for the invasion of Europe. On board the *Queen Mary*
were Mrs Churchill and their daughter Mary, in addition to a
number of WRNS, cypher officers (called 'cypherenes' if female)
and clerks. Because there was too much work for one person, staff
cohesion was taken to its limits. Despite the added workload,
there was time for romance. Kinna mentions that a 'particularly
attractive cypher clerk named Judy Love' fell in love with Leslie
Rowan, one of Churchill's Private Secretaries, and later married
him. The Rowans remained fast friends with the Churchill family
even after Winston died. Sir Leslie was one of only five non-family
members at Churchill's interment.[37] Much later, Lady Rowan

continued to visit Kinna, who was then living in retirement in Brighton.

Kinna was burdened with responsibilities that Churchill would assign to very few. After intense meetings in Quebec (Quadrant) and at Hyde Park in August 1943, Churchill and his entourage decided to have a fishing vacation and rest on the shore of Lac des Neiges in the Laurentian Mountains. Kinna was charged with a file labelled 'TA', which meant nothing to him at the time. TA stood for Tube Alloys, code for the work on the atom bomb, and Kinna had to keep this essential file with him at all times.

> [W]e couldn't even let our trusty and well-known marine order-lies... carry this. I had to carry it. When we got to the side of the lake we were put in... little skiffs without outboard motors... to go to some attractive log cabins. And we're swaying from side to side and I thought at any moment now this is going to turn over... don't worry about yourself. Keep hold of the TA file.

He didn't know the reason for the importance of the file, but did as he was ordered, holding it close during his stay in the cabins, along with 'one or two mice going along the logs'.

Later that year, at the Big Three meeting in Teheran in November, arranged so that Roosevelt could meet Stalin for the first time, Kinna was charged with the responsibility of taking care of the Sword of Stalingrad.[38] King George VI had commanded that a four-foot ceremonial sword be forged, inscribed and presented to Marshal Stalin as a tribute from the British people to the Soviet victors at the Battle of Stalingrad, some ten months earlier. Amid an almost balletic ceremony at the Russian legation, Kinna handed the sword to a British lieutenant, who then handed it to Churchill. The prime minister then presented it in its red Morocco-leather scabbard to Stalin, who took it, kissed it, and then showed it to the American president in his wheelchair. Roosevelt, not one to be upstaged by the leaders of Great Britain and the Soviet Union, ceremoniously drew the sword from its scabbard, as Kinna watched. Kinna had been trusted enough to have charge of the sword all the time before the ceremony, but was not of sufficient rank or standing to be the one to offer it to Churchill to start the ceremony. Still, he had been involved and was present, a testimonial to the importance Churchill attached to him.

After the meetings in Teheran, at which May 1944 was agreed as the date for the invasion of Europe (Operation Overlord), Churchill flew to Cairo for more meetings and planning sessions. 'At no time since the war began had he [Churchill] been so exhausted.'[39] After meetings in Cairo he flew to Tunisia, taking Kinna with him, to meet with some of his commanders and General Eisenhower at his villa (called the White House) overlooking the sea near Carthage.[40] Two of Churchill's children, Randolph and Sarah, were there, as guests of the American military, Sarah reading *Pride and Prejudice* to her exhausted, enervated father. By mid-December Churchill was more than tired. He had developed pneumonia. According to medical reports, 'It was characterized by fever that lasted six days, left lower lobe pneumonia and two episodes of atrial fibrillation.'[41] It was a serious enough matter to require the continued attendance of Lord Moran, Churchill's doctor, assisted by two (in one report three) nurses and a pathologist called in from Cairo. 'It is remarkable,' noted Drs Vale and Scadding, 'that, despite the severity of his illness, he continued to direct the affairs of State from his bed'.[42] This, with an ailment commonly referred to as 'the old man's friend', because it was seen as a swift, relatively painless way to die.

Kinna recalls 'we were all very worried and in fact Lady Churchill came out [from London] with Grace Hamblin' and Jock Colville. Despite the medical emergency, Churchill continued to dictate to Kinna, against doctors' orders, which were 'to no avail'.[43]

When well enough to travel, Churchill proceeded to Marrakesh for a period of recuperation, although not for a complete rest. That was hardly possible, since accompanying Churchill were most of the military leaders, their staff, plus some medical advisors to keep an eye on the prime minister, and Churchill's usual secretarial staff. Planning for the assault on Anzio was being debated, as were the initial plans for Overlord, so it cannot have been a moment for recuperation. However, work slowed enough for Kinna to be able to find some time off.

That was when Kinna (like Hamblin, who described that period when she and Layton shared a room at La Mamounia[44] as 'three lovely weeks in Marrakesh, never to be forgotten') seized an opportunity for a period of liberation from the demands of his boss. When the work pace slowed during Churchill's recuperation, Kinna was not called for by the patient as frequently as was usually the case. So he planned to try to visit his brother, who was serving somewhere in Italy. General Alexander, a Kinna favourite, arranged to have him flown to Naples and 'dropped... on the runway... I walked along to some officers and said please can... you find out where [my brother] was. They were very helpful, found out where he was stationed and gave me a jeep. I stayed the night [with him] in his mess.' Later his brother asked the Americans if they had a plane going back to Tunis.

> [T]hey had a Dakota and I was put on board.... I was beginning to get worried that my absence might be noticed. The pilot said... I'm coming down in Sicily. I'll stay a few hours. I've got a girl-friend there I want to visit. I could have killed him... but had to wait patiently in the plane.

This adventure was made possible by the fact that Kinna had earlier formed a relationship with General Alexander. No such bond existed between the general and any female staff, none would have dared make such a request.

During this stay in North Africa, one of Kinna's most moving moments was on Christmas Eve. Kinna and Sawyers, both Roman Catholics,[45]

> had heard there was going to be a midnight mass in Carthage Cathedral high up on a hill overlooking the city of Tunis... we

arranged for someone to take us there in their jeep and as we were getting nearer this enormous cathedral, the bells were being pealed and when we went inside, we found the cathedral full of [armed] forces people in their various uniforms and various nationalities... all started singing hymns... I think it was the most memorable midnight mass I have ever attended.

And an experience that made the difficulties and, at times, lack of consideration by Churchill well worth bearing.

With time and, for the most part, some rest, Churchill improved, helped by his own robust constitution and the Americans who provided many of his medical requirements, as well as food and lodgings for the prime minister's staff. In fact, the Americans had imported a nutritionist* to watch over Churchill's menus – although she cooked the partridges for 'an hour and half: the result was concrete. Sawyers rashly informed the American cook that Mrs Landemare cooks partridges for only fifteen minutes.'[46] The New Year's Eve party went rather better. Churchill invited everyone regardless of rank or status to see in the new year at his Villa Taylor (owned by rich Americans). 'All formed a circle to sing Auld Lang Syne,'[47] 'followed by the prime minister complaining in stentorian voice – "Clemmie – there's a wasp in my punch."'[48]

The party had flown to Marrakesh with the plan that Churchill would recuperate more fully there. But as Churchill improved, his work increased, despite his family's pleadings to slow down enough until he was completely recovered – a plea they knew he would never heed. As a result, Kinna's workload also increased, although he, too, was understandably exhausted. But he recalls that he made many good friends in Tunis and, after the war, returned often to visit them.

Throughout the war Kinna met the famous politicians and military men who were planning and conducting what was a war

---

* This shows the concern that the Americans felt for the prime minister's well-being.

to save Western civilization – an opportunity routinely denied the female secretaries who had no basis on which to form opinions and therefore none are expressed during their oral history interviews.

Here's Kinna on various famous people he encountered.

Roosevelt: 'He was very friendly. Always very considerate.' One day, while working at Roosevelt's Hyde Park weekend home he 'heard a terrific noise and was nearly trampled to death because Eleanor Roosevelt was rushing out in her riding habit... I was nearly knocked for six.'* Kinna believed that

> if Roosevelt had not more or less got on the side of Stalin, I think the world today would have been very different. I blame him for a lot of the present-day situation... I'm sure the Americans might be very angry if I said this but one had the impression, at least I had the impression, that the Americans all the time were trying to push the English aside. I think they were jealous of our empire.

Stalin: 'I shook the bloody hand of Stalin... I was terrified. He had the coldest eyes... cunning and very evil... Very uncouth and rather a tough chap.'[49] 'A very powerful evil treacherous man but very impressive... I remember so well at the conference he criticized British intelligence saying your intelligence is not as good as Russian intelligence. I think that was probably fairly true because we all know the Russians are pretty ruthless at getting the information they want and spend a lot of time and money on it.†

General Smuts: 'A humanitarian who always seemed a little concerned about me' (as we saw in his concern for Kinna working in Egyptian heat).

---

*   An expression derived from cricket (when hitting the ball over the boundary scores six runs, the maximum for one shot), meaning devastated, shocked or upset.
†   It is unusual to have a secretary express stout political opinions, as few of the female secretaries did in their oral histories.

General Ismay: '[A]n absolute dear... a great man.' Kinna had
first worked for him in Paris at the Hotel de Crillon, just before
the war started when he had to

> type up the preliminary minutes of decisions taken at the War
> Council in Paris... [Churchill] thought the world of General
> Ismay as he always called him. [Ismay] always knew his work
> on the military side and would express his own opinions in a
> nice gentle way and Winston used to listen to him very very
> carefully. He would say Pug [Ismay's nickname] did a wonderful
> job during the war... I kept in touch with him after the war
> as well.

General Alexander was a Kinna favourite: 'everyone liked him
very much'.
General Montgomery was not a Kinna favourite:

> Although a very good general, he didn't like the lower echelons
> very much. I remember on one occasion a cable went from the
> PM's office to Montgomery saying he was planning to come
> out to see him [to watch the battle of the Rhine] and his party
> would consist of the following two: Leslie Rowan and myself
> and would he arrange accommodation. A very curt reply came
> back saying: 'I will be pleased to see you, prime minister, but
> I cannot accommodate your staff.' Fortunately, Field Marshal
> Alexander accommodated Leslie Rowan and me and so we had
> the great pleasure of dining in his mess with him, which was
> much nicer than being with Monty I can assure you.

The prime minister solved the problem created by the not-always-
easy-to-deal-with Montgomery by advising:

> it would be necessary for me to have somewhere twenty or thirty
> miles further back in a train, or perhaps a railway coach, where
> I can keep a Private Secretary and Mr Kinna who deals with

facilities for scrambling messages... I do not need them all at the front... A motor cyclist or two would keep in contact with this 'base'.[50]

The prime minister deemed Kinna essential, even on a short trip to a battle site.

Randolph Churchill:

Randolph I didn't like at all... not many people did unfortunately. He was an awkward person and I always used to be sad or rather worried when I knew he was flying from somewhere to meet his father on these trips abroad because I knew it would cause great arguments between father and son... I think it was in Cairo one day, he came up to me and started telling me what to do – what he wanted done... the only time I was ever rude to him or anyone in the Churchill family when I told him exactly what my functions were... I didn't come all this way to work for him.

No female shorthand typist would have had the temerity to say this to a man, no matter how rude, and especially not to the son of their employer, the prime minister.

Sarah Churchill:

I adored Sarah. Everybody did. She was my favourite... [because] she realizes we were poor slaves and didn't have much of a let up... she might perhaps when dinner was over and Winston and whoever was visiting were having conferences, she would come into my office in her Women's Auxiliary Air Force (WAAF) uniform looking terribly beautiful, sit on the desk and talk... very very friendly and no side at all... everyone stopped working for a while to gossip with Sarah.

And despite what at times seemed to be Churchill's inhumane treatment of him, Kinna fondly remembered his boss's humour, which had a way of showing Kinna that he was one of a small, very special group. He recalled that on a flight back from Europe, the Dakota on which he and Churchill were flying began to lose altitude. Churchill jokingly suggested they might have 'to jettison one or more of the passengers'. Turning to Kinna, he said, 'No use throwing you out, there's not enough of you to make a ham sandwich.'[51] Much later, in February 1945, while waiting to fly back to Britain from Cairo, Churchill again teased Kinna about his slight build, saying, 'If we come down in the desert, you would not be much good as a meal.'[52]

And there was the kindness – a characteristic often subordinated to the pressures of war. Kinna recalls

> when the prime minister had time which wasn't very often he could be very considerate, very kind. I remember we were flying somewhere or other in a converted bomber… and it was becoming very cold. We didn't have any modern comforts. [Churchill] had the only bunk bed quite rightly, and I had to sleep in the bomb bay with one or two others… I remember he said you are going to be very cold tonight. [He] was dressed in his RAF gear and took off his RAF overcoat and put it around me. I thought that was really something.

Much like when the two secretaries were working in the cold Hawtrey Room at Chequers without a fire and Churchill insisted on lighting a fire for them. Or when Churchill insisted on getting a spare coat for Holmes during the Christmas 1944 visit to Athens, of which more below.

After the election defeat of 1945 Churchill wished to say goodbye personally to his closest staff and assembled them in the Private Secretaries' room, just outside the cabinet room. And

> to my surprise [Churchill] said: come in, Mr Kinna, so he had me in first – probably thought he'd get rid of me first, I don't know. I closed the door. He sat at his usual seat at the cabinet table. I sat directly opposite and then he started reminiscing about all our

perilous trips together abroad, and mentioned various countries we'd been to and the people we'd met... becoming very sad... and then he said the British people don't want me anymore. And he had tears running down his cheeks and I had tears running down mine as well. It was all rather sad.[53]

Kinna was here exposed to Churchill's well-known willingness to cry unashamedly when overcome with emotion. Virginia Cowles reports him in tears when seeing a small shop in ruins after a bombing raid, because the owner had lost both his home and his livelihood. At the christening of Randolph's son, Winston Junior, Churchill, 'with tears streaming down his cheeks', murmured, 'Poor infant, to be born into such a world as this.'[54] And Ismay is reported to have said that Churchill 'cries equally from pleasure or from sadness, [and] cried and sobbed from the moment he set foot in France [in December 1944].'[55] His show of emotion was not confined to weeping. 'Anyone who ever heard Churchill chuckle cannot realize the fun that lay in that noise. It was between a chuckle and a snort, and it was apt to be followed by a sound from deep in his chest that sounded like "oomph", repeated several times as the joke was rolling around and maturing.'[56]

Sometime later Kinna was summoned to Claridge's to meet Churchill, who offered him the job of being secretary to the Leader of the Opposition, as Churchill then had become. Kinna recalled:

I again felt I could not do justice because after all these years, really long hours, so, I hope, I gracefully declined. But I suggested Elizabeth Gilliatt would be ideal. And that I think was more or less the end of my very delightful, very hard, wonderful connection with Winston Churchill.

Kinna then spent some years working as a secretary to Ernest Bevin at the Foreign Office until Bevin's death in 1951. After that, Kinna worked in the private sector as a company director and retired to Brighton in 1973.

Churchill recommended him for an MBE in 1945 and, it is said, the two men exchanged white geraniums on their birthdays.[57]

In 1984 Kinna was one of a group of secretaries that had worked with Churchill who, in the presence of the queen, attended the opening of the museum now known as the Cabinet War Rooms, so beautifully preserved that 'you can practically still smell the cigar smoke'.[58] He was the last surviving male member of Churchill's wartime private office.[59] Kinna died in March 2009 aged ninety-five.

5

Jo Sturdee

'We all dressed quietly… we did not
dress flamboyantly.'

'You see we were meant to merge into the
background and not be noticed.'

'It was his joy to work.'

Jo Sturdee, oral history

NINA EDITH STURDEE – always known as 'Jo', later Countess of Onslow – was one of the most significant of Churchill's personal secretaries, and not only because she was responsible for vetting and training many of the women whose recollections of working with Churchill are related here. She served Churchill during the war years of 1942 to 1945, after which she became his main personal secretary from 1945 to 1953. That gave her an almost unique view of the man in and out of office, as a leader of his wartime government, as the Leader of the Opposition to the first post-war government, and once again as prime minister, this time struggling to prevent the nuclearized post-war world from repeating the mistakes of the last war and bringing about still another conflict.

Born in 1922 and 'educated at a convent', Sturdee trained as a shorthand typist at the Mayfair Secretarial College and then worked in a solicitor's office. In October 1941, feeling she ought to do something more for the war effort, and having been turned down by the WRNS, she applied to Mrs Hoster's agency which kept a listing of available jobs, although she had not trained with them. 'If you went to [any] of those so-called smart secretarial colleges in London they guaranteed you a job at the end of their training at not less than two pounds ten [shillings] a week (about £110 in today's money) which was big stuff in those days.' She was offered an interview with a cabinet minister whom the agency refused to identify, and who stressed that several others were also being considered. In her interviews at Downing Street, she first saw Kathleen Hill and then Mags Stenhouse, a civil servant in charge of Number 10 staffing, about whom we will learn more.

Sturdee is one of the few who mentioned a security vetting process – probably because she was being hired straight into Downing Street during the war. She recalled her father having a sandwich and beer for lunch one day when a stranger sat down next to him, asking 'a whole lot of impertinent questions'. In retrospect, Sturdee and her father decided the man had been checking her background for potential security risks. She was hired, in part because Hill noticed her 'impeccable manners'.[1]

Sturdee was finally told she would be working for the prime minister, on his personal staff, under Kathleen Hill who was also supervising Elizabeth Layton. No one instructed her in proper office attire: 'We all dressed quietly... we did not dress flamboyantly... You see we were meant to merge into the background and not be noticed.' She says she wore 'a neat little suit and a white blouse half the time, or a twin set and pearls, dark colours'. Layton notes, 'We were not able to be very smartly dressed – neither time nor [ration] coupons allowed for that; but one and all we made it a rule always to appear neat and groomed, hair in order and properly made-up.'[2] There was no formal dress code to guide these women, merely a sense of what was proper and what was not. However, Vanda Salmon, who worked for Churchill when he was Leader of the Opposition, might have stretched things a bit when she appeared for her interview 'wearing my best navy-blue suit and a rather fetching hat with a red feather in it (we all wore hats to work in those days)'.[3]

The Churchills did not give Sturdee a clothing allowance, but Mrs Churchill did advise her always to wear white gloves if she were meeting royalty, '[you] must never present a bare hand to [them]... they must not ever touch anything but white.' And, as we shall see, Sturdee learned to 'Never, ever go abroad without a long dress. You always had to have at least one, if not two, long dresses.' Joan Bright, as always, an independent civilian woman, but who worked closely with military men and women, said that she 'kept her own clothes on the dark side and tailored, looking uniformed, thinking that this gave me more authority'.[4] And she had a great deal of authority as General Ismay's de facto office manager.[5]

It would be some months before Sturdee met the prime minister. Before that fateful day, she worked on constituency matters, copying out letters that Hill had drafted in order to get the hang of answering letters. She called herself happy to be the dogsbody*... doing the 'ruddy' press clippings. A whole packet came in every day depending on what the prime minister had been up to. [I] had to read them all and decide [which to keep]... and so I think we kept... probably depending on which was the best report, probably *The Times* or the *Telegraph* and then always the lesser ones like the *Mirror*.

But, she added, they kept all the bad reports too, as well as the ones from the 'left-wing newspapers'. Churchill had every national and several regional newspapers on his bed when he woke up every morning and he read them all, beginning with the 'left-wing [ones] and finishing with *The Times*'.

Her first interview with the prime minister was the usual affair, experienced by all other secretaries when first introduced to Churchill – more of a looking-over than what we would call an interview. Her first impression at that moment was 'what beautiful hands he had. <u>Beautiful</u> hands I thought to myself,' an observation also made by 'Chips' Gemmell; and decades later Jane Portal vividly remembered Churchill's 'beautiful hands... with the signet ring given to him, I think, by his father with the Marlborough coat of arms on it.' Some years later, when Cecil Beaton, the famed photographer and stage designer (of *My Fair Lady*, among others), met 'the great hero dethroned' – this was December 1945 – he was taken by what he describes in his diary as Churchill's 'feminine hands with pointed nails and fingers'.[6] Pugh also commented on his 'lovely hands'.

Sturdee goes on to say that Churchill 'scowled at me like anything' when she first entered the cabinet room to take down his words directly onto the typewriter; it was either his usual, automatic reaction when faced with a new staff member, or designed to intimidate. Sturdee was nervous, but had been well enough trained by Hill to know that when 'he dictated prime minister to

---

* In British English, a 'dogsbody' is someone who does drudge work. A rough American equivalent would be a 'gofer,' 'grunt' or 'lackey'.

CIGS… you put a heading… at the top and underline it. [I'd] been taught how to do it,' even though she claimed she had no idea at the time what the CIGS (Chief of the Imperial General Staff) was. But now she was inside the Secret Circle, accepted by Churchill. Consequently, Sturdee's hours increased radically as she was now part of the group that shared the massive amount of work – and secrets – the wartime prime minister generated. In addition to her work at Number 10, she alternated weekends at Chequers with Hill and Layton, where the male Principal Private Secretaries, who also worked alternate weekends there, were always present. Everyone worked round the clock to keep up with the enormous flow of incoming and outgoing memoranda, reports and other materials that flooded in to a prime minister, who also served as his own Minister of Defence, and who chose to involve himself in all the details of his government, including rationing and matters normally left to the Foreign Secretary. In this as in many other things, he was different from Chamberlain, who 'hated to be disturbed at weekends. He never took a Private Secretary with him to Chequers, or his typist, Miss Watson. Until the outbreak of war, he had communicated with the world from a single telephone in the pantry, to be used for emergencies.'[7]

Working at Chequers, and at the pace set by Churchill, was not easy, in part because of the lack of adequate office space. Two 'young ladies' had to share a small room with the Private Secretaries, and with a large amount of equipment – typewriters, files, sacks of letters, ringing telephones, the scramblers. In addition, there was a chair by the fireplace where the prime minister would sit during his frequent drop-ins. Commander Thompson, Churchill's principal aide, also had a desk in this cramped workroom. There might be a war on, and he might now have realized his long-held ambition of becoming prime minister, but Churchill's routine remained what it had always been: only the scene of the action changed. One of the women was with the prime minister, taking dictation early in the morning, often in his bedroom, surrounded with papers, pets, cigars, military officers and Private Secretaries.

'The routine at Chequers was like that at No. 10, but more so. That is to say the work and the flow of papers, telegrams, minutes, etc., was just as intense, but in addition there were the mealtimes, at which discussion could take place, and there was the night... bedtime was not often before 2.30 am.'[8]

Sturdee recalls: 'he never treated us like servants... although we didn't eat with him, we ate with Miss Lamont, [then running Chequers], but [he was] always most concerned about whether we were comfortable.'

At Downing Street the office was more spacious. Churchill's personal secretaries – Sturdee, Layton and their 'boss' Hill, who was working for Mrs Churchill – worked in a very large room outside the Cabinet Room, sharing that space with the civil servants' secretaries, all of them women. British protocol is that civil servants do not work on political (constituency) or private (family and financial) matters. Those matters were handled by his personal secretaries. Sturdee says there was little interaction between the female staffs – but certainly no animosity between them.

Sometimes, Sturdee recalls, one of the shorthand typists would be called into the Cabinet Room to take dictation straight onto the Remington noiseless typewriter with special large print, which was kept there in case 'it was wanted in a crisis'. The machine had been imported from America, because Churchill 'insisted on a quiet working environment'.[9] The typewriter was so heavy that one of the male Private Secretaries would have to carry it across the room and place it on the Cabinet Room table, opposite the prime minister, who traditionally sat with his back to the fireplace, in the only chair with arms. Sturdee often used the silent typewriter in that room – decades later she bought one, perhaps as a reminder of her days with Churchill. While Churchill dictated, there might be cabinet members in the room, telephones ringing and Private Secretaries bringing in notes and files. It must have been difficult to hear the prime minister's words and concentrate on typing – especially since news and events during 1941 were so important, so riveting and changing every minute.

When there were air raids, work continued, but in the Annexe. 'We had terrible bombings in London... and air raids... and several weeks on end when Security knew that the Germans were going to concentrate on bombing London.' On those nights, Churchill could 'be persuaded to sleep over at the Annexe'. The Annexe contained a complete duplicate office for the entire staff, and all the needed papers were transported back and forth in large black boxes between Downing Street and the Annexe, depending on the Germans' bombing schedule. Even Mrs Landemare, the long-time cook for Churchill and his family, 'had to trundle over with her kitchen maid and staff and her 26 pounds of butter and whatever'. The staff, Sturdee included, ate in 'the Cabinet Office canteen in the Annexe'.

Sturdee recalls that some time during the war, President Roosevelt sent two very early model electric typewriters as a gift to the prime minister for use by his staff. 'All of us found them most difficult [to use] when you were taking dictation straight onto the typewriter. Even the prime minister saw that it was impossible... and they were noisy... I am sorry to say we didn't use them very much. I trust the President never knew.'[10] So far as we know, neither Churchill nor any member of his staff shared the secret of the unusability of the president's generous gift with FDR.

Another gift, this one from the film director Alexander Korda, was a Dictaphone, which was installed at Chartwell. Jane Portal tells us that 'after a night of fun, I was suddenly summoned to Churchill's room. Upon entering he said to me, "Take it away. I don't like it. I can never work like this. I must be able to dictate to hear the English language as I speak it and not to a machine" – so it was removed.'[11]

When Sturdee accompanied Churchill to his meeting in Quebec with President Roosevelt (Octagon, September 1944), she benefitted from advice from two veterans of such international conferences. Both Hamblin, who by then was working for Mrs Churchill, and Layton had been at the first Quebec conference (Quadrant, August 1943). They were able to tell Sturdee what to

expect, both during the trip to Canada aboard the *Queen Mary**
and at the conference itself. Since all those oral histories mention
teamwork frequently, and competitive back-biting never, we can
assume the advice was offered. Since Sturdee was extraordinarily
bright, we can also assume that it was gratefully taken.

Four secretaries (Hill, Holmes, Layton and Sturdee) travelled
with the prime minister and Mrs Churchill, along with 'hundreds
[of] service staff, chiefs of staff, coders and decipherers'. Many of
the female service staff and cypherenes suffered from seasickness,
so Sturdee says she had to step in and 'type their [the chiefs of staff]
things'. Work was incessant. Just as the transfers from Downing
Street to the Annexe and back were not allowed to interrupt the
work flow, neither was the transfer from Downing Street to the
Queen Mary (nicknamed 'The Grey Ghost') and to Quebec, leaving
little time for socializing.

In fact, the only social life on the boat, amidst all the work, was
at meals. And what meals they were. 'We had a compartment set
aside for us,' reports Sturdee and, as reported by Jock Colville,
'the meals were gargantuan in scale and epicurean in quality,
rather shamingly so'.[12] And the feast continued after the *Queen
Mary* docked and the party moved on to the train from Halifax
to Quebec. Sturdee recalls the 'enormous steaks' served on board
the train. Fond remembrances of meals past, even decades after
they were consumed, should come as no surprise, since they were
served to British travellers who had lived under rationing for
some three years. Sturdee recalls that some crew members left on
their plates more food than she would have had under rationing.
There is no mention in her oral history of worries about German
U-boats, although that threat must have been real.

On board the ship, Sturdee shared a cabin and bathroom with

---

* After the war, between February and September 1946, on thirteen
crossings, her Cunard colours repainted, the *Queen Mary* carried more
than 12,000 European war brides and children to the United States and
Canada.

Layton. Holmes and Hill shared another cabin* – they must have
decided among themselves who would room with whom, as they
often decided among themselves who would work weekends and
who would be off. Moving from cabin to work, Sturdee had to
run the gauntlet of 4,000 homeward-bound, wounded American
troops to the accompaniment of 'wolf whistles galore', although
in recounting the memory she does not sound at all aggrieved by
these attentions. Both Churchills, of course, had outside cabins;
the staff were allocated inside.

When they arrived in Quebec, Sturdee and the secretaries
stayed at the Hotel Chateau Frontenac, while the Churchills and
the military chiefs of staff were housed at The Citadel, a military
installation and the official residence of the Governor General of
Canada. Cars were arranged to shuttle the secretaries back and
forth between their hotel and The Citadel daily.

While in Quebec, Sturdee celebrated her twenty-first birthday
with a party – even now it is difficult to imagine what these experiences must have been like for one so young – arranged by Hill,
for what she called the 'serfs club', meaning all the 'underlings...
[the personal secretaries], the detectives and the photographers...
people like that... I've still got the menu signed by them all with
little messages.' As we shall see with Holmes and others, in Quebec
and elsewhere, there were some moments for fun. Although in this
case not for one of the secretaries, who undoubtedly had to miss
the party in order to remain on duty should the prime minister
need her.

Sturdee not only helped when needed by the chiefs of staff –
the lines between Churchill's personal staff (paid by him) and the
civil servants (paid by the government) were often crossed in the
interests of getting done whatever had to be done for him and in
the country's interests – but also had some chores to do for Mrs
Churchill, of which typing was the least of Sturdee's problems. The

---

* Sturdee sketched a floor plan of the cabin they shared and enclosed it in
a letter to her family.

added difficulty stemmed from the fact that Mrs Churchill was travelling without a maid, which was unusual for her. So Sturdee, the junior, was warned that she would be asked to go 'through the dresses to see if anything needed pressing'. She recalls: 'Anyway, I went with Mrs Churchill to the second [Quebec] conference and as long as I didn't mind, as well as doing any typing which she may need or anything like that, as long as I didn't mind doing her ladies mending as well, I said "Crumbs! I can't even iron the handkerchief."' 'Oh yes you can,' Mrs Hill told her when the roster for the trip was being compiled. '"You['ll] do perfectly well. She wants you to do that; otherwise you can't go." So I said, "I will try!"'

Sturdee goes on to explain that Mrs Churchill wore 'those stays with long laces… must have been ten feet long. And every day those stay-laces had to come out of her stays and be ironed… she had clean… laces in those stays every day.' Sturdee goes on to say that

> everything Mrs Churchill wore had to pressed… pressing her beautiful modern new clothes. I was petrified. I took some lessons… you have to iron them on the wrong side… with a damp cloth. I never knew that… I was never told don't press velvet… she had one of those lovely long black velvet tea gowns [with] tomato red cuffs. I thought it needed ironing… and of course you got the mark of the iron.

She sought out Layton for advice. The two repaired to their shared cabin and hung the gown up in the bathroom in order to stream out the ironing indentations. She says 'everyone was so sweet… dear General Ismay… you had to have someone to confide in… [He was] always on one's side. Always helpful.' So easy to confide in that she told him about her near disaster with the velvet dress. Of course, 'it was all around all the men… Yes [the mark] came out… And all the people were looking because it was behind you see… They all said that's all right. Got away with that one, Jo.'

Accompanied by Holmes and Hill, the Churchills went on to Hyde Park, the Roosevelt family's long-time home north of New

York City, to visit the Roosevelts. The entire party then reconvened for the trip home on the *Queen Mary*, carrying more than 15,000 American and Canadian troops back to the European war. On that homeward voyage Churchill continued his usual practice of speaking to the American and Allied soldiers aboard the ship just before docking, soldiers arriving to fight in Europe, sensibly nervous about their futures, and who certainly could benefit from a Churchillian pep talk.

A few months after returning from Quebec in September 1944, Sturdee was asked to travel with the prime minister to the Yalta Conference in February 1945, along with Layton, Holmes and Kinna. On 3 February 1945 Churchill and his party, after a seven-hour flight, landed at Saki Field on the Crimean Peninsula with President Roosevelt's plane landing shortly thereafter. Each leader's plane was escorted by six fighter planes apiece.[13] Churchill wired Mrs Churchill, 'My friend has arrived in the best of health and spirits.'[14] 'No one else who saw the President that day described him as "in the best of health",'[15] Sturdee recalls. 'Oh, he [Roosevelt] was so ill, it was sad.' And Holmes, also present when Churchill greeted the president, recorded in her diary that the president 'seems to have lost so much weight, has dark circles under his eyes, looks altogether frail and he is hardly in this world at all'.[16] Twelve days later, at his last meeting with Roosevelt, and after seeing him in action for several days at Yalta, the prime minister revised his opinion: 'I felt he had a slender contact with life.'[17] Less than two months later, on 12 April, Roosevelt died.

Two limousines and numerous other vehicles had been transported from Britain and ferried to the nearest port, Sevastopol, along with civil service drivers employed at Number 10 to transport the prime ministerial entourage to the conference site. Roosevelt and the Americans brought their own vehicles. Because of the primitive condition of the snowy mountain roads and numerous switchbacks, that ninety-mile trip took six or seven hours. Joan Bright says that forty-three army motorcars plus some RAF trucks 'containing wireless equipment' arrived early by ship. They were frozen to the deck and everything had to be unscrambled by Bright and moved to the meeting site.[18]

The British team recalls with delight the enormous banquets of foods laid out by the Russians at every stop for the visiting dignitaries. The president's group by-passed the feasts, with Anna Roosevelt along to look after her frail father's health and eager for him to have some rest, making their apologies to Soviet Foreign Minister Molotov's interpreter.[19]

Once in Yalta, the vehicles imported from Britain were used to transport the personal secretaries between their rooms in what was then unromantically called Sanatorium B Corpus 1* and the prime minister's office and residence, the Vorontsov Palace.

Joining him in that vast 150-room palace (only two bathrooms) were his daughter Sarah, two Private Secretaries, Commander Thompson, Patrick Kinna and Churchill's valet Sawyers, as well as many senior military officers. There were clearly not enough bathrooms to accommodate all who wished to bathe. The women had a 'bathhouse in the garden with a Russian girl standing by to scrub bathers of either sex... [one officer] drew up a roster of bath-times.'[20] Sturdee and Layton describe the bathrooms having

> great big sinks... with one cold tap over each, a row of loos... and men and women had to wash [there]... it's sometimes rather difficult as you could not strip down... the men trying to shave in front of you and you trying to make yourself up... in your nighty and the men in their pyjamas... no hot water tap [at all].

All these men were senior military officers fighting a war, advising Churchill on how to deal with Stalin on very weighty matters, and usually assigned private toilet and bathing facilities. Cramped though some of the members of the British delegation were, 'we

---

* Small villas on the grounds of the former Czarist palaces had been turned into sanatoria for wounded and sick Soviet soldiers, hence their names.

are much better off than many of the delegates, for instance the sixteen American colonels who shared a single bedroom.'[21] An added problem was the plague of bed bugs, which were everywhere until the Americans sprayed DDT, not only in the quarters of the US delegation, but in the facilities assigned to their very grateful British allies. One British squadron leader is quoted as having come to regard the bed bugs as 'part of the normal flora [sic] of the Russian bedroom'.[22]

Meals for staff were in the communal dining room known as Sanatorium A Corpus 1. Breakfast was an 'Enormous spread of the most delectable cold meats and cheeses and champagne if you wanted it... [plus] tisanes [herbal teas] in long glasses and lovely rye bread and delicious butter,'[23] all in contrast to the rations on which the British team survived at home and, presumably, to what was available to the average citizen of the Soviet Union.

And, of course, the travelling office had to be set up so that the women could be completely self-sufficient and ready to work the minute the prime minister arrived. Each secretary had to bring her own typewriter: Sturdee describes 'the civil-service-[made] wooden boxes... covered in black material with a great handle on the top so that our typewriters [fit precisely] and didn't wiggle about... And the black tin boxes full of headed paper and carbon paper and copy paper and tags and klops and labels and whatever we'd need.' At the conference, the Allies had agreed to what Churchill and Roosevelt thought would be the structure of the post-war world: Roosevelt's (undetailed) plan for a United Nations and a conference to prepare its charter; Churchill's proposed deal on Poland with which he professed to be 'content', although fearful of the reaction of parliament.[24] Then the packing up began. The goal was to leave nothing behind lest it prove of use to the Soviet security services.

Only three months after the team's return to London, the European phase of the Second World War ended. Sturdee remembers three things about VE Day, 8 May 1945. First, the tumultuous crowds outside Buckingham Palace applauding the king and queen. Second, the fact that Churchill's modesty and respect for the monarchy caused him to stand slightly behind the royal couple. As Sturdee puts it, Churchill 'never once acknowledged that applause which of course was partly for him'. Third, his duty to his sovereigns done, Churchill received the congratulations due him. He went from Buckingham Palace directly to his beloved House of Commons to announce the victory and was mobbed in the road. Characteristically, he continued working. Whenever he had a moment between celebrations, Churchill dictated telegrams and answered congratulatory messages from around the world. Then he went to the Ministry of Health (later named the Home Office), stood on the balcony and received his own thunderous applause. When going to the Ministry of Health he walked through the Number 10 garden along a line of his secretaries who 'clapped and cheered like anything'.[25] Sturdee recalls that Churchill missed Mrs Churchill, who was still in Russia, but telegraphed her several times during that day to suggest what she should broadcast to the Soviet people. At home, Sturdee says there was no 'bubbly… no special celebration… we were all jolly thankful and so pleased for him'. But they had work to do.

A few months later, Churchill's coalition government was defeated in the first general election since 1935. Sturdee was with him the entire day as the votes were counted and she recalls 'A dire day… The ghastly realization that Churchill had not won the general election. It seemed unbelievable… [loss] never occurred to us… a tragedy… such gloom… shattering.'

The challenge facing Sturdee after the Conservative Party's unexpected loss of the election was complex indeed. Not for the British the American system of allowing two months between the election of a president and his inauguration, with a well-funded transition period in which staff can be marshalled; the defeated incumbent packed up immediately and was sent on his way. In Britain, you lose, you so advise the queen, and you at once turn over the reins and your residence to the leader of the victorious party.

Sturdee's problem was not made easier by four circumstances. First, the election came in the midst of a meeting of world leaders at Potsdam. Second, there had been little advance planning for the Tories' defeat. Very few expected Churchill's return to Britain for the election to be other than the first part of a round-trip back to Potsdam and a resumption of the conference. Third, Mrs Churchill, who would have to help organize the move from Number 10, was worn out from her war duties. Finally, Sturdee was moving not any prime minister, but one who had led a wartime government for five years, during which all the resources of that government were his to command.

Now Churchill was to become not a retired elder statesman, but a very active Leader of the Opposition, and one who was a prolific author, with war memoirs to research and write, and not one to let the little matter of a change of office, a change of residence and a sudden reduction in staff interfere with his demands on himself and, now, on a diminished staff. But Sturdee says that Churchill was knocked off 'his perch' by the election results: 'he was shoved off bounds for the first week [but] brave like a solid war ship... mortally wounded... the whole nation had left him'. He initially took little consolation from the fact that he had won re-election in his own constituency and would now become leader of his now-minority party and therefore Leader of the Opposition. Churchill told the American diplomat Averell Harriman, who stopped in London on 8 August, en route from a meeting with Stalin, that as Leader of the Opposition 'he only missed one thing being out of office. He had been accustomed, upon waking up in the morning, to press buttons and give directions which would set important matters in motion. He could not get used to not being able to do this.'[26] The world around him might change, be thrown into chaos: he had no intention of changing a lifelong pattern of work, and his literary and political life. The problems of transition were Sturdee's to solve, the adjustments hers to make, with the exception of the not insignificant problem of finding adequate housing for the Churchills and their personal staff, which was Mrs Churchill's to solve.

Mrs Churchill immediately moved the family and personal staff out of Number 10 and into suites at Claridge's. Sturdee, Hill and

Layton – the 'serfs club' as she calls herself and her colleagues – had to squeeze into a tiny vestibule outside the sitting room, along with the detectives who remained on twenty-four-hour security detail. 'No longer civil-service private secretaries, black boxes, official switchboard, office car,' but Churchill's work continued at almost the same pace. Layton was engaged to be married soon and move to South Africa; Hill had been asked to take over the Chequers Trust; and Hamblin was by then working for Mrs Churchill, putting Sturdee in a senior position, but with no civil service backing. Sturdee was unsure whether the Churchills would keep her on – 'would have to put up with her' was her wry assessment of her new circumstance. Because of the high cost of a penthouse suite at Claridge's, the Churchills then moved briefly into Westminster Gardens (on loan from Duncan and Diana Sandys), which was 'madly uncomfortable' even though the staff was smaller, but the 'sacksful of letters had to be opened, sorted and answered' as they and other papers requiring attention continued to arrive, some addressed to Claridge's, some to Westminster Gardens, and some still coming into Number 10 and the Annexe. Churchill's personal effects had to be removed from Number 10 and sent down to Chartwell. Lena, Mrs Churchill's maid, and Sawyers took care of these, but the serfs had to pack up the 'stuff' from the personal office. Collegiality was so great – and the smooth change in government paramount – that there did not have to be one boss directing this complicated move. Civil servants' secretaries helped: 'they didn't want us to feel we were being pushed out'. The Private Secretaries and Churchill's personal staff rallied 'round, with one goal: an orderly transition from a wartime coalition government to a Labour government' – there had not been a Labour government since the 1920s.

Churchill decided to take what we now call 'a break' before assuming his new duties. Not a rest, but a change of scene. 'I don't need rest, but change is a great refreshment,' he once said.[27] Field Marshal Harold Alexander made his plane available to Churchill and served as his host during Churchill's stay in Moltrasio, Italy, in the Villa delle Rose on the shore of Lake Como, owned by an Italian industrialist who had apparently disappeared. Alexander also arranged for a detachment of the 4th Hussars – Churchill's old regiment of which he was still colonel – to guard and honour him during his stay in Italy.[28] His new Detective Evan Davies (known to one and all as 'Bish') joined the party.

Accompanied by Layton, Lord Moran, his valet Sawyers and daughter Sarah, Churchill worked on his books and his painting. But a period of all play and no work was not possible for Churchill. He interrupted his vacation to dine with a variety of military men with stories to tell about various battles and the conditions in Soviet-occupied Europe, and to review memoranda about the reasons for the Conservatives' electoral defeat. As for Layton, this was perhaps her last trip before her marriage and move to South Africa. She returned to London while Churchill was finding new scenes to paint,[29] leaving the secretarial chores to others who would follow her.

Churchill as Leader of the Opposition needed a London base, so Mrs Churchill bought 28 Hyde Park Gate and with Hamblin's help renovated the house. Sawyers, Mrs Churchill's maid and the cook Mrs Landemare had to share rooms on the top floor, 'which left only one small room for the office up there'. Sturdee quickly realized they could not work in such cramped quarters, so the family bought the house next door at 27 Hyde Park Gate and installed the office there – with space both for the personal office and the official work that Churchill had as Leader of the Opposition. The office took up the main ground-floor room and the basement, which included the kitchen and a bathroom. In order to generate a bit of income, Mrs Churchill, who always worried about finances and was married to a man with extravagant tastes,[30] leased the top two floors to a man whom Sturdee describes as 'a frightfully dishy actor'.

With Hamblin working for Mrs Churchill and renovating Chartwell, Hill beginning her transition to run Chequers, and Layton in South Africa, Sturdee found herself in a key administrative position, as well as trying to manage the numerous building works that Numbers 27 and 28 required, renovations that Mrs Churchill suggested be carried out. The two houses had to function both for family living as well as offices and meeting rooms.

Sturdee's doubts about whether she would be kept on ended after three weeks when Churchill, 'prompted by Mrs Hill', asked her to stay. He told her 'Now you do realize, don't you, that you are head of my private office? I want there to be no misunderstanding. Is that all right? If you have any complaints will you come to me?' 'But certainly I knew I could always go to him if there were any troubles,' Sturdee says that Churchill continued: 'You know what I want and… I expect to have it… I will expect the service that I have had up to now from my private office, full stop.' This is a rare instance in which Churchill involved himself in the staffing and organization of his private office; a necessity, since he had no one else to do this for him.

Sturdee was then asked if there were someone remaining at Number 10 that she would like to work with and that would be willing to leave the civil service. Elizabeth Gilliatt, Sturdee's first choice, accepted the offer and listened carefully to Sturdee's stern warning against disclosure of anything about her work or the Churchill family. Even when he was out of office, confidentiality was of the utmost importance – he was writing about the war and there was much still to keep secret. In addition, the worldwide press was desperate for news – any news – about Churchill and his family. Gilliatt joined the team at the beginning of 1946. Her first chore was to shape the Secret Session speeches* into book format. (For more about Gilliatt, see Chapter 7.)

---

* Secret Session speeches is the seventh and final volume of Churchill's war speeches. The book contains five speeches Churchill delivered in the House of Commons sitting in Secret Session – those of 20 June and 17 September 1940, 25 June 1941, and 23 April and 10 December 1942. These speeches were never meant to be publicly distributed and there were no recorded versions. The compiler of the speeches later relied on Churchill's drafts and full texts – as saved by the personal secretaries – to reprint them. (Charles Eade is the editor.)

But even the addition of Gilliatt did not bring the staff up to adequate levels. Because Churchill was organizing documents and considering how to write his history of the Second World War, while also resuming work on *A History of the English-Speaking Peoples*, it became clear that more shorthand typists/personal secretaries would be needed. Sturdee was in America with Churchill on his visit to meet the new American president, Harry S. Truman, so Hill asked General Ismay, who 'was close to all', whether there was anyone he thought fit and suitable. He suggested Lettice Marston; Hill interviewed her and, when Churchill returned from America, received final approval to take her on. At which point the staff was set: Sturdee, Lettice Marston and Gilliatt.

But this was small compared with his staffing when he had been prime minister: six Private Secretaries and 'lots of Garden Room Girls', who, according to Gilliatt, did not take dictation directly from him, but nevertheless were helpful and on call when needed. Plus he had all the services that Number 10 provided, such as mailings, messengers, chauffeurs, twelve girls on the switchboard twenty-four hours a day. Now Sturdee and her staff had to take on all these chores.

True, Churchill no longer bore the burdens of a prime minister, but his work expanded to fill his working hours. In addition to his considerable duties as Leader of the Opposition, a post that most holders have viewed and still view as full-time work, he planned to write *A History of the English-Speaking Peoples* and his war memoirs – famously stating, 'I will leave judgments of this matter to history – but I will be one of the historians.' That inevitably affected his narrative: Arthur Balfour described one of Churchill's histories, *The World Crisis*, as 'Winston's brilliant autobiography, disguised as a history of the universe'.[31]

The workload inevitably required still more staff, with Churchill resisting every such request due to worries about expenses. Sacks of letters continued to come in – sometimes as many as eighty letters a day, Sturdee guesses. She was able to convince Churchill that extra help was needed to handle that flood of correspondence, and, when it was his birthday, the flowers, cakes, gifts and mementos added to the incoming deliveries. Someone had sent him a giant cheese, which was to be cut into pieces and those pieces sent off as gifts – with attached cards – all arranged by the personal secretary.[32] Taking charge, she recalls: 'So I had to say, look, we can't do this, to Mr Churchill but would you agree – may I ask on your behalf please the Conservative Central Office, may I ring up and say that you wonder whether [they] might… Yes, he said, do it.' Like all skilful administrators, Sturdee won the day by presenting her boss not only with a problem, but with a solution – and a costless one at that. She would not find such cost-less solutions to understaffing in the future.

But even with the help of Central Office, she knew 'we weren't doing justice to the [ongoing] volume of work in the office', as well as the beginning of the organization for the massive job of research for the war memoirs. 'So I had to measure up [again] and said, sorry, [Mr Churchill] we need somebody else. Wasn't an easy battle to win, either. He could not believe it. [He said] "I don't see what you are complaining [about]"… "We're not complaining, Mr Churchill. We're just saying we can't go on doing it." "Oh, all right, if you say so" [he agreed].' So Cecily 'Chips' Gemmell was added to the staff in the summer of 1946* and began working with Denis Kelly, classifying and categorizing the documents in the Chartwell muniment room – the documents on which Churchill would rely when writing the six volumes of his history of the Second World War.

To keep the staffing as lean as possible, given the workload, Sturdee adopted advanced techniques and an efficient division of labour. Before she left with Churchill on the trip to America, she had a switchboard installed 'with two lines into Number 28 and Number 27, with twelve or thirteen extensions'.

She had Churchill sign his name, had it 'Photostatted' on Chartwell as well as Hyde Park Gate stationery and used it so that

---

*   memories for dates are imprecise; see footnote, p. 198

thank-you letters could be sent to thousands of correspondents. She explains that in the 1940s the signature looked very real indeed. For efficiency, Sturdee, now in full command, decided that 'we all must be responsible for a subject. There were many different aspects of Mr Churchill's life... let's all make ourselves responsible for one, two or three... aspects.' Gilliatt took over politics, and Marston was in charge of engagements. Sturdee had a broad remit, retaining responsibility for personal, financial, legal and family matters. The remit was sufficiently broad, and by 1949 Sturdee's confidence that her advice might matter was sufficiently high, that when Churchill decided to follow his father into the world of racing, she did not hesitate to send him a memo warning of 'the risk of damage to his great reputation' and to his standing with the electorate.[33] Beaverbrook echoed her concerns, pointing out the risk of alienating the voters: 'The public will back it [your horse], and it won't win.'[34] He worried, too, that staff might bet on a Churchill horse and lose their money. In the event, Churchill ignored that advice. Sturdee put 'a bob or two' on his horses and the venture did not prove a financial disaster as Mrs Churchill feared it would. Churchill enjoyed himself hugely, and his racing activities brought him closer to Queen Elizabeth II and to the average punter, as well as to his son-in-law Christopher Soames.[35] In addition, it provided Churchill with an opportunity to chide the deputy editor of the *Telegraph* (who then became the long-serving editor) for referring to his first racehorse Colonist II as a gelding. Churchill replied, 'He is, of course, entire, and will eventually go to stud.' Churchill delighted in recounting 'in a whimsical way, how the animal responded to promises of a first-class harem if he won'.[36]

He might have ignored advice about going into racing, but in other matters Churchill relied on advisors. There were tax, banking and legal considerations, and, Sturdee says, Churchill sought advice from Brendan Bracken, Emery Reves, Lord Camrose (Sturdee calls him 'a darling'), Mr Moir, his solicitor, and Leslie Graham-Dixon, a barrister and Churchill's tax expert. Sturdee interacted with all of these advisors. Such government documents as Churchill was receiving were placed in government black boxes he had taken with him (with government permission) and, as before, the secretaries placed the most important documents in the top box for him to see first.

Throughout his life, Churchill's work habits remained surprisingly the same. He was a man who expected the surrounding world to adjust to him regardless of changing circumstances. And his personal staff did the adjusting, with Sturdee often devising the means of making that adjustment; a job made easier by the cooperation of the other women who worked for Winston. The young ladies arranged the working rota among themselves for his benefit; for example, staggering their lunch hours so that the telephone was never unmanned. Sandwiches would be brought in at lunchtime and, if they were working through dinner, the valet Sawyers or the domestic staff would bring them meals on a tray. Work done, they could call a taxi to take them home, paid for by the Churchills.

When working at Chartwell, the women lived in different cottages on the grounds and had somewhat different arrangements for meals than when they were in London. They 'used to get their own breakfast which was toast and coffee or tea… For lunch or dinner, we went out every day to a local thing [sic] at the Churchills' expense.' From the descriptions of the vast amount of work it seems unlikely they would have had the time. Sturdee's memory as to meal arrangements differs a bit from those of her co-workers, which might be due to the fact that they were describing meals at different places and at different times.

With fully functioning offices set up at Hyde Park Gate, Chartwell and in the Leader of the Opposition's offices at the House of Commons, Churchill felt it was safe to take a prolonged working vacation – he knew no other kind – in America. The Churchills accepted an offer of his Miami house from Colonel Frank Clarke, a wealthy Canadian shipowner, who had provided the then-prime minister with a guest house outside of Quebec during the first

(1943) conference in that city. Mrs Churchill was delighted, and wrote, 'I think it would do Winston such a lot of good.'[37]

So they set off on a three-month trip to the United States in January 1946, partly for a vacation in the sun, more importantly, to meet with President Truman. The president of Westminster College, a small men's college in the Midwest, had invited the most famous man in the world to give a lecture. That college president was a friend of President Truman, a fellow native of the state of Missouri. Truman had added a handwritten note on the bottom of the official invitation letter, agreeing to introduce Churchill. Churchill quickly accepted the invitation, as he planned to sound the alarm of the increasing Soviet threat to Europe and knew that Truman's presence would give his speech the publicity he felt it merited. In addition, Churchill was closely following the meetings in Washington on a new US loan to Great Britain.

Sturdee had demonstrated so many skills setting up the offices that Churchill was confident they would run smoothly in his absence, and hers, and asked her to accompany him on the long trip to the United States. The woman who had begun her career working with Churchill, clipping and filing, was now in charge of organizing his working life, both in the UK and abroad. Before setting sail to Miami via New York, Sturdee had to pack up an entire duplicate office, as always. She arranged to take the minutes and telegrams he had been allowed to take away from Number 10 Downing Street, as a basis for his history of the Second World War. Negotiations were ongoing as to publishers, due dates, rights and payment schedules, a complex business overlooked by Emery Reves and Lord Camrose on Churchill's behalf. With Sturdee overseeing and keeping track of all the moving parts, she and Churchill sailed for New York on the RMS *Queen Elizabeth* on 9 January 1946, although her boss 'took it fairly easily on the boat' and had not started writing what became known as the Fulton 'Iron Curtain' speech or working on the memoirs. But he was thinking deeply about both.

Arriving by train at Miami from New York, Sturdee set up the office in Colonel Clarke's Florida vacation home. He was a

Canadian friend of Churchill's and Sturdee was grateful too for the help of Clarke's secretary Lorraine Bonar, because almost at once sacks full of letters arrived three times a day – mostly from American fans. Churchill did not have to get accustomed to a new face on his staff, something he always tried to avoid ('at times it would put him off his work to see a strange face opposite him'[38]), and he directed all the work to Sturdee, who then had Bonar help get it done. Bonar told her parents: 'the great man has arrived and he's just wonderful – entirely captivated me... really charming to everyone. Today Mr Churchill and I had a chat about the goldfish, of which I am the keeper... he thought he might try to take some back with him.' Knowing his fondness for goldfish, we can easily imagine his thinking about how to get this done. Bonar must have come face to face with him, perhaps he only resented new faces when they worked for him as they might interfere with his thinking and dictating. He could be charming; he was after all a politician. However, she goes on to say: 'he wasn't above being very difficult and contrary.'[39]

Once again, the resources available proved insufficient to meet the workload. And once again Sturdee confronted Churchill with that fact and persuaded him to ask the British Consul's office in Miami to help by answering the letters from the public. It remained Sturdee's job to open, sort and decide which letters Churchill had to answer and which could be answered routinely by the consul's staff. That staff proved unable to keep up with the workload and so called upon the Consul General in New York to send reinforcements. In addition, the British Embassy in Washington flew down two additional secretaries to help.[40] All to assist Churchill during his 'vacation'.

Sturdee calls Clarke's 'a small house' in which Detective George Williams had to sleep in the office as there was no other room for him. Sturdee slept 'at a place nearby', but Sawyers 'had a little box up there somewhere', presumably near Churchill. American FBI and local police kept the crowds away from the house. Kathleen Hill, still supervising some of Churchill's arrangements, had asked

Scotland Yard's Special Branch to make sure that whomever they sent to protect Churchill would be able to work with the American police. She had requested Sergeant Evan Davies (known to all as Bish), but Special Branch of Scotland Yard sent Detective George Williams instead.[41]

Sturdee 'worked from half-past eight until ever so late', but there must have been some time off as she, Bonar and Detective Williams occasionally went to a hotel and bar called the 'Ole King Cole... with a <u>marvellous</u> display of fruit'. She and Bonar were often included in invitations to join the Churchills at the Surf Club,* where Churchill would bathe and lunch, or at an animal centre, which she thinks was called something like Parrot Land or Jungle, 'where the parrots would come and settle on your shoulder... [he] loved going there'. But she was invariably too busy and '[I] could not get away... wouldn't be happy leaving all that stuff'.

This was when Churchill began his war memoirs. Sturdee says: 'You could see he had to wind himself up into a whole new world and this had to be his future... this was going to be his work.'† He would take out the first box of minutes and telegrams and start dictating from them. Sturdee typed it up and returned it to him for editing. She continues: 'not a great deal was done but certainly a start was made'. And she says he began to dictate his Fulton speech to her. As usual Churchill could work on two big projects at the same time, separating each in his mind and concentrating on one at a time. Secretaries were meant to keep up with his wide-ranging personal, diplomatic and, in some cases, political output, as well as the personal chores he assigned.

She says: 'Mr Churchill [had] got a yen about going to Cuba' even before he had left Great Britain, asking how long it would

---

* The young ladies shared many jokes about the differences between the Surf Club and the Serf Club.

† Much like he had to do after resigning in 1955, as he turned his mind to completing *A History of the English-Speaking Peoples*.

take to fly there from Miami. Perhaps he was recollecting the excitement of his earlier days there in a prior century, or perhaps thinking about visiting some cigar factories, or both. In any case, President Truman put an American air force plane at his disposal for the trip to Cuba, as well as for the trips back to Washington and New York.

After a few weeks in Miami, the Churchills – taking Sturdee as the only personal secretary – flew to Havana. Mrs Churchill's maid flew with them, so there was no danger this time of Sturdee having to do double-duty ironing. The velvet gowns were safe. Decades later, Sturdee recalls with great affection that one of the American commanders, a Major General William Plummer, who also piloted the plane, taught her the rhumba. It wasn't <u>all</u> work.

The British Embassy in Havana did not have enough room for the entire party. The British Ambassador suggested they all stay at the Hotel Nacional. Arrangements were made to accommodate everyone there, including the necessary offices – they had an entire floor to themselves, staff and offices included. A very rich Cuban cigar manufacturer, Antonio Giraudier, lent the group his private house and beach as the hotel had no accessible beach for Churchill, who loved swimming in the surf. Sturdee recalls the 'gorgeous imported silver sand' and the vast number of attentive servants: 'if [I] got a drop of water on my toe, [they] would wipe it off with a clean towel.' Still, she went there only a few times as she didn't like to leave any work undone.

She recalls Giraudier with great fondness. Later, he had to flee Castro's regime and moved to the United States. He not only supplied Churchill with cigars until his death, but also sent packages to all the typists, even the ones he had never met. He had asked Sturdee for a list of all the personal secretaries, and frequently sent them food parcels from Fortnum & Mason, silk stockings, perfumes, lipsticks and even brandy.[42] They nicknamed him Uncle Antonio, and Jane Portal (now Lady Williams) told me recently that she still remembers him fondly some seventy years later.

Sturdee was surprised that Churchill did not paint in Cuba,

despite the brilliant sunshine and bright colours. After returning from Cuba, Sturdee had to pack up to leave the Florida vacation home in 'a mad rush, clearing the place of muck and rubble',* and only one night off to go dancing. To get that one night off after weeks of working at night, she writes 'it means asking Mr C at 7 o'clock or something like that "Will you be wanting me any more tonight?" Grunt, grunt, grumble, grumble, mumble mumble. [Finally, he says] "No, I can manage."'

Sturdee was in such a frenzy because she thought (as it turns out incorrectly) that Churchill would be going on to Fulton without her, leaving her plenty of time to close up the Miami operation.

> As neither Mrs C nor Mrs Truman were going as the President preferred a male party for such dos.† I naturally assumed that Mr C would not take me... [So I was] scurrying as fast as possible through the [Fulton] speech trying to get it typed in time for him to take away, ignoring the piles of correspondence strewn all over the place.[43]

Churchill was demanding 'Come along, come along. Where are all the telegrams? Hasn't anything come from England? Surely there is a newspaper I can look at. What have you done with my red pen?‡ Tell the ambassador I want to see him. Where's Sawyers? Haven't you opened the post yet?'[44] These rapid-fire requests and demands are typical of Churchill's wide-ranging and eclectic

---

*   Sturdee, letter home (8 March 1946), WSC Archives. At the end of her letters home, Sturdee asks her family to 'pass this letter to the... girls at No. 28 to read' so they could all share the news. Not only did they agree among themselves to share the work, they also shared the news freely, knowing that it would all be kept confidential. When she was abroad, her letters to her family were sent back to Britain via the diplomatic bags and left unsealed so the girls 'back home' could read the news before sending them onwards to her family.

†   And for many other 'dos', as Bess Truman stayed in Independence, Missouri, while Truman was in the White House.

‡   Churchill usually edited his speeches with a red pen. See Layton, p. 28.

interests and demands, not to mention his unreasonableness when it came to work. In any case, he said he needed her with him there to work on *the* speech – as he always made changes and edits right up to delivery time. He also needed her secretarial help for a speech he had agreed to give a few days after the Fulton trip to the General Assembly in Richmond, Virginia – followed by a visit (this time with Mrs Churchill) to Williamsburg with General Eisenhower and his wife Mamie – all in one day.

Sturdee wrote home that week that Churchill said to her:

> Of course you must come, with various reasons why... after hav-ing flung office papers and a tooth brush into a suitcase, which had not been unpacked or thought about since Miami... I tagged along looking like something... emptied into the dust bin. I felt self-conscious... about being added at the last minute and being the only female.[45]

In March 1946 Sturdee travelled with Churchill and the presi-dent on the presidential train inherited from President Roosevelt, named the *Ferdinand Magellan*, from Washington, DC, to Fulton, Missouri, where Churchill was to give his now-famous 'Iron Cur-tain' speech. She recalls that a 'sweet' Dr Robert Harris (a former navy officer) from Miami was also on the train, as both a friend and doctor for Churchill. Missouri was then a dry state and it seemed that only Churchill and Truman could have their whisky on the train. At one point on the journey within Missouri, Dr Harris asked to see her and she followed him down the corridor into a private lavatory. She worried and thought, 'Oh dear, Sir Winston has been taken ill in the lavatory and Dr Harris [needed her help]. But no, the good doctor pulled out a whisky flask, offered it to her and said, "It will do you a power of good."' She refused, but Dr Harris needed a swallow and took one himself. She goes on: 'He thought perhaps with all the work and worry I had it would do me good.' Another 'sweet' man was President Truman, 'honest and perfectly sweet... a nice man.' It was highly unusual that a secretary should have such personal contact with Churchill's also-famous colleagues. Recall that Churchill neglected to introduce Kathleen Hill to President Roosevelt when they were at Hyde Park. Perhaps Truman was less forbidding, or a long trip in the confines of a train produced a more casual atmosphere.

After a twenty-five-mile drive to Fulton from the rail depot, with Churchill and the president in an open car, and Sturdee and Sawyers in following cars, they arrived at the College President's house to face stacks of incoming mail for Churchill; and since Sturdee was not included in the official lunch before the speech, 'one of those G-Men... took us over... for a scrum with the press men... for a sandwich and a Coca-Cola.' 'Out of the bottle or with a straw?' they asked her.[46]

About the Fulton speech itself, she wrote to her family: 'I wonder if you heard it on the wireless? I feel it was or will be proved in the future to be quite a historic speech.'[47] After the speech, they all returned to the president's house hoping for a drink. But no alcohol, she complained, as

> it is a Presbyterian house [and a dry state]. Fortunately, Dr Harris... who had been requested by Mr C to come along [from Miami] had... brought along a little bottle 'just in case of anything'. So one by one, we were tapped on the shoulder, informed that Dr Harris thought we needed medical attention and would we step into... the w.c.

'Ah, heaven!' she concluded. 'Dr Harris was a true dear,' as he had proved to be on the train to Fulton.[48]

At Fulton, Sturdee recalls that she thought the Westminster College gymnasium not very grand and the audience smaller than she had expected. But she admits that 'only afterwards [did I] realize what importance [the speech] had... everything, certainly to me, everything he did and said was important and right.' Churchill never meant the speech only for the audience present on 6 March 1946. He meant it as a warning to the world.

Churchill and his travelling office returned from Fulton to Washington and the British Embassy, where Lord Halifax was in his last months as Ambassador (he would head home in May 1946). The Washington embassy had few bedrooms and certainly no provision for a secretarial office for visiting dignitaries, so Sturdee set up her office in her bedroom. She was

> in a frightful flap about all the urgent stuff awaiting us at the Embassy, telephone calls, etc. and the Virginia speech... get the speech done two minutes before he leaves that night... [she] ask[ed] to be excused from the trip to Virginia... but glad to get one day... [in order] to get a little order into the chaos.[49]

Sturdee recollected with great fondness how kind Lady Halifax was to her, the only female personal secretary with the Churchill entourage. Sturdee says that during the war when she had been abroad she was usually ignored, 'not paid much attention to'. Lady Halifax was a different sort. She came to Sturdee's office/bedroom several times a day, asking if she was all right and did she need anything. Lady Halifax told her that lunch was served 'at one and we meet for a drink at half past twelve... and we have dinner at eight... we are always there at half-past seven, so you come in when you like.' Unusual this, to be included with the official guests at an embassy dinner. Sturdee responded, 'I don't think I'm included in dinner,' but Lady Halifax said, 'In this house you certainly are included.' The problem was the length of the dresses: Sturdee did not have a long dress with her. So Lady Halifax arranged that she and Mrs Churchill would be wearing short dresses that night, so that Sturdee in her short dress would not feel out of place. No wonder Sturdee recalls her affectionate kindness. Lady Halifax was the aunt of the man Sturdee would later marry, Lord Arthur Onslow.

Sturdee gives Lady Halifax (or Aunt Dorothy, as she later would be called) credit for 'breaking the mould', making the young ladies feel they were important, that we 'were <u>private</u> secretaries... it was rather good for us [all]... it brought us on.' Class lines and assumptions were indeed breaking down across Britain, even in the British Embassy, thanks in good part to the ambassador's wife, who had a reputation for directness as Churchill well knew.

Lady Halifax was known for her forcefulness and speaking her mind, even directly to the prime minister at Downing Street. When he appointed Halifax as Ambassador to the United States in December 1940, a post he did not want and considered 'banishment', Lady Halifax argued with the prime minister against the appointment with vigour and some 'tough talking'.[50]

Before returning to Britain, Churchill visited FDR's grave at Hyde Park – he had not attended the funeral of the man he described as the 'greatest American friend we [Britain] have ever known'[51] – laid a commemorative wreath, and by one account, sighed 'Lord, how I loved that man.'[52] Then, back to work at Chartwell and Hyde Park Gate in late March 1946, where Sturdee met Lettice Marston, who had begun working at Hyde Park Gate alongside Liz Gilliatt. Churchill told Sturdee 'let me see the new girl'. Marston had settled in well with Hill's help and was welcomed by Sturdee and, more importantly, by Churchill, and turned out to be 'a good appointment. The best appointment that could be made'. For the remainder of 1946 Churchill would work on his war memoirs, taking several foreign trips, while his private office hummed along with Sturdee, the senior personal secretary in charge, working side by side with Liz Gilliatt and Lettice Marston.

After the war, several European governments invited Churchill for an official visit so that they could thank and honour him, often conferring honorary degrees or bestowing the freedom of the city on him. He did not work on those usually short trips, merely acknowledging their thanks, enjoying the tributes and 'taking it in his stride'.

On one such trip, Churchill travelled to Holland at the invitation of Queen Wilhelmina and took Sturdee with him. Sturdee recalls the innumerable details that had to be arranged between the Dutch monarch's offices, the Dutch ambassador in London, the British ambassador in Amsterdam, and the British Foreign Office: what newspapers did he want (all!), what did he want for breakfast, whom did he want to see privately, approval for the seating at all the dinners. Sturdee managed the coordination between these elements and, on arrival, stayed at the Dam Square Royal Palace. Protocol demanded that all guests be in the drawing room before the sovereign, but occasionally Sturdee was delayed working for Churchill, so she had to explain to him why she was rushing out, needing time to dress and get to the reception before the queen. Churchill, of course, was aware of and respected this protocol, and so, unusually, allowed her to rush off.

She says: 'If you're staying at the royal palaces, you always dine with the party: the king and queen or whoever it is... you had your own footman standing behind your chair if you were lunching or dining' – shades of the splendour that awed Kathleen Hill when she accompanied Churchill to the Sassoon's Port Lympne, with the important difference that Hill was an observer, but Sturdee was the beneficiary of her very own footman. Sturdee seems different from the other secretaries as she was included in social events that would not have been open to prior young ladies. Earlier and later secretaries would not have stayed in royal palaces or been included in dinners at the British embassy in Washington. We can only speculate about why Sturdee was able to fit in like this.

In late December 1949 Churchill, hoping to paint, decided on a sunny vacation. He flew to Madeira, taking Mrs Churchill and two secretaries, Sturdee and Gilliatt. They sailed down, staying at Reid's Hotel, where the owners assigned a manager to look after the Churchills and, no doubt, help the young ladies set up their office. Because there was no airfield on the island the work bags took longer to arrive by ship. Sturdee wrote home that 'I must say that it has been nice not to get a bag full of work every day, as usual.'[53] Although she found the English community there provincial, she did write home that, one day, she and Gilliatt were invited out to lunch to meet some 'eligibles and returned to the office at 4.30 to check on Mr C to be told he was working... someone must work sometimes [he said]. He is being very sweet though and after dinner, when we flit in in our long dresses (hoping he won't work)... he always relents and says all right, you can go and enjoy yourselves.' But she found 'the standing and dancing all the time tiring.... Bathing a bit... it is best in the mornings between 8.30 and 2.'[54] This is a rare view of the very few hours off the young ladies had – perhaps because the bags of work and newspapers could not arrive every day.

In February 1950 the Tories narrowly lost a general election called by Prime Minister Attlee, leaving Churchill free to resume his travels. Early in October Sturdee travelled with him on an official trip to Copenhagen, Denmark, staying at the Fredensborg or Frederiksberg Palace (different palaces, but the audio recording on file at the archives is unclear). She was told that 'members of the resistance were the only ones allowed to meet Mr Churchill and his party... the Court was now made up of people who had fought in the resistance.' At one dinner, unusual for Churchill secretaries, Sturdee was seated next to Admiral Vedel, Commander of the Danish Navy during the Second World War. He told her: 'I think I had the worst job of anyone in the war... I was the one who had to scuttle the Danish Navy so the Germans wouldn't get it... we were a maritime nation and it was all we had.' As on most trips, to mark the end of his working day, Churchill liked his chilled consommé, usually brought to him by his valet. On one occasion, the valet had gone home early, so Sturdee – with the help of some Danish aides-de-camp – bought Churchill his good-night soup. Or so one story goes. Another has it that the Danish king brought it to him – memories fade and recollections can vary.[55] Either way, Churchill got his soup and slept as soundly as he always did.

Then, in December, it was off once more to Marrakesh, with Gemmell and Sturdee in tow. That work/play trip ended early in the new year, 1951, when the responsibilities of the Leader of the Opposition required a return to Britain and attention to politics. Churchill undoubtedly recognized that Labour's majority was insufficient to keep it in power for very long, and that Attlee would soon call a new general election, but he decided on still another European trip, this one ending in Venice. Jane Portal and Lettice Marston accompanied him to help complete the last volume of his memoirs before the general election he was certain would return him to power.[56] As he expected, a general election was called for 25 October, cutting short his stay in Venice and requiring a quick flight back to Britain. Sturdee, back home, arranged the complicated flight details on a private charter aircraft to get them home in time to campaign throughout the country.

Sturdee often accompanied Churchill on his campaign trips across Great Britain, during which he somehow managed to continue work on his memoirs. She was relieved to find that all the political events were handled by the Conservative Central Office apparatus. But not travel details. Churchill travelled the country in a special train – with all meals, communications, stops and other travellers arranged by Sturdee, with help from the Conservative Party, including several detectives and telephone operators to handle the vast number of phone calls into and out from the train. She set up her 'office on the train even if you were not going very far... because he would want to dictate'. Often one secretary stayed on the train, while the other one attended the speech in person. She explains that she often sat in to listen to Churchill's speeches, because 'it was a good thing to be there so that [I] could alter any alternations he made to his text... it was important that any alterations to his speeches' be made, so that an accurate record would be kept of what he actually said. Nothing had changed from the days in which a secretary would attend his speeches in the House of Commons and take down his speeches so that historians would have an accurate record of what he said. Churchill wanted his part in the history through which he lived recorded properly.

No surprise to Churchill, the Tories won, and Churchill became prime minister again at the age of seventy-seven, when the world seemed headed for a Cold War or worse. He took Gilliatt and Portal to Number 10 with him, where they would work closely with the existing civil-service typists already in Downing Street. Sturdee would help out as much as she could. Marston remained at Hyde Park Gate to handle secretarial matters related to the memoirs, and constituency matters. These women also experienced something new. With the pressures for 'Action This Day' less severe than during Churchill's wartime service in Downing Street, Sturdee had introduced an innovation: annual two-week vacations for secretaries.

Sturdee recalls that in Downing Street the Churchills each had a bedroom on the top floor and a drawing room with the secretaries' office on that floor as well. Other secretaries have different memories, which might explain why Churchill would complain to her: 'Why don't I see you these days… I can't have you out there [meaning in the Downing Street pool]. Let's make changes. I'll see to it.' And he did. There was no precedent, as she says:

> Mr Churchill had been the first prime minister to have his own personal secretaries… he broke the mould… during the war… We kept our own dignity even if we were pushed to one side… the civil side had forgotten probably that Mr Churchill had been used to having his personal secretaries… [but] the main thing is the work. The work just goes on just the same [at Chequers and Downing Street and also at Chartwell].

In 1952, when George VI died, Churchill, working from bed at Downing Street, dictated to Sturdee the speech he would deliver to the House of Commons five days later. 'I could hardly see for the tears. They were going plunk plunk on my notebook,' she says, 'while the guns [were] being fired by His Majesty's soldiers… in a royal salute.' Big Ben was silenced during the state funeral.[57] But it was Jane Portal who was with Churchill when he welcomed the new queen home from Kenya and it was Portal who took down the immediate and very moving words of his tribute to George VI, broadcast to the nation the afternoon of Queen Elizabeth's arrival.

Sturdee recalls Churchill's first impressions of the new queen:

We must protect her. She's such a young girl. And we must save some of those boring things that she has to do... [The prime minister] suggested to her that she might ease up on these investitures, they need not be so long. She need not have so many of them... [If] she gave up doing the junior ranks and just do the senior ranks of the various orders. Her reply was that the junior ones were the very ones [she] would do because the senior ranks know me anyway.

Sturdee's last trip with Churchill, she thinks, was to Jamaica in January 1953, when he was writing and editing the last few chapters of his war memoirs. Churchill took his personal secretaries with him on this trip – not ones from the government – as the work was personal and not related to his prime ministerial chores. Gilliatt was there as well, although her oral history does not mention the work she did there.

After returning from Jamaica, Sturdee 'decided the time had come... they of course tried to persuade me not to, but I said no, it's time [for her to resign].' Towards the end of her work with Churchill, she describes some pressures from MPs for Churchill to resign, but she is reluctant in her oral history to describe either Churchill's increasing deafness or his thoughts about whether or not Anthony Eden should or could succeed him.

In 1953, at the ripe old age of thirty-one, Sturdee resigned. But, as with many other 'former' secretaries, she returned to help out when the existing staff could not handle the load. Delia Morton (now Drummond)* tells me that in 1956 she was hired by Sturdee to work through the backlog of fan mail that flooded in after

---

*   Delia Morton worked for Churchill for two years from 1956 to 1958, and was interviewed and hired by Sturdee to handle the enormous volume of general and fan mail. She worked mostly at 27 Hyde Park Gate alongside Doreen Pugh.

Churchill's resignation as prime minister. She organized the mail so that communications from 'pottykins' – another of Churchill's invented words,[58] this one for incoherent correspondents – were filed under 'P'. Churchill was in the habit of stopping by her desk and asking to see the pottykins letters, which it turned out, included scribbles from Ezra Pound, filed of course under 'P' in bins called 'pottykins'.[59]

Jo Sturdee had seen the world's greatest statesman through a global war, a period as Leader of the Opposition, and then again as prime minister as he tried to prevent the Cold War from triggering a nuclear exchange between the Soviet Union and the West. She had travelled the world with him, participated in the drafting of a treasure trove of histories and memoirs, and made it possible for him to accomplish most, but not all, of his goals. In that year Sturdee was named in Elizabeth II's Coronation Honours and awarded an MBE (Most Excellent Order of the British Empire), among other things for public service outside the civil service. She went on to marry the Earl of Onslow, and passed away at the age of eighty-four in 2006. In his will, Churchill left her £200, about £3,750 today.

6

Marian Holmes

'You know, you must never ever be frightened of me when I shout. I'm not snapping at you, but thinking of the work.'

Winston Churchill to Marian Holmes[1]

'He seems to have an insatiable thirst for work.'

Marian Holmes, 1945[2]

'You are the indispensable slave.'

Field Marshal Jan Smuts to Marian Holmes, 1945[3]

'There just wasn't anybody to match him on the world scene.'

Marian Holmes, oral history

Born in 1921, Marian Holmes worked with Churchill from March 1943 until July 1945, when he was replaced as prime minister by the Labour Party's Clement Attlee. In addition to working closely with Churchill at Number 10 Downing Street, Chartwell and other locations in the United Kingdom, Holmes travelled with Churchill as his personal secretary to several critical meetings: with President Roosevelt in Quebec and Hyde Park, to Athens in December 1944 to try to broker a settlement in the Greek civil war, and to summit meetings with the American president and Joseph Stalin in Yalta and Potsdam.

After graduating from Notre Dame School, an independent Catholic girls' day school in Cobham, at the age of eighteen, Holmes attended a secretarial course, and then took the civil service exam, qualifying as a 'copy typist'. Because Holmes came out at the top of the list of candidates taking the exam, she was first posted to the Treasury, considered the most important government agency, entitled to draw the best people. She was required to take a further exam in shorthand, as well as courses in maths, history, English and geography (that must have come in very handy later during her planning for and travelling with Churchill!). The Treasury job, she says in her oral history on file at the Churchill College Archives, had become a training ground and a path for many young women into private-sector jobs in the City – especially desirable since those jobs were only five days a week, whereas civil-service jobs included Saturdays.

But Holmes's rise in the civil service was sufficiently rapid to induce her to stay on, rather than migrate to the City. After only two weeks at the Treasury she was sent to Number 10 for an interview. Neville Chamberlain was then prime minister and the prime minister's entire staff numbered only twenty-three people. Holmes was accepted at the starting level in Downing Street, in part, she believed, because her diction had been perfected at the convent and because her high ranking on the civil service exam led the examiners to decide she was worth training. It was probably less to do with her diction than she imagined, since all the secretarial candidates were speech-perfect. I asked Andrew Roberts about that at a gathering of Churchillians; his response is worth noting: 'That's how we avoid revolutions, by having lower-class people aspire to and absorb the manners of the upper classes. You can bet that, with the exception of Jane Portal, who came from a higher-class family than the others, the parents of Churchill's secretaries didn't speak the language of their daughters.'

As was to become usual for Holmes, she passed several more exams and became a clerical office secretary. Like other secretaries with shorthand and typing skills, she was expected at times to remain overnight, available should she be needed. Beds were provided and breakfast was served by the prime minister's personal 'domestic' staff.

When Holmes joined Downing Street, there were only two women employed in non-secretarial positions. One, Edith Watson, 'a spinster in her late fifties',[4] was, according to Elizabeth Gilliatt, 'an elderly lady who handled the parliamentary questions'; she had been there since the time of Lloyd George and would receive an MBE in June 1941. The other, a civil servant, Mrs Margaret Stenhouse, known as 'Mags', was in charge of Downing Street staffing and of Honours – meaning she probably received recommendations, sorted them and advised – a sensitive position, certainly. Holmes recalls that Stenhouse was 'head girl at Cheltenham Ladies College. I think that says a lot [about her].' And she later referred to her as 'the top female banana at No. 10'. Holmes described Chamberlain's office as 'quiet' – this is just before Munich.

All of that changed when Churchill became prime minister in May 1940. 'It was as if an electric current had gone through the place... suddenly all bustle and work and action this day... He cut out all the verbiage, the staff increased and the weekends vanished altogether.' 'Churchill arrived on the scene like a jet-propelled rocket,' wrote Colville.[5] 'The late nights really were late nights.'[6] 'The air tingled.'[7] By moving from the Admiralty to Number 10, Churchill went from the 'periphery' to the 'centre'. 'We [the War cabinet] had not the experience or the imagination to realise the difference between a human dynamo when humming on the periphery and when driving at the centre.'[8] Having been vetted and chosen by Treasury staff for transfer to Number 10, John Martin reported to Downing Street for duty as one of the new PM's Principal Private Secretaries, a post that despite its deceptive title is hardly secretarial as that designation is generally understood. Principal Private Secretaries – always male, their titles always capitalized – were the equivalent of senior policy staff and advisors. Not surprisingly, it being early May 1940, the prime minister was 'too busy to see him [Martin]' for a personal interview. So Stenhouse, who was then 'head of the permanent staff of assistants in the Prime Minster's office',[9] took Martin in hand and introduced him around. Martin, who stayed with Churchill until the end of the war, says of Stenhouse that to her 'expert knowledge, wisdom and splendid leadership of "the girls" so much was due in the coming years'.[10] The 'girls' are the Garden Room Girls, civil servants as distinct from Churchill's personal secretaries. These typists were so named because they worked in an office facing onto the Downing Street garden. The secretaries today are still known as the Garden Room Girls.*

Martin encouraged friendly relations between all staff levels at Downing Street, believing this would make the work more enjoyable and the tense, long and late hours worked more tolerable. He became friendly enough with Watson to ask her to join him for lunch to act as a sort of chaperone, the other guest being the woman to whom he would soon become engaged and eventually marry. On Christmas Day 1942 Martin became engaged to his future wife. He 'arranged a lunch party for all the shorthand writers and others on duty' in order to introduce his fiancée to the staff. Someone had given him a Welsh turkey and 'our Swedish cook produced an excellent meal,'[11] writes Holmes. Watson reported back to Martin that 'everyone was captivated by her'.[12] The

---

* According to Charles Moore, there has only ever been one Garden Room Boy.

camaraderie and mutual support among all of Churchill's staff was to last through the war years and beyond, their shared devotion to him making common ground. Churchill, of course, was aware of Martin's efforts to maintain morale, and despite the pressures on the wartime prime minister to cope with the enormous paper flow and other work for which he was responsible, never interfered with this use of his staff's time to create loyalty and affection between his staff members. Churchill was capable of being as sensitive to his staff's morale as he was to the morale of the British people, suffering under wartime restrictions, especially rationing.

Churchill's method of interviewing was idiosyncratic. When Martin was finally ushered into the prime minister's office in the House of Commons several weeks after coming to Number 10, Churchill looked him up and down with a 'searching gaze' and said, 'I understand that you are going to be one of my Secretaries.'[13] That was it. Martin assumed he had been hired. This method of taking on new staff after only a 'searching gaze' probably reflects Churchill's faith in the vetting process that preceded his initial meeting with new additions, perhaps supplemented by private calls to the many informed sources he had accumulated in a lifetime of journalism and politics. It was repeated with many of the female personal secretaries.

Marian Holmes's days as a Downing Street typist came to an end when one of Churchill's female secretaries became ill, creating an opening on the prime minister's personal staff. Holmes believes that the Private Secretaries took an informal vote and settled on promoting one of the typists to work directly with Churchill – she thinks her sponsor was John Martin.

Holmes's interview, if we can call it that, was similar to Martin's. She was working nights and Churchill needed to dictate. Leslie Rowan, one of the Private Secretaries, brought Holmes into Churchill's office at around 11 p.m. and said, 'Excuse me, Sir, this is Miss Holmes.' She writes: 'he was sitting... in a deep armchair reading some documents.'[14] The prime minister did not respond to Rowan, and instead started dictating. Holmes immediately sat down and began to type on 'the relatively silent typewriter'.[15] When Churchill finished dictating, he simply said, 'Give me' or simply 'Give' (meaning the typed sheets). She handed them over and rose to leave the room. She reports that Churchill said something like, 'Where the hell are you going?' Or in a 'loud voice DAMMIT! Don't go. I've only just started.'[16] Finally, he looked up at her and 'his face changed totally, there was that beatific grin, and he said, "Do sit down... when I shout, I'm not shouting at you, I'm thinking of the work"... I'd been accepted.'[17] She learned, as did others, that Churchill never let his temper simmer; he allowed it to boil over, but it always came off the boil very quickly. Barely a week later he said to her: 'You are doing very well,' in effect making her a member of the prime ministerial work family.[18] Like the other personal secretaries, Holmes signed the Official Secrets Act, which placed strict limits on what she could tell outsiders about her work. This is one reason she declined an invitation to give a talk about her experiences in Moscow when she returned with Churchill after his meetings with Stalin in October 1944. 'I would be billed as "Just Back From Moscow". Declined of course,'[19] she notes in her diary – which, of course, she was prohibited from keeping,[20] a prohibition she, like Colville and many others, ignored, to the benefit of historians.

In addition to the Official Secrets Act there was an additional constraint: there could be only one star, one person reporting Churchill's version of what transpired in the Soviet Union. Personal secretaries, and all others on the prime minister's staff, were meant to stay in the background, and not only for security reasons.

Like Holmes, many staff members kept notes and diaries; others wrote letters home when accompanying the prime minister on his travels. Luckily for historians, these documents eventually found their way into the Churchill Archives. They provide exciting insights into Churchill's work habits, his interactions with his staff, and his own reactions as he travelled the world managing the war. We do not know whether Churchill knew of Holmes's diary, but we do know he learned to trust her completely. And in July 1944 Churchill

▲ 12. WSC dictates on a
train with a silent typewriter, June 1941.

▼ 13. WSC broadcasts from the White
House after victory in North Africa,
May 1943.

▲ 14. WSC works en route to Quebec,
August 1943. Mrs Churchill and Private
Secretary John Martin assist.

The Unsung Women

▲ 15. Marian Holmes.
◀ 16. Violet Pearman.
▼ 17. Cecily 'Chips' Gemmell, painted by Churchill, *c*.1952.

▲ 18. Jane Portal.
▶ 19. Jo Sturdee.

▲ 20. Kathleen Hill takes down WSC's instructions, aboard HMS *Prince of Wales*, as he leaves for Placentia Bay to meet President Roosevelt, August 1941.

▼ 21. Marian Holmes disembarking HMS *Ajax*, off Athens, a city under fire during the Greek Civil War, December 1944.

▲ 22. Lettice Fisher at Sussex Square, 1924.

▲ 23. Elizabeth Layton at her desk at Chequers during the war, early 1940s.

▲ 24. Kathleen Hill, leaving Morpeth Mansions with WSC, September 1939. Versions of this photograph crop Hill out.

was heard to say that she is the 'sort of girl who'd rather die than have secrets torn out of her'.[21] The prime minister and the military leadership depended on the fact that the personal secretaries were entirely reliable – during the war many of them were privy to secrets known to very few indeed. Grace Hamblin describes Holmes as 'fair-haired and blue-eyed, like a fairy… Apparently he [Churchill] said to Mrs Churchill when she first appeared, "Oh dear, she's very young. I mustn't frighten her."'[22]

Asked about her usual day, Holmes explains that because she never knew when Churchill would call for her, she was always on her toes, ready to be summoned seven days a week, at any time during the twenty-four-hour day. If there were any gaps in the flow of work to her from the prime minister, the Private Secretaries would ask her to file FCO telegrams, cabinet minutes and other private memos. Or Holmes and her co-workers would work for one of the Private Secretaries and for visiting ministers such as Anthony Eden: 'Occasionally, we might do something for him. Certainly when we were bored we did.' Perhaps Eden didn't know this …

Often there were two personal secretaries on duty, one to work from 7 a.m. until dinner time, the other to be on call from dinner until the prime minister went to bed, usually between 2 and 3 a.m.

Holmes emphasizes that Churchill dictated to her everywhere, 'wherever we were: in cars, on trains, on planes, on ships every-where', including walking in the garden. She describes it all as being 'very stimulating'. She recalls driving 'back to town with the PM. He dictated most of the way and it was a balancing act, as we were driven at great speed, trying to keep dispatch boxes from falling on the flowers,* finding the right papers and taking dictation all at the same time.' And using her ankle to hold open the black dispatch box on which he was working. These black boxes accompanied him everywhere and only Churchill and his personal staff carried the keys. They contained the filing system

---

* Flowers were generally brought from either Chequers or Chartwell back to Downing Street.

that Churchill himself had organized[23] to handle the 'farrago of operational, civil, political and scientific matter' descending on him.[24] Not to mention the cigar smoke.

Holmes most loved working at Chequers,[25] where it was, if anything, busier than in London, with military officers, politicians, friends and family gathered there every weekend. Even 'baby Winston [aged about four] knocked on [her] door and I let him come into play for a while'. Once as they drove away, some of the grandchildren were waving and yelling: 'Don't go, Grandpa!'[26]

Churchill 'used the opportunity of having these... distinguished visitors down, there was also purpose to it... there'd be a mass of generals... John Winant [American Ambassador to Great Britain] and all kinds of people.'[27] Plus the Private Secretaries and, of course, Mrs Churchill. No relaxation on these weekends: constant work. Holmes's diary lists her bedtimes when she was finished with work, most often 3 or 3.30 a.m., when the prime minister had finished dictating.[28]

Holmes did have help at Chequers. The arrangement was that two of Churchill's four personal secretaries would go down to Chequers every weekend, the other two getting alternate weekends off. Holmes usually worked with Kathleen Hill, the senior personal secretary. When she was working there, she and Hill dined, not with the family, as did the Private Secretaries, but with the guards and security personnel and the manager of Chequers (later called the Curator)[29] in a small private dining room elsewhere. Levels of social distinction were maintained at Chequers, even in wartime.

At times when at Chequers, Holmes worked for Mrs Churchill, sometimes 'just listening, actually'. Holmes recalls that someone once described Mrs Churchill's conversations as being 'like chasing a butterfly with a dragnet. But I much enjoyed her lively talk about prefabricated houses, flying bombs, rest centres and all manner of diverse subjects.'[30] On another occasion, Mrs Churchill's conversation was 'as lively as ever. It ranged from elections to the best method of committing suicide.'[31] Not unlike her husband, whose curiosity was boundless and who encouraged conversations covering wide-ranging topics. Except, of course, suicide (see Chapter 7).

The schedule was gruelling and Churchill unrelenting in his production of work. Although he imposed an unreasonable schedule on his secretaries, he was not otherwise inconsiderate. He instructed one of his Private Secretaries that Holmes, who had not gone to bed until 3.30 a.m.,[32] 'was not to be called until at least 10.30 in the morning'. And aware that Chequers was not an ideal work site – it was notoriously cold* – he did his best at times to make their work place as comfortably warm as he possibly could.

The room in which the personal secretaries waited for the prime minister's summons and typed his dictation had a fireplace, which the women often lit. But at times they worked in the Hawtrey Room, one of the grand public rooms at Chequers, so grand that the secretaries would not dare to light a fire, especially when they would be working there only for a short time. One evening the prime minister 'caught me working in the Hawtrey Room and ticked me off for not lighting the fire. "You'll catch your death of cold… Why do you do such mad things?"'[33] On another occasion, Churchill literally took matters into his own hands. Worried that Holmes and Layton would be cold as they worked, and although the Hawtrey Room is quite wide and with only one fireplace on the long side of the room, quite hard to heat, Churchill knelt down and built up the fire himself, saying to them: 'Oh, you poor things. You must light a fire and get your coats. It's just as well I came in.'[34] And when Churchill believed Holmes had succumbed to a cold, he told Sawyers, his valet, to send up a hot whisky toddy. Naturally, this consideration for their comfort endeared him to the secretaries, and more than made up for his occasional grumpiness and for the demanding work schedule.

And he was not unaware that a bit of praise could have a

---

* When Harry Hopkins, FDR's closest advisor, was visiting, he held meetings in the downstairs guest bathroom, with his coat on, as it was the only reliably heated room in the house.

wondrous effect on morale. On one occasion, the prime minister said to John Martin in Holmes's presence: 'We could always get some more young ladies down here [to handle increased work]. Of course, they won't be as sweet and charming as the ones we've got here now.' She was embarrassed, but the compliment undoubtedly made up for the many late nights, for many of the times he snapped at her or couldn't control his impatience. Another compensation for this arduous schedule was to earn a place among those on whom Churchill, as a mark of affection, bestowed a nickname, in her case 'Miss Sherlock'. In the case of Eric Seal, one of his Private Secretaries, Churchill played off the fact that seals can be found on ice floes and dubbed him Ice Floe, one of Churchill's favourite puns on someone's name.

It might seem odd that these incidents of consideration, and some flattery, offset the punishing work schedule in his secretaries' minds. The answer lies in their understanding of the importance of their task helping to win the war. In addition, the work was exciting and very varied, and their boss was at times funny. And in the fact that he would accept their suggestions for making their jobs easier and him more efficient. Holmes noticed that Churchill had 'been getting into the habit of dictating into shorthand. He used to dictate this way only for speeches. Tonight, I persuaded him to revert to dictating straight on to the silent typewriter... He can see straight away what he has said and sign it... The majority of comments and directives he dictates never need correction.'[35] He quickly saw the sense of that change, that it would permit him to get his work done more easily and quickly. That, after all, was what mattered most to him. When asked what could put Churchill in a bad mood, she thought whatever 'he'd regard as inefficient'.

Indeed, it was hard work and difficult problems that very often lifted Churchill's mood, as Holmes – and indeed others on his team – could not help noticing. In October of 1943 he was consumed with the Italian campaign, the preliminary plans for Overlord and the thorny question of who would lead the invasion of continental Europe, as well as organizing a summit with President

Roosevelt and Stalin. Noting his exhilaration at the combination of great challenges and hard work, Holmes wrote in her diary: 'P.M. worked hard all morning. He was in high spirits and seems to have an insatiable thirst for work.'[36] Such high spirits that she recalls he 'began but did not finish, the jingle "There was a young lady of Crewe".' This is similar to Layton's observation: 'The prime minister always seemed at his most approachable and considerate and easiest to work for when there was a crisis on... In calmer times, when there was less to worry about, he would sometimes be irritable and easily upset.'[37]

Holmes's fondness for working at Chequers did not mean that she was not excited when the opportunity for foreign travel presented itself. She saw it as a great treat, even though the workload increased substantially. At the beginning of the war, foreign travel was considered too dangerous for women, so only Patrick Kinna, the only male personal secretary, and a whizz at shorthand, travelled with Churchill and his all-male entourage. However, as the war progressed, female secretaries were asked to make dangerous trips to distant locations for summits and other meetings. Holmes described her first trip, which was to the second Quebec Conference (Octagon, September 1944): 'I was just told... would you like to go?' Of course she would! She had never been abroad and called it her 'first big travel adventure!'[38] She had been secretly storing up clothing coupons and borrowing 'some undies. It might be windy'[39] and other clothes from Edith Watson, whose chores at Downing Street meant she would not be a candidate to accompany the prime minister. Secretly, not only because Churchill's trip, destination and route were highly confidential, but because it would be the first time a female secretary had been allowed to travel and other candidates might have been more than a little put out at not being asked to go. Travel, after all, would become a major perk of the job.

The trek to Quebec began on 5 September 1944. George VI lent the prime minister one of his special trains to transport Churchill and his large delegation to Greenock, Scotland, there to board the *Queen Mary*, lying offshore, for her trip across the Atlantic to Quebec. The *Queen Mary* had once been the most luxurious liner in the world, but since the outbreak of the war she had been used only to transport soldiers back and forth between the United States and the United Kingdom. The ship was now leased to the Americans to transport thousands of soldiers returning from the Normandy Campaign. Only three months earlier, Holmes, Layton and Hill had tensely awaited that invasion, on the prime minister's special train, parked on a siding at Southampton, spending two and a half days there, in order to be near Southwick Manor, General Eisenhower's command headquarters.

For its VIP guest (and his staff), the top deck of the *Queen Mary* had been refurbished to its past luxury, the bar and dining rooms opened. Holmes shared a cabin with Kathleen Hill, 'most luxurious for us'.

Enemy submarines followed the *Queen Mary*, but Captain Pim maintained the map room that showed where the submarines were.[40] Either because Churchill's presence ensured adequate protection by destroyers or because, as Holmes put it, 'One could never, ever, feel scared in the company of Churchill,' she felt reassured – just as the British public seem to have been reassured by a Churchill walkabout or wireless broadcast in the worst days of the war. That feeling of safety was not confined to the crossing to Quebec. Holmes's diary mentions that she 'had to tell the PM that London was again under severe air attack', when, like other Londoners, she was one of the targets of the bombing, and she notes later, 'still ducking the doodlebugs... Heavy raids. Spent the night ducking, both at the office and at lunchtime at Victoria.'[41]

Some work was done on this voyage, but less than usual as Churchill, just two months shy of his seventieth birthday, was 'quite ill... [we] feared that he was going to get pneumonia'. Brigadier Lionel Whitby, a doctor, and Nurse Pugh were also on board in case Lord Moran, Churchill's regular doctor, needed their help. Downing Street had advised that the presence of the brigadier, a medical colleague of Lord Moran's and an expert in blood transfusions, and Mrs Pugh (as she was to be known, and no relation of Doreen Pugh) was not to be disclosed as it might cause comment and worry. Churchill called the brigadier 'Vampire' (another Churchillian affectionate nickname), because of his medical speciality. Despite being ill – illness rarely stood between Churchill and a good dinner – the prime minister and his Private Secretaries dined on oysters and champagne on the first night out. We have seen Colville's description of meals aboard ship in Chapter 5. Although they did not dine with Churchill and his advisors, it seems the staff had access to the same good and plentiful food, as meals on board were not subject to rationing.

Using his leisure time to pursue his consuming interest in politics in all its forms,* Churchill read Antony Trollope's *Phineas Finn* and later *The Duke's Children*, both drawing heavily on politics. One wonders why he skipped the in-between volumes; it is almost certain that he had read them all before. Holmes recalls the trip as a 'jolly time, very jolly time, yes, terrific time'.

During the voyage, Churchill discovered that the US servicemen on board had been granted leave, but only from the date of embarkation. Because the *Queen Mary* had been delayed a week to allow the prime minister and his party to arrive in Scotland and board, the soldiers would lose a week of their leave and pay. Churchill cabled FDR at once, asking that the week's leave be made up to all. Roosevelt agreed and thanked Churchill for his 'thoughtfulness',[42] a virtue with which Holmes and his staff were quite familiar, and all the more notable and surprising because of the pressures on the prime minister. We can only guess how Churchill learned of the plight of the servicemen. Perhaps Mrs Churchill reported to him her visit with the 400 or so blind American servicemen on board. Perhaps his natural curiosity and

---

* This shows Churchill's absorption in politics even during his leisure hours, as when he described the Battle of Jutland using the cutlery on his dinner table during a social dinner, and his choice of plays and films, such as *Henry V*.

his concern for the plight of all servicemen led him to ask about the troops below decks, their condition and morale.

The *Queen Mary* docked in Halifax on 10 September 1944 to be met by 'a tumultuous crowd of hundreds... [T]he smiling Churchill led them in song after song up until the train pulled out.'[43] Churchill and his staff of about 100 then took a train to Quebec City, where they were met by Roosevelt and his staff of about 250. Holmes's recollections are basically in line with those of Hill, recalling the 'massive menu'. Churchill's Principal Private Secretary John Martin remembers a '10-course dinner' on the train.[44] Coming as they did from rationed Britain with 'no lights, no white bread and rolls', this must have been a great thrill for the British contingent. In Quebec, the president and Mrs Roosevelt, the Churchills and his personal staff stayed at the Citadel, the official residence of the Governor General of Canada. The remainder of the staffs, both British and American, stayed at the luxurious Hotel Frontenac. Holmes recalls that although she worked very long hours, she managed to find some time to shop for nylons[45] and clothes, and to go dancing one night. Also time to have a mild flirtation with one of the Canadian Mounties, who promised her a flight over Niagara Falls. Alas, before she could accept, she was ordered back to The Citadel, then to go with the prime minister to Hyde Park, the president's private home in upstate New York. She regretted not seeing the Falls, but 'as it turned out, of course, it was far more interesting to go down' with Churchill to Hyde Park. Once there, Holmes and Hill were put up in a hotel close to the president's house, always ready to answer a summons to work.

On 19 September, Holmes recalls she 'had to read out a minute to the prime minister while he was still reclining in his bath'.[46] Other secretaries who had similar experiences report that they sat outside the bathroom door, with no sightline in to the bathing prime minister. She also recalls on the train to New York to board the *Queen Mary* for their return to Britain: 'the PM dictated something so funny that it reduced Mr Martin, Cmdr. ['Tommy'] Thompson and me to tears of laughter.'[47] In one of the ironies of history, as Churchill sailed home, 'Private Henry Kissinger, by contrast, was on an overcrowded troopship, bound for the front line in Western Europe.'[48]

Like others of the ladies who joined Churchill on visits to America, Holmes vividly recalls the difference between the security arrangements at Chequers, Hyde Park and on the prime minister's trips, and the more massive and intrusive arrangements made by the Secret Service to protect President Roosevelt. There was no such group of protectors, or security measures, at Chequers, 'when we were close to invasion by the Germans… just a few miles as the crow flew, from us, and there'd be one English bobby. The president's security was amazing… electric fences… roads cleared and there were masses of G-men on all the running boards.' Initially, the secretaries found the Secret Service squad rather intimidating, but later in the war became more relaxed in their gun-toting presence. In fact, at Yalta, Holmes, part of the prime minister's large entourage, joined Layton in inviting six of the men to dinner, and a merry affair it proved to be.[49]

Despite the omnipresence of the president's security detail, Hyde Park was 'very relaxed', Mrs Roosevelt unassuming and bustling and with 'a thing about picnics',[50] which of course suited Churchill.[51] Much to her excitement, Holmes spied a luncheon guest invited by the Roosevelts, possibly at Churchill's request: the former Prince of Wales, now the Duke of Windsor, whom Churchill had loyally defended – and at considerable political cost – during the abdication crisis, only later to be rewarded by the Windsors' flirtation with Hitler. To Holmes's regret, the duchess did not accompany her husband. Holmes also saw the president, who, she delightedly noted, smiled at her. A regretful Churchill, too absorbed in other matters to tend to the needs of his staff, realized only too late that an introduction to the American president would have been a highlight of Holmes's trip; he later apologized to her for not introducing her personally to the president,[52] a treat Harry Hopkins had conferred on a flustered Layton the previous year.[53]

A day later they were off to the *Queen Mary*, with 'high security and all the traffic stopped everywhere'.[54] On the return voyage to Britain, Holmes's diary records:

> PM dictated a further two thousand words of his speech [to be delivered in the House of Commons, reporting on the Quebec summit]. I got the best view of his behind that I have ever had. He stepped out of bed still dictating, and oblivious of his all-too-short bed jacket. Anyway, he was in a kind and conciliatory mood and I felt waves of his approval.[55]

'Oblivious' is a word well chosen by Holmes. Churchill, when focused on his work, could be impervious to his surroundings or the people around him or to his current state of dress. But as Holmes reports, not always: while dictating in bed early one morning, 'an enormous fly started buzzing around his bedroom. He asked me to ring for Sawyers and said: "Get hold of that bloody fly and wring its neck."'[56] Churchill hated any noises like whistling or buzzing or, as we shall see, the clanging of cow bells, when he was concentrating on his work.

Later, working on the same speech, she recalls: 'When I told him that he had repeated himself, he said "All right, all right. Don't break your heart about it – I can always cross it out," rather snappishly.' Then off he went to play bezique* with Jock Colville until 3 a.m.[57] The impatience that resulted in all those 'Action This Day' memoranda would contribute so much to the efficient execution of the war, but at times was not appreciated by his overworked but loyal staff.

On 26 September the *Queen Mary* docked at Greenock. Although he had been away for three weeks, Churchill did not pause for a detailed briefing on happenings in his absence. Instead, he went directly to the House of Commons for Prime Minister's Questions, and a few days later reported to the House on the Quebec Summit,

---

* A favourite card game of Churchill's. Played by two people with two packs of cards.

demonstrating his respect for his beloved House of Commons, his understanding of the need to keep its members informed, and an energy, drive and work ethic unusual in those days for a man close to seventy years old.

Barely two weeks later, Holmes learned that she was to pack again, this time to head for Moscow, where Churchill would be meeting with Stalin. Holmes and Joan Bright flew out in advance of Churchill and his delegation, along with Elizabeth Layton, stopping in Teheran for refuelling for forty-eight hours before proceeding to Moscow. The pair were in Moscow when the prime minister landed on 9 October 1944. Asked why she and Bright had travelled out earlier, Holmes explained that Churchill 'did like to see a familiar face whenever he went... he liked his own.' And he relied on Bright to 'arrange the accommodation for the British delegation',[58] which of course meant she had to arrive in advance of the delegation.

Churchill and his staff were driven directly to Minister of Foreign Affairs Vyacheslav Molotov's dacha, where Churchill indulged himself in one of his favourite pastimes: he took a bath. Holmes and Bright stayed at a guest house on the grounds of the dacha in order to be on call should Churchill require secretarial help. The 'hospitality was amazing... caviar and vodka for breakfast... huge buffets... we were entirely spoiled'. She also reports that Soviet women would insist on staying in the bathroom when she took a bath and that they would scrub her back and dry her – it was not easy for her to get used to. She compared her own important war work with that of the women who were attending her and showed them photos of British women working in factories and in uniform. We have no report of the reaction of the Soviet women.

The nine days of long meetings with Stalin, Molotov and Soviet generals and their British and American colleagues exhausted Churchill. Holmes says

> he wandered into the office [in their Moscow town house] very sleepy-eyed in his dressing gown... I followed him back to the

bedroom with some telegrams. He asked if I were going to the ballet tonight... and then [I] poured him another a cup of tea, [unusual for Churchill to drink tea]... [He said] The hand that rocks the cradle ought to be able to pour me a cup of tea. He had been eating chicken with his fingers. Sawyers brought him a finger bowl. What's this? [he asked] To wash your hands, Sir [he answered]. [Churchill] cried out Good heavens! I'm going to wash me [*sic*] whole body in a minute.[59]

Holmes records that Stalin arranged for a performance of the Bolshoi Ballet, which both he and the prime minister were to attend. With the Soviet leader intent on spreading 'a carpet of goodwill', Joan Bright 'put in demands for tickets to opera and ballet; if I asked for double I usually got the number I wanted,' making it possible for Churchill's staff and some embassy and mission staffs ('who seldom got seats') to attend several performances.[60] Although it is not certain that even Bright could cadge all the tickets she wanted for the gala to be attended by Churchill and Stalin. Churchill, however, made certain that Holmes could attend the gala, saying to her: '"You're going. Oh, you must go." It's not true that he wasn't concerned about one enjoying things also... Churchill was very kind. He wanted very much for us to see the ballet and to partici-pate.' The programme began with the 'first act of the ballet *Giselle*, then two hours of Red Army singing and dancing... with the PM thoroughly enjoying the martial songs... and beating time to them with his hands.'[61] Churchill also loved music-hall songs, was not shy about singing and knew many songs by heart. After two consecutive showings of the film *The Mikado* at Chequers, Holmes describes Churchill as being 'in a highly entertaining mood... sat in the office singing *The Mikado* songs – he seems to know all the lyrics by heart.'[62] His prodigious memory for people and politics extended to poetry and songs.

Soviet security was even more pervasive than what Holmes had experienced during Churchill's visit to FDR at Hyde Park. When the secretaries travelled between the dacha grounds and the ballet it was in armoured cars. When she returned late at night, there were guards and checkpoints everywhere. When she went for a walk in the surrounding pine forest, 'one of the trees would move and you'd realize it was a soldier... dressed in grey'.

When the nine-day meeting with Stalin ended on 18 October, Churchill held a press conference at the British Embassy for American, British and Russian correspondents. Sitting behind the prime minister and Anthony Eden, both Layton and Holmes were to take down in shorthand everything said. Holmes recalls 'afterwards, Churchill said to us "You didn't take down all that tripe, did you?"'[63]

In her book, Elizabeth Layton, who was also on this trip, gives us an insight into Churchill's unexpected, impish humour. The flight out of Moscow had to make an overnight stop at Simferopol, in the centre of the Crimea. At a dinner that night, Churchill insisted that Layton, Sawyers and Inspector Hughes* join the main group as there was no other dining room. Layton and the two men

> found a small table and sat together... There was a toast to the King, then to Marshal Stalin... Then I saw Mr Churchill look-ing at me with a wicked twinkle and wondered what was going to happen. He rose to his feet and proposed the health of 'Miss Layton, the only lady present', at which all that grand company got good-naturedly to its feet, laughing... General Yermetchenko [one of the guests/minders] seized the flowers out of a bowl on the table, and dumped them dripping, into my lap... and then the company called for a speech. Feeling fairly idiotic, and scarlet-faced, I stood up and said 'Thank you very much. I feel greatly honoured.'

She knew Churchill was teasing, singling her out for attention. Holmes had flown home in another aircraft.[64]

A little more than two months later, a few days before Christmas 1944, Holmes (and Layton) were working late at Chequers. For once,

---

*   Detective Inspector Bill Hughes, one of Churchill's regular bodyguards.

Holmes was unhappy to be on call – it would be her first Christmas away from her family. Then everything changed, as it so often did for people working for Churchill: the prime minister decided that – Christmas Eve or not – he had to fly to Athens to try to broker a peace in the civil war raging in Greece and in which British soldiers were heavily involved in street fighting. Typically, he felt that his personal intervention might make a difference, bringing the warring factions to some compromise solution. He asked Holmes and Layton, 'the PM's two most attractive typists',[65] to handle the secretarial chores on that journey. 'Tremendously exciting, yes, because it was totally unexpected… we work up until 8 o'clock that night [Christmas Eve] and we had to sort of rapidly pack… we were all slightly merry… whisked off to Northolt for our first flight on this marvellous new aircraft, the C-54… a beautifully appointed aircraft' given by President Roosevelt.[66] Or as Pierson Dixon, Eden's Principal Private Secretary, disparagingly described the Skymaster, 'alas American'.[67] Pierson, recalls Holmes, 'had his hat on the back of his head… I thought perhaps he had had quite a bit of brandy or something.'

Sir Martin Gilbert describes the Skymaster: 'There are bunks for eight besides the PM and a dining salon and six of the bunks turn into three Pullman seats during the day, for the lower members of the staff… The whole aircraft is most sumptuously fitted up, swivel chairs and satin curtains, carpets etc.'[68] At the back of the plane was a simple bedroom where Churchill continued to work, his pens, klop and tags laid out beside the bed. He would dictate to the two women, 'anywhere really and everywhere', or as we noted from Holmes's earlier statement, 'wherever we were: in cars, on trains, on planes, on ships everywhere'.

Once airborne, it being almost midnight on Christmas Eve, the staff were all served 'whiskys and sodas', leading to massive headaches due to lack of oxygen when the C-54 landed in Naples, en route to Athens. Probably for security reasons, the Skymaster had to fly at high altitudes, but only Churchill was supplied with oxygen. 'A breakfast under battle conditions' was served at a military airport outside Naples.

Then back on the plane and on to Athens. As they flew over the Greek islands Churchill shared with Holmes and Layton his joy at being in – or in this case, thousands of feet above – an historically important part of the world. He pointed out the islands: 'There we [Holmes and Layton] were, lying across the bed, looking out... at these Greek Islands.' The prime minister's enthusiasm and his desire to share it were infectious and overcame his fatigue and that of Holmes and Layton. Holmes was learning that Churchill's curiosity about the places to which his management of the war and his search for peace took him, his delight at discovering historically significant places, was never far below the surface, even on dangerous journeys to convene or attend fraught meetings. She was learning, too, of Churchill's special delight at sharing with his staff his knowledge of the history of the places to which they would travel together. Much like his delight and pleasure at arranging to show President Roosevelt his favourite sunset view of the Atlas Mountains after the Casablanca Conference.

The party landed in 'freezing cold' Athens at lunchtime on Christmas Day in the middle of the civil war, a shooting war at that time. Churchill had hopes of bringing that civil war to an end. But Churchill's work habits never changed. Sitting on the runway in Athens, still aboard the Skymaster, he continued to dictate in his bedroom at the tail end of the plane. Holmes said Layton 'found it very hard to type because her hands were so cold'.

General Scobie (British Army Commander in Greece) and Harold Macmillan (Resident Minister in the Middle East) came aboard the plane for meetings, after which the team transferred to HMS *Ajax*, waiting in Piraeus Harbour, where Churchill, Holmes and others would live throughout their Greek stay. Holmes recalls they were advised to transfer to HMS *Ajax* as it would be much safer, warmer and a functioning office could be set up there for them. The *Spectator* reported that 'German agents were known to abound [in Athens]'.[69]

Later that day, at 6 p.m., back aboard the *Ajax*, a Christmas Day costume party was in full swing and carols were being sung, a

Royal Navy tradition. Churchill had arranged separate meetings in separate cabins with representatives of two of the factions warring, literally, for control of Greece, which Stalin had conceded to Britain during his meeting with Churchill in return for concessions from Churchill. As these representatives came aboard for their separate meetings, they must have been surprised to see British naval personnel outfitted in dresses and beards, with 'glasses of gin in each hand... I think the Captain just moved [the Archbishop, who had a real black beard] away in time to save [him from] a beard-pulling contest.'[70]

Holmes and Layton shared a cabin, and both had to share a bathroom with the admiral whose flagship the *Ajax* was. Holmes records, 'It was a wonderful time there. And [Layton] and I were sort of entertained and we had our meals in the ward room where the officers were.' When the two women exercised on deck, an American destroyer saw them and signalled the *Ajax* 'How many have you got?' and *Ajax* replied, 'We've got two but they're ours', thereby passing up an opportunity to cement the Anglo-American naval special relationship. 'It was great enormous fun.' This amidst gunfire and shelling. Colville says the ship was 'straddled by shells'.[71]

The following day the party returned to Athens. As she climbed down the ladder from *Ajax* into the tender taking them into Athens for the meetings, Holmes recalls that Churchill asked her: '"Are you sure you have enough clothes on? You don't look warm enough to me." He gave instructions that a spare overcoat was to be brought from *Ajax* for me.' She and Layton had only the shortest notice that they would be leaving for Athens on Christmas Eve. Both had planned that they might have to work at Chequers over the holiday and had no time to pack properly for a trip to cold and dangerous Athens. Whether it was the hasty departure or rationing that left Holmes without a coat, we do not know. We do know that the secretaries had become skilled at converting pieces of fabric into clothing: 'one girl even had a fine winter coat made out of an army blanket'.[72]

Holmes goes on to report that 'we were again shelled as the motor launch reached the shore. We drove in an armoured car… to the British Embassy. The building was under siege.'[73] Although the party was under fire much of the time in Athens, none of the oral histories and memoirs complain about the danger and discomfort. The only fear, expressed earlier by Layton, was 'I suddenly began to feel frightened. What would happen if HE caught cold in this bitter wind? Where was there we could go?'[74] Just as Churchill worried about Holmes, Layton worried about him.

Churchill and his staff went to the Greek Foreign Ministry, then under attack, with parts of the building on fire. Separate meetings were scheduled with Archbishop Damaskinos, representing the royals, and with Georgios Papandreou, prime minister of the Greek government-in-exile, anti-royalist and anti-communist. The only lighting was provided by hurricane lamps as the electricity supply had been damaged during the fighting.

After the meetings in Athens, Churchill and the others returned to the *Ajax*, but Holmes and Colville went to the British Embassy so she could type up her notes from the meeting and Colville could cable them to the cabinet. That accomplished, the pair set out to reboard the *Ajax*. Colville, some three decades later, recalls, or claimed to recall, perhaps with tongue in cheek, that he and Holmes shared the sight of the Acropolis and Mount Lycabettus

> by the light of the full moon. It was no less thrilling to share that romantic pleasure with Marian Holmes who was not only shyly charming and highly efficient, but closely resembled one of the prettier species of gazelle. What rapture it was going to be to glide with her across the smooth moon-lit waters of Phaleron Bay in the snug warmth of a spacious and spotless naval pinnace… In the moonlight Marian Holmes's long golden hair transformed her into the Lorelei.[75]

The event did not quite match up to the alleged fantasy. Holmes recalls:

An armoured car drove us back to the Piraeus Harbour, where there was supposed to be a motorboat waiting for us [to return them to the *Ajax*]... the driver [of the car] had to get back so Jock and I were stranded... Some Greek soldiers came up and Jock was in danger of being arrested because he was in a RAF uniform. They thought we were a hangover from the Germans... it was all a bit dicey.

The Greeks did not speak English and neither Colville nor Holmes had any Greek. Colville spoke a few lines of ancient Greek, to no avail: he says he tried this line from Sophocles' play *Ajax*: 'My son, mayest thou be more fortunate than thy father.' He certainly picked the apposite source, but his 'accent bore no resemblance at all to modern Greek'.[76] Matters got worse when Colville tried a few words of German. Dicey, indeed. But finally, all was settled and they were returned safely to the *Ajax*. In recalling this incident Holmes makes no mention of any romantic approaches by Colville, either because his longing was just that or because she thought them not proper to discuss.

In the thoughtfulness of which he often was capable, Churchill, while aboard the *Ajax*, asked for the names of the fifteen 'plucky women on Embassy staff' and requested that they all receive the British Empire Medal, because 'these ladies have been living for three weeks under the constant fire of the enemy, in spite of which they have carried out their duty with utmost credit and tireless devotion to duty'.[77] Just as he had found time on the voyage to Quebec on the *Queen Mary* to cable President Roosevelt, requesting added leave time for the wounded American soldiers on board, so under fire and enormous pressure to work out a settlement of the Greek civil war, he found time to think of those women whose unheralded contributions he knew from first-hand observation to be crucial to a successful war effort.

After addressing the crew of the *Ajax*, thanking them for their work, Churchill and his staff boarded his Skymaster for the flight home, via Naples. Before sailing, Holmes says that 'Bearers of gifts knocked on the door of our cabin all morning. There were sponges, grapefruit, butter, pictures of *Ajax* framed for us by the ship's carpenters… The most cherished offering was a good conduct certificate which read, in part… She [Holmes] has conducted herself most excellently under difficult conditions. She has been an asset to the ship,' signed by the captain of HMS *Ajax*. Layton probably received a similar certificate.

In Naples Churchill stopped off to meet with Field Marshal Alexander and Admiral Cunningham. The field marshal had arranged for the two secretaries (Holmes and Layton) to stay in a fully staffed chalet in the grounds of his Villa Rivalta. The admiral had further arranged a dinner for the two women at his HQ, the Villa Emma, and insisted that they 'be served with some of his best brandy', which they enjoyed sitting on a terrace overlooking Capri with 'garlands of flowers'[78] in the house where Admiral Nelson had lived with his mistress Emma, Lady Hamilton, a tale recounted in *That Hamilton Woman* (1941),* one of Churchill's favourite films, watched, and not for the first time, on a sea voyage to meet with President Roosevelt and at Chequers.

While in Naples Churchill had time to dictate a loving note to Mrs Churchill. Holmes recalls that he was a bit grumpy and that she 'could not hear what he was saying… he often abandoned his dentures and would be smoking a cigar and he also had a slight impediment.' So she asked him to repeat two words. 'Tender love,'

---

*   A black-and-white film starring Vivien Leigh and Laurence Olivier, *That Hamilton Woman* was shot in the United States in late 1940 and released in 1941. On 2 August 1941, as Churchill prepared to sail to meet President Roosevelt for the first time, he insisted on seeing the film again. He was so disappointed that the film had already been sent back to Korda's offices that he ordered: 'put people across the road to stop them [the film delivery van and driver]'. *The Churchill Documents,* Vol. 16, p. 1027, from Oliver Hoare's Diary. On 8 August Cadogan's Diary notes that the prime minister and his officers aboard the *Prince of Wales* watched the film for the fifth time and Churchill was 'moved to tears'. This was the night before his first meeting with Roosevelt aboard the USS *Augusta*. We can assume that Kinna also saw the film.

he said, but still inaudibly. She told the prime minister that she still could not hear him. 'Tender love,' he repeated. 'You ought to know what that is.' One of the less endearing aspects of the prime minister was his occasional and ill-concealed irritability, especially when tired, as he had every right to be in this instance after his frustrating exertions with the combative Greek factions and while under fire. There were, of course, more substantial reasons for any irritability, especially in the early days of the war when disaster followed disaster. But that tale has been well told by others, viewing history from the top down, rather than from the staff level up.

But exhaustion rarely lasted. When asked about Churchill's health in general, Holmes described his 'stamina as amazing... He seems to throw off illness in a stubborn way.' And he had 'this marvellous ability to sleep, to sort of catnap really... awake early and working.'

Churchill's eagerness to share with Holmes and others on his staff his sense of history in each of the venues they visited, and his courteous inclusion of them in events such as the ballet in Moscow, does not mean that for someone born at Blenheim, hierarchy did not matter. When asked, Holmes admitted that she had never had dinner with Churchill's intimate circle, with the exception of one occasion, aboard a flight from Cairo to Naples. She was working in the back of the plane 'on a rather rickety table with a typewriter... planning to have lunch with Sawyers.' The prime minister sent back a message asking her to come forward for lunch with him and Field Marshal Lord Alanbrooke, Chief of the Imperial General Staff (CIGS), and the others. She did as asked and Churchill offered her some brandy. She goes on: 'I had to desist because I thought I'd never get any work done... I thought I was going to fall flat on my face if I had brandy. Never be able to do any work, in these conditions... on an aircraft.' But, she says, 'Generally, I didn't eat with the family, not really, no.'

One of Holmes's most interesting recollections is her private moments with Churchill, after the day's work had been done, when he was 'wanting to unwind'.[79] These times were 'totally fascinating... He would recite Tennyson... with all the emotions and tears falling down... a poem called "Locksley Hall". Then he would talk about his early life... when he was in India. He was very mellow... but his invective was quite memorable too.' Elizabeth Layton said she could 'hear the tears in his voice'.[80]

Churchill had a lively and imaginative vocabulary. Without naming names, she reports Churchill saying someone should 'be swatting flies in his wife's boudoir'; someone else was 'a yapping dog... Occasionally he would swear and then sort of profusely apologize – especially if a lady was present.' On another occasion he described someone as 'a bladder with a name on it'.[81] She wrote: 'I would not have missed his reminiscences for anything.'[82]

After Athens, Holmes was not surprised when the prime minister said to her: 'You know I can't give you the excitement of Athens every day.'[83] He was wrong. Her next trip would be even more exciting: Yalta in February 1945, when Churchill met President Roosevelt and Marshal Stalin. After only a few weeks of routine work at Downing Street and Chequers, Churchill asked her if she was coming with him to Yalta. When she said 'no', he told Leslie Rowan to add her name to the list of those travelling with him to Yalta. Because the staff was a cohesive unit and worked well together with no friction, Holmes was worried that she might be replacing Jo Sturdee on this trip, which she told Rowan she would not do. Rowan assured her that 'what the Boss says, goes and orders is orders'[84] and that both she and Sturdee would be travelling to Yalta.

Churchill's party was flown to Malta and there boarded the HMS *Orion*, where Churchill and his daughter Sarah joined them. When President Roosevelt's ship, the USS *Quincy*, sailed into the harbour, the two leaders waved to each other from their respective bridges. Layton and Holmes say they were invited to drinks and dinners by each of the officers' levels (by rank) aboard ship. She wrote that Churchill 'visited the Wardroom and stood at the bar and had a drink with all the officers crowding around him. He is simply wonderful at these impromptu chats.'[85] He urged the officers to be 'kind to my lady secretaries. They travel everywhere with me, sometimes under most difficult conditions and they put up with all my bad tempers.'[86] Hard to resist that Churchillian charm. The officers sang 'Goodnight, Ladies' to Holmes and Layton as they left the wardroom. The party then flew on to Yalta, where, on 'late night duty, we are sleeping in a nearby sanatorium', with scarce bathroom and washing facilities, and having to wait in a queue with Field Marshal Alexander for a bath. 'What a hole I've brought you to,' the prime minister apologized to Holmes. But the days and work contained sufficient excitement to offset the physical hardships.[87]

The prime minister gave a dinner for the leaders at the Vorontsov Palace on 10 February 1945.[88] Holmes recalls that Commander 'Tommy' Thompson 'came in to get the PM's approval of the table plan. He [Churchill] thought some of the courses ought to be cut out.' With his usual attention to the details of dinner gatherings, and his use of the dinner table to advance his policies, Churchill 'finally approved the table plan saying that what they would lose in pleasure they could gain in business'.[89] Consumed with work, even at dinners, and planning ahead.

Churchill's personal secretaries had dinner that night in another dining room with the staff of the president, many of whom they knew from the meetings at Quebec and Hyde Park. The special relationship was – and is – deep.

Before leaving, Churchill toured the site of the Battle of Bala-clava. The entourage then boarded the SS *Franconia* so the prime minister could work there. Holmes could sleep in her own cabin aboard the ship. But not for long. The staff was to fly home shortly after its stay on the SS *Franconia* to get some work done. They were escorted to Saki airbase, where the Soviets had arranged a grand buffet. British and Russian toasts were 'ad nauseam – our private toast was: Here's Saki in your eye.'[90] With typical Chur-chillian curiosity and knowledge, he regretted merely flying over the island of Samothrace – a site of ancient renown because of the discovery of the justly famed statue of Nike, now prominently displayed in the Louvre.

On the way home, Holmes landed at Athens in February 1945,

for the second time in her career, where the Churchill party was greeted as heroes for having brought to an end the Greek civil war. Holmes had a dinner that night with the officers aboard HMS *Ajax*, many of whom she knew from her previous visits aboard that ship. Then she flew to Cairo's famous Mena House Hotel, with its glorious views of the Sphinx.

When preparing to fly back to Britain, the prime minister asked who would be on the plane with him. When told it would be Miss Layton this time, he commented, 'And so my bevy is to be divided.'[91] Holmes flew back through Marseilles, where she was given a 'hot meal in "The Blitz" café'.[92]

Back at home, the work continued. As did the excitement of working for Churchill. With some understatement, Holmes describes the week of 29 April 1945 as 'very exciting. Liz [Layton] and I hope that, as well as the surrender in Italy, the whole war will come to an end while we are on duty.'[93] Grinning, the prime minister said to her, 'It's nice to be winning, isn't it?' as the German armies in Italy surrendered to the Allies.[94]

At 3 p.m. on 8 May 1945 Churchill spoke to the nation. Holmes's diary records: 'We have come though the greatest and hardest trial in our long history – as victors. The PM's voice broke as he said "Onward Britannia". We all rushed into the garden [at Downing Street]… we clapped him as he passed between us and he thanked us warmly, his own staff.'[95] Churchill knew, and his staff knew he knew, that his personal secretaries, privy to all the secret information during the war, working tirelessly and enduring arduous and dangerous trips, were a key part of the war effort, having done much to enable him to be effective in conducting that battle.

Big Ben was now lit and striking, and victory parties were held all over the country. Churchill continued his routine of dictating memos, speeches and bulletins late into the night, keeping the same work pace he had established during the earlier years of the war. But he did find time to issue an order ensuring that there be enough beer in the capital for the celebration.[96]

By June he had started dictating his election campaign speech. As a civil servant, Holmes was not allowed to do any election work, only the work of the ongoing government. But she did occasionally type speeches related to the upcoming election, as did Jo Sturdee. Holmes notes that 'at one point he was completely overwhelmed with emotion [considering the upcoming election]. The sight of this great and fearless man sobbing made tears well up in my own eyes. His compassion is so deep.'[97] The only problem she faced that night was Randolph standing over her as she typed the speech, 'breathing whisky and onions down my neck'.[98] But exhilaration prevailed. One night after the prime minister went to bed at 2.30, she and others on the late-night shift 'skipped into St James's Park and had a go on the swings and seesaw at 3 a.m.'[99]

Holmes had not seen the last of exciting travel. She was asked to accompany the prime minister to the upcoming Potsdam Conference and she wrote: 'Am being taken to Berlin! Hooray. Tottered off to bed at three a.m.'[100] There were perks, certainly, but there was also a daunting amount of full-time work. By mid-July Holmes was landing at a military airfield near Berlin and being driven to a 'beautiful villa' in the Soviet zone near Potsdam. The prime minister arrived the next day, with his daughter Mary and a 'galaxy of Field Marshals'. Some problem, which Holmes does not identify, had the Private Secretary on duty 'jumping around like a parched pea on a shovel', so the atmosphere was far from tension-free. Churchill, at one point, 'wandered into the office about 1 a.m. and looked at some pictures on the wall. He said he could paint those kinds of scenes until the cows come home and do them much better what's more.'[101]

The morning after his evening arrival in Potsdam, Churchill deviated from his usual work-in-bed-until-noon routine and walked over to President Truman's villa for a first meeting. Churchill very much liked the president and decided they could work together, which must have been a relief.[102] Holmes saw Truman at a later lunch between the two men in Churchill's villa and describes him as 'a nice crisp man with an air of determination'.[103] Recall that

Sturdee also used the word 'nice' about Truman. The president had a more nuanced reaction to the prime minister: Churchill 'gave me a lot of hooey about how great my country is. I am sure we can get along if he does not try to give me too much soft soap.'[104] Holmes deemed it sufficiently noteworthy to record that Truman walked over to the prime minister's villa alone, with none of the security detail around FDR when in Hyde Park.[105] Of course the entire Potsdam conference area was sealed off by Soviet troops, so security within the perimeter was assured.

When the conference was interrupted so that Churchill could fly back to Britain to await the results of the general election, Holmes flew back with him on Churchill's beloved Skymaster.* By now the 'ace RAF crew' knew her pretty well, as she notes: 'The crew have got into the habit of coming back to our compartment asking very formally if Miss Holmes could come up front "for ballast".'[106] We cannot be certain she accepted the invitation, but we do know that lunch was served after take-off.

She writes of the election: '[T]he most depressing atmosphere I could ever have imagined... Ministers being bowled out one after another. Labour gaining fast over Conservatives. It became obvious by the afternoon that Labour had won the Election with an overwhelming majority. Everyone at the office completely stunned... Mr Attlee is now the prime minister.'[107] Churchill, knowing that a general election was imminent, had included the deputy prime minister Clement Attlee at Potsdam, so that he would be fully informed should the up-coming election not favour the Tories. Attlee had stayed in Britain during previous conferences to run the country's domestic affairs.

Holmes had met the new prime minister in Potsdam when they had drinks at the mess together with General Ismay, but 'it is difficult always to hear what he says in his staccato mode of speech'.[108] At once she flew back to Potsdam with Attlee and the

---

*   Given to the British by the Americans, but really on loan. Prime Minister Attlee later returned the plane to the United States.

new Foreign Secretary Ernest Bevin to be available at the resumption of the interrupted Potsdam Conference. As a permanent civil
servant, Holmes was now working for the new prime minister along
with John Peck. Such is the smooth transition that is arranged by
the civil service at its best. Smooth it may have been, but also a
transition to a far duller assignment. Holmes noted in her diary: 'It
is the difference between champagne and unsalted water. He calls
us in only when he wants to dictate something. No conversation or
pleasantries, wit or capricious behaviour.'[109]

But this happened only after she had said goodbye to the wartime
prime minister with whom she had shared so many adventures.
'Determined not to seem upset,' she approached Churchill while
he was still in bed.[110] Holmes's last entry as Churchill's secretary is
worth quoting fully. He said to her:

'Perhaps they can do better than me, especially on housing and
coal... It must have been very hard putting up with all my bad
tempers. You have been wonderful, sharing all the secrets and
flying off with me... [You will] always have a place in my memory.'
It was very emotional and by this time we were both in tears...
as I withdrew from the room, he blew me a kiss. What a sadness
to so suddenly stop working for what surely must be the greatest
P.M. we will ever have. There was never a dull moment.[111]

In 1965 she was invited to Churchill's funeral at St Paul's and
recalls the very emotional moment when his face came up on the
monitor, a photograph taken some time in 1940. Then, she said,
she and the others 'dissolved into tears... and with some former
colleagues went back to No. 10 [she was working there at the time]
and... cried into our gin... We knew we were happy [then], as
Dylan Thomas would say.'

In 1957 Holmes had married Steve Walker, a history master at
St Benedict's School, Ealing, with whom she had three sons and a
daughter. Following Walker's death in 1974, Holmes married James
Spicer, an engineer, in 1979. She died in 2001, at the age of eighty.[112]

7

Elizabeth Gilliatt

'It was hard work indeed. We didn't get any break
for the work there.'

Gilliatt describing a trip to Switzerland with Churchill,
Elizabeth Gilliatt, oral history.

'The thing I thought was so marvellous about him was
that he did not waste an instant and he did not waste any
of the talents that the almighty had given him.'

Elizabeth Gilliatt, oral history

'I noticed the gift for intense concentration: while he
worked away, everything else ceased to exist for him.
"I like working," Churchill said with satisfaction.'

A. L. Rowse[1]

ELIZABETH GILLIATT WAS born in 1920. She started working in Downing Street as a shorthand typist in 1943. Thanks to a recommendation from friends of her father, Sir William Gilliatt, consulting gynaecologist to the queen,[2] she was elevated to a Garden Room Girl slot, where she worked for the five Private Secretaries, including the 'remarkable lady, Miss Watson', who handled the parliamentary questions. Incoming mail from the general public – and there was a lot of it – had to be acknowledged. Gilliatt had been warned there would be a great deal of such mail addressed to the prime minister to sort and mark. Private Secretaries marked some of it 'ACK', for 'acknowledge', some 'AFS' for 'acknowledge with Churchill signature' and a short note. The Churchill Archives are filled with personal letters, on a wide variety of subjects, written and signed by Gilliatt and other personal secretaries, as well as by Churchill himself.

Her first contact with Churchill was the day of the 'terrible election in 1945', when he passed her in a hallway and said 'Good morning, good afternoon or whatever and no sign of upset at all. I thought it was wonderful.' At that time, she was working for Churchill's successor, Clement Attlee, and discovered that working for Mr Attlee 'wasn't quite so much fun [although he was] a nice person'. She decided that she would seek a post with Churchill, who had retained his parliamentary seat and was then Leader of the Opposition. She explained to Patrick Kinna that working for Attlee was not as exciting as working for Churchill. 'It's not the same… it's not the same,' she repeated. Kinna recommended her for a position with Churchill and she interviewed with Kathleen Hill, who was retiring and whom Gilliatt would replace. Hill took her in to see Churchill, then living at 28 Hyde Park Gate. In his typically informal interviewing style, Churchill, who was in bed, said, 'I hear you'd like to come and work for me. I said yes, very much, thank you,' and that was it. In short, Churchill interviewed Gilliatt as he did others – in a perfunctory manner. 'Churchill believed he could sum up a man in… swift scrutiny. Later I was to see him reject a candidate after an equally abrupt examination,' said one of his Private Secretaries.[3]

Of course, it might also have been that he was confident that his staff, who performed the initial interviews and checked references, knew what he needed. Gilliatt worked for him for the next nine years. After all, Gilliatt had been recommended by the queen's physician, then by Kinna, vetted by Miss Watson and interviewed by Hill – an impressive gauntlet to have run. It proved a good choice. Only one year later, Churchill trusted her enough to advise Mohammed Ali Jinnah, the Indian Muslim leader, to communicate with him only through Gilliatt and that in his responses he should always sign himself 'Gilliatt'.[4]

When Gilliatt joined his staff in early 1946, Churchill was moving between 28 Hyde Park Gate, the Commons office of the Leader of the Opposition, and Chartwell. When he was returned to office in 1951, Chequers was his again to use, and was added to the list of offices and residences among which the secretaries would shuffle.

Gilliatt was

> expected to go to Chartwell with him at weekends; he was never without anyone... even if he went from Hyde Park Gate to the [nearby] House of Commons he always had a secretary with him... We used to go everywhere with him: to the House, if he went away to stay with a friend, accommodation would be booked for us nearby and we could come in every day and work in the friend's house.

She said of typing his speeches, 'It's just that you were in a different place when you typed them,' either Hyde Park Gate or Chartwell or in-between. As we have seen, Churchill worked and dictated everywhere, on trains, aeroplanes and in cars. Gilliatt recalls that trains were the most difficult, 'because the train would jerk and you'd land on the wrong letter. It was very difficult indeed and you couldn't keep the blinds down or else someone... on the station [would say] "Oh look!" That sort of thing.' And the personal secretaries went with him everywhere. 'That really was very tiring,' she recalled, and even once fell asleep while working for him. 'But he was so nice about it. I think he was horrified to see how much he tired us out.'

Churchill continued his lifelong habit of taking a rest in the afternoon, and had a bed installed in his room at the Commons. Gilliatt recalls that one day she had to fill his hot-water bottle for his afternoon nap. She ran along to the 'ladies cloakroom [reserved for members only] to fill the hot water bottle from the tap... And a lady member came in and she said: "What are you doing?"' Gilliatt answered truthfully, but not completely, saying she 'was filling a hot water bottle' and fled – members covet their privileges, of which exclusive use of strategically placed toilets is one.

Gilliatt's first assignment was to type from his complete notes some of the speeches Churchill had delivered to secret sessions of the House of Commons during the war, for inclusion in the *Secret Sessions Speeches* book that was subsequently published.[5] She also learned to use the new telephone that had two separate lines – it is hard to imagine today how advanced that must have seemed then. For nearly a decade, Gilliatt worked for Churchill, 'a devoted member of the small inner circle which made possible Churchill's mastery of so many spheres of activity'. One of her recollections of those years was that Churchill 'didn't waste a single talent'.[6]

The personal secretaries divided the work among themselves, with each getting separate responsibilities. But they were nevertheless a team. As Gilliatt explains: '[A]part from dividing the correspondence up a bit, if we were with him, we had to do whatever he did and it didn't matter whether it was your section or not.' One advantage of this arrangement is that it permitted each secretary to snatch some much-treasured time off, with the others picking up the load. Gilliatt recalls that they 'used to have a fortnight [off]... it was simply that the others worked harder than ever when one of us was away.'

It should be noted that teamwork and a willingness to go that extra mile for one's boss was not characteristic of all of Britain's working men and women. The smooth functioning of Churchill's overworked staff is a tribute to his ability to exact huge amounts of work by communicating to them the importance of what they were doing and by distributing such perks as the jobs permitted. With what appears to have been a smile and approval at just the right time.

Jo Sturdee was on the Churchill team when Gilliatt arrived – and Lettice Marston arrived later from General Ismay's office. As the work increased, two more personal secretaries – Cecily 'Chips' Gemmell and Jane Portal – were added. Nevertheless, the late nights continued – 'even sometimes until 3 or 3.30 a.m.' But, says Gilliatt: '[H]e was the most lovable person... I don't say you didn't mind, you sort of cursed under your breath, but it didn't spoil the enjoyment of the job.'

Although 'enjoyment' was not always the right word to describe the job of being Churchill's secretary. Very rarely was Churchill's office closed for holidays. Gilliatt recalls one Christmas Eve at Chartwell when she was 'the last one left... about half past five, and I think the police were going to take [me] back to London... I was frightfully tired... and he wouldn't let me go. So I wiped off my makeup and hoped that Mrs Churchill would come, which she did.' Using a technique deployed decades earlier by Hamblin, Gilliatt appealed to Mrs Churchill to intervene with her husband. She obligingly did, saying, 'Darling, Miss Gilliatt looks terribly tired. You'd very [sic] much let her go.' He did. Gilliatt then said goodnight to Sir Winston and thanked him for letting her go, adding, 'I do hope everything will be all right.' He said: 'It won't be, it won't be!' Not always the cheery optimist, he could succumb to despondency, in this instance because he was totally dependent on the office staffs, who had decided to take off Christmas Eve.

As if the workload of a Leader of the Opposition were not enough, Churchill proceeded with his history of the Second World War, which he was determined to complete, because he wanted his history to become the standard version of that great conflict. One of Gilliatt's tasks was to take dictation for those books or 'he would possibly have drafts from some of the people helping him write it, [then] he would either order out the draft and give it to you to type or dictate from the draft changing it. We did a lot on that.'

Churchill never did separate his personal and private lives and duties, which added still another dimension to the work days of his secretaries. In addition to her secretarial duties she had the task of arranging for the shipment of special worms from Yorkshire to feed the golden orfe.* And when the worms arrived at Westerham train station (closest to Chartwell), Gilliatt would have to collect them and bring the worms to Chartwell. Not your average job! Churchill's care and even love for animals (and butterflies, which he called his 'flying fairies')[7] lasted throughout his life.

Gilliatt and the other personal secretaries had as little contact with their boss as possible when he was painting. 'You had to be jolly careful if you had to go and ask him a question not to interrupt in a vital minute, otherwise there was a bit of an explosion. But if you waited until he got to the end of a cloud or whatever it was, you could somehow get away with it' – if it were really important.

They also tried to avoid direct contact when it was necessary to inform Churchill of the death of a friend or relative – or, in fact, just about anyone he knew. The very emotional Churchill always became visibly upset – although in the case of Franklin D. Roosevelt, not sufficiently upset to attend the funeral of his war-time ally. Rather than be the direct bearer of bad news, Gilliatt discovered the best way to deal with such news: inform Mrs Churchill and ask her to tell her husband.

Because the division of labour among the staff was organized informally, when it came to arranging engagements, mistakes were almost inevitable. Churchill asked Gilliatt to invite a certain

---

* A specimen fish that can reach up to twenty-four inches in length and weigh as much as four pounds. It is golden in colour and lives just below the water's surface, so they are easily seen. Churchill loved feeding them. During the war, Harrods asked Churchill to take twenty-two varieties of rare fish from the store into his lakes for safekeeping. As a thank-you, Harrods agreed Churchill could keep as many of them as he wished. In Lough, *No More Champagne*, p. 282.

maharajah to lunch, naming the particular one he wanted to see. But, somehow, the maharajahs' names got mixed up. When the wrong maharajah arrived, Churchill rushed along to the office saying, 'You've asked the wrong maharaja,'* but Gilliatt's voice and inflection on the oral history tapes don't tell us whether Churchill was angry. Perhaps the years that have passed since the event have softened her memory, perhaps he wasn't really angry, just bemused. Much like the mix-up when Churchill said, 'invite Berlin to lunch', but somehow Irving Berlin showed up instead of Isaiah Berlin. So far as can be determined, no staff members were either chastised or dismissed, even though Churchill took special care to arrange invitations to his table to suit his needs and interests.

Then there was the time, as related by Gilliatt, when arrangements were being made to get Churchill's special bed onto a train taking him to Scotland to give a speech. Whether it was the very same bed that Churchill had installed in the office of the Leader of the Opposition we do not know – but sleep was a balm, essential to Churchill. However, the very fact that such a bed-installing process was once again underway reminds us that as a junior officer during the First World War – before he became famous for leading his nation from the brink of disaster to victory in the following conflict – Churchill did not think it odd to have his bathtub shipped to him on the Western Front. In one case, both what Gilliatt describes as 'the little man from British Rail' charged with the responsibility of moving the bed onto the train, and Sir Alan Lascelles, private secretary to George VI, arrived at the same time to meet with Churchill. The secretaries confused the two. We do not know how Sir Alan or Churchill reacted when the confusion unfolded, or whether Sir Alan demanded that heads roll. They didn't. Gilliatt dryly recalls: 'We had our moments.'

Nevertheless there were some perks to working for Churchill. Principal among them were the extra coupons issued to allow the secretaries to 'have at least one exceptionally smart outfit for receptions,

---

*   Gemmell tells the story in much the same way.

and to purchase decent trousers for wearing on the battleships that would carry them overseas.' Especially prized were coupons for 'the luxury of new shoes', because leather was severely rationed.[8]

There were visits to Switzerland, Jamaica, Bermuda, the United States and, of course, to La Capponcina, Lord Beaverbrook's villa in Cap-d'Ail in the South of France, and to Marrakesh. Her first long trip with Churchill was one of what would prove to be several to America, often on the *Queen Mary*. This was a time when Churchill was crossing the ocean regularly to visit with President Truman, or to travel to Canada to deliver a speech, or to Fulton to warn of Soviet intentions. Or to reacquaint himself with Eisenhower.

On the trips to America Gilliatt thoroughly enjoyed the *Queen Mary*, for reason obvious from the descriptions from several of her colleagues. And because the routine was often broken with memorable events, even though not all of them were pleasant. On one, the voyage was 'quite rough' and she did not feel well at all. Just as she was recovering a bit, Colville 'breezed into the cabin and said, "I'm just going downstairs. I'll have a steak and I'll be feeling better."' This prompted Gilliatt, who until then 'was doing all right', to retreat quickly to her own cabin. But all of the trips to America aboard the *Queen Mary* allowed for meetings and chats with notables and VIPs, and some diversions, which was compensation enough for a bit of seasickness.

On another trip in 1949, scheduled by Churchill because he was told President Truman would be in the audience to hear him speak at the Massachusetts Institute of Technology (MIT), Churchill learned that the president would not be able to attend after all. Churchill wanted to order the big ship to turn around and return to Britain, 'but thank goodness Lady Churchill was there and she calmed him down... Very interesting.' Gilliatt characterizes that trip as 'a busy one. I don't remember having much time off then.'

On still another of their visits to America, Churchill decided, after five days of meetings in New York and Washington, some of them with president-elect Eisenhower, that he would like to have some time in sunny Jamaica. President Truman graciously lent his plane, the *Independence*, named after his Missouri home town. The flight was rough enough for his staff to worry about his health. But Churchill 'ate a huge steak for lunch and had his usual brandy and cigar in President Truman's magnificently fitted aircraft'.[9] The weather in Jamaica was not good, but Gilliatt recalls she 'ran into frightful trouble one day because he was sitting on the beach painting and I was swimming and I am not a good swimmer... I was swimming away busily on my breast stroke and there was Sir Winston back on the beach. Churchill worriedly asked, "Has she got to the buoys yet?", repeating the question. When Gilliatt came ashore from her swim, Churchill said "You really mustn't do that, Miss. I'm responsible for you and you went out much too far."' He could at times worry about his staff and they appreciated it. A cynic might attribute Churchill's concern to the fact that Gilliatt was in Jamaica not to swim but to take dictation as Churchill revised the third volume of his war memoirs.

Gilliatt learned early on – when she accompanied Churchill to a villa on Lake Geneva to work on a major speech to be given in Zurich, and on his memoirs – that these trips could be exhausting, even if a second secretary, in this case Marston, came along. 'It was hard work indeed. We didn't get any break for the work there.' Several years later she put the same thought a bit differently: when Churchill was working on his memoirs, 'he really did go at it hammer and tongs'. Even when sitting for a portrait, this one by Sir Oswald Birley, he would dictate to Gilliatt, 'because he could not relax'.[10]

To the lesson that work was the dominant feature of Churchill's life, add two more, these learned on a trip to La Capponcina: pack carefully, and use the power conveyed by working for Winston.[11] Gilliatt forgot her little teddy bear at the hotel at which she was put up. The teddy was a favourite which she had had since she was five years old. So she cabled the hotel and asked to have it returned to her. Three weeks later the little bear arrived in a matchbox, addressed to Gilliatt c/o The Right Honourable Winston Churchill. If Churchill had heard about this, he would have found it amusing, I'm sure.

And the hotel's obliging attitude was still another perk, a less famous guest might not have such attention paid to left-behind articles.

Still another trip took Gilliatt to Marrakesh, which she 'loved', although she had to work the usual long hours. But it was not all work. On Churchill's trip to Marrakesh in December 1947 Gilliatt and Sturdee were included in a festive Christmas Eve dinner party, along with Sarah Churchill (then Mrs Vic Oliver) at La Mamounia. Churchill wanted all those who had forgone their Christmas at home to enjoy the evening, which Gilliatt and Sturdee most certainly did, since Churchill danced with each of them, as well as with Sarah and Mrs Deakin, and 'a good-looking fair lady, otherwise unidentified'.[12]

Even when Churchill and his guests went on 'long lunch picnics we were always along. [We] probably didn't have lunch at the same table necessarily, but [we] were certainly allowed to go. It was a most elaborate picnic... tables and chairs and napkins and knives and forks.' She also went along on picnics in the South of France, as Churchill was very fond of eating outdoors, even during the war. But at 'jaunts', as Gilliatt called them, he had to have a secretary or two present, primarily because he might want to dictate, but also because he sought to include his secretaries in such adventures whenever he could, just as he included Holmes and Layton when Stalin invited him to the Bolshoi Ballet during the prime minister's 1944 visit to Moscow.

Travel was not the only perquisite the secretaries enjoyed. Another was the opportunity of meeting, or more precisely, getting to see the world's VIPs, especially at Chequers, once Churchill became prime minister for the second time in October 1951. Gilliatt recalls that 'at Chequers, the secretary's office was just inside the door, so quite a lot of them [the VIPS] used to wander into the office before they saw him... They'd come in and see what the situation was.' On trips abroad, she said, she would 'see more of the VIPs... perhaps the Chiefs of Staff would come in and have to wait a bit, so they'd be in our office chatting together. That was the interesting thing about abroad.' Of course, the staff never asked for autographs or to pose for photos. This was not yet the selfie era; they knew to keep to the background.

Another perk became available when Churchill developed his love for horse racing. When he was seventy-five he bought his first horse, a grey, called Colonist II, chosen with the help of his son-in-law Christopher Soames.[13] As usual, when he went to the races he took a personal secretary with him in the car. Churchill had an enormous capacity to switch topics, dictating in the car on the way to the races, at times right up until the gate was raised. And even dictating in a dark car while driving with Elizabeth Layton in Moscow, although covered with 'huge Russian fur rugs'.[14] Knowing him so well, Gilliatt thought that there [must have been] something wrong if he hadn't… been able to change his focus on such short notice.'

Gilliatt thought that Churchill was pleased when the personal secretaries bet on his horses, and so they did – and shared his joy when Colonist II won so many races. And Gilliatt was delighted when he had her join him in the paddock and enclosure, after all, he might have needed her to take down some idea or instruction.

Sometime in the spring of 1951 Elizabeth Gilliatt requested permission to leave, so she could travel with her father Sir William, the eminent physician, who was making a worldwide teaching and lecture tour, and he needed Liz as hostess because her mother was too ill to make the trip. Churchill was of course not happy at the temporary loss, but reluctantly agreed when her father explained to Churchill that he had 'more right to her as she was his daughter. IF someone suitable could be found to fill in and if she promised to return.' In her place Vanda Salmon was hired.

The return to Number 10 required some rearranging of the private and personal secretaries. Gilliatt was 'delighted' to have been asked to return to Downing Street with the once-again prime minister. In addition to staffing there were also some changes in the way Gilliatt worked for the prime minister, although she continued to take dictation and type for him. There was now a layer of officials between her and Churchill. If she had something urgent for him to see, she would have to 'say very politely [to the Private Secretary on duty] "could this get into the box?" meaning would they put it into the box of work that they were preparing for the prime minister. She regretted not seeing as much of Churchill as she had when he was a private citizen: 'And once I didn't see him for a fortnight. I was rather annoyed about it. But it was perfectly normal.' Sturdee also found herself cut off from regular contact with Churchill, but he somehow had the barriers removed in her case (as noted in Chapter 5). Such was Gilliatt's personal loyalty to Churchill and the power of his charm that although no longer in continuous, direct contact with him, she continued to work uncomplainingly at her several tasks.

In June 1953, at a dinner party in Downing Street in honour of the Italian prime minister, Churchill suffered a major stroke. He was seventy-eight. 'Things weren't at all good,' reflected Gilliatt. The appositely named Dr Russell Brain, Churchill's neurologist, examined him and advised against his taking a scheduled cabinet meeting and an appearance later in the week in the House of Commons, which Churchill was insisting on attending. He did attend the cabinet meeting, but was driven to Chartwell the next day. Gilliatt, who was with him in the car, noticed that he was 'walking very unsteadily and his speech was slurred'. The personal secretaries and everyone in Downing Street knew 'there was something wrong. I mean it was all around the office'. But it was not reported in the press, by agreement of the so-called press lords who tightly controlled the media in those days when print news was just about all that mattered in Britain.

Within two or three months the prime minister had recuperated sufficiently to be able to work on a speech he was to give at the upcoming Conservative Party Conference in Margate in October. '[Brendan] Bracken, one of the few men who knew of Churchill's stroke, wrote "cheering beyond telling is this marvellous recovery."'[15] Gilliatt recalls that at Margate 'all went well' and Churchill could celebrate his eightieth birthday in good spirits. In poured 'an awful lot of letters... They didn't bring the mail up to us in trays but in huge wire baskets.' The personal secretaries reviewed each letter or birthday card to determine whether or not the prime minister would see it, which depended on who sent it. For example, a letter and card from Madame Odette Pol-Roger would of course be sent into Churchill.* Some signatures were illegible, requiring close cooperation between the private and the personal secretaries to identify the sender. Gifts were another problem – there were hundreds of them from people and institutions around the globe. The secretaries opened all of them, logged them in and decided how they were acknowledged. Even when 'a little boy, let's say from Doncaster, a little boy of nine wrote in and sent a little present or something... somebody did send him a photograph. Important ones [gifts] had their destinations'; one a 'marvellous cabinet of cigars, and that of course would have an honoured place. Books would mostly be at Chartwell.' Gilliatt makes no mention of the gifts of large cheeses remembered by Sturdee.

There were many birthday parties, both public and private. The secretaries generally were not included, but Gilliatt was invited to Churchill's eightieth and the unveiling in Westminster Hall of the infamous Sutherland portrait, which 'I didn't like... they hated it.'

Because of his stroke, Churchill had been forced to cancel his proposed summit meeting in Bermuda with President Eisenhower and the French – putting it off in the expectation of making a complete recovery. He rescheduled it for December 1953, hoping to persuade the Americans to agree to a summit with the new Soviet leader Georgy Malenkov. Unfortunately for Churchill, Eisenhower and his principal foreign policy advisor John Foster Dulles opposed any summit with the Soviets.

---

* Pol Roger champagne was Churchill's favourite drink. He met Madame Pol-Roger at the British Embassy in Paris in 1944 and they became friends. He named one of his racehorses Pol Roger and it won the Black Prince Stakes in 1953. When Churchill died, she ordered that all bottles of champagne exported to Britain have a wide mourning band across the label. Champagne Pol Roger created their Prestige Cuvée Sir Winston Churchill in his honour.

From Gilliatt's point of view, the trip to Bermuda was somewhat more successful. For one thing, she got another dip in the sea, although Churchill – put off by the water's temperature of 67 degrees – did not. For another, she had a rare, short but personal conversation with Churchill. Rare, because her relationship with him was purely business, with minimal exchanges of personal remarks or information, as with all the other secretaries. Churchill's mind was on work. She had been surprised once when he asked her how old her father was. She said, 'Sixty-two, Sir Winston.' He replied, 'Oh, he's a mere chicken. I am seventy-two.' As Gilliatt recalls, 'There might be the odd remark like that, but no, there was no question of discussing things with him'.

No matter how long these women had worked for Churchill he never called them by their first names. It was always 'Miss', 'the young lady' or, rarely, 'Miss Gilliatt', or 'Where's the Miss?' Unless he had a nickname for them, such as 'The Portal' for Jane Portal and 'Miss Sherlock' for Holmes, but these were not used regularly. He had a reason for calling them interchangeably 'Miss', as we saw in Chapter 2.

However, in Bermuda Churchill engaged Gilliatt in another rare personal conversation. She notes in her oral history on file at the Archives that there was no time on Sundays for

church or anything like that. But if one could go, one did. And he said to me one day, 'Have you been to church, Miss?' I said, 'Well, no, Sir Winston,' hoping to go later on. Churchill replied: 'I'll tell the Pope about you.'... I had a feeling – he had sort of a sympathy for the Catholic Church. I remember him giving me a lecture at Chartwell once... he said, 'The attitude of your church to sex is absolutely marvellous' or something like that.

Gilliatt, like those of her colleagues whom Churchill occasionally teased, and to whom he playfully assigned nicknames, felt special, singled out, as a result of this attention.

Churchill returned to Britain to face increasing pressure from

Opposition leaders to resign, and, more importantly, from Anthony Eden, who had been pressing since 1945 to step into his shoes. Gilliatt hoped that Churchill would stay in office until he would 'drop in his tracks... because I felt that he had so much still to give'. President Eisenhower privately felt that Churchill ought to resign and let Eden take over. Ike even went so far as to think that 'Churchill should began planning his farewell address.'[16] Gilliatt thought that 'He'd hate resigning and I thought it a pity that he shouldn't be allowed to carry on till he dropped. But I mean when a whole country depends on it, you can't really do that, I think, – I'm afraid I wish he had been able to.'

Not surprisingly, Gilliatt was part of Churchill's team until the last minute. 'When he finally drove away from No 10, the day of his resignation [as prime minister], it was announced that he... drove away with an unknown woman. That was me.'[17] Even under the most stressful and emotional situations Churchill needed a personal secretary with him, perhaps to take down, perhaps as a symbol that there was work still to be done, of which there was enough to sap the energies of a much younger man.

After his resignation, Churchill flew to Syracuse in Sicily for a much needed and well-earned vacation, taking Gilliatt along. She 'didn't find this trip easy at all... I don't think he had settled to the fact [of his resignation] yet and I think he wasn't very happy... but there was the dickens of a lot of work to do. Thankfully Jock Colville was with us and also Lady Churchill [as she had by then become] who helped to calm troubled waters when necessary.' Lord Cherwell (Frederick Lindemann), a wartime colleague and one of Churchill's closest friends, was also there. They stayed at the Grand Hotel Villa Politi, which on its current website announces 'I never slept so well,' signed W. Churchill and Lady Clementina, April 1955.

Friends, secretaries and Lady Churchill could not console him. The weather was not good and the Italians less than helpful: Gilliatt had 'to ask about four times' to get a response to her questions. 'I mean if he wanted his room hotter, so you didn't ask once for extra fire, you had to ask two or three times. And when you're as busy as we were it made it very difficult and altogether a great loss.' Churchill's theory about the Italians' lack of urgency is that they were angry with him for bringing English weather with him and were glad to see him leave Sicily and take his weather with him. The trip was not a success.

How could it be? Gilliatt thought 'he was rather depressed'. Despite that, work continued at its usual pace. There were speeches to be written and delivered. He was still working on *A History of the English-Speaking Peoples*, and there was an election coming up in which Churchill would have to defend his seat for the nineteenth time.[18] Churchill's success in so doing contributed to a Tory majority of fifty-nine seats.

When they returned to Britain, Gilliatt was exhausted, and two new secretaries, Doreen Pugh and Gillian Maturin, were taken on staff, presumably to clear up post-election correspondence and help with the completion of *A History of the English-Speaking Peoples*. Maturin stayed for three and a half years and Pugh for nearly ten years. As we shall see, both were 'overcome by how sweet he was', according to Pugh.[19]

In 1955 Gilliatt left Churchill's employment. He bequeathed her £400 in his will, some £7,500 today. She died in 2004.

In his last letter to the queen after his resignation, Churchill wrote:

> The historical atmosphere of Syracuse grows perceptibly upon me and my companions here as the days pass. Our hotel rises out of the sinister quarries in which six thousand Athenian prisoners of war were toiled and starved to death in 413 BC, and I am trying to paint a picture of a cavern's mouth near the listening gallery whose echoes brought secrets to the ears of Dionysius. All this is agreeable to the mental and psychological processes of laying down direct responsibility for the guidance of great affairs and falling back upon the comforting reflection 'I have done my best.'[20]

Indeed, he had.

8

Lettice Marston

'Do you think that you could endure the
vicissitudes of this life?'

Lettice Marston, quoting Churchill, as she started work for him.
Lettice Marston, oral history

He could be 'in a bad mood… Perhaps things had gone
wrong in the House of Commons… so [we] kept out of his
way… It soon disappeared, [amid] twinkling blue eyes.'

Lettice Marston, oral history

L ETTICE MARSTON WAS born in 1919. She had been with the Auxiliary Territorial Service (ATS) during the Second World War, and after Germany's surrender was sent to Berlin to work with the Control Commission for Germany.* She had worked with Lord Ismay to set up the accommodations for the Potsdam Conference, refusing to assent to those arrangements until 'they had got the kitchen range working in Churchill's residence'.[1] Later, she worked for the Anglo-Iranian Oil Company, but didn't fancy 'working for a large organization', although her boss there had also recommended her to Lord Ismay. Lord Ismay put her in touch with Kathleen Hill, who interviewed Marston over lunch in a London restaurant. Churchill was in America at the time, but Hill hired her on a month's probation. Marston started working for Churchill in March 1946, after the loss of the 1945 general election. When she started work, Churchill had to sign her employment card, meaning that she would receive moneys from the government, with contributions by the employee, employer and the state. This was the result of a plan that Churchill had been instrumental in setting up in 1909 – the first national insurance scheme. Churchill said to her: 'I pay both parts. It's all my fault.'[2]

A month later, and before Marston was exposed to the pace of life as a Churchill secretary, an American company suggested to Churchill that he might like to experiment with what is now called a voice-activated recording machine. Sturdee, always on the alert for new efficiencies, must have agreed to having it tested at Chartwell. It 'was first acclaimed by us secretaries, as relieving us of some of the long hours of night dictation... Indeed, Churchill

---

*   After the defeat of Germany in 1945, a Control Commission was set up to support the military government, which was in place at that time. The military government was gradually phased out and the Control Commission took over the role of 'local government'. It was responsible for Public Safety, Health, Transport, Housing and Intelligence. The forward HQ was in Cumberland House, Berlin. Recruits had to be over twenty-one, and were recruited from civil servants, the Foreign Office and demobbed military personnel. See the BRIXMIS website: http://www.brixmis.co.uk.

was so delighted with the device that he dismissed his secretaries for the weekend. They rejoiced in this unexpected change in their routine.' Alas, it was not to be a success: Churchill kept tripping over the wires of his lapel microphone and the machine. 'The machine had to go and the secretaries returned.'[3]

Marston began working at Hyde Park Gate alongside Gilliatt, because Jo Sturdee was with him in America, and Hill had become Curator at Chequers. Three weeks later the Churchill entourage returned from the United States, 'family members, staff and luggage and everything'. Churchill told Sturdee, 'Let me see the new girl,' so up she went to his bedroom and started taking down. Nothing was said until much later, when, sorting books at Chartwell, he tossed her one which landed on her foot, so 'we had a good laugh' and he unexpectedly asked her, 'Do you think that you could endure the vicissitudes of this life?' And she answered, 'Yes, if you think I am capable.' And that was that.

Marston lived in a flat in Kensington, but when she was working at Chartwell she stayed overnight either in the house or in a cottage on the grounds if there were too many guests staying overnight in the house. She had meals at the Kings Arms Hotel or at Pitts Cottage in Westerham, but usually at her desk, in the office. Rare were the 'working lunches' when she would sit at the table with her pad and pencil, perhaps with family members and others.

Her first task in the morning was to sort the mail: she and the other secretaries decided what Churchill should see: 'Obviously political matters, letters from anyone of repute... anything from the public that was of great importance, or something new that he should know about or deal with. There was a lot of trivialities, of course, and a lot of correspondence from madmen.'

They had great discretion and Churchill trusted them to decide in his interest. Marston says that she grew in confidence to decide what post Churchill should see. She also had to ring people up, make appointments, set up meetings, arrange for cars and drivers if he were going to the House of Commons or elsewhere.

And she, and the others as well, all took part in taking dictation on Churchill's war memoirs, which he worked on 'a certain amount every day'. Because he found it 'comfortable and relaxing', he worked in bed all morning, as usual – which had a certain advantage: 'it was good to have him out of the office... We could get on with things in the morning alone.' He seldom worked in the office set up at Chartwell, which Marston considered a good thing as 'He'd make a muddle of one's arrangements.' The papers strewn around the bedroom looked 'like a pudding mixture on his bed', and when he had trouble finding what he wanted, she 'would have to sort things out'. One advantage of the Chartwell office was its location: at the front of the house, 'so [we] could see everybody who came and went... and say [so and so] is on the horizon. Of course, there were times when he had to get up, like going to see the king.'

The women were in charge of setting the rota of their own work; one would be on nights, another would be working alternate weekends. Churchill 'did no organizing like that'.[4] He simply expected the secretaries to be there when he needed them – two on duty at a time, one to take the dictation and then type it up, while the other one was ready to take his new dictation. Such was their loyalty to him and his work that they ensured he was always covered.

He was a hard taskmaster, as all the women have said, but they agree that he could make 'things much brighter... he would turn and smile and say, "Poor lamb", "I've done too much" [or] "You must go to bed" [or] "Go home."' But he could also be

in a bad mood, and you had to take a cue from it... Perhaps things had gone wrong in the House of Commons... nasty remarks... or there was some bad vote... something gone wrong in some way. So [we] kept out of his way... it soon disappeared, [amid] twinkling blue eyes. But there were other times when he was elated and excited by things.

But the work was varied and interesting. She recalls:

He'd want you sometimes to go with him to feed the fish, and all the time he'd be saying 'We need some more worms or something for them'... and you'd have to make notes all the time and remember to order whatever it was... You were making notes fairly all the time he was talking, because he was wanting this, that and the other.

In other words, a full-time job with no division between his work, his hobbies and his friends and family.

Like the other secretaries, Marston enjoyed going with Churchill to the races – she even won money betting on Colonist II – in between working, while Churchill watched his horses. She tells of a Dutch businessman who gave Churchill a famous horse and brought it to Chartwell to present to him. 'He [Churchill] didn't keep it at Chartwell so he had it at Knightsbridge Barracks, where Elizabeth [Gilliatt] and I would use to go ride him... It was great fun... Elizabeth and I used to go in the evenings sometimes, exercise this horse... It was a beautiful horse.' There were unusual perks for working with the Churchill family.

Marston also took charge of the constituency work, recalling that Churchill went down to Woodford in Essex once or twice a year, more frequently during election time. But she often travelled down there and met with constituency officers and agents when they came up to London. Churchill went to the House of Commons as often as he could, 'sometimes pop[ping] in at odd times, perhaps on his way back from Chartwell at night. If the House was sitting, he saw the lights on, he would pop in... for half an hour. It was his life, really.'

When Churchill was writing his war memoirs, she helped (with Gemmell) to organize the muniment room, so the principal researchers, William Deakin and Denis Kelly, could start work. Those researchers, along with secretaries and research materials, had to be organized and transported between Chartwell and Hyde Park Gate, depending on which chapter Churchill was working on and where he was working. All the documents Churchill needed had to be on hand when he wanted them. Marston 'would ask for things from the cabinet office... They would be sent around by hand,' and she would make sure Churchill's own papers – for the most part at Chartwell – were available when and where needed. But, she says, he just dictated 'out of his head, with the aid of [some] documents... but long long passages from his own mind'.

And it was not just the researchers who had to be organized, but also the guests – both political and social, including family – who often stayed overnight at Chartwell or came in for dinners at Hyde Park Gate. She recalls the food being good, because Mrs Landemare was a 'supercook', but Churchill could be

> very cross when it wasn't right... Once at Chartwell, Grace had... got him some fruit for breakfast. And you know how difficult pears are to assess, whether they are ripe or not, and he had a pear he could not get his knife into and he was absolutely livid about it... What can you do? It's just bad luck.

And a more than slightly spoiled boss.

'But he did love his food,' Marston says.

> He had particular likes: oysters, one of his favourites, and smoked salmon, of course, and smelly cheese like Stilton, and things like gulls' eggs and strawberry jam and turtle soup were the two great things. Turtle soup [consommé] every night before going to bed... Yes, always... We used to have to get it out of the fridge... and give it to him before he went to bed. One day when he was in Marrakesh, he cabled back to London asking for strawberry jam and turtle soup, and Lady Churchill made us cable back... saying, 'Did he really mean it?', because it was such an effort to get it sent out to Marrakesh, but that's how he was.

One of his historical researchers, Alan Hodge, heard Churchill explain why it was good to eat cream: 'it cushions the nerve ends'.[5]

And of course, the champagne. Marston recalls: 'Very often one had to go down to put the champagne in the fridge at the right time for the meal.'

Social guests seldom varied. The same names are mentioned by all the other secretaries: Lady Lytton, Venetia Montagu and Violet Bonham Carter – Churchill liked to see the familiar faces of his old friends, with whom he could relax and play cards. Lord Ismay and Lord Cherwell, Leo Amery and Brendan Bracken were constant guests at both Chartwell and Hyde Park Gate. Churchill would occasionally ask them questions about something he wanted to include in his war memoirs, but the visits were mainly social, with much card-playing, especially the two-pack bezique. And, as always, there were family members visiting, especially Mary and Christopher Soames.

Marston, as the other secretaries have mentioned, had little to do with Churchill's painting, but she did have opinions – which she kept to herself, as he 'wasn't really interested in what you thought about what he did'. Nevertheless, he did value advice from other painters. Marston thought his best paintings were done in France during the First World War, 'which were very striking with the bursting shells over the battlefields'. She thought him 'very good at painting three subjects which I think are very difficult… water, metals like gold and silver and copper, and glass'. Fortunately, she only infrequently had to clean the brushes, as Churchill's valet and at times Gemmell did that. The valet 'always used to curse at having to do it' and, as we shall see, Gemmell complained about this chore, although decades after the fact to the interviewer but never to Churchill.

After 1945 Churchill received many awards, honours, freedoms and honorary degrees, both at home in Britain and in Europe. Marston, who joined his staff shortly after these honours started to come in, went along on several of these trips, but the trips she most enjoyed were the painting holidays to France and Venice. Her first trip, she recalled, was to a Villa Choisi on Lake Geneva, with Liz Gilliatt, to prepare for Churchill's speech at Zurich; then later to Paris and Cap-d'Ail to stay at Lord Beaverbrook's villa, whose owner regarded Churchill as 'a glittering bird of paradise'.[6] She also went along on Churchill's visit to the Windsors' villa in the South of France, where she stayed for two nights, ready should Churchill need a document to show the duke – although she describes the visit as social.

The women decided not only who would work which hours, but also who would go on which foreign trips – they shared the burdens as well as the perks. Only occasionally would Churchill ask that a specific person accompany him. Whoever was to travel had the full responsibility of organizing everything: the travel and security arrangements; coordinating detectives and drivers; packing the painting paraphernalia; moving the office and all the work material that might be needed and logging in and out of all the luggage. As many as 100 personnel – all with their own office and luggage requirements – might be included on foreign trips, complicating arrangements and increasing security concerns. Churchill's personal secretaries were privy to all these decisions, working with Special Branch and its counterparts. On 'working' holidays or electioneering, he always travelled with an entourage – a valet, a secretary or two and what Marston called his 'flying circus'. And when Mrs Churchill came along, her lady's maid.

Marston did have some help from Thomas Cook and British Rail. When he was first out of office after 1945, Churchill could use RAF planes out of Biggin Hill, she says, but 'seldom did he go in public transport'.* Churchill also used 'private air companies and when he first came out of office he used to use the RAF planes'. Frequently trips were cancelled or changed, so all the

---

* It was rare for Churchill to be on the streets by himself. In late 1947 Sturdee says that Churchill got stuck in a dense fog and was unable to be driven home. So 'he walked from Hyde Park Corner to Knightsbridge, got fed up, I suppose, and spent the night at the Hyde Park Hotel'. Marston, summoned to the hotel, to work, noted 'I found him in bed. He spent the day there. He rather enjoyed it.' In Gilbert, *Winston S. Churchill: Never Despair 1945–1965*, Vol. VIII, p. 306.

arrangements had to be redone. She recalls: 'then at a moment's notice you had to rearrange everything. That was rather a headache, but... these things can be done.' And, as always, the young ladies cooperated closely with each other, communicating between the offices, within Britain and abroad. Especially when abroad, urgent messages and telegrams flew back and forth on arrangements for receiving page proofs, editing them, and sending them back to the London printers, all necessitating a staff working very closely indeed.

Sometimes the messages were wryly amusing, as when Marston telegrammed back to London: 'Lots of curses as we are trying to get ready for a picnic.'[7] So close were the relationships among the secretaries that when Sturdee travelled abroad with Churchill, she directed that the newsy letters she was sending in the official pouch to her family remain unsealed, so that all the secretaries could read about her news and adventures, before sending them on to her family.

Flying circus, indeed: when Churchill went out painting 'the whole lot of you went, the valet and everybody, detectives, [sometimes] Lady Churchill went, plus lunch, sometimes one of the waiters to serve it, all the cutlery and knives and forks and plates and tablecloths and napkins... umbrellas and chairs'.

If the trip was a long one, Churchill usually planned to have two secretaries along, so they could alternate the dictation and typing: one would take a few hours of dictation, then go to the office to type it up. The other woman would then be available to take dictation, so they would work in tandem with one always available to Churchill, wherever he was and whatever he was working on. When abroad, all the mail was sent on to his travelling office. Mail included correspondence, gifts, 'flowers, books to sign, asking for cigars and all this sort of nonsense... and then, of course, thank-you letters for all these presents'. And if the workload became too heavy, she 'always got help from the British Embassy wherever [we] were'.

When abroad, Marston might stay in the villa they were visiting if there was room; if not, she stayed in a nearby hotel, as described by Gilliatt. Both women agreed it was lovely to be able to get away, as 'he couldn't get at you except on the telephone, which was unlikely'. Given the long hours they worked, an escape even for a few hours was probably most welcome.

On a trip to Oslo, Norway, in May 1948, Churchill and his wife were guests of King Haakon. While there, he gave several speeches and received an honorary degree from the University of Oslo. Marston went with him and recalls that the king himself greeted Churchill on arrival at the airport – an unusual honour from a monarch. While there, Churchill visited the Viking Ships Museum – his curiosity was never-ending – and, of course, his hosts would have been proud to show off their heritage to so famous a man.[8]

Marston was working with Churchill in August 1949 at La Capponcina, when Churchill developed some cramps in his right hand and realized that he could not write his name properly; although, as Gilliatt recalled, 'he kept on practising it, asking one again and again, "Is it all right?"'[9] A local English doctor was called in and Lord Moran (as he had by then become) was summoned from London. Churchill had suffered a minor stroke, but only his doctors and Beaverbrook knew the truth. Marston observed that 'it was pretty obvious something had happened, because his face was slightly collapsed... the side of his face.' Both she and Gilliatt remembered how worried he was about being able to write his name; after all, his writing (and dictating) is what kept his working life – and his finances – going. Understandably, he worried, too, that he might have another stroke that would interfere with his participation in the upcoming general election, and the chance to become prime minister again. Fortunately, Churchill's amazing recuperative powers helped, as Marston says that he did recover almost completely, although 'perhaps he was not so active... physically... He would not walk around as much... around Chartwell. He would always go in the car over the fields rather than walk.'

But Churchill felt well enough to continue as Leader of the

Opposition after Labour narrowly won the general election in February 1950. Knowing that Labour's majority was unstable and that another election might soon occur, Churchill took the opportunity to take yet another trip abroad, this one to Venice in August 1951 with both Marston and Portal. To his neurologist, Dr Brain, Churchill wrote:

> I am going to Venice for a fortnight and there will be beautiful bathing at the Lido. I think it would do me good provided that first, the water is well over 70° and secondly, that I do not plunge in but change the temperature gradually, taking two minutes or more in the process. This is after all only what I do in my bath. Will you kindly telegraph your advice to me at the Excelsior Hotel, Lido, Venice.

Taking the honeymoon suite and the entire top floor, and no doubt several other rooms at the Excelsior, the 'flying circus' arrived with fifty-five suitcases and sixty-five smaller articles, including, of course, work relating to Volume V of the war memoirs. This volume was about to be printed, and last-minute telegrams flew back and forth between Venice and London with queries that only Churchill could answer. Denis Kelly, working at the London office, cabled Marston: 'For God's sake, or at any rate for mine, get Mr C. to read Prof's [Cherwell's] comments carefully. If necessary type them out as his pencil scribbles will put him [Churchill] off.' But Volume V was finished: 'twelve years had passed since the outbreak of war, the story of which he was now so near completing'.[10]

Marston toured Venice with Mrs Churchill,

> [if] she wanted company... The food was always marvellous... It was great fun. And there were all the islands to visit around Venice, Torcello, Murano and Burano. And we used to go off for the day and ring up beforehand and order lunch at some marvellous place overhung with vines. And all the locals used to get

terribly excited that he [or his party, sometimes, including Jane
Portal, were] coming.

Ample compensation for the fact that when with Churchill she
often had to take dictation 'as they flew along in a motor launch'
through the canals of Venice.[11]

Churchill was right: Attlee was forced to call a general election
for October 1951. The Tories won and Churchill was again prime
minister. Marston says that 'One woke up and found oneself going
to Number 10... There were great preparations for sort of moving to Number 10 and shutting up the house of Hyde Park Gate.'
Almost all his personal staff went with him, but, as with his first
stay in Number 10, they 'had a separate office apart from the civil
service side... the government side was quite separate [from his
personal staff]'. However, the increased workload forced Churchill
to use some of the Number 10 staff as well as his own. He had
known some of the senior civil-service secretaries at Number 10,
so there was no need for him to do what he disliked – adjust to
new faces.

But Marston did sense a slight loss. She felt that the personal
secretaries 'didn't have quite the same status... I wouldn't say I
enjoyed it. It was just different. It was all very official... the government servants and messengers.' But Churchill's way of working
never changed: 'he didn't alter his way of living... apart from the
fact that he was sort of slowing down... he was not working so late
at night,' and his increasing deafness made his usual schedule take
longer and tire him out more.

Marston continued to work for Churchill from Hyde Park Gate
– and occasionally at Chequers, dealing with constituency matters,
as well as being 'in charge of all secretarial matters relating to the
war memoirs'.[12] In 1953 she married Robert Shillingford, a pilot
she had met when touring an RAF base with Churchill. After her
marriage, she lived in Wells and did all Churchill's constituency
work, which was sent to her. She volunteered, as several other
former secretaries did, to help for big events such as his eightieth

birthday in 1954 and his golden wedding anniversary in 1958, both of which generated 'massive correspondence to deal with' and presents to acknowledge from around the world. Two days before his eighty-ninth birthday in 1963, Churchill went to the House of Commons in a wheelchair, and that night he dined at The Other Club. But his working life was winding down.[13] Marston volunteered to help with the massive amounts of congratulatory letters, telegrams and presents that came flooding in. Churchill dictated a letter to her on 6 December 1963, thanking her for her work and saying, 'Thank you for your kindness in helping to deal with my correspondence on November 30. I understand that you wish me to regard this [work] as a gift for my birthday and I much appreciate all your valuable assistance,' signed personally by him 'with every good wish, yours very sincerely'.

When Churchill died in 1965 Marston went back to work at Hyde Park Gate to help with funeral arrangements and the masses of correspondence. She was 'devastated' when he died, but 'he had certainly earned his rest'.

Marston and her husband Robert Shillingford established a branch of the Cancer Research campaign. She died in 1988, aged sixty-nine, and had worked for Churchill for nineteen years. When Churchill died in 1965, he left her £200, about £3,700 in today's money.

9

Cecily 'Chips' Gemmell

'I'd have thrown myself under the bus
practically for the Old Man.'*

'Chips' Gemmell, oral history

'Contemporaries forgave his many foibles, attributing all
these traits to the eccentricity of genius.'

General Walter Bedell Smith[1]

---

* 'Old Man' was used affectionately by many of the secretaries.

BORN IN 1929, Cecily 'Chips' Gemmell was another graduate from Mrs Hoster's Employment Agency, the secretarial college and placement service for women, highly regarded by employers. She applied for employment with Churchill and was interviewed by Jo Sturdee, who was managing Churchill's staff and offices at a time when Churchill was Leader of the Opposition. Sturdee says Gemmell described herself as 'a country girl [who] would much rather work at Chartwell', which was fine with Churchill, since 'they needed extra help there too'. She was hired, aged eighteen, she thinks because she 'looked the toughest and having passed Sturdee's eagle eye, I then went to see the Old Man who had just come back from the hospital'. He was in the downstairs dining room at 28 Hyde Park Gate, where 'I was ushered into... this terrifying presence sitting up in bed'. She was offered the job and accepted, despite a fear of working for Churchill. 'If it had been somebody like [Franklin] Roosevelt, who I somehow pictured as a very kindly person... I would have no hesitation accepting a job like that.'

She began work in the summer of 1947 and remained with Churchill for four years, before transferring to Mrs Churchill for another two. Since her father was in India and her mother was staying with friends in Britain, Gemmell was housed in a cottage called Over the Way (opposite the Pitts Cottage restaurant) in Westerham, the town in which Chartwell is located, bicycling daily to Chartwell ('up an incredibly steep hill'). But since Churchill was unwilling to pay for the rental of the cottage on weekends, and Gemmell had nowhere to go, she was forced to pay for her weekend stays in the cottage. When hiring Gemmell, Sturdee emphasized the importance of secrecy and discretion, as she did with all the secretaries she approved for hire or hired herself. Gemmell says 'Jo [Sturdee] put the fear of God into one. One must not say anything about the Churchills because the press was very interested and we were privy to EVERYTHING there and we were TRUSTED completely and expected to keep our mouths shut.' Of course this was essential during the war years when national security was of grave concern and they were all required to sign the Official Secrets Act. But even after 1945 secrecy was maintained to ensure the Churchills' privacy and safety.

Gemmell's first big task was working as a typist with Denis Kelly, who set up the muniment room at Chartwell to sort, date and catalogue all of Churchill's papers in preparation for writing his war memoirs, and to establish an archive on which he could draw. Churchill had charged Kelly with 'making Cosmos out of Chaos'.[2] In other words, establish the Archives[3] and then help out with writing the war memoirs, a chore that could not start until the archiving was completed, and a determination made of whether Churchill or the government owned the papers. Kelly was a lawyer who continued to handle his legal cases up in London, so when he left Chartwell, carrying his gown and wig in what looked like his dirty laundry bag (but was in fact his barrister's bag), Gemmell continued on her own, working regular office hours, 9 a.m. to 5 p.m., in a semi-basement area converted into a muniment room.*

Gemmell, now working as an archivist as well as a trained typist, had had no training in creating an archive, except what Kelly taught her – and it is not clear what, if anything, Kelly knew about archiving before he undertook this task.† But whatever experience he lacked as an archivist, he seems to have made up for in enthusiasm. Sturdee recalls that Kelly would come into her office and excitedly announce, 'Oh, I found a most interesting document today.'

Inexperienced in the real world of work, untrained and largely untutored, with an employer who struck fear into her heart, Gemmell confronted hundreds of black tin boxes and literally

---

* She could not see out completely, but the small window to the front of the house gave her a good view of visitors' shoes and socks. She called it her view of 'the socks of the famous'. She especially recalls Anthony Eden's pink socks.
† What is clear is that all future historians will thank Kelly and Gemmell for their initial work setting up what became the invaluable Churchill Archives.

thousands of unsorted documents. The physical work environment didn't make her life any easier: the rooms were next to the
oil-burning furnace, which 'roared away most of the year since
Churchill hated a cold house'. Electrical wiring was 'distinctly
primitive... and Churchill reluctantly agreed to purchase fire-
resistant steel cabinets'[4] in which Gemmell filed the archived
materials; probably pursuant to a system she developed, just as
Grace Hamblin earlier developed a system for keeping track of
and controlling Chartwell expenses. It cannot have been easy for
Gemmell to work under these conditions, but she persevered,
recalling 'total confusion'.

At this point, she was not yet working for Churchill directly,
but she did smell his cigar smoke and hear his voice, all of which
made her 'tremble, and in a way thinking I would never get to
the point where I was going to work for him'. But get to that point
she did.

When the archiving was complete, she was transferred to Churchill's secretarial staff and summoned one night, after dinner, to
his bedroom, to take dictation, or 'take down' as the chore was
called. There this fearsome figure was, sitting in his four-poster
bed amid the inevitable newspapers, brandy, cigars and ashtrays
and an occasional cat. Sitting on the card table next to him was
the noiseless typewriter. She recalls: 'I don't know why I just didn't
fall on the floor. So frightened I was shaking.' It was unusual
for him to dictate from his bed after dinner and he did so only
when he had dined alone. But Churchill started dictating and she
started 'typing away like mad', having to type extra hard as the
silent typewriter required extra pressure on the keys. She 'kept
thinking this is a nightmare. I'm going to wake up. This isn't for
real... The thought kept me going and I went typing, typing away
and he went dictating, dictating away.' He stopped, she handed
him what she had typed, he said goodnight 'with a big smile' and
she left the room. But the next morning Churchill came into the
office, dressed in his siren suit (called by his staff, although not in
his presence, 'his rompers')[5] and monogramed slippers, 'THREW

the papers on the ground and he said to me "You haven't got one word in fifty right!"'

A big part of the problem was that Churchill had been working on a speech, composing it as he dictated, always a tense time. Gemmell confirms that he spent many hours crafting each speech. When dictating one to her, she says 'He probably did have little themes on pieces of paper, but it was straight out of the mind... It was very hard for him to do speeches... This was something he'd spent a lot of time and energy on, and to have it come out as gobbledygook was terrible to him... Goodness knows why he accepted me after. That was what was so wonderful about him.'

After lunch, he wanted to dictate again and Sturdee sent her up the back stairs – probably believing in the old axiom that getting back on the horse after being thrown is a good idea. She typed his words and handed them to him: 'He looked at it and he said, "I knew you could do it," and then one was okay... He was terribly magnanimous. After the yell, it was then forgotten and you started again.' That characteristic, noted earlier by Kinna and later by Portal, has been clear to all students of Churchill's character: 'For Churchill, the greatest error was to indulge in the emotions of revenge and spite,' notes one scholar of Churchill's behaviour during the fraught negotiations over Irish neutrality during the Second World War.[6] Gemmell recalls:

On the whole, after you had been reprimanded and shouted at... then you were accepted again with a clean slate... Yes, I used to get shouted at. The typewriter wasn't in the car when he wanted it [or] on the plane. Things like that... one had done something silly, one would get shouted at. So I think he could get irritated quite easily. But then once the shouting was over, then start again... He could make you feel absolutely down in the dumps or absolutely walking on a cloud.

Gemmell was eighteen, the other secretary was nineteen, and after working on a speech for Churchill, when he was getting ready to leave to give the talk, he called for 'the young ladies and he would say, "Thank you very much. You did very well," and then he would be off in a flurry of coats, drivers and detectives. And one just felt wonderful, which was sweet of him.' Gemmell and Portal were the 'young ladies', Sturdee and Gilliatt the older ones, although they were only in their mid-twenties. Magnanimity, of course, was practised not only in private, but lauded as a virtue in several speeches, as well as being part of the moral of his war memoirs: 'In victory, magnanimity.'*

Taking down speeches and transcribing them was only one use to which Gemmell put her training in her early days with Churchill. In addition to his duties in the House, and his large and varied social obligations, Churchill was writing his war memoirs. As Churchill dictated, Gemmell would type on to 'long galley sheets, the backs of the galleys he had seen proofs on, and we'd type on those, double spacing'. Because she had been so young during the war, many of the proper names he used were unfamiliar to her, requiring her to check her transcription against a list of names. Churchill would then correct her draft with a pen, most likely the 'beautiful gold one'[7] he prized. 'And then, after you'd done a night's work, it would be packed up in a package and left in the pantry and the car would come and pick it up and take it down to the station [at Westerham] and it would go straight up to the printers. Usually the printers would be able to run it off during the day and it would come back... in galley form, which must have been incredibly expensive.' Fortunately, 'Churchill had a special contractual provision, allowing for excess printing costs to be met,' presumably by the publisher.[8]

On one occasion, while dictating his war memoirs, Churchill quoted the famous phrase 'never in the field of human conflict'. Gemmell, a teenager during the war, does not believe she had ever heard it. When she 'typed "never in the field of human

---

* Examples abound. Notably Churchill's agreement to allow de Gaulle to share the glory of the liberation of Paris.

consciousness" and he read it, he was almost crying, and said "It's clear you haven't heard one of the greatest quotations in the world." Almost crying because he was quite conceited.' Graebner says that Churchill 'was always pleased to be reminded of his own great phrases and was particularly happy when someone corrected his misquoting himself – something he frequently did as he grew older.'[9]

Because Gemmell preferred working in Chartwell to working in London, Sturdee did her best to arrange an accommodating work schedule more easily done on weekends, because Churchill usually moved his base to Chartwell from London on Thursday evening. Gemmell would bicycle or hike up to Chartwell on Friday morning, over the fields and hills, to arrive at about 9 a.m. Churchill would have arrived the night before, bringing with him the black and red boxes which Gemmell then sorted and arranged for him to work from. The other secretary on duty at Chartwell on weekends would arrive about noon, driven down from London in a police car, bringing with her the London mail and additional work and several newspapers. On these weekends at Chartwell, Gemmell would work nights, with other secretaries working days. When working very late into the night, she would sleep at Chartwell in one of the maids' rooms or down the road at the butler's cottage, waking early to complete the transcription of whatever Churchill had dictated that evening. Churchill took no part in arranging their schedules, their camaraderie allowing them to work things out in Churchill's interests.

Looking back, she recalls:

It was hard work… He would go to bed anytime up to five or six in the morning… and then he would say, 'What time do you think you could get up in the morning?' When he asked you something like that, one would have done anything for him… and say, 'Would you like me in sort of early?' He would say, 'Oh, that would be very nice.' And one would say… when he asked you something like that, <u>one would have done anything for him</u>…

Sometimes there would be lovely, lovely evenings, but they didn't happen very often, when he would buzz down to the office and he would say, 'You can go to bed. I'm not going to work.'

Whenever the secretaries needed a break, they would get up and excuse themselves. Churchill would invariably say, 'Where are you going?' 'I'm just going downstairs to the office for a moment.' 'Well, don't be long,' he would say. While Gemmell was gone, he would sign a few copies of his books, which he meant to give as gifts, especially thank-you gifts, usually signing only his name, with no further inscription.* A chore he hated.

At Chartwell, dictation of the war memoirs went on, and the advisors arrived to 'dine and sleep', as the engagement cards put it. The advisors were Lieutenant General Sir Henry Pownall (military), Commodore G. R. G. Allen (naval, known as 'full steam ahead and damn the consequences Allen') – both of whom Gemmell adored, as did the other secretaries. And William Deakin, who had helped Churchill on his biography of Marlborough and who, Gemmell says, was the political advisor. Sometimes these advisors were at Chartwell alone, sometimes all at the same time, having arguments and discussions, 'all mucking in… Sometimes I would not know when one was being dictated to and when one was not, because they would all be talking.'

Churchill would ask for 'a background of the battle of something or some situation and they would type him up a history of whatever it was… He would look at it… From there his memory would seem to come to the fore… He would never use their things. He would then dictate his memory of what had happened.' Churchill wrote the story of the war based on the minutes he had dictated himself during the actual war – minutes that he had kept and 'interleaved into the narrative… with a lot of cutting and

---

* He was urged, too, to sign photographs of himself, which he also used as thank-you gifts to staff and others.

pasting of everything... a lot of klopping and tagging.'* Leather treasury bands held proofs and chapters together, and there were 'things tied up with pink Treasury ribbons'. With so many inputs, organization was a huge administrative chore, usually managed by the (always male) Private Secretary on duty.

As was the case with other secretaries employed by Churchill throughout his life, Gemmell's workload was not confined to preparing speeches, helping with the memoirs and doing what might be considered chores of a secretarial nature. There were also a huge number of menial chores. Walking Rufus II† was one such. Churchill asked that Gemmell walk his dog last thing at night, so that Rufus could sleep through the night on the floor in Churchill's bedroom. No one, not even Rufus, was allowed to interrupt Churchill's sleep. After their walk, when she brought Rufus upstairs into the bedroom, Churchill asked her 'Did the little dog do his duty?' and when she answered 'Yes', Churchill said, 'Oh good, you may go to bed now. Thank you very much.'

Rufus II (and the detective following behind) always tagged along with Churchill as he toured his Chartwell garden, wearing his 'garden hat with swan feathers sticking in it... And they'd feed the golden orfe [and] call out the swans.' Sometimes he would visit the pig farm and say to the detective: 'I'm going down to the pigsty. You come down in the car and pick me up. You'll know me by my hat... It was funny every time he said it... You had to laugh, because he had such a puckish look on his face.' Gemmell also recalled that 'There was often a touch of humour in his expression, as if he had just said something funny – which he frequently did. We were very intent on work, so I didn't exactly study his face a great deal. I certainly would say that he smiled quite a bit. But I never saw his teeth.'[10]

---

* Tagging was done with 'little pieces of material with a wire at the end, which you put through the Treasury tags.' Belly bands were the leather straps. Compare with the 'Bellybandoes' for his cigars.

† Rufus I had been run over by a car while Churchill was away in Brighton at the Conservative Party Conference in October 1947.

Gemmell says that she was also asked to wash his paintbrushes at the end of a weekend, but in their oral histories other secretaries say the valet or detectives did that. Gemmell's recollection included how she hated doing that assignment because it roughened her hands, so her version is likely correct. She might not have objected to cleaning brushes when the portrait painter Oswald Birley (the father of club entrepreneur Mark Birley) came around. He painted four portraits of Churchill and gave him painting hints when he visited Chartwell, and helped Churchill paint Gemmell's portrait, a portrait Portal says Gemmell still has.

Another chore that she disliked intensely was 'to look after the tropical fish, seeing that the tank was clean'. Sturdee says, 'Oh, poor 'Chips'. She used to get so bored with it... we tried to encourage her, say it did look clean or [teasingly] "What went wrong this week? They're not looking as clean."' And of course Churchill would be the first to point out that something was wrong with his beloved pet fish. Churchill often wrote to Mrs Churchill giving up-to-date news on his beloved black mollies, an intensely black fish.[11] A five-year-old boy had once brought them to the door as a present for the prime minister's birthday. (See Appendix 2.) As they were a tropical fish, Churchill called for experts to advise him and new tanks were ordered. 'We had a lovely lot of them.'[12] But when Churchill became prime minister in 1951 the fish in their special tanks were moved to Chequers into 'the Hawtrey room which was lined with tapestries... [the] five tanks looked simply beautiful against this backdrop.'[13] When he resigned as prime minister, he kept one tank and the remainder were donated to the London Zoo.

He was nothing if not eccentric, with a sense of humour at times perhaps best appreciated by himself. A careful reading of the source material suggests that, like secretaries who preceded her and followed her into Churchill's employ, Gemmell 'did whatever had to be done'. It is difficult in this day and age to imagine any secretary being asked to do some of these chores, and, if asked, to agree. But this is now, that was then; Churchill was an imposing figure, jobs were scarce and other aspects of the job – excitement, travel, a sense of being part of his Secret Circle – were seen as powerful incentives to do as he asked.

What was most exasperating to Gemmell was Churchill's capacity to put off work or chores he didn't want to do. He hated signing copies of his books and had schemes and ploys to avoid doing that, such as marking in his very own 'shorthand "Top of Box" or "T of B", which meant he didn't want to do it now... He would get around to it.' She recounts that Emery Reves, his literary agent, gave him one of a series of paintings of Charing Cross Bridge by Monet and in return expected that Churchill would sign multiple copies of his books for Reves to send around. Churchill refused to inscribe the books, despite Gemmell's pleading with him to do so. At times, he could delay signing by picking up one of his own books, reading in it, and saying appreciatively, 'He's very good, you know,' about his own words.

Occasionally, she would be asked to go up to London from Chartwell for the day to help in a crisis, so she would have to bring Rufus back from London on the 'Green Line bus', if Churchill wanted Rufus with him. One day she and the dog got off the Green Line bus, walked up the hill towards Chartwell and noticed a large American car parked by the side of the road. The occupants were peering over the wall into the gardens. She and Rufus went into the house and

> shortly after the doorbell rings... Here is this chauffeur, and he said, 'Excuse me, I am driving Mr Spencer Tracy, the actor, and he is a great admirer of Mr Churchill's. Would it be possible to come in and look at the grounds a little?' Ham [Hamblin] wasn't there to run and ask. I am sure if I had said to her, she would have said yes... I thought... suppose they wander around the grounds and they run into Christopher Soames?... I'll get the blame if Christopher does not approve. And so I said, 'I am terribly sorry... it is a private house.'

If Churchill had seen the Spencer Tracy film *State of the Union*

(1948), in which Tracy plays an industrialist considering a run for the presidency and Katharine Hepburn his wife and conscience when difficult compromises present themselves, he might well have invited the star in for a drink. Gemmell, who knew how much Churchill enjoyed films, regretted not having the authority to allow Tracy to tour the grounds.

She felt badly, too, when one of the films she selected for viewing by the Churchills and their guests did not meet with approval, even though it had been sent by film-maker Alexander Korda's office. On one occasion, she or one of the other secretaries, or perhaps Churchill himself, chose *49th Parallel* (1941), a film in which several Germans who are trying to infiltrate the United States through Canada are killed off, one by one. She recalls: 'On this occasion two German prisoners of war who stayed on at Chartwell after the war as farm workers had been invited to the movie… After it was all over, the Old Man went up to them and said: "I'm so sorry. Forgive me for inviting you to this movie"… Incredible… The Old Man apologizing for any embarrassment.' His magnanimity in victory extended even to German farm workers.[14]

Churchill, as is well known, loved the theatre as much as films. Gemmell recounts the famous story of Churchill going to see Richard Burton play Hamlet. Sitting in the front row, Churchill recited the lines as Burton said them – she thinks 'Burton found it rather off-putting.'[15] And after the play ended, Churchill went back to see Burton in his dressing room and said to the actor: 'My Lord Hamlet, may I use your bathroom?' She must have heard this story from the other staff members or from someone who was present: there is no record of Burton's reaction in his diaries.

There may have been many chores, not all pleasant, odd hours, demanding standards, and at times sharp mood swings. Gemmell recalls that once, when she was talking to General Pownall, they got 'on to the topic of suicide'. When Churchill heard, he erupted and said, '"Shut up, shut up… Don't talk like that"… This was something he didn't like to hear people talking about.' He had once said he worried about standing too close to the edge of a railway track, perhaps afraid of what he might do, although his zest for life, curiosity and his love for his wife would have precluded any such action. Significantly, his black dog depression generally only lasted as long as he was not in office – working hard set him back on his usual upbeat energetic mood.

Against these negatives must be set not only the excitement of working for Churchill, but the many perks, such as going to the races with Churchill, although Gemmell recalls some moments of unease.

> I was supposed to only go as far as the race course and then I was to go back to London, but I think he relented and said I could go to the races... He said, 'I am going to Lord Derby's box. You can't come there'... glaring at one... When there was an awkward situation and you didn't quite know what to do, he fixed on the terrible glare. You got the point that you just had to fix something else up... I think we [she and Detective Evan Davies, called 'Bish'] went to the Jockey Club dining room and watched the Derby from there.

And while at the races she spotted Lord Ismay at the rails, smiled and said hello to him. 'He looked straight through me and I thought it's not the place to – perhaps he didn't see me... I thought: a lesson learned.' Meaning she knew her place and so did Lord Ismay, who in other places and at other times was 'far more approachable than most of the British officers.[16] I must say that no other recollection of General Ismay's character supports this type of arrogance. More characteristic of the general was that he sometimes before dinner would bring glasses of sherry into the office for the personal staff – amid many giggles.'[17] Marston had a similarly positive recollection of Ismay when she worked with him at Potsdam, just prior to the meeting of the Big Three in July 1945. She reported that General Ismay, 'unlike other attendees, appreciated how much they had slaved... to get the place ready. The rest of the delegates assumed the Russians had done it all.'[18]

Even though she was privy to all the highest and most impor-tant secrets of the land, Gemmell could not breach the class barriers of the Britain of her day. She rarely was invited to dine with the Churchill family. On one occasion when the separation was breached, Gemmell was seated next to Randolph, famous for his rudeness to staff – even when he needed them to do some chore like taking dictation. Gemmell says, 'I thought I should make conversation. He wasn't talking to me for a very good reason. He probably wished we weren't there. [I said to him] "We are going to Monte Carlo tomorrow. I have never been to Monte Carlo." That was the end of our conversation.' No surprise. When he was twenty-one, Maxine Elliott, who often welcomed Churchill to the Chateau de l'Horizon, her villa in the south of France, described Randolph

> as handsome as a matinee idol... an arrogant young man... con-vinced that he would... be prime minister by the time he was twenty-five... but he failed to take into account an Englishman's natural distaste of bumptiousness. He was heartily disliked... He lacked his father's humanity and... common sense.[19]

Another observer, a historian, describes Randolph's behaviour as a young man visiting America with his father a bit floridly, but not inaccurately, according to the secretaries who later worked with his father: 'An Etonian Old Boy fully eighteen years of age and a student at Christ Church College, Oxford, Randolph had the facility for elevating his nose to heights considerably more lofty than are deemed physiologically feasible and then looking down at what he regarded as upstartism and impertinence.'[20]

No surprise that Randolph was all of the secretaries' – and many others' – least favourite person, as 'there was always chaos when he came, chaos because he just rubbed them [the Churchills] both up the wrong way... He had a very good mind. He was just very difficult.' Another irritating presence was Duncan Sandys, whom Churchill's eldest daughter Diana married in 1935; they

were divorced in 1960. Gemmell says Sandys was around much of
the time, but that

> he exasperated Churchill very often... I remember once it was
> my early night. I was having a bath in the servant's wing [and
> I was] hauled out because Duncan wanted to dictate... He was
> so bad and he changed his mind constantly. After about half an
> hour, Churchill came shuffling down and [asked], 'Well, my girl,
> what have you done?' I read what he [Duncan] had dictated: 'The
> Council of Europe', and then I think there were two more sen-
> tences. The Old Man was beside himself [with laughter. Duncan]
> sort of put his foot into it and wasn't very sensitive to Churchill's
> reactions. Sarah was another matter. Everyone liked her.

In part, because Sarah opened up to some of the older secretaries
about her troubled life.

Class distinctions were made not only between the Churchills
and their staff. Intra-staff differences also mattered, especially to
Mrs Churchill. On one trip to Marrakesh, Mrs Churchill 'thought
it was not proper for the secretaries to have to have their meals with
the personal servants, which is sweet of her... She said, "You girls
don't have to sit with Walter [Churchill's new Swiss butler]. Walter
can have his meals in his room."' When Churchill heard about
this he was 'very upset', saying in a mocking tone of voice, 'Poor
Walter, poor Walter. Meals in his room.' Churchill pleaded with
them, 'I suppose Walter couldn't have his meals with you, could
he?' And so Walter did, breaching one of the fine class distinctions
that were applied to the staffs of the upper class. Not quite a case
of upstairs, downstairs. More a case of in-house servants ranking
below professional secretarial staff.

Top of the list of favourite perks were foreign trips. It was very
rare for young working women of the day to have an opportunity
to travel abroad. It would have been beyond their financial reach,
unless accompanying an employer and his family in a serving
capacity; in most cases sufficient vacation time was not available,

and there were questions of the propriety of single young women travelling alone. It was even rarer for young working women to travel abroad as part of the entourage of perhaps the most famous man in the world. Even if there would be little time off from taking dictation, a foreign trip was a cherished perk.

In the summer of 1949 Gemmell travelled with Churchill's party to Lake Garda in northern Italy, landing at an old airbase to ensure Churchill's privacy, and staying at the Grand Hotel Gardone Riviera. Gemmell and Marston had arranged for twelve rooms and for special telephone lines to be installed. But Churchill's arrival could not have been much of a secret as the Ferrari company had arranged for a fleet of cars to collect the party at the private airport. Suddenly

> The Old Man was pushed into a very sleek Ferrari car and whizzed off to the hotel... and they had gone apparently at 160 miles an hour... Wonderful picture of him probably with his cheeks all flattened while speeding. And we went in another one... a bright red model... I've never driven so fast in my life... He got out frightfully shaken and said, 'Never again. Now I'll have the hotel car.'

Detective Sergeant Davies ('Bish') must have had another tense moment when on a boat trip to an island for dinner, a motorboat crammed with photographers almost ploughed into the Churchill's speedboat. Bish was able to threaten them enough that they sped off. It must have been an incongruous sight: Churchill travelling incognito as 'Mr Smith', in a ten-gallon hat and smoking a big cigar, looking like 'a little old man from Texas' fooled no one.

Escaping the heat, the party travelled to Carezza in the foot-hills of the Dolomites, where Churchill found 'the most paintable scenery'.[21] It would be interesting to know how and why Carezza was chosen. Did a staff person scout for possible locales for him to paint? There, Churchill was disturbed by the sound of cowbells. 'He summoned the manager of the hotel and said that he simply could not work with all the tinkling of the cowbells. So all the cows were driven away… one terrible hour… and the most ghastly sound as all the cows were chased away with their bells clanging up into the mountains and then there was peace.' The bells were only one problem. Either because she measured it incorrectly or her measurements were garbled when transmitted to Lettice Marston, one of Churchill's Alpine paintings did not fit in a frame he had asked her to order. Churchill, accustomed to having his orders carried out correctly and instantly – and in addition impatient to see his painting properly framed – was deeply disappointed. He called his mortified secretary a 'bloody fool'. As usual, all was soon forgotten – but not by Gemmell, who seems to have had a vivid recollection of the incident some six decades later.

From there the entire entourage moved on to Monte Carlo, to stay, first, at the Hotel de Paris and later at La Capponcina. Churchill was 'incorporating the final new material for Volume III… working hard to "meet the deadlines" on his war memoirs.'[22] *Life* magazine, which was to serialize the memoirs, and (Gemmell says) the *Daily Telegraph* paid for the entire trip,* so she and Detective Davies decided 'to work our way through the wine list… They picked up the bills and you could have what you liked. It was carte blanche' at the Hotel de Paris, where Churchill's party was staying. Such largesse was either a foolish move on Time-Life's part, or a tribute to the bargaining power of the author they were funding. On a work/play trip just two months earlier, Churchill had reflected the same disrespect for expenses as he did when dealing with his own money. The editor of the magazine later reported that Churchill had claimed $60,000–$70,000 (between $550,000 and $650,000 in today's money) 'on those trips to work on the book… These were very lavish trips…. He had the best in food and hotels… and the last expedition to Marrakesh presented an expense account I wouldn't want anyone to peer into.'[23] Little wonder that Gemmell and her

---

* Time-Life also paid for many of the trips on RMS *Queen Mary* and RMS *Queen Elizabeth*.

colleagues regarded the terms of their trip as a wondrous perk, its cost not noticeable on expense sheets submitted to Henry Luce, the very wealthy owner of *Time* and *Life* magazines. Assuming, of course, Churchill's staff had the time to enjoy it.

On other trips to Monte Carlo, when Churchill stayed with Beaverbrook at La Capponcina, Gemmell stayed in a small hotel in the town and went back and forth to work at the villa by taxi. As usual, Churchill managed to find time to paint and to swim off the beach. He 'turned somersaults in the sea to amuse [Merle Oberon, the beautiful actress and wife of Alexander Korda].[24] He also tutored her in the art of painting and was delighted to teach her and she patterned her painting on his.'[25]

Churchill suffered a minor stroke while visiting Beaverbrook, serious enough that Lord Moran was summoned from London, arriving with his golf clubs 'so that it would not seem that anything was amiss'.[26] Gemmell remembers only that Churchill had a few colds and this stroke – but she does not recall fearing that the stroke was likely to cause permanent damage or prove fatal.

She does, however, recall Mrs Churchill's disapproval of her husband's visits to the casinos in Monte Carlo. Clementine had a lifelong fear of gambling, losing money and facing bankruptcy, which was no surprise given her impoverished and itinerant childhood. Her mother Lady Blanche 'enjoyed the casino [when they lived in France], quickly becoming a regular. Needless to say, she lost money she did not have, and to Clementine's shame, the family was forced to ask for credit in the local shops.'[27] With this background, being married to a man who 'lived from pen to mouth'[28] must have been unnerving indeed. Especially given his often-all-consuming passion for the casino. In 1938, en route from Daisy Fellowes's villa near Monte Carlo to the train station, Mary Penman[29] recalls that 'Churchill ordered the car to stop as they were passing the Casino. Although we had little time to spare before catching the train, he dashed in to the Casino and returned triumphantly, "I have just won enough to pay for our fares home – what do you think of that?"'[30] Fortunately for his family's ability to maintain the lifestyle to which Churchill was accustomed, they did not have to rely on his winnings: he sold more history books than any other twentieth-century historian, according to Andrew Roberts, his latest biographer.[31]

During their 1947 stay in Morocco, Thami El Glaoui, the Pasha of Marrakesh, gave a dinner for Churchill's party and unusually the entire entourage was invited, including the female secretaries. His palace was in the Medina, the old fortified city. 'We were ushered through lots of courtyards and into a tiny little room hung with carpets or silk or something... No sign of the Glaoui and drinks were being passed around... so I reached up for my drink and the Old Man said: "Oh Miss, be careful, it might be an aphrodisiac. Ho ho ho!!"' When the Glaoui appeared they were invited in to dinner to sit on rugs on the floor, but Churchill, however, sat on a low bunk. 'Then they brought in these great earthenware pots of food, absolute lovely. I remember chicken with wonderful pastry... We ate with our fingers[32] and we all took little bits out and then the pot would go to the wives and from the wives all the way down. But we had the first thing.' And they were served champagne, although the Muslim hosts did not drink it. She says they were expecting undulating dancing girls, belly dancers perhaps, but were disappointed as the only dancers turned out to be boys, covered head-to-toe in white, carrying musical instruments. Churchill, however, writing to Mrs Churchill, remembers it differently: first Berber female dancers, then female Arab dancers, neither of which he found either enticing or interesting. In fact, Churchill wrote: 'I have great regard for the Glaoui who no doubt had endured all this and many other afflictions in his journey through this vale of sin and even more woe.'[33]

Churchill had admired some paintings in the La Mamounia Hotel and asked to meet the French artist to ask him how he painted such 'beautiful blue skies'. Invited to his studio, Churchill took Gemmell with him, expecting to work on the drive. It was hot in the studio and Churchill fell asleep – or so Gemmell thought. While the artist explained in French how he used tempera[34] and 'blew the paint on to his canvases', Gemmell, who did not speak French, nodded knowingly, while the artist said he hoped she would be able to explain it all to Churchill. Suddenly Churchill woke up and said, '"No good talking to her, she can't understand a word." Wasn't that awful? I [was] mortified and a figure of fun.' Churchill could be momentarily cruel.

And impetuous. 'Lili Marlene' was one of the most popular songs of the Second World War. Although originally a German song, it was later picked up by the Allied armies in North Africa and its lyrics changed to English. Churchill hated the 'Lili Marlene' tune and 'was absolutely terrified that they might play "Lili Marlene", because once he got that tune in his head he had not been able to get it out.' To get away from the tune, he decided to flee Marrakesh. The party first flew to a French Foreign Legion base with an old runway in the foothills of the Atlas Mountains. The French Commandant of the base welcomed Churchill's party – with offerings of dates and goat's milk and some more-welcome French coffee. The Commandant, a real Beau Geste figure, dressed in a navy cape and red hat along with his most attractive wife, entertained Churchill and his staff. Gemmell remembers that she sat for a meal with the detectives until Churchill asked that she join his table – an unusual gesture.*

The entourage then drove to a tiny village called Tinehir for a few days, where Churchill 'found a sunlight painting paradise'. In a letter he promised Mrs Churchill he would take her when she arrived a few days later.[35] They stayed in a small hotel where, Gemmell recalls, the bathrooms were all downstairs. One night, needing to go to the bathroom, she wandered down the stairs in the dark. She 'put my foot out and something rose and rattled to its feet... and found the next morning that the Berbers were sleeping downstairs, guarding him.' Not sounding very concerned, she says she felt no 'danger of being raped perhaps by a Berber'.

---

*   One of the Scotland Yard detectives told Gemmell that he had helped build the road they were driving on when he was serving in the French Foreign Legion.

Back in Marrakesh, there were multiple picnics, 'star turns and he [Churchill] expected all his guests to attend. Probably no man in the twentieth century organized an outing on such a lavish scale. The site was selected some days in advance after Mrs Churchill... had explored the region with a careful eye on what would make good subjects for Mr Churchill's brush. Departure time was usually eleven sharp.'[36] Gemmell says that the family sat at one table and the staff another, but that all the secretaries were invited – should he have an idea or a letter to dictate. Presumably they were included, too, in the Indian army toasts learned from General Pownall. She adds that they all adored and wanted to marry the recently widowed 'Darling General Pownall'.

Later that year, Gemmell decided to live in London and began to work for Churchill at Hyde Park Gate, with occasional trips to Chartwell. In London the taxi service they used to ferry the secretaries home was called Godfrey Davis, so when work was over for the night, Churchill would say to her 'Go and order your Davy Jones,' another Churchillian wordplay.

In December 1950 Churchill returned to Marrakesh to paint and work, mostly on the final volume of the war memoirs. He took Gemmell as well as Sturdee, 'a detective; Sergeant Murray, Churchill's bodyguard; and Norman McGowan his new valet. Also on the expedition was Lord Cherwell and his valet Mr Harvey.'[37] While the secretaries were unpacking the office supplies and type-writers to set up the offices – as they did on all trips – and the airline crew, staying at another hotel for the month, were settling in, Churchill scouted around for the 'most paintacious' spots, and cabled home to ask how Rufus II was doing.[38] Graebner describes this type of office:

The office was always installed in the middle of the Churchill wing [of the hotel],* since it functioned as the nerve centre for

---

* Usually the Churchill party took an entire floor. In this case, it was a renovated wing of the hotel.

the entire party. All mail, for example, was delivered to the office, not to the rooms of any individuals. If anyone wanted to find out who was coming to dinner, he inquired at the office. All plans for the day were issued through the office. The management of this vital part of the holiday operation was entrusted to secretaries [Sturdee and Gemmell] from the London staff, one of whom was available whenever Churchill called between 8 a.m. and 2 a.m.[39]

In October 1951 a general election brought Churchill back to Downing Street as prime minister for the second time. Churchill immediately went to work at 28 Hyde Park Gate, doing what he called 'putting chickens in coops', meaning filling cabinets posts. But once again Gemmell's confidence ebbed and she became fearful of not knowing what to do in the new situation. Jane Portal, being junior to her, was offered the post of working for Mrs Churchill, but turned it down. That gave Gemmell an opportunity to offer herself, which she did because she was very afraid of 'going to No. 10 with him. I think I thought it was going to be terribly responsible and… I saw a way out by going to work for Mrs Churchill. So then we all moved over to No. 10.' Although back in Number 10, but now working for Mrs Churchill, she saw less of her old colleagues. Sturdee,[40] Portal and Gilliatt went with the prime minister, Gemmell with Mrs Churchill. Gilliatt recalls that the three of them did all his shorthand and typing, creating some resentment for Churchill's personal secretaries from the Garden Room Girls, who had been anticipating doing that work.

Gemmell wasn't in the clear yet. She was in her office when one of the Private Secretaries asked her to please come to the cabinet room as the prime minister needed to dictate and everyone else had gone to lunch. 'I go shaking into the Cabinet Room. I think it was the first time I had been in there… He wanted to dictate something… about the Yalu River.' Because papers discarded at Downing Street had to be burned and not thrown out, she had a little pile of black ash on her desk – she was so nervous typing that there were quite a few sheets of paper that needed to be burned. But she 'got through it somehow'.

The work Gemmell did for Mrs Churchill was

mostly personal: remind people to come to lunch, shopping for her, [buying] things on approval... She would say, 'Could you go and get my camelhair coat, dear?' I used to go to Fortnum & Mason and, [pointing to items], say 'That's nice, that's nice, that's nice... Could you send them, please, to No. 10 on approval?' I'd get the car and chauffeur and it was very pleasant.

Mrs Churchill's biographer points out that as Churchill aged and sank into 'apathy and indifference',[41] Mrs Churchill 'in her loneliness turned to the young women she employed as secretaries.'[42] Because they had been warned to be discreet and agreed to those terms, she could count on them to be discreet and not sell stories to the tabloids or otherwise be the source of gossip about the Churchill family.

Mrs Churchill was not the only one on whom loneliness descended.

On some days [the Churchills] would have lunch or dinner alone. There were days when nobody [came] to lunch... He'd say, 'Who's coming to lunch today?'... and one would sometimes say, 'You're alone.' [He would] say, 'Well, you'd better have lunch with me.' And so to lunch with one's [shorthand] book, mind you. And then no conversation. He hated being alone... and then the Old Man would become very mellow with the champagne. There would be meringues, perhaps, with dessert... His favourite things were Irish Stew and meringues... [He'd say], 'I bet you like those, Miss, don't you?' Talking to the dog. You were there to take down.

She says he did not drink a lot, but sipped a weak whisky and soda throughout the day, champagne for lunch and dinner, and then a brandy after dinner. She sometimes had to mix his whiskies and soda, especially when Walter ('the most charming Swiss butler… he was sweet') was on vacation, or sometimes the Swiss maids served his drinks. Churchill complained once that one of the Swiss maids made his drinks too strong, but he was reluctant to tell her as he thought it might hurt her feelings. And this is the same man that could yell at his personal secretaries, clashing characteristics in one person.

When Churchill was knighted in April 1953 the secretaries had to decide what to call him. He hated being called 'Sir', even before he became a knight. He wanted to be called simply 'Mr Churchill'. However, when Gemmell 'met him in the passage at Number 10, said, "Good morning, Sir Winston." He went, "Hummm, don't be so cheeky, Miss," which was sweet.'

In early 1953, before Gemmell moved to New York to work for *Life* magazine, she went to say goodbye to both Churchills. She was told the prime minister would see her in the Cabinet Room. He was just off to the races and dressed in shepherd's plaid.* 'I think he kissed me and I practically died on the spot. He offered her a photograph… and that was it.'

By July 1954 Gemmell was living in New York, where she still lives today. Churchill was there at the same time, visiting President Eisenhower. As he boarded the *Queen Elizabeth* for home, she and other guests, among them Bernard Baruch,† came aboard the ship to say goodbye to Churchill. When she saw her old boss, she recalls

> He was so sweet. I think I got a kiss. I practically burst into tears…
> [H]e must have asked where I worked. I… said *Life* magazine,
> and he said 'Do you see Mr Luce often?' [Henry Luce was as
> grand to Time Incorporated as Churchill was to the world.] So
> I said, 'Not very often.' 'Well, give him my regards,' answered

---

*   A black-and-white tartan plaid.
†   Gemmell recalls that Baruch was very kind, and not only because he gave the secretaries pocket money.

Winston: All Work and No Play...

◀ 25. WSC Chutes into the Mediterranean, at Chateau de l'Horizon, Maxine Elliott's villa in the South of France, c.1935.

▼ 26. WSC feeds his golden orfe at Chartwell, 1950.

▲ 27. 'If it weren't for painting, I could not bear the strain.' WSC in Aix-en-Provence, South of France, 1948.

► 28. WSC and Colonist II at Newmarket, 1950.

The Secretaries: All Work and No Play…

▲ 29. Violet Pearman tours Rhodes with WSC, *c.*1934.

▼ 30. Christmas at La Mamounia, 1947. Left to right: Bill Deakin, facing the camera, Jo Sturdee, Elizabeth Gilliatt, and Sarah Churchill in a festive hat.

▲ 31. Jane Portal, far right, touring Venice in a water taxi with the Churchills, 1951.

▲ 32. Taking the plunge off the rocks, Cap d'Ail, 1949. Left to right: 'Chips' Gemmell, Lettice Marston, Denis Kelly and Evan Davies.

▼ 33. Grace Hamblin finds time for a camel ride in Tunisia, *c.*1964, repeating Mrs Churchill's 1921 adventure.

▼ 34. 'Chips' Gemmell with naval escorts aboard a ship at Portsmouth, early 1950s.

The Secretaries witness history

▲ 35. Female members of WSC's staff aboard the *Queen Mary*, September 1944. From left to right: Marian Holmes, Nurse Dorothy Pugh, Jo Sturdee and Elizabeth Layton.

► 36. Marian Holmes on tarmac at Aboukir RAF base, outside Alexandria, en route home from the Yalta Conference, February 1945.

▼► 37–8. Lettice Marston's security passes for the Potsdam Conference which took place between 17 July and 2 August 1945.

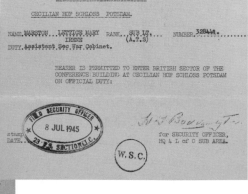

Churchill. When I got back to the office, Mr Luce was there, and he said, 'Hi, young lady. Where have you been?'... 'Just down to see the prime minister and he sends Mr Luce his regards,' she answered. 'I got a look [that said] you're very good at making up stories.'

On trips back to London Gemmell visited the Churchills and was invited to Chartwell for lunch. Lady Churchill (as she had become) warned her that 'Winston was very changed, dear.' At the table, a thoughtful host as always, Churchill asked if she wanted mustard? Then asked her, 'Have I got soup on my face or something?' (She was so taken with her placement on his right and was looking at him intensely.) Then he continued, 'Do I know you?' 'Oh yes,' she said. 'I used to work for you.' 'For how long?' he asked. 'For four years,' she answered. She then went to say goodbye to him and he 'sweetly said, "Thank you for coming to see me."' She never saw him again.

Gemmell's recollections are of two sorts – the first is her semi-humorous description of his work-above-all attitude:

We always used to laugh, but the old man really just wanted us to be there to take down. We always used to laugh that if anything happened to us and one went in and one said, 'Mr Churchill, I'm terribly sorry, but' – let's say it was me – 'Miss Gemmell has been run over by a tram.' We always [used to think] what the old man would say – no, not run over, 'She's been hurt in an accident' – and the old man would say, 'Oh, oh, I am sorry. Will she be able still to take down?' And then if the answer was 'No, I don't think so. It's going to be a long time.' 'Oh well, well, send her parents a copy of *My Early Life*. I'll sign it.' We always used to laugh about this, but we never really believed it… And then [on] one of the picnics, General Pownall took Jo [Sturdee] and me up a hillside for a walk, and coming down Jo caught her ankle in a hole or something and did sprain it very badly; and General Pownall said, 'Take the car back to the hotel,' and – she was in quite a lot

of pain – and 'Get the doctor and they'll bind it up for you.' Jo
got into the car and was driven back to the hotel and General P.
went over to the old man, who was painting, and he said, 'Miss
Sturdee has had a small accident. She sprained her ankle and I
sent her back to the hotel.' And the old man looked up and said
to General P., 'Can she still take down?' I heard it and it was too
good to be true. So if one only had the courage, I would have
said, 'Well, it's her ankle, not her hand. So she was still able to
take down.'

The second is a completely serious description of her deep
affection for Churchill, using many of the same words the other
secretaries used.

He was lovable… so funny… sort of a lovable teddy bear, except
when he was barking at you, shouting at you. And appreciative…
the way he would call me into the hall and say goodbye… and
thank one. [And] charm, he had bags of charm. Bags of it. Now
whether he was being just Winston Churchill, the squire tending
to his sheep, would he still have gotten one to love him as much?
I don't know… the greatness …

10

Jane Portal

'[Churchill] felt it was his last deed in his life to bring about world peace. He felt he could get through to him [Stalin]. And everybody told him he could not.'

Jane Portal, oral history

'If I remain in public life… it is because… I believe that I may be able to make an important contribution to the prevention of a Third World War… It is the last prize I seek to win.'

Winston Churchill, 23 October 1951[1]

BORN IN 1931 in India, Jane Portal was the niece of both Air Chief Marshal Charles ('Peter') Portal and of 'Rab' Butler, who served as president of the board of education in Churchill's wartime coalition government, and as chancellor of the exchequer when Churchill returned to power in 1951. Portal was reared in the Smith Square home of Rab and his wife, Courtauld heiress Sydney Elizabeth, which was crucial to Portal's future career. When only eighteen, she graduated from a secretarial college and signed on to an employment agency. She heard, undoubtedly from her uncles, that Churchill was looking for what she describes as a

> donkey in the office. Somebody who was young and strong and could do the night shift... He had only gotten to Volume II, *Their Finest Hour*, of his [six-volume] *The Second World War*, and I think he had a premonition that he would again go to Number 10. There was an election due in 1950 and he wanted to get as much of his war memoirs written as possible so he needed a good typist.

Thanks to recommendations from her uncles, she was interviewed at Hyde Park Gate by Jo Sturdee, the 'head girl', as Portal called her. She was then called back for an interview with Churchill. She was 'terrified... paralyzed with fear', as most of the secretaries report they were when they first met him. Portal recalls 'There was always this feeling until you got to know Mr Churchill that he was a terrifying figure... I saw Monty [General Montgomery] go in to have an interview with him and he was, I could see, nervous.' Sturdee told her that Churchill would come in to see her and when he did, he just 'walked around [her], not saying a word... then he said, "You'll do", and that was all the interview I had... [A]lmost like a heifer being inspected at a sale.' An experience no different from that of any of the secretaries Churchill hired during his long life, a tribute to his faith that the vetting process that preceded his inspection was comprehensive, his interest in the appearance of those who worked for him, almost as if he were memorizing their faces. Also, too, his confidence that the trial-by-fire to which he customarily subjected new members of his staff would separate the capable 'heifers' from those unable to survive the pace or work set by a man always in a hurry – except perhaps when painting.

In Portal's case there was an added factor. As she puts it in her keen yet fond reminiscence:

> [Churchill] liked relationships and I believe that is how I got the job. He had a great sense of people being related to each other and belonging to each other... maybe this went back to his childhood. He took on an even sweeter atmosphere when there were people who were related around him. He became more affectionate and I think he liked the relationship that Rab had with me.

No need for her to guess that she was hired because of her relationship to both Portal ('Uncle Pete' as she calls him) and Butler, and because she was brought up in a political family, and not any political family, but the Butlers. At one point Churchill admitted to her that 'I took you because of your uncles.' Churchill also knew Gilliatt's father, Sir William Gilliatt, and Vanda Salmon's grandfather, with whom Churchill 'would sit on the low wall in the sun having a drink and talking [about] trees'.[2]

In late December 1949 'I went to work for him straightaway,' Portal recalls, 'and for six months I never went near him.' This mirrors the experience Sturdee and others had when first hired. It was standard operating procedure for Churchill, who apparently preferred to have his new hires gain some experience and be tested before he trusted them with 'taking down' and other important chores. And, perhaps most important, to make certain that they worked in harmony with other members of his team.

Portal was assigned to do the filing, which had not been kept up to date, and to manage the 'old-fashioned switchboard with levers' at Hyde Park Gate, with extensions in almost every room,

including Churchill's bedroom. Hers was the awesome responsibility of deciding which calls would be routed directly to Churchill. She survived, although making many mistakes 'and cut
people off and put the wrong people through', an experience she
later characterized as 'very good training', but at the time it must
have been a little unnerving.

Her initiation apparently completed, Sturdee found a good time
for Portal to confront the man himself. At 3.30 in the afternoon of
12 May 1949 Churchill, as Leader of the Opposition in the House
of Commons, was to respond to Labour's position on the North
Atlantic Treaty, a speech he considered very important. Labour's
foreign secretary Ernest Bevin was proposing to support the new
North Atlantic Treaty, and Churchill was eager to have his Conservative MPs, as he said later that afternoon in the Commons,
'approve this Atlantic Pact... the only opposition to it expected
from that small band of Communists, crypto-Communists and
fellow-travellers whose dimensions have been very accurately
ascertained in recent times'.[3] But by 2 p.m., working at Hyde Park
Gate, he had gone through three or four drafts and was still dis-
satisfied. Because all the other young ladies were busy still typing
up his dictation from the night before, early that morning Sturdee
had to send Portal up to Churchill's bedroom to take dictation
on a last-minute draft. Sturdee 'took me up and flung me into
his bedroom... He said in a voice of horror, "Isn't there anyone
else?"' Portal fled back downstairs, telling Sturdee: 'He doesn't
like me.' Sturdee, responsible not only for seeing to her boss's
immediate needs, but for the long-term efficient functioning of his
organization, was not prepared to lose a good secretary. She 'frog-
marched me up to his bedroom... giving him a steely look from
her flashing blue eyes, saying she has got to do, there is no one else'.
Before long, as with other secretaries, Churchill 'felt that even in
that tense moment, when he was working against the clock, that
he had been unkind. And he always made up for being rough, if
ever he was, which was very seldom. He always made up for it by
some kind of gesture, not an apology, which would have been out

of place, but a gesture.' That Portal thought an apology 'would have been out of place' says a great deal about the professional and social distance between Churchill and the women who worked with him; a kind 'gesture' showing Churchill's willingness to recognize an obligation to make amends for his harsh treatment of a frightened young woman.

She fit in well with the other staff – Vanda Salmon, who worked with her, describes Portal as 'an amazing and pleasant person'[4] – and with the family, which came in and out, as the door to the Hyde Park Gate office was always open. Portal recalls she worked there in 'a beautiful two-room office knocked into one, with a garden on one side with lots of light and comfortable chairs... for people [to] come in and sit down and relax.' The two detectives waited in this office as well as politicians, researchers helping with the memoirs, and others, all waiting for meetings with Churchill. Next to the office was a small waiting room for formal visitors like Jan Smuts, Anthony Eden and Bernard Baruch, and, according to Salmon, Lieutenant General Sir Frederick 'Boy' Browning, who was Commander of the First Airborne division at Arnhem, which Browning had predicted might be 'a bridge too far'.[5] Portal recalls that the John Singer Sargent portrait of Churchill's mother dominated that small room.

As always, everyone worked in concert, in Churchill's interest; intra-staff bickering was minimal, even when one of the women found chores such as feeding the tropical fish, cleaning the tanks or cleaning paintbrushes highly undesirable, as did Gemmell. Portal says, 'They all did everything,' which was true when events so required. But Sturdee had established a system in which each of the young ladies had several areas of responsibility and could develop expertise. Portal's responsibilities were acknowledging gifts, helping with constituency matters, and seeing to Churchill's painting supplies and arrangements. She had to make certain that he always had available the paints, brushes and frames he wanted and needed. She worked closely with a famous framer who would come to Chartwell to frame all of Churchill's paintings. At one point, Churchill wanted to try his hand at painting portraits and asked Gemmell and Portal to sit for him. Gemmell still has her portrait, as we have learned in her chapter, but Portal does not know where hers is – probably '[it] has sunk into oblivion, I'm thankful to say, because he wasn't really a good portrait painter,' and besides she wore a 'multi-coloured ugly dress', which certainly did not help.[6]

In addition to these ongoing chores, Portal had responsibility for some one-off special events, such as the arrangements for the Conservative Party Conference scheduled for October 1951. Was the hotel adequate? Were enough rooms ordered? Was the furniture adequate for Churchill? Was the bed in his rooms in the right place? Was there enough space for his office to be set up in or near his rooms? Were there enough telephones? These were only some of the details to be seen to. She might have had some help from the party officials, but she alone spoke for Churchill.

Hyde Park Gate, of course, had been selected because of its proximity to the House of Commons, a ten-minute drive in which Churchill was always accompanied by a secretary, those suffering from car sickness generally being excused from this duty, even for a short trip, with the other secretaries working out the alternative rota. A police car eased his way through the traffic. From the Speaker's entrance, into the 'rickety old lift which was quite private'. But there was a problem. The lift was small, Churchill was 'substantial, not fat', and the detective insisted on being in the lift with him. And all the while Churchill was 'in mid-sentence', continuing to dictate, so that Portal had to run with him and squeeze into the lift to continue taking down. '[I was] really his shadow.'

Once in the House, Churchill worked in the Leader of the Opposition's rooms. Portal describes a wide-windowed room with a table large enough to accommodate a meeting of the shadow cabinet. Next to that room was the secretaries' room, situated so that anyone meeting with Churchill had to pass by the young ladies. 'We could ward off MPs if that was appropriate, or let them in. So we got to know the members of the party pretty well.'

Portal confirms Churchill's daily routine: awake at 7 a.m. and, after breakfast, by 8 a.m. he would start working from his bed, going through the correspondence – letters had been opened, decisions made as to what he ought to see, and the secretary who had not worked the night before would be in the bedroom, waiting to take down. Churchill wore a 'very beautiful brocade dressing gown that came down halfway to his thighs, so as to be comfortable in bed. Everything was arranged so that he could work comfortably and efficiently while in bed; [there was a] mahogany tray which fitted snugly over his torso [and] was fitted with a set of small rubber pads on which he could rest his elbows.'[7] There were also 'pens laid out and various instruments for putting papers together... He liked to call it "klopping", which was an instrument that made a hole in the corner of a paper so that it could be attached to other papers, NOT with a paper clip but with a tag. He liked to do this himself... but we handed him the klop.' And of course, the pets on the bed, the cigars and ashtrays and the telephone ringing all the while, all going on at the same time as Portal took down his words.

Portal estimates Churchill read about a third of all the mail that came in, often asking 'Aren't there any ordinary people [the general public] writing to me?' He would see official government letters and memos and family correspondence the instant they arrived. If the handwriting were recognized as that of a close friend or family member, or marked 'private' or 'personal', the envelope was delivered to Churchill unopened, even though he disliked opening his own mail. Staff members came and went during the morning bedroom hours, and 'usually the Chief Whip would come to see him to talk about what was going on in the party... [then] lunch.'

After lunch Churchill was taken on the short drive to the House, especially on days when it was Prime Minister's Questions. When he returned to Hyde Park Gate he 'always fitted in a two-hour sleep'. If the business of the House meant he had to stay there, 'he would sleep there [in] a bed that went up against the wall [of his office], but he preferred to come back about six and have his sleep [at home]. He always had to have a sleep during the day.' Perhaps because he was able to nap during the day, perhaps because he had 'very good health indeed... never any sign of fatigue' in a man seventy-five years old when Portal first observed him, he could work the long hours described by all secretaries. Portal believes that only young staff could maintain the working pace set by Churchill, one reason he selected secretaries in or just out of their teens. By the time Portal joined the staff, Sturdee insisted that the secretaries have regular two-week vacations. Portal spent the first four days of her vacation sound asleep, recovering from exhaustion. Not much time for 'social life... I got exhausted at one point,' she recalls. Portal attributes her boss's stamina to several facts. He was 'a very good walker... He walked very fast, [striding] out with his stick. He ate very little' – small portions of the items on the very extensive menus he confronted at most dinners – 'and drank very sparingly... amazing constitution'. He 'never inhaled his cigars [but] was sucking on [them] so', she says, 'they did not smell', a fond recollection which this author's experience belies. 'When they got all soggy at the end, he used to just throw them down and... souvenir-hunters... used to get into the gardens especially to look for cigar stumps.'

Once when she was in the car with him, Churchill rolled down his window and handed over his cigar butt in exchange for the latest *Evening Standard* – no words were exchanged with the news agent. It seems none were needed. There is no record of the value of this exchange. Churchill saved the price of a newspaper; the news vendor if he had saved the cigar butt for several years, might well have auctioned it off for £9,500 ($12,000), the price paid by a collector in Palm Beach, Florida.[8]

Portal worked Monday to Friday in London, at Hyde Park Gate, often going with Churchill to the House. At this time, he was dictating his war memoirs and she was taking it down straight on to the silent typewriter, 'a huge contraption which had muffled pads on it... very heavy to move.' She claims

I never could do shorthand properly... which was a problem, because he liked things read back very regularly. He would dictate a sentence and then say, 'Read it back.' I learned my own form of shorthand, which was half-written out... When he became prime minister... one had to go in after a cabinet meeting and read documents back to the cabinet. That was quite alarming. This was a way he had of making the work go more quickly, so that when you typed it, it was a final copy, as he wanted it. He dictated very slowly, because he was composing... the thought process was going on all the time.

Churchill would finish dictating at around two or three in the morning, which meant Portal would be transcribing until break of day. If the dictation had been for his histories, she had to have those pages ready to be sent off to the printer first thing in the morning. The pages, as Gemmell tells us, 'would be placed in the pantry for pickup and run it off during the day and it would come back [by 6 p.m.] in galley form, which must have been incredibly expensive.' All the typed memos and minutes from the night before had to be ready in the morning.

A relaxing and pleasant interlude in the work week occurred on the Friday arrivals at Chartwell. Portal, Churchill and a detective, along with Rufus II, would 'walk around the gardens which he had designed... with the waterfalls coming down the hill to the pool at the bottom... to feed the fish.' Churchill always claimed that 'they came especially to say hello to him', but of course they came for the food, not something anyone felt compelled to make clear to this sentimental man. A pleasant half hour – even though there was no conversation between them – 'he had no small talk', perhaps an instruction or two – and then back to work. 'The prime minister always found social conversation superfluous, as indeed did Rab... It was all politics, world affairs, serious business.'

'Arrange for Rufus II to be poozled,' Churchill would order. So Portal would set up an appointment for his 'hairdo', in a special dogs' parlour in Beauchamp Place. Sitting in the front seat, Rufus II would be driven to his appointment by the chauffeur, who waited there the entire day to drive the dog back to Chartwell, 'looking absolutely wonderful'. Hamblin also took great care with Rufus II, as we saw, and several secretaries report that Rufus II was in the car on trips between Chequers, Chartwell and Hyde Park, and, no doubt, other visits as well. None mention any of the cats moving back and forth with Churchill between houses, perhaps because those resident in Number 10 and at Chartwell had mouse-keeping chores to attend to.

From about 1949 through 1951 Bill Deakin and Denis Kelly spent nearly every weekend at Chartwell, providing the required research materials, presumably for Volume III of the history of the Second World War,[9] and obtaining government permission to use official papers. Often, Portal recalls, Ismay and Lord Cherwell were also there, refreshing Churchill's memories, although Portal says that Churchill was 'a tremendously fast reader and had a photographic memory'. He refreshed that memory by reading what his researchers provided and then would dictate his version of events, mostly after dinner, either in the study at Chartwell or in the dining room at Hyde Park Gate.

When Churchill needed a secretary, he would simply

shout 'MISS!'... done in a way that nobody could possibly have resented this bellowing... then one of us would go... It didn't matter who it was. Sometimes he called me 'Joan'... but my aunt, who was married to Air Marshal Charles Portal, was Joan Portal and I'm sure that was the connection... Sometimes he called me 'The Portal'.

When annoyed he could have an 'outburst of irritation, more than anger at some stupidity. It would always be something that I had done... that was different from the anger of some event that distressed him.' She describes his occasional 'temper like lightning and gone quickly. And a quiet smile was all [we] needed to feel appreciated, [he had] no grudges, no malice, hated vendettas and

witch hunts.'[10] This lack of malice, what Churchill called 'magnanimity' and 'good will', was so prominent a part of his personality
that historian Lewis Lehrman pairs Churchill's use of those words
in each volume of his Second World War memoirs with Abraham
Lincoln's 'malice towards none' inaugural address in his com-
parison of the two men – which would come as no surprise to
any of the secretaries who so often benefitted from Churchill's
instant forgiveness of major errors.[11] And John Maynard Keynes,
at times a fierce critic of Churchill, writes in his review of *The
World Crisis, 1916–1918*: 'He pursues no vendettas, discloses no
malice.'[12]

As Lord Chandos, a member of Churchill's cabinet in both of
his administrations, observed:

> One of his [Churchill's] most signal virtues is his magnanim-
> ity. He seldom carries forward from the ledger of today into
> tomorrow's account. It has befallen me more than once to have a
> sharp and almost bitter argument with him of an evening, when
> hard blows were exchanged, and to find him the next morning
> benign and smiling and affectionate. He regards the bouts with
> friends as dialectics and not personal contests... It is difficult to
> describe how endearing this can be.[13]

A sentiment with which all the secretaries would agree.

Portal, like those with whom Churchill worked all of his life, was
expected not only to satisfy his demands, but to anticipate them.
That required two things: reading his moods and being aware of
events in the political and social worlds in which he operated.

> There was a lot of tuning in to the way he way thinking... That
> is what he looked for in people who had the most to do with him,
> was the quickness of their reaction and their sensitivity to what
> he was thinking without putting it into words... I could sense

his moods very easily. For one thing they showed on his face. And, if one was aware of the events that were going on in the world, one [had to] read the papers carefully and listen to the news.

Like many of the other secretaries, Portal listened in on all his telephone conversations – something we now pretty much take for granted – but was unusual then. She had to be certain that a record was made of any arrangements for speaking engagements, meetings or social events and the like, and circulated to others if necessary. She explains 'that was part of the process of making the office work efficiently'. One of the calls she overheard was received by Churchill at Chartwell from the 'resident clerk at the Foreign Office. So I put the call through and listened in, as it was our duty to make a note. I remember the resident saying, "Your neighbour has flown." Churchill replied, "Thank you for letting me know. Do keep me in touch."'[14] The flown neighbour was Guy Burgess, who famously spied for the Soviets while working for the Foreign Office and the British Embassy in the United States.

Like many of the secretaries, Portal selected films for the Saturday night showings in Chartwell's lower-floor cinema – a 'magnificent cinema with a full-size screen', an amenity not available either at Hyde Park Gate or at Chequers; although at Chequers the Long Gallery could serve the purpose of a cinema, with the Ministry of Information providing some news and propaganda films.[15] Portal believes that Churchill might have got the idea of a home cinema from Roosevelt's White House, where one was installed in 1942. In any case, its installation at Chartwell was one of Alexander Korda's many gifts to Churchill.

Portal would call Korda's personal secretary to ask which films were available that week, and select one or, at times, send the list to Churchill, who 'would tick the one he wanted. I asked him to tick two, because sometimes one wasn't available'. Portal, it should be noted, alone among the secretaries from whom we have recollections, recalls that Churchill sometimes made his own choices.

But he more often delegated these choices to his secretaries, with an occasional nod to Mrs Churchill's preferences.

All staff, some twenty in all, were invited to see the film, including the outdoor garden workers, among them the German ex-POWs, as verified by Gemmell. Like so many other events in Churchill's life, film-watching remained an unchanging ritual. The Churchills entered last, after everyone else was seated. As they walked in, everyone rose to their feet and remained standing until the Churchills had seated themselves in the front-row armchairs, with cigar paraphernalia and whisky close by. Then Churchill would say, 'Let 'er roll.' At the end of the film, staff rose to their feet while the Churchills left the room. Quite 'feudal' in a way, thought Portal, but it was an Edwardian household, with a large indoor and outdoor staff, accustomed to an age of deference.

One film chosen was not a success: it ended with the death of a white horse, which so upset Churchill that he summoned Portal to his office and

> with tears still pouring down his face, an expression of his own distress. He said to me, 'You must be very cruel.' I was completely taken aback, because I had been very upset by this film, too. He said, 'You must never show me films with animals that are tortured in this manner'... He was very soft-hearted... almost sentimental... The cinema played a great part in his life and... he did have a fantasy world like all of us, but his was very open for everybody to intrude into. He was a schoolboy in some ways.

Churchill was more than a passive audience for films, and Alexander Korda more than a mere film-maker. Korda was a spy. He sent film crews to photograph strategic locations in Africa and Europe, spied on both the Germans and the Americans for the British during the Second World War, and acted as personal courier for Churchill on his own flights back and forth across the Atlantic. 'It's possible to suspect the hidden involvement of British intelligence at just about every stage in Alex's career in Britain.'[16]

And, thanks to Korda, Churchill was offered and accepted a contract to write a 'screenplay to mark George V's Silver Jubilee in 1935... accepting an offer of a £10,000 guarantee [worth just under £700,000 today] and 25 per cent of the film's net profits'.[17] Churchill wrote the screenplay, but the film was not to be, and Churchill's payment was reduced to £5,000. The ever-generous Korda, however, did pay him a retainer of £4,000 for work on other films (on *Lawrence of Arabia* and *Lord Kitchener*), but nothing came of these projects.*[18]

He also offered £50,000 for the film rights to *A History of the English-Speaking Peoples*, which was as yet unpublished. Churchill's 'hoped for break-through into the lucrative world of film... remained just that, a hope'.[19] But at least he did have the pleasure of meeting Korda's wife, Merle Oberon, described by Portal as 'a very beautiful young starlet'. As noted in Chapter 9, Churchill sought to amuse Oberon by turning somersaults for her in the Mediterranean, while vacationing in the South of France at La Capponcina, a villa at which she was also a guest.[20]

Churchill, Portal tells us, 'liked pretty girls', but adds 'just to look at'. Apparently, his interest might have extended, but only might have, extended beyond 'looking at'. If some interpretations of Colville's later oral history are to be believed, Churchill's interest extended beyond 'looking' in the case of the notoriously 'promiscuous' Doris Castlerosse.[21] Those interpretations have been disputed by most scholars. Andrew Roberts points out that this is a hearsay statement 'with nothing substantial to back them up, by a man who did not join Churchill's staff until some half a dozen years after the alleged event'.[22]

Colville also wrote of the women with whom Churchill chose to spend time: 'he was susceptible to good looks and to wit... and if, like Clare Boothe Luce, they were at the same time well-informed

---

* Churchill was diligent in suggestions about the screen play, and even wrote dialogue for it that found its way into the script of David Lean's *Lawrence of Arabia* twenty-five years later.

and highly geared, that was a gratefully received bonus.'[23] He must have been impressed with Luce when she arrived for a tea-time visit at Chartwell. He 'not only changed from his zip outfit to a sporty summer suit to honour her presence, [but he] was clearly fascinated by the succinct and amusing way she made her points.'[24] The author's father, who met Mrs Luce, praised her as 'having a mind like a steel trap'.

The Churchill family was always in and out of the houses, spending weekends at Chartwell or, later, at Chequers. Portal says she and the other secretaries all

> met [the Churchill children] constantly. [They had] difficult upbringings... They had a need when they came to visit their father to have his whole attention and they didn't always get it. Time with his family was one of the reasons that Churchill loved Chartwell. But it used to upset Churchill that Randolph would be so aggressive towards him during these family visits. We used to try to keep out of the way of these really horrendous rows.

Churchill loved his children deeply and 'had an enormous capacity for love... It wasn't always apparent to the children. I always thought Sarah was his favourite child.'

Churchill loved his grandchildren, too. They were 'a great joy' to him, says Snelling. She remembers Churchill feeding his grandson Rupert, who was born in 1962, 'bits and pieces of cucumber sandwiches... The greatest fun... They loved each other... Really enjoyed each other.'

Portal reports a similar affection for 'the marvellous child, little Winston', as he was called. Portal recalls putting him to bed one night in his monogrammed pyjamas when he had arrived alone, aged nine. She thought then 'Poor little boy, [but] he was very nice and Churchill was very proud of him.' Churchill was particularly close to Mary and Mary's children. 'Wherever Churchill went there was a family atmosphere. Sometimes it was explosive, but it was always there.'

Much of which she attributes to Mrs (later Lady) Churchill, of whom she was inordinately fond, and about whom she comments extensively, and with whom she 'had quite a lot to do'. Portal recalls:

> She was a very unselfish person... a very strong character... physically incredibly beautiful until the day she died... given to periods of depression. He worshipped her. They had this marvellous communication with each other and when she was in her down moods, he was deeply affected. He was quite selfish about this, in that his work still came first, but he would find time to see more of her to try to make it better for her, because she was very isolated. [Clemmie] 'was a wonderful hostess... so that everything was always very agreeable for him and she was doing this for him.

Her husband, it seems, was not much help. 'The problems of housekeeping on a comparatively small budget were something he never grasped... Clementine would do her best, for she did not wish to jeopardize her husband's political career or snub his friends; but she resented the late nights, the excessive consumption of brandy, the noise and the rowdiness which were inseparable from the garrulous evenings.'[25] Rather like her American counterpart, Eleanor Roosevelt, who had a decidedly negative reaction when Churchill introduced her husband to the joy of conversation long into the early hours.

There is only one recorded instance of Churchill being persuaded to abandon his lifelong procedure of beginning work long after midnight. And it was not spousal pressure that accomplished that feat, but Field Marshal Jan Smuts of South Africa, who on that historic evening was a guest of Churchill at Chequers, as were the chiefs of staff and Earl Mountbatten of Burma, commander of Britain's forces in Southeast Asia. After dinner and a film, at around 1 a.m., Churchill announced, 'Well, gentlemen, now we will start work.' Mountbatten tells what happened next:

Smuts whose usual bed time was 10 p.m., said, 'I am not going to start work. I am not going to be a party to killing your Chiefs of Staff... They have to be back in the office at 9 o'clock in the morning, ready for meetings at 9.30; you will still be lying in bed with a fat cigar, dictating to your secretary. They will have to work all morning and all afternoon; in the afternoon you have a siesta... You will kill them and I not going to be a party to that.'

With that, Smuts got up and went off to bed. There was a stunned silence for a minute or two; nobody spoke. After a long pause, Winston stood up and said, 'Well gentlemen, perhaps we'd better go to bed.'[26]

Portal continues her description of Mrs Churchill:

She was brilliant as a wife, as a political wife, and the wife of a great man, in that she never imposed herself on his work. She was exceptionally intelligent... She would give him advice and he would take her advice, but it was not a foregone conclusion... that he would show her his speeches or anything like that. He didn't do that. She never came up to interrupt his work, ever. For instance, this business of always having the secretaries around: a lot of wives would not like this at all. [But] she was sweet to us... She was always very very nice to me. I was always very businesslike with her because I felt slightly frightened of her... I had plenty to do. Hamblin was with her the whole time, then Gemmell... Lady Churchill was very fond of Gemmell.

Although Portal thought it not unusual to put little Winston to bed, dining with the family was a rare event, perhaps only at a lunch or a dinner at which there were too many men. And if dining alone with Churchill, 'he would dictate the whole way through the meal. One just took a mouthful whenever you could.' Portal and, indeed, all of the secretaries knew they were there to work, even when dining alone with Churchill. 'We made ourselves scarce when he wasn't working and I think he appreciated that without probably knowing it.' Time away also meant that the secretaries could get on with work left undone.

Jock Colville and his wife, on the other hand, did include Portal in Churchill's seventy-eighth birthday lunch at the Turf Club, along with Mrs Churchill and their daughter Mary. They were in the Ladies Annex, of course, as women were not allowed in the main club rooms.[27] This is a very rare occasion when a personal secretary was included in what was otherwise a family event and it says much about the family's feelings for young Jane Portal.

In February 1950, shortly after Portal joined Churchill's 'Secret Circle', Prime Minister Attlee called a general election. Portal, along with Sturdee, travelled all over the country in 'an almost presidential train... liv[ing] on the train... [We] were shunted into a siding at night.' Labour won. Attlee was returned as prime minister, although with a much-reduced majority, giving Churchill more time to finish his memoirs, which he hoped to do before the next election. Attlee would have to call another one soon in order to obtain a working majority in the Commons. Churchill decided to use the interval between the elections to work on his memoirs in France, and to take Portal along – her first trip abroad with him. Their first stop was Annecy in France near the Swiss border, but Churchill complained of the cold rain and decided to take the train to Venice. Portal 'told him that the train did not stop at Annecy and we would have to drive to Geneva [to connect to a train for Venice]. "Kindly remember that I am Winston Churchill. Tell the station master to stop the train."'[28] He did.

The change of venue was no minor logistical matter: as Marston, who was also along to help with the memoirs, pointed out, the party travelled with a huge amount of luggage (fifty-five suit-cases and trunks),[29] including all that was necessary for Portal and Marston to set up his office the moment they arrived at the hotel. Nor was the trip without incident. Churchill's then-valet, Norman McGowan, describes a nearly fatal accident as the train neared Venice. In his excitement to see Venice, Churchill 'leaned out of the train window, but suddenly the detective [standing next to Churchill] wrenched Mr Churchill backwards by the shoulder. A split second later a concrete pylon carrying the overhead wires for the electric train flashed past, only about a foot from the side of the train.' McGowan recalls that 'my Guv'nor's smiling comment was: "Anthony Eden nearly got a new job then, didn't he?"'[30]

Once in Venice, the usual routine for a Churchill overseas visit was established. The party took the entire top floor of the famed Excelsior Hotel, on the Lido, including the honeymoon suite. Time-Life was paying for everything, as it was in the magazine's interest to publish the serialization of Churchill's war memoirs as soon as possible, with Houghton Mifflin to publish in book form in the United States and Cassell in the United Kingdom. It was Portal's job to keep track of all the expenses, all the accounts for Time-Life, 'cash in and cash out', as she described it.[31]

So pressured was Churchill to finish the last volume of his *The Second World War* (he was so 'absolutely certain that he would win the [next] election', notes Portal) that he 'summoned' C. C. Wood to Venice for proof-reading, although he knew Wood was not well-liked by the staff. Churchill, heavily dependent on Wood for his proof-reading skills, declared, 'If none of you will be nice to him, I will lunch with him alone.' Portal puts that reaction down to the fact that Churchill 'was very much aware of people who were being persecuted by other people',[32] proof that he could be sensitive to the feelings of others – just not all of the time.

The team worked until late in the day, when Churchill's love of bathing in a warm sea became irresistible. 'There would be a parade going down to swim in the sea… All the crowds would gather on the beach of the Lido… He would go wading in… The photographers would crowd around and the detectives would beat them off.' However, McGowan regretted that no press photographer got a coloured photo of '[my] Guv'nor wearing a pair of fire-red bathing trunks'.[33]

Portal was invited to swim, but felt shy – she was just twenty – although they had 'a wonderful set of bathing huts' which could have been used to change into swimsuits. At that young age, she was also impressed that she was 'sitting in the restaurant looking at Errol Flynn… All the film world was there [at the 1951 Venice Film Festival][34]… It was a very glamorous period, but a serious period too, because [Churchill was on a deadline and under pressure to] finish the last volume of the war memoirs.' One of the advantages of Portal's trip to Venice was that she, and at times Marston, could go sightseeing with Mrs Churchill, but only if she or Marston had any time off. It is unlikely that Mrs Churchill would have interfered with the work schedule.

Another general election was indeed called for October 1951. Churchill, almost seventy-seven years old, campaigned in earnest, once again travelling the country in the 'almost presidential' train, with scores of staff. His love of campaigning, which had not yet deserted him, and his optimism about the outcome of the election had him in good humour, and produced still another play on someone's name. 'There was somebody called George Christ from Conservative Central Office… Mr Churchill used to say… "Ask Christ to come down."'[35]

Sturdee had organized the campaign office at 27 Hyde Park Gate, 'with charts of all the constituencies… We had a red pencil for the Labour Party and blue one for the Conservatives, and as the results came in we wrote them up on the charts, working throughout the night, as Churchill eagerly watched, but pretty sure of the outcome.' Despite the fact that Labour polled almost a quarter of a million more votes than the Conservatives and their National Liberal allies, and won the most votes any political party in Britain's history had ever won, the Conservative Party obtained a seventeen-seat majority. At Buckingham Palace Churchill agreed to form a government at the request of George VI, and Mrs Churchill and the secretarial staff scrambled to move Churchill back into Downing Street without any interruption in his working day, while he began to put 'his chickens in coops', as Gemmell recalls his description of putting together his cabinet.

Senior members came to Hyde Park Gate to accept their new

places, among them Portal's uncle Rab Butler, who became chancellor of the exchequer, second in rank only to the prime minister. Once the 'inner cabinet' was formed, Churchill wanted to go to Chartwell to get some rest and asked Mrs Churchill to open the house. Advisors opposed this move, saying he had not completed his government and that it could not be done from Chartwell. Churchill promised that he 'would take one of my young ladies down to Chartwell and as long as they have got the telephone numbers it's going to be perfectly simple. They will get them [prospective ministers] on the telephone and I will appoint them.' This caused pandemonium. However, Churchill got his way and as Portals notes, 'I went down with him to Chartwell.' Chartwell was not fully staffed, so the valet had to do the cooking for Churchill, Portal and the detectives. At least Churchill did not have to carry out the now-famous threat made earlier when Chartwell was closed and without staff but he longed to go there: 'I shall cook for myself. I can boil an egg. I have seen it done.'[36]

At Chartwell, Portal set up her own system for ministerial appointments, with three columns listing names of potential government ministers and pencilling in the decisions made by Churchill. But either because pressure on the new prime minister to return to London increased, or because he had all the rest he required, they drove back to London, where he 'moved into this totally different environment of Number 10 with the official machine working'. Churchill asked Jock Colville to return with him to Downing Street. Although Colville was reluctant to 'disrupt his domestic life', according to Portal, he agreed. 'We always gave up everything willingly and quite rightly.' The organizational structure was not characterized by rigid lines. Portal and Gilliatt were transferred to the government payroll – or at least Portal so recollects – and all Churchill's personal secretaries worked in tandem with the in-place civil-servant Garden Room Girls, who were the 'young, highly qualified, bright girls who looked after the prime minister and the Private Secretaries' needs'. The Head of the Garden Room Girls, Sheila Minto,[37] sorted the mail, sending the personal items upstairs, and leaving the bulk of it to be handled by her staff. Later, when needed, she would become a personal secretary to the prime minister.

The relations between the private and personal offices at Number 10 are complicated and can differ under every prime minister. But they were even more complex now because of Churchill's insatiable demand for secretarial help and his ability to work simultaneously on both personal and public matters. For our purposes all we need to know is that, as Portal explains, they

> did all his dictation and all his personal affairs [family and household matters, book contract negotiations, etc.]. We were the communication between the upstairs and the private office [downstairs]... [Occasionally] he would use a certain member of the Garden Room [staff]. All telephone calls would go through the private office. If they decided the prime minister should speak to whoever it was, then they would come to us and we would listen in and [a record of the call would be kept].

The goal was the same for everyone: keep the office running as smoothly and efficiently as possible in the nation's interest. That goal at times required one of the Garden Room Girls to take dictation from Churchill when the workload overwhelmed his personal secretaries. And unlike the ladies who worked with Churchill, that chore was not always greeted with joy. Jane Parsons, who worked as a Garden Room Girl from 1946 until 1981, complained that Churchill was incapable of considering the needs of others when the mood was upon him. She hated taking dictation in the car, the budgie flying around, smoke pouring from Churchill's cigar.[38] Fortunately for all, occasions when he called on Garden Room Girls, whose main job was taking down from the Private Secretaries, were rare. But Sheila Minto thrived under pressure, as many of Churchill's earlier secretaries had.

Churchill's decision to bring with him his own personal

secretaries, something done only once before (and by Churchill in his first premiership), reflected what Portal calls his 'habit of plucking people out and taking them with him'. This allowed him to recognize and reward talent, hard work and loyalty, and avoid accustoming himself to new faces, which he very much disliked doing.

The Churchills' flat was at the top of Number 10 Downing Street. It had a large 'beautiful room with windows overlooking Horse Guards Parade', and the young ladies had their office on that floor as well. He left 'his bedroom door open and we left our office door open, so all the had to do was to shout for us... "MISS!"'

In or out of office, at home at Chartwell or Chequers or at Downing Street, Churchill's work habits did not change. He remained in bed in the mornings, and met with staff and visitors, both British and foreign, in his bedroom, at the top of the house. Pets on the bed and Toby, his budgie, flying around the room, with an affection for Rab Butler's bald head,[39] and, 'there were times when a secretary would be taking dictation with Toby busy biting at her ear'.[40] Churchill would go downstairs for cabinet meetings or 'if there were a crisis'.

With Churchill ageing, it is no surprise that jockeying to succeed him was the order of the day. Portal, brought up as she had been in Rab Butler's very political house, was acutely aware of what was going on. Eden was 'certainly impatient' and Rab Butler, too, saw 'his chances' to become prime minister should Churchill resign. Butler, as chancellors of the exchequer do, was living at Number 11 Downing Street and could come and go frequently through the door that connected Numbers 10 and 11, so Portal saw her uncle regularly. She says that 'Churchill was very sweet about Rab being my uncle and he liked me to be around if Rab were there. And if Rab was making a big speech, he always said, "See that The Portal is in the chamber"... arranging that I sat in the Private Secretary's box in the House of Commons on the floor of the House'. Churchill at his thoughtful best.

Portal confirms that she, too, had to take down his many

speeches in the House verbatim and reconcile them for printing in Hansard.* That took precedence over almost all other work flowing from a prime minister whose capacity for work was undiminished by age, at least so far. Despite the help from the Garden Room Girls, Portal and her cohorts worked long hours. She was on duty at night and, if Churchill had an official dinner, she would leave her telephone number with the ever-helpful switchboard girls and return at once to Downing Street or Chequers, usually about four nights out of seven. If she were out with friends, the switchboard would call to say, 'Would Miss Portal please ring her mother as soon as possible?', indicating she was to go at once to Downing Street, but without revealing her destination. Sometimes the ever-helpful switchboard girls would hang up her work dresses, so that the Misses could quickly change into appropriate clothing before going into Churchill's presence to take down.

Portal and Gilliatt, who became the closest of friends,† a friendship that would last a lifetime, established a work system. Churchill alternated weekends at Chartwell and Chequers: Portal liked working at Chartwell, and Gilliatt preferred Chequers. But as always, such an arrangement was flexible, subject to change to meet the prime minister's needs. Chequers was used for large official parties for heads of state, as Chartwell was too small, so they worked wherever they were needed, whenever they were needed. There was a noticeable difference between working at Chartwell and Chequers: 'a different atmosphere at [Chequers]. We were more distant... We waited to be called for. We weren't just around the house. Each women's armed service took it in turn to cook and run Chequers, to be the valets... the WRNS in the war, [with] the WAFS looking after Chequers [when we were there].' Kathleen Hill had been appointed Curator there and had 'her own flat and we

---

*   Portal had taken down the text for the speech that Churchill gave at Westminster Hall on his eightieth birthday, 30 November 1954. When the actor Robert Hardy later recited that speech in 2015, Portal was in the audience.
†   Elizabeth Gilliatt is godmother to Portal's son, Justin Welby, now the Archbishop of Canterbury.

would have our meals with Mrs Hill [always referred to that way] in her flat, unless we were invited to join the official party which was not very often. If Rab came, I would often be included unless there were a lot of cabinet ministers there.'

When at Chequers, Portal worked in the secretaries' office in front of the house, overlooking the lawn. She recalls watching as Churchill and Attlee met – Attlee, who lived nearby, came over very often on a Sunday and they would go and sit: 'Two old men sitting in the garden and talk[ing] about the war. It was very private. A very special friendship.' Another frequent visitor, close friend and wartime colleague in the coalition government was Ernest Bevin – but that was a 'London friendship' and Churchill would often go to Bevin's chambers in the House for visits. The friendships that had been formed while working together during the war endured in the face of later partisan differences, and even survived Churchill's ill-conceived 'Gestapo' campaign broadcast (in which he had warned that Attlee's socialist government 'would have to fall back on some form of Gestapo').

One night, returning late from a dinner at The Other Club, with many of his oldest friends, accompanied by Portal, the driver hit and killed a badger in the road. Churchill at once had the car stopped, got out and took the badger in his arms, saying kindly as he patted it, 'Poor, poor, badger, it's not your fault.' Churchill had the badger skinned and stuffed and kept it over his bedside.[41] He was, of course, responsible for the death and stuffing of the badger. There is no other record of any interest in animals that were stuffed. In 1908, however, he seems to have been contacted by a firm selling

modelled heads of '1 Rhinoceros, 1 zebra, 1 warthog, 1 wildebeest... 1 Thomson's gazelle and the dressing of three zebra skins at a total cost of £32.7.0'... The firm, believing it had an order from Colonel Gordon Wilson on Churchill's behalf, asked, 'We have no instructions to put in hand a Rhinoceros Table. Do you wish us to do so?'

Churchill declined: reminders of dead animals upset him, as did the film Portal selected showing the death of a white horse.[42]

Mags Stenhouse had ordered that all the young ladies who travelled with the prime minister had to wear a hat; a 'great expenditure,' Portal recalls

> a great addition to my wardrobe. [It] would be stuffed on to my head in the hall... I felt thoroughly self-conscious about it. The prime minister would come down – he always walked very quickly and before you knew it he would be in the car and everybody would be waiting [for you] with the door open so you had to be on your toes... and [ready] with our notebooks, the pencil, the hat... Sometimes Rufus II... and a messenger carrying our enormous typewriter, in case the speech was not perfect. [Churchill] was a perfectionist.

Bullock, the chauffeur, was ready and would have the 'occasional' seat down and the typewriter put on top of the seat and I would sit... and type as we drove. It was appalling.'

This astonishing pace of his work sometimes left Churchill time for a bit of fun with those with whom he was working. When there were gaps in the typing, Churchill would burst out with doggerel, such as: 'She was the Admiral's daughter, but her bathing suit never got wet.'[43] President Roosevelt noticed this at their first meeting in 1941 at Placentia Bay. FDR cabled Churchill shortly after the conference: 'It's fun to be in the same decade with you.'

There were larks, too. In August 1950, Portal was sitting by Churchill's side as he painted in his Chartwell studio,* 'should he need anything', as she put it to me in a recent private conversation. Quite suddenly he said: 'I need a crocodile' for a painting of Marrakesh, on which he was working. Being inventive, Portal searched for and found a children's book in the house and traced a

---

* Chartwell is the only one of his houses in which he had a permanent studio and gallery.

picture of a crocodile from it. Since every communication between Churchill and his staff had to be memorialized, Portal typed a note saying: 'Mr Churchill. You wanted a picture of a crocodile. Will this one do?' and handed him the note and tracing.[44] Crocodiles, it seems, were often on Churchill's mind, perhaps a reminder of his East Africa trip in 1907, and he used them to illustrate a point. In 1940, referring to nations attempting to appease Hitler, he famously said: 'Each one hopes that if he feeds the crocodile enough, the crocodile will eat him last.'[45]

On 6 February 1952, a few months after Churchill became prime minister for the second time, George VI died, having suffered from emphysema and a lung removal for a cancerous tumour. Churchill had worked closely with the king, as his wartime prime minister from 1940 to 1945, and now once again as prime minister. Although the king's death was not unexpected, it was a shock to his daughter and heir, the twenty-six-year-old Elizabeth, who at the time was on a tour in Kenya. Churchill was deeply moved both by the death of his sovereign and by a realization of the tremendous burden the young woman faced. He drove to the airport to greet Elizabeth and her husband Philip on their arrival from Kenya,[46] taking Portal in the car with him, so that he could dictate his speech on the death of the king, which was scheduled to be broadcast that afternoon. He said, 'I could do the broadcast. I know what I want to say, but I need to work at it very, very particularly. And so I would dictate in the car because I would have <u>peace</u> there.' Portal goes on to recall:

No such things as car telephones then. And so he dictated the speech between Downing Street and Heathrow and it just came straight out. As he was sitting in the car dictating, the tears were pouring down his face and he was heaving with sobs... he was weeping at his own words and his own thoughts. [Churchill] was very moved, very obviously deeply moved... because he had this historical feeling [about] events.

As Churchill put it in his very moving BBC broadcast: 'The king walked with death, as if death were a companion, an acquaintance, whom he recognized and did not fear. In the end, death came as a friend.'

At the airport, Portal and Evelyn Shuckburgh, Eden's Principal Private Secretary, hid themselves behind another plane so they could witness this historic event, this passing of an era. She could see the entire cabinet, waiting on the tarmac for the plane to land with the prime minister closest to the bottom of the gangway.

Portal recalls that Princess Elizabeth shook hands with each member of the cabinet. Churchill continued to work on the broadcast when they arrived back at Downing Street. At one point, Colville and the other Principal Private Secretary, David Pitblado, asked her if he had finalized the speech, as they were eager to get broadcast mechanisms set up. She answered, 'No, he had not, which was a bit naughty of me... I was trying to protect him... They must let him be for a time... He had a rest and the broadcast was marvellous.' She took down the speech as delivered on the night of 7 February 1952 and had stayed up all night typing it for the permanent records.

The speech done, Churchill turned his attention to the relatively young queen-to-be. Portal speculates that Churchill was thinking of Lord Melbourne, who in the early nineteenth century mentored Queen Victoria when she was still a teenager.[47]

> Churchill usually had a great sense of history [that came] into everything he did. [Churchill] did teach her [Elizabeth], educate her and protect her and serve her and he was a deeply fond of her... he used to come back from his weekly Tuesday audiences and say, 'She is so lovely, so beautiful.' Apart from being true, it was also a romance, just part of his own character. But I think she must have felt the greatest dependence and affection for him.

Sixteen months later, on 2 June 1953, Elizabeth was crowned queen, an event to which Churchill had 'looked forward... enormously,' but about which he was greatly concerned. So concerned, says Portal, that 'he asked his staff to sleep that night at Downing Street... We all had to sleep on camp beds' to be ready for the ceremony and to be sure that they would not be delayed by traffic disruptions. One of his concerns was that the decision to televise the event – a decision he had unsuccessfully opposed – would add to the stress on the queen. Another was that the preparations 'took up a lot of time. [He] was slightly impatient about all the events that [were] involved.' So concerned was he about being diverted from foreign policy and other matters, that 'when the day came [he was] almost reluctant to go. But go he did, in a closed, two-horse carriage with Clementine Churchill at his side.'[48] After the coronation, Churchill unexpectedly did not finish the whole procession in his state coach, directing them to turn off to Downing Street, saying, 'the government must go on and he must read the foreign telegrams and carry on' with his search for peace with the Soviets.

'He had wanted the cabinet to allow him to visit Stalin and they would not let him. Anthony [Eden] in particular would not let him go.' Churchill 'felt it was his last deed in his life to bring about world peace. He felt he could get through to him [Stalin]. And everybody told him he could not.' Stalin's death, in March, a few months before the coronation, increased Churchill's eagerness to meet with the Russians, to see if he could strike some sort of deal with Uncle Joe's successor, Nikita Khrushchev. That was not to be.

After the coronation, Portal describes the seventy-nine-year-old Churchill as 'totally exhausted'. Two weeks later, while still at dinner in Downing Street for the Italian prime minister, Churchill had a serious stroke. Portal was not on duty that night, but when she arrived at Number 10 at 8 a.m. the next morning she was told the prime minister was not well. In the office, 'Lord Moran, Colville, the Soames and, of course, Mrs Churchill were all trying to persuade the PM not to take a cabinet meeting that morning, and Prime Minister's Question Time in the House that afternoon.' Churchill insisted on chairing the cabinet, but agreed not to attend the House. Dr Russell Brain, Churchill's neurologist, was summoned and he 'insisted' that Churchill go to Chartwell for a complete rest.

Not surprisingly, the accounts of Churchill's secretaries vary. Portal went down to Chartwell in the car behind his, because 'he said he was not going to work in the car and that was very significant'. But Gilliatt, the senior young lady, did accompany the prime minister in the first car, and she says the prime minister was in no condition to work: 'He was walking unsteadily. Oh! Things weren't at all good.' Gilliatt reports that Churchill's speech was slurred, and Portal noticed that 'he had to be helped up the two steps that go up to [the house at] Chartwell.' In the days that followed, neither seems to have been in constant contact with a very ill Churchill, as Portal says that she and Gilliatt 'were kept away'. Portal believes the more serious stroke occurred that night at Chartwell, as 'he could not get out of bed'. Colville and the family then decided 'that the queen should be informed and that the prime minister wished to continue in office, but he must have a complete rest, providing the queen agreed, [an agreement] made through her private secretary Sir Alan Lascelles that he should continue.' At Colville's suggestion, the press barons agreed among themselves to keep the knowledge of the seriousness of his illness away from the public, a decision still much debated today. Bulletins were issued saying simply the prime minister needs a complete rest, and freeing the press to cover the Princess Margaret–Peter Townsend story.

The crisis was compounded by the fact that Foreign Secretary Eden was in America being treated for a serious ailment. That left the chancellor of the exchequer, Portal's uncle Rab Butler, in charge. His niece, who stayed at Chartwell for three months, at one point told him that Churchill was 'probably going to die, he's very ill.' Portal's concern was understandable, given the seriousness of the stroke and its rather horrifying symptoms. But she did not reckon with what Colville described as her boss's 'recuperative powers, both physical and mental, [which] invariably outstrip all expectations and after a week he began rapidly to improve, although his powers of concentration appeared slight.'[49] Portal adds

I don't believe he thought he was going to die or else it was masked
by an absolute determination to live… We fixed up a special desk
for him to be able to put a book on, because he could not move
his left side… He just sat in bed totally immersed in the whole of
the political novels of Trollope.* If he got tired one of us would
spend a half an hour and turn pages for him. He would still say
has anything come in. [I would] take the [ministerial] box up and
show him a few things. But really work was not coming through.
In fact, Rab was doing the work… Somehow we got through the
months… Miss Gilliatt and I were there to run the office[50]… The
use of his limbs came back really remarkably quickly. He had a
limp… a slight slur… He had physical therapy.

In early September Churchill 'had to – I say had to, because he
really wasn't up to it – he went to stay at Balmoral to visit the
queen… [It] tired him.' It apparently took more than a stroke to
force Churchill to cancel this regularly scheduled visit by every
one of her prime ministers.

By mid-September Portal says he was well enough to travel to
Lord Beaverbrook's villa, La Capponcina, taking her, the Soameses
and the Colvilles. As Churchill wrote to the queen in his thank-you
letter for the Balmoral stay: 'I am now here in warm sunshine and
delightful villa built by the dressmaker, Molyneux… I shall not
often leave the garden where I am installing my painting tackle,
and reading for the first time (!) Coningsby [a political novel by
Disraeli, published in 1844].'[51]

As the guests departed, Portal found herself alone with Churchill, and her record of that experience may be one of the most
revealing ever recorded about Churchill the man, and therefore
worth extended citation here.

INTERVIEWER: You were really his companion.

---

* The Palliser novels by Anthony Trollope.

PORTAL: Yes. One never felt as if one was a companion. I never felt like... because what I felt was that I was actually employed by him. The family was the companions. I was always very much aware of this – that we were there to do our job, and this made no difference to the emotional feeling of loyalty and affection – deep, deep affection. But there was a border line that you didn't cross, because it wouldn't have been right and it wouldn't have been welcome... We would work through meals or just sit in silence. There would never be any question of conversation with... Churchill. I never had a conversation with him the whole of the time I worked with him. He wasn't interested in me and I didn't expect him to be. I would have been horrified if he had been, I think. It was not the way the relationship existed. And I'm sure that was the same for all of us... He wanted his own privacy in his own world.

I always knew that he was very fond of me, because his face used to light up and his face was always full of expression, and if he didn't like somebody it was perfectly obvious and if he did it was perfectly obvious.

After returning to London in late September, Churchill approved the final preface to the final volume of his war memoirs, a volume he titled *Triumph and Tragedy*, because 'the overwhelming victory of the Grand Alliance has failed so far to bring general peace to our anxious world'.[52] A peace that Churchill would continue to pursue for the remainder of his working life.

Most important, he was back at work, determined to finish *A History of the English-Speaking Peoples*, which he had been contracted for in late 1932, to be completed by 1939. Hitler upset that schedule, and in late 1953, more than two decades after the original contract had been signed, the seventy-nine-year-old author began thinking about how to organize the research and writing for *A History of the English-Speaking Peoples* by reading the sections he had already drafted. He also continued working on the speech he was scheduled to deliver at the Conservative Party Conference in

Margate in mid-October. Churchill had written to Moran from the South of France: 'Everything depends on whether I can face October 10 [the Margate speech]. I could not walk up the floor of the House of Commons at present. You must help me, Charles.'[53] And Portal had written to her uncle Rab: 'The PM has been in the depths of depression. He broods continually whether to give up or not... He is preparing a speech for Margate but wonders how long he can be on his pins to deliver it.'[54]

Churchill knew that Eden – not in the best of health himself – Butler and others eager for him to step down, would be watching for any sign of physical or mental weakness. When the time arrived for the speech, Portal travelled to Margate to 'prepare the living quarters and the practical arrangements... We rented a house in Margate... seeing that all the telephones were put in and all [the] scramblers' that allowed conversations to be conducted in complete secrecy.[55] Churchill spoke, standing on those 'pins' for fifty minutes, and, says Portal, agreeing with the clear majority of the audience,[56] it was an 'enormous success... There was a tremendous feeling of euphoria afterwards that he'd made it, and he himself was so relieved. He felt that nobody had the right then to pressure him to go,' Portal recalls. 'Very few men can have got over such a paralysis in so lion-hearted a manner,' wrote Butler.[57]

After they returned to London, a black cat was found on the front steps of Downing Street. '"It has brought me luck," [Churchill] said, stroking the purring cat. "It shall be called Margate. Rufus II... has gone to bed in a sulk"... Churchill later reported to his wife "Rufus is becoming gradually reconciled. Generally, the domestic situation is tranquil."'[58] Whichever secretary typed that letter must have smiled knowingly, or ruefully if she was not as enthusiastic about caring for Churchill's pets as he was.

The potential threat of a Margate fiasco having been successfully met, and having been awarded the prestigious honour, the Order of the Garter, by the queen, Sir Winston, as he had become, turned to resurrecting the Bermuda meeting with President Eisenhower, which had been cancelled when he had a stroke. Because of

Churchill's amazing recovery, the meeting was now reset, this time for December 1953, shortly after his seventy-ninth birthday. Colville, Pitblado and Eden were on the seventeen-hour flight, with only two stops, as was Portal, the lone personal secretary to make the trip, but several Garden Room Girls, as well as some Foreign Office girls, were in Bermuda to assist the Principal Private Secretaries. Portal (perhaps unaware that Churchill had selected Bermuda in part because he thought its golf course would be an added attraction for Eisenhower) explains that Bermuda was chosen because of the good weather at that time of the year and very good hotels and facilities. Churchill may also have had in mind showing off a British colony at its best. There were no cars on the island, but two had been sent ahead for Churchill's use. 'Nothing of importance happened… just an ordinary normal summit. What he really wanted was to be able to see and talk with Eisenhower to whom he was absolutely devoted and [they] had a great friendship because of the war… They were close friends, real friends.'

Portal was there for about a week of glorious weather with 'midnight bathing parties… I had a good time. Churchill was still working away… he could not stop this dictating.' One midnight, as she was on the beach bathing with others, 'a message came down that that the prime minister wished to work and would I kindly go back at once. I'd been swimming and I went back to the hotel with my hair dripping down my neck, into his bedroom where he was dictating telegrams to Lord Moran [his doctor, who] looked rather irritated, naturally.' The doctor may have been good at some things, but taking down was not his job. Another account says that the prime minister was trying to dictate to Anthony Eden, who also resented it. Portal goes on: 'Churchill looked up at me in that typical way that I have such a vivid memory of, this rotund lovely complexioned face that was totally unlined, with blue eyes and the petulant look that said, "Where have you been? You look like a drowned rat."' Eden's Private Secretary said that 'poor Jane Portal took the brunt of it [abandoning Churchill]. The old boy kept repeating, "You left me all alone."'[59]

'It was a wonderful experience for me,' Portal says, 'for the prime minister it was a journey to see an old friend.' However, she notes that 'nothing was achieved at that summit'. Bermuda might not have achieved anything, but Churchill did not give up and returned to Washington in June 1954, the third visit of his peacetime premiership. Portal was along on all these trips, and on this one travelled with him in the Stratocruiser, which had been nicknamed 'Canopus',* on a nine-hour flight with one stop at Gander. Colville describes the purpose of this trip 'was to convince the President that we must cooperate more fruitfully in the atomic and hydrogen sphere and that we, the Americans and British, must go and talk to the Russians in an effort to avert war.'[60] To no avail.

In Washington, Portal stayed in a hotel, but set up her office within the White House, next to Churchill's bedroom, and

did all work there... a great deal of very hard work. Wandering around the White House and feeling that it was very much like being at Chequers, that you could go anywhere, walk out a door and there would be the President... all very relaxed... and we had the cinema... and I think Churchill felt he had achieved something at that conference.

He then proceeded to New York to visit his old friend, financier Bernard Baruch, while Portal 'was allowed to come back [to Britain] for personal reasons, in that my sister was getting married and I could come back by air'. Which meant that when Churchill decided to return home on the *Queen Elizabeth* 'to give him a rest', Gilliatt was on board, so he could continue, as he always did, to dictate. It would have been impossible for Churchill to guess the storm he would confront some months after returning home.

In September 1954 the House of Commons had voted that a fitting tribute and gift on Churchill's eightieth birthday in November

---

* The name of a star, as well as a navigator for King Menelaus of Sparta during the Trojan War.

1954 would be a portrait. Portal says that Aneurin Bevan's wife
Jennie Lee, a committed socialist and MP, knew and recommended
the painter Graham Sutherland. Churchill 'agreed to it [the sittings]
reluctantly, as he had seen the Beaverbrook portrait [by Sutherland
and thought it] an awful portrait'. Perhaps he was encouraged to
agree by the fact that the art historian and broadcaster Sir Kenneth
Clark (Lord Clark) had also recommended Sutherland for this
portrait. In the event, Churchill posed in his own studio at Chartwell, and Sutherland came over from Saltwood, Clark's Norman
castle in Kent, where he was living as a guest. Painters usually
do not like to have their work seen in progress and Sutherland
allowed no one to see his painting, covering it and locking the
studio after each sitting. However, in October, Clark invited Lady
Churchill (as she had become) to view the picture. Lady Churchill,
Portal tells us, 'was very quiet and subdued when she returned
from Saltwood, but said nothing'.

Later, the prime minister obtained a black and white photograph
of the painting and showed it to Portal, asking her opinion. This
rather contradicts the image of a man who would never engage her
in conversation and with whom she did not deem it proper to have
one. Or perhaps the stroke had softened his personality or he had
a softness for Portal, because of her uncles. She

> said at once, 'I think it's terrible... how awful'... He said, 'My
> dear, I've got to accept it.' The others were called in to see the
> photograph, and the people who loved him said 'How terrible'...
> It made him look like a senile old man who had not done up his
> fly buttons... It was not the man I knew. [There was] something
> malevolent about it which I never felt about him. [There was] no
> malevolence... He was deeply wounded by it. To him it was an
> insult and to Lady Churchill it was a deep insult [too].

Portal says Churchill saw the painting

> as a similar rejection... to the blow of 1945... This was another

rejection, but worse... For an old man of eighty to leave this world on that note [for] posterity... It's cruel. And he minded. He was upset about it, and we didn't want him to be upset about anything. I think that is another way that we should have noticed his age... We didn't like him being upset about things. We protected him from anything that was going to upset him. We kept messages from him.

There was much discussion as to whether he could or should turn it down, but he finally agreed to accept the portrait, and gave 'an extremely amusing speech about it'. And we now know from Grace Hamblin's history what happened to the painting: it was secretly destroyed and never again discussed within the family (see Chapter 2).

In March 1955 Churchill told Portal he would resign on 5 April and then go on a private holiday. When he returned, he would start work at once and asked Portal to go to the muniment room at Chartwell and get all his manuscripts – and A. J. P. Taylor's notes – so that he could complete *A History of the English-Speaking Peoples*. She found the yellowing pages, which he had begun in the 1930s, and, handing them to him, he said:

> 'I am going to get to work straightaway on writing... and will you come?' No, he would never have said 'Will you come?'... He said, 'I want you to come.' I believe they were going to take a villa in Crete and have a period there for him to adjust to retirement. I believe they did go, but in early April I left because I got married.

In fact, the villa was in Syracuse in Sicily, not Crete.

Portal left, but not before one last, arduous task. On 1 March Churchill delivered what he knew would be his last major speech in the Commons, introducing the annual Defence White Paper. In it, he would announce Britain's plans to build its own hydrogen bomb. It was fifty-four years after he had first spoken there.[61] According to Portal, he spent a total of twenty hours preparing the speech and 'Dictated it all by himself.'[62] Portal's memories of Churchill are how 'exhilarating, romantic, expansive, humane and generous a person he was'.

In 1975 Portal married Charles Williams, Baron Williams of Elvel. Lord and Lady Williams live in London and until recently Portal had been the Secretary to The Other Club, which, founded in 1911, continues to meet.

11

Doreen Pugh

'After the announcement in May 1963 that he would not contest the approaching election, the last stimulus was taken from his life.'

Doreen Pugh, oral history

'it was a cruel fate which ordained that Churchill should survive till the age of ninety.'

Anthony Storr[1]

APRIL 1955 WAS not the happiest of times for Churchill. He had just resigned as prime minister. He and Mrs Churchill were on holiday in Syracuse, Sicily, when a general election was called for May, requiring their immediate return to Britain so that Churchill could once again defend his seat in the House of Commons. He probably had mixed feelings about that interruption to their trip. He had found the Greek ruins interesting and a worthy subject for his paintbrush. In the long letter to the queen, cited earlier (see Chapter 7), he wrote, 'Our hotel rises out of the sinister quarries in which six thousand Athenian prisoners of war toiled and slaved to death in 413 BC... [I am painting] a picture of a cavern's mouth near the listening gallery whose echoes brought secrets to the ears of Dionysius.'[2]

On the other hand, the weather was vile, a condition he always found disagreeable when on a painting trip. On Churchill's return, he met with two new secretaries that Jo Sturdee had interviewed and provisionally hired as one-month temporaries to help handle the mountain of work that still descended on his office. One was Doreen Pugh, who had returned to Britain from her travels in Australia and needed to find work. She was later described as 'short, rather petite, brunette'.[3] She registered with Mrs Hoster's agency. She was then asked to interview with Jo Sturdee in her Mayfair office, mainly because 'they thought I knew about pressure and speed and that sort of thing,' as she had worked for Reuters. Because the electricity had failed in the office, it was too dark for Pugh and Sturdee to see each other clearly, but they persisted and the interview was successfully concluded. Sturdee sent Pugh off to the Hyde Park Hotel where Sir Winston (as he had by then become) was 'camping' until the house at 28 Hyde Park Gate could be re-established. The secretaries worked next door at 27 Hyde Park Gate, now set up as an 'airy, agreeable and accessible' office after it was found that Number 28 was not large enough to accommodate Churchill's office and staff. Anthony Montague Browne, his Private Secretary, would also have his office at Number 27, next door to the new secretaries' office.[4]

Interviewed at the same time was another woman who would become a Churchill secretary, Gillian Maturin, who had come over from New Zealand and was temporarily cooking in Scotland for the Queen Mother. Churchill had lost most of his staff after his resignation as prime minister. As Pugh recalls: 'Jane Portal had left to get married and Liz Gilliatt was tired out, so they thought they'd better get someone in for a month' to cope with the increase in correspondence since the resignation. Both were hired, but on a one-month temporary basis. In the event, Maturin stayed with Churchill for a little more than three years, while Pugh remained with him until his death some ten years later.

Both Pugh and Maturin survived the usual interview process, which was either carelessly perfunctory or a mere formality after Sturdee approved of the applicants. Pugh was so nervous at the prospect of being interviewed by Churchill that her hands were shaking as she was taken up to meet the former prime minister in 'this great bed'. Her first impression of him, she recalls, despite her nervousness at being interviewed by a man who by then was widely recognized as one of the all-time greatest statesmen, was of his 'beautiful skin... lovely skin and a lovely expression. It was sort of sweet really. And lovely hands,' as so many others have noticed.

Pugh's later recollection, perhaps having heard from Gilliatt who had been on this trip with the Churchills, is that the Syracuse holiday wasn't 'at all happy or successful', and she sympathized with his unhappiness. After all, 'he had just given up being Prime [sic]... and it was an ominous sort of place I think, awful ruins'. This characterization of the Greek ruins was more likely hers than his. Pugh could not have known that an important success of the Syracuse trip was the idea for Churchill College, planned and mostly financed with funds raised by Jock Colville and Lord Cherwell.

In typical Churchill fashion, she and Maturin, both presumably having survived the Churchill 'searching gaze' described by John Martin when he was interviewed some fifteen years earlier (see Chapter 6), started work the next morning. 'Incredible, really! And we rolled off to Chartwell with him and the detectives'. No vetting beyond the Sturdee interview, no security protocols – at least none are recorded.

Because Chartwell was not yet fully open, they all 'camped together in the cottage [in the grounds of Chartwell] and [Maturin] cooked his breakfast'. Like Maturin, Pugh did not distinguish between ordinary secretarial work and personal chores. Like all the other Churchill staffers, she interpreted her job to include non-election work: she fretted over 'a tank of tropical fish and he [Churchill] was very concerned that the right thing happen to them and it was arranged that they should go to the zoo.' When the chauffeur or detective was not available, she drove him around the grounds of Chartwell over 'tracks to visit his pig farm'. Churchill slotted in his hobbies, while Pugh typed his speeches for the election and worked on canvassing and other schedules. An unusual overlap of political and personal work. 'The pleasures of Chartwell' were myriad.

Pugh might have been nervous at first, but 'after about a week I wasn't frightened anymore and I went on and on in my diary*… saying how endearing and funny and sweet he was.' At the same time, she understood how 'shattering it was for him to retire'.[5] Hers was much the same reaction as the other personal secretaries: fear gave way to respect, and eventually, as these women worked closely with him, they learned to adore Churchill the man.

Pugh vividly recalls two features of her experience working with Churchill: the enduring loyalty of former secretaries, and how hard everyone worked to keep up with the relentless pace of her boss. 'How kind everybody was, the old secretaries who came back and were <u>always</u> on the end of the phone. How kind they were.' The former secretaries in a very real sense remained part of the team of women that made it possible for Churchill to work as productively as he did. That is surely a testimonial to the enduring loyalty his kindness elicited from an often-overworked staff. Listening to the

---

*   What Pugh called her 'little handbag diary', which she kept in spite of the rules.

oral histories these women left suggests that they very much liked being called in to help, because even after retirement most of them felt close to – and responsible for – Churchill and his work, which they knew from their own experience to be so important to him and the nation.

As for the hard work, 'I think I'd also forgotten how terribly <u>hard</u> we worked, actually. We worked very long hours because there was a terrific backlog.' This is no surprise, since Maturin and Pugh – both new, both presumably temporary – constituted almost the entire secretarial staff. At Chartwell she worked on all aspects of the 1955 election, yet more unusual overlap. Churchill was to canvass in his constituency – he was running for re-election in Woodford – and there were constituency visits to be coordinated with the police, detectives and local politicians. This was his nineteenth contest and, as he wrote to Bernard Baruch, 'I cannot say it is either a novelty or a pleasure.'⁶ He was eighty years old and beginning to consider how to finish the volumes of *A History of the English-Speaking Peoples*.

And there were the speeches. Churchill dictated a 'large portion of it himself… a lot of dictating, and that was quite nerve-wracking very quickly learning to hear it and get it and to spell… It was lovely learning [to type] speech notes… which I didn't find difficult, because it was just like journalese… those sorts of shortenings they used in newspaper writing' when she worked at Reuters, proving that Sturdee was wise to see prior work experience as an important qualification for the secretarial job for which Pugh was applying. Pugh took down the dictation in shorthand, then typed it up as a draft, which Churchill edited, returning it to the secretaries, who converted it into Churchill's famous 'psalm' format, 'based on how we heard him speaking, and he never seemed to object'.⁷ Churchill found it easier to memorize from that format and then deliver his speeches, allowing him to put his emphases in the right places. 'And all the time there was a lot of other work to do and a lot of catching up and mountains of things which wanted attention.'

There was also the problems of becoming accustomed to working in a speeding car and of the clunky, silent typewriter, but these difficulties had some rewards. Pugh recalled with fondness a car trip to Chequers to discuss the Suez crisis with Anthony Eden, then prime minister. Churchill had notes with him, but wanted to dictate additional points in the car, so he ordered Pugh to bring the typewriter. It was a high-speed journey, probably with a police escort. She said: 'He dictated and I could not type with the car going along… It was a huge, heavy typewriter. [But] he was being terribly helpful in helping me turn the paper and handing me pencils and rubbers and being very sweet and funny.' They stopped in a lay-by for a few minutes to allow her to finish the notes. 'When we arrived, Eden came racing down the steps to greet him. Sir Winston had all the papers clutched in his hand. He said: <u>she typed this</u>. Eden went on about something and not really paying much attention. [Churchill repeated] <u>She typed it in the car!</u> It was awfully sweet.' Churchill was proud of her efforts and let her – and Eden – know it.

The month went by and these two 'temporary' secretaries stayed in place. No one asked them to stay, it was simply assumed they would stay and, of course, work as hard as ever. Pugh recollects that 'there was a <u>terrific</u> lot going on and after the election he was seeing ever so many people… people to meet with and going out to dinners… He was going all the time… being given various freedoms and honours… They all needed a speech from him.' When Churchill needed to dictate, he would call out '"Miss Um-Uh" or "MISS", said loud enough it should bring you.' 'MISS' was his traditional summons for a shorthand/typist/secretary to come to him, dictation pad and pencil at the ready. He had no need to abandon the lifetime experience of having his commands obeyed: to Churchill, that was the natural order of things, and somehow he had no need to persuade his staff of that fact. I attribute this to the excitement of the job, his treatment of those who laboured on his behalf, and the structure of society at the time.

Pugh believes he would never have used her Christian name, as he was from 'a past age… and treated everyone with terrific respect... tremendously polite'. Mrs Churchill, on the other hand, always called the secretaries by their Christian names and was deeply interested in their private lives, 'very keen on romance'. But, Pugh thought, it would never have 'crossed his mind that we had any other lives. But he wasn't being selfish, it was just the way he operated.' On the other hand, Mrs Churchill, as she aged, lost much of her comfort in her husband's company, and sought friendships with some of the female personal secretaries, as she trusted their discretion and their shared histories. Pugh often lunched with her from 'one to two-thirty, exactly as she got tired'.[8]

Churchill resumed the work on *A History of the English-Speaking Peoples* that he had laid aside during the war, and the several volumes of which would be published between 1956 and 1958. These volumes were a large part of Pugh's workload and she thought of it as 'very enjoyable'. He had received the first cheque for £500 from Cassell, the publishers, in September 1934, some twenty-two years and one world war earlier.[9,10]

That workload began early in the morning with sorting the mail before Churchill rang for her. Pugh then took the mail up to him in bed and put it on 'a little rickety round table' with two files on it: one marked 'To See' and the other 'To Sign'. The Private Secretary on duty also marked some letters 'GP' for 'General Public'. Among them were 'mad letters... certain mad people that wrote every day. Because I think great people attract certain regular maddies. We got very few obscene ones, I'm happy to say.' Pugh reports that the 'mad letters' were turned over to Monica Graham, a friend of Lettice Marston's, perhaps for transmission to the security services. At times the Private Secretary on duty would have sorted the mail, putting the most important items on top, but Pugh quickly learned what Churchill should see immediately, or in some instances not at all. He would go through the mail and 'mark them all, dictate on them or whatever'. She also brought him the engagement cards for that day, showing his appointments, often filled in in pen by different hands, making it hard to make changes or additions.

After working in bed all morning and getting up in time for lunch, Churchill would 'go to the House if it was midweek, straight after lunch, smartly' – this is after his resignation as prime minister. It was at this time, after his re-election to the House at the age of eighty, that Pugh began to notice a certain decline both in his capacity to work and in the demands made upon him, a decline she felt was very gradual. The secretaries continued to treat him as they had in the past, but 'towards the end of the day when there wasn't so much [work or news] he'd ring the bell and say, "Is there anything?" You'd hope <u>desperately</u> that there was something.'

His workload expanded significantly around his eightieth birthday in late November. Even out of office, the former prime minister received 'hundreds and hundreds of telegrams wishing him a happy birthday and he sent hundreds of replies… Every single one he saw' and replied to. Christmas was very busy as well, although Lady Churchill and her staff did all the buying and present-giving, including the gifts for his female secretaries.

The spurt in late-life activity for both Sir Winston and Lady Churchill naturally translated into a heavy, feverish workload for the secretaries. This led to the usual priority: work comes first. At 'that first Christmas, he let us go off, I think, it was 8 p.m., the pair of us', on Christmas Eve. Where work was concerned he could be less considerate. Doreen Pugh told Sir Martin Gilbert that 'Sir Winston never quite understood why he had to let us off on that day!' On the other hand, he did give each of the two secretaries £5 (about £130 in today's money).* In fact, Churchill was not particularly insensitive to the needs of his staff at Christmas. But his need to work trumped that sensitivity. He was always torn between his desire to treat his secretaries with consideration and the unrelieved drive to get still more work done. As Pugh puts it, days and time

---

* 'The secretaries kept extensive detailed lists of the Churchills' Christmas gifts to family, staff and friends. Gifts included 'carolina ducks, pâté de foie gras, silk cravat, silk nylons, chicken and shawl' and several dolls presumably for staff's children. Also many gifts of wines, port and champagnes.' CHUR 2/387/106

off were 'a sad story... about the first two years we got a fortnight, but our holidays were taxing, because the other person had to work through it for you.'

Even at this late time of his life, in Churchill's office everything was still put in writing, including a report by Pugh that Maturin would miss a few days because of the flu, acknowledged by him with his initials. Record-keeping in those days was considered necessary to orderly government, and Churchill as prime minister had taken the writing of official memoranda seeking 'Action This Day' to a high art. As he directed the War Cabinet Secretariat: 'Let it be clearly understood that all directions emanating from me are made in writing, or should be immediately afterwards confirmed in writing, and that I do not accept any responsibility for matters relating to national defence on which I am alleged to have given decisions unless they are recorded in writing.'[11] And Clementine once advised General Spears that her husband 'often does not listen or does not hear if he is thinking of something else. But he will always consider a paper carefully in all its implications. He never forgets anything he sees in writing.'[12] This directive is one reason – and an important one – why the secretaries found themselves struggling to keep up with Churchill's flow of communications to his staff and government departments. This insistence by the prime minister was in sharp contrast to the policy of his American ally. It was 'typical of Roosevelt's meetings [that] no one kept minutes for the afternoon session at the White House' preparing for the Casablanca meeting.[13]

Knowing the importance of a written communication, Pugh and Maturin decided to put before Churchill a written request for a three-week holiday. They explained that three weeks were more restful than two, to which Churchill responded, with a grin, as Pugh remembers, 'I know that three weeks is better than two, but I can't spare you.' She had to accept his verdict, but the following year she and Maturin appealed to Lady Churchill, who took their side. This direct appeal to Lady Churchill was a bit unusual. Although the secretaries could always count on her for support, it was difficult for them to complain to her – they had to wait for her to notice their exhaustion or concern at workdays that generally ran from 9 a.m. to 11 p.m., and perhaps later if a film was shown. For Christmas time off, they acted a bit more boldly.

Knowing that they had his wife's support, the secretaries followed the procedure laid down by their boss and noted their three-week holiday dates in a written memo to him. 'Any message you wanted to get over to him, it was always in writing. It was just the way [he] always operated.' Because 'he wasn't very good at figures and he probably didn't quite understand, so he said, "Yes, that's all right," and he always signed things to affirm it… so after that we had our three weeks.'*

The routine of correspondence, visits to the House, speeches and other chores was followed by dinners, many of which I have described elsewhere.[14] At Chartwell, he no longer had his long-time cook, the fabled Mrs Landemare, who had retired. But Pugh recalls that a gardener's wife cooked occasionally for the Churchills; and there was a butler, Rose, and a valet, Kirkwood. One night when Mrs Churchill was away, Grace Hamblin was organizing the dinner. Churchill wanted to know what was for dinner, as Lord Cherwell, a vegetarian, would be dining with him. Grace told Churchill she was serving stuffed marrow, to which Churchill replied, 'Oh, I don't think he'd like that.' Grace Hamblin explained that it was vegetable marrow. Churchill retorted, 'Well put, that!' Churchill once said:

> Almost all of the food faddists I have ever known, nut-eaters and the like, have died young after a period of senile decay. The British soldier is far more likely to be right than the scientists. All he cares about is beef. The way to lose the war is to try to force the British public into a diet of milk, oatmeal, potatoes, etc., washed down on gala occasions with a little lime juice.[15]

---

* Luckily for historians, most of the documents that Churchill wrote or saw are now filed by date and by person in the Churchill Archives.

Lord Cherwell was not the only one of his oldest friends to visit.
Two others, Brendan Bracken and Lord Beaverbrook, were frequent guests, as were Lord Ismay and Field Marshal Montgomery.

When Churchill's powers began to fail, Monty was not one to
desert… His mission was one of companionship and comfort.
His name appears twelve times in sequence in the visitor's book
at Chartwell. There the two old men would sit together, Churchill
mainly silent while Monty reminisced about the triumphs and
tragedies of days gone by. It was a radiant and peaceful evening.[16]

Pugh recalls that Montgomery 'was quite a difficult friend, but
he was a close friend… and there [visiting] a lot… one of the most
companionable friends… One of the ones that bothered to come at
the end of the day when things weren't so much fun.' The difficult
years of their relationship had not been forgotten only a few years
earlier, when Churchill, aged eighty-seven, was recovering from a
broken hip at Middlesex Hospital in London. Lady Churchill and
Montague Browne carefully protected the patient from visitors who
might upset him and cause a stroke. Because the two old warriors –
a term later used by Peter O'Toole to describe Churchill[17] – had had
'heated discussions', 'It was decided that Monty should not come.'
Nor should Randolph[18] – no surprise there. The field marshal did
send a large 'V' of red, white and blue flowers.[19]

Pugh notes that a young Ted Heath, who was disliked by the
Garden Room Girls, perhaps because he 'could not get on with
women [and] never knew what a single one of them was called',[20] was
a great admirer of Churchill and visited often. Intermingled with
men at the various dinners and lunches were many of the women
with whom Churchill had remained friendly for decades. Lady Juliet
Duff, Violet Bonham Carter and Lady Lytton were all old friends,
all welcome at Chartwell. Among the oldest of his friends, only
Montgomery, Eden, Moran and, with the exception of a few others,
his first love Pamela Lytton (née Plowden), outlived their host.

Dinners generally did not include the secretaries. Pugh

remembers that she rarely, if ever, had a meal with the family. At Hyde Park Gate the female secretaries had 'a little cooking place adjoining their office... We could cook lunch and make tea and coffee.' When working at Chartwell, life was a bit different, a bit slower and

> everything was done for us... tea was brought to us in the early days; we went out to lunch on weekdays into the village. At the weekend, everything was given to us on a tray in the office, and it was lovely. Dinner was <u>always</u> given to us in the office... Sometimes if there was a nice family gathering we might be invited. And sometimes if he was alone. But not very often.

Churchill didn't like to be alone, so he sometimes included Pugh in a lunch, expecting her to come to the table with pad and pencil. She recalls: 'He was a very good host... saying "Do have some more" and that sort of thing... always wanting us to do things, like "Do go and have a swim"... Although there was so much work to do, he still wanted you to have a good time.' She says they were spoiled – getting the best champagnes, for example. His personal and warm concern for these women – just not all the time – is echoed by all the others who worked for Churchill.

Churchill loved to watch a film after dinner, as we know, even when he was a wartime prime minister and the movie lengthened an already long work day. In later years, when Pugh was working for him, Churchill spent weekends at Chartwell, usually a long Friday afternoon to Monday afternoon, although that could change if the House were sitting. At Chartwell, he continued to watch films, sometimes asking the secretaries to order three or four for each weekend. 'Everybody, gardeners and all [attended the films]. And he was jolly upset if everybody wasn't here.' She recalls that 'Any film with Vivien Leigh was absolutely safe to be had again.[21] Anything about the American Civil War, if it was well made, was pretty safe. He liked a good western... anything in French... things about animals tended to be good [for him],' provided nothing bad happened to them, as we saw in Chapter 10.

The elaborate process for selecting films is best described by Catherine Snelling and others, whose recollection of Churchill's preferences differ somewhat from Pugh's. (This is no surprise, given the time lapse between the events and the recording of their oral histories.) The women ordered the selected films through Alexander Korda and the Kinematograph Rental Society, an early film distributor, neither of which organizations charged Churchill for the loan of the films – it was seen as a modest repayment of the nation's enormous debt to him. Pugh's belief that anything about the American Civil War was likely to please Churchill proved misplaced in the case of one such film. It proved too complex or too disjointed for Churchill to follow. He knew the history of that war in some detail, and indeed described it in seven chapters of the fourth volume of his *A History of the English-Speaking Peoples*. Even with that knowledge, he could not follow the events in the film. Finally, after fruitlessly asking others in the audience to explain what was going on, he said: 'I am watching it. I am watching it like a cat watches a mouse, but I still can't get it.'

There were visits from family friends as well; there were stays at Blenheim,* of course, and at Hatfield, but rarely did Pugh stay at those houses. When secretaries did go along, they were put up in nearby hotels or, occasionally but rarely, stayed at the houses. But most of all, Pugh says that Churchill liked people to visit him at his own house, 'to dine <u>and</u> sleep, because they [he and Lady Churchill] both thought that was civilized'. She said visitors to Chartwell rarely brought their own staffs with them – there would not have been room in any case, but when he visited others it was more like a royal tour, with civil servants, detectives and secretaries in attendance, even after he had resigned as prime minister.

Although Churchill much enjoyed his social life at Chartwell, and visits to the often-grand homes of friends, as we have noted, he also took as many holidays as he could and enjoyed them enormously,

---

* Understandably one of the few places he liked going to, as he preferred people to come to visit him. Pugh: 'To some extent he felt he was going home.'

especially during the winter when he sought the sun and the scenery he wanted to paint. But work went with him, as did the secretaries. They had planned to travel with him on alternate trips, but as the workload continued, often both Pugh and other secretaries accompanied him. Churchill planned his holidays, mainly to the South of France, to Lord Beaverbrook's villa La Capponcina, on a beautiful rocky promontory close to the coast of Monaco. There he could work uninterrupted on his *A History of the English-Speaking Peoples*. Even in these circumstances, his restless desire to be at – or to participate in – a wide variety of events was still part of his life. He would frequently fly back to London to sit in the House or see his horses race* or to dine at The Other Club – three of his continuing outside-of-work interests. He rarely missed a dinner of The Other Club – every other Thursday when parliament was sitting – and, if out of the country, he would fly back for these dinners. Churchill continued to recommend members – Pugh recalls 'he brought in Mr Onassis, which was probably fairly unusual'.†

The trips, of course, required more than merely the presence of the secretaries. The ongoing work had to be transported as well: 'mountains of stuff went. As if we were going to a desert island or something', Pugh remembers. There was so much paraphernalia for Churchill's routine trips that one of the secretaries went in a second car with 'maids, luggage, black boxes and the dog and the budgerigar... Every black box in existence was packed with papers and tin trunks' – tin, presumably so that the papers would not get chewed, mildewed or drowned.‡ And the large, heavy typewriters from Number 10 all went into their own specially built crates.

---

* Pugh rarely went with him to races and stud. But Churchill sometimes would 'charter a little aeroplane and fly off to Newmarket with some friends'. When he won he gave each of them 'a tenner' (£10, around £300 in today's money), as 'he loved having these successes'.

† It is assumed Mr Onassis supported the Club with gifts of champagne, but as the members and rules are still secret, one cannot be sure.

‡ The more familiar red boxes were used within Britain, but black boxes were also used, especially for trips abroad.

'All as if we were going to a desert island, a cavalcade' of cars, as Snelling describes it. Other secretaries remained in London to manage the daily flow of packets of work back and forth between the two offices. Also travelling would be the detectives, and, often, Mrs Churchill's lady's maid, plus assorted drivers.*

The packets of work contained hundreds of memos, telegrams and letters that staff back in London thought Churchill should see, as well as the latest proofs of his books. In the mornings, once all the mail had been dealt with and answered, memos dictated and typed, Pugh and the others were responsible for getting them to the post – she had a car and driver waiting at the door, presumably to catch the waiting courier. If they were abroad, the women were also responsible for collecting the latest proofs from the airport and putting them in order for Churchill to work on, and, importantly, for sending proofs to Mrs Churchill, requesting her comments.[22] Occasionally, Denis Kelly and Alan Hodge came down to stay – for literary and historical advice[23] – staying mostly at La Cappon-cina, which Lord Beaverbrook had bought from Captain Edward Molyneux, a well-known English dress designer with shops in London, Paris and Cannes. Pugh said the villa 'smelled of France. We all loved La Capponcina,' as well she might.

Visits to La Capponcina – really working holidays – were a bit

> more relaxed... and great fun when we were there with the Beaverbrook party as well. And his (male) secretaries used to be thrown off his yacht and swim back to it. I think Lord Beaver-brook enjoyed showing off... They were thrown off the boat, it seemed miles [away], but it wasn't really. And they swim back to the villa [or yacht].

She went on the yacht, but was not made to swim back, saying, 'I wasn't made to do that.'

---

* Drivers did not usually stay over, but went back and forth between places.

When Churchill and his extended party arrived at La Capponcina the secretaries went to work setting up the office, unpacking
the typewriters and sorting the mail. If it was summer, Churchill
put

> on a pair of blue bathing drawers and, walking down to the sea,
> down a hundred steps through Beaverbrook's enchanted garden,
> [he] plunged into his holiday. He wallowed like a porpoise; he
> blew spouts of water like a whale, and he swam round and round
> like a schoolboy. He turned, and he twisted, and he lost his baggy
> blue bathing drawers. It didn't matter for there was no one there
> to see him but Beaverbrook and me.[24]

He bathed three or four times a day, when visiting other villas in
the South of France.[25]

Lady Churchill didn't seem to agree with Beaverbrook's sense of
fun, and seldom accompanied Churchill when he visited La Capponcina. But Churchill wasn't lonely – there were always many
guests – selected and invited by Beaverbrook 'to keep Churchill
amused'.[26] Churchill disliked social gossip and insisted on guests
who could inform him and with whom he could discuss politics –
and on those who admired him. As with old, familiar-face secretaries, so, too, he 'was comfortable with old friends around him',
selected from guest lists that his hosts carefully managed.[27] One
guest described listening to Churchill at dinner as 'the best feast of
conversational entertainment ever enjoyed… with an infectious
spirit of delight'.[28]

Although Churchill liked his work routine and stuck to it regardless of where he was, while relaxing in the South of France he varied
his days, among other things immersing himself in his painting.
As Pugh explained, they did little work after dinner – unlike his
usual London working schedule. Also, he had no after-dinner
films in France, but, she goes on to explain: 'it was very different. He was more with his hosts… more social… nice, because we
had the variety.' Pugh and the female secretaries had little to do

with Churchill's painting forays into the French countryside, as the detectives (English and French) or his personal valets usually packed his painting supplies and set up the easel, once Churchill had selected the vista he wanted to capture on canvas.

In another change of routine in France, Churchill would get out of bed early, 'bathing in the sea after a session with his secretary on his war books, then out to paint with his ten-gallon hat and his five-man retinue',[29] carrying his paints and brushes, including, of course, his cigars, cutters and ashtrays.

In addition to visiting with Beaverbrook, Churchill often was the guest of Emery Reves at his South of France villa known as La Pausa, but known familiarly to Churchill as 'Pausaland'. Reves was his literary agent, who sold the rights of Churchill's books to publishers and magazines throughout the world with much financial success. In the early spring of 1958 Churchill stayed there, with Pugh in attendance, as work on *A History of the English-Speaking Peoples* was ongoing. She said that after three weeks there 'he seemed twenty years younger'.[30]

Churchill later accepted the hospitality of a new friend: Aristotle Onassis, to whom he was introduced by Randolph. Churchill often sailed with friends on Onassis's yacht, the *Christina* – but never, according to Pugh, with his usual secretarial staff – a 'dreadful disappointment' to her. She was afraid that he would be without staff. 'There was no mail and they didn't need one [secretary].' A holiday without a secretary in attendance was unthinkable in the past, but times were changing.

Ever restless, ever curious, ever in search of new subjects for his paintbrush, Churchill at times travelled to one of his favourite hotels, La Mamounia in Marrakesh, Morocco, flying there with his party on one of Onassis's Olympic Airways planes. Pugh had wonderful memories of that trip. The hotel was 'lovely... all scented oranges and lemons... He just loved it and he loved painting [there]... lovely gardens... and olive groves.' The Colvilles and Montague Brownes were invited, and they – secretaries included – all joined him on the 'amazing picnics. A pantechnicon would go ahead of us to the foothills of the Atlas Mountains… long tables and fine linens, silver, endless tea-making things, all set up, awaiting his arrival, with delicious, marvellous meals.' Pugh had an opportunity to take some time off and would go 'wandering down the souks… not that he did that!'

Pugh, like others who worked for Churchill, not only had to attend to his extraordinary workload, his extensive social sched-ule, including organizing dinners and films, and endure what she called his 'toing and froing', while serving as a zookeeper. On drives between offices and houses, when she was frantically taking down, Toby the budgerigar was always there, 'out of his cage and fussing about and chewing edges of papers and generally enjoying himself, which made a nice diversion'. Although one would have assumed that when the bird travelled in the car he was caged, Pugh says he was not and is supported by the complaints of the unhappy Jane Parsons, a Garden Room Girl who took dictation in the car on occasion. Toby also travelled with them on the vacations in France, requiring 'endless forms and Minister of Agriculture permits and visas and French Embassy and everything you could think of, and you had to swear that he hadn't met another budgie and might carry parrot's disease.' Once, when working and painting in France, Churchill decided

it would be rather fun for Toby to meet another budgie, which was strictly against all these regulations. He got a lovely real, local peasant-type man to bring some young virgin budgies for Toby to meet… Anthony Eden was terribly upset, as he knew the Foreign Office wouldn't like it and we'd sworn about parrot disease… Diana Sandys was there and thought it was wonder-fully romantic… It was really dreadful, because these dear little young budgies were brought in a very humble cage and Toby was embarrassed… He had never met another budgie and [he] sat in the corner and didn't look at them. It wasn't a success.

Toby, of course, was only one and probably the smallest member of Churchill's menagerie. Churchill always insisted that no list of his friends was complete without inclusion of his animal friends, a view more common in some circles today than it was then. He had special affection for those he knew personally. In his squiggles to Clementine he depicted himself as a pig. He refused to eat suckling pig, as he had raised pigs at Chartwell and claimed to know them. During the First World War when food was in short supply, he refused to carve a goose from his farm at Lullenden, saying: 'You'll have to carve it, Clemmie. He was a friend of mine.'[31] He made sure that bees had sufficient sugar to manufacture honey. He had a special fondness for his several cats and he sometimes fed one at The Other Club dinners. He took his budgie on trips.

Pugh tells us that 'all his animals and birds and fish were very close friends. And he had a lion [called] "Rota" at the London Zoo, whom he used to visit... He had a photograph of him in his bedroom.' She thinks Rota had been a gift to him. There was sadness when the zoo called to say Rota was ageing, as we all do, and ought to be put to sleep: 'Sir Winston took it rather personally... He thought he and Rota were going along together... Pretty upsetting.' The zoo also took his tropical fish, 'because it was more than he thought he could look after'. Rufus I and II are famous as being Churchill's dogs, spoiled by everyone, but mostly by Churchill. Rufus II's successor was named Robbie, in whom Churchill insisted Grace Hamblin share ownership and responsibility. Churchill would 'be having breakfast in bed and it was sweet, because he'd throw Robbie sugar lumps'. So much for budgies and dogs. There were also lambs, bantams, fox cubs, bees, butterflies and goats, among other members of the Churchill menagerie, a continuing source of pleasure at his advanced age. Most loved were the many cats Churchill owned during his lifetime. 'He loved cats,' Hamblin tells us.[32] During the Second World War, Churchill said that Nelson, the Chequers cat, 'served as the prime ministerial hot-water bottle' – one cat's contribution to the war effort.[33] John Martin, another of Churchill's Principal Private Secretaries, was less fond of Nelson, who in July 1943, when guests at Chequers were sleeping with their windows open, 'flopped in at my window and woke me at 4 a.m., after I had only gone to bed at 3 a.m.'[34] Churchill also had a special place in his heart for Smokey, a grey, fluffy Persian, famous in the Secret Circle.

One morning, Churchill, still in bed, was on the telephone with the Chief of the Imperial General Staff (CIGS), General Sir Alan Brooke, as he then was, when Smokey bit Churchill's exposed, wriggling toes, prompting a yell, 'Get off, you fool!' – followed by an explanation to the startled general that the fool in question was not the CIGS, and an apology to Smokey, who had been sent flying across the room by a mighty kick. 'Poor little thing,' a remorseful Churchill said.[35] Months later, when Churchill left for the Casablanca Conference, he sought out Smokey from the crowd gathered to see him off, hugged him, and specifically instructed Layton 'to see he was not lonely'.[36] Finally, Jock Colville gave Churchill a ginger cat to be named Jock, 'who was a huge success and was there when he died'. To this day there is a ginger cat named Jock living at Chartwell (see Chapter 2).

Churchill might have signed himself as 'pig' when writing to Lady Churchill, but he clearly envisioned himself as a more heroic animal. On one visit to Aristotle Onassis, he was asked, 'What would you have been, Sir Winston, if you hadn't been born a man?' and without any hesitation, Churchill replied, 'I would have been a lovely tiger.'[37]

The softer side of Churchill was displayed not only in his treatment of animals, but also in a playful sense of humour. Although we have no reason to believe that Churchill's sense of humour was more in display when working with Pugh than with other secretaries, she did spend more time during her oral history recounting such displays. Pugh 'remembers one sweet little time when I was fairly new, he suddenly said, "Come here, darling, I want to kiss you." And then he'd look up, mischievously, obviously hoping to embarrass you. [He then said] "I meant the cat."'

That sort of playfulness was also reflected when he commented on his habit of travelling between London and Chartwell on week-ends without secretaries in the car, because Mrs Churchill was available and he wanted to be with her. Pugh remembered his once remarking, with a wicked grin, that 'it was a waste travelling with Lady Churchill, because you couldn't dictate to her'. He loved travelling with her, but couldn't quite repress his constant need for his secretaries.

There was more wordplay on Armistice Day. There was a tradition that Churchill would be photographed buying a poppy and the picture would appear in the evening papers. Pugh asked Churchill to come along and be photographed buying the poppy. He refused. She was surprised and emphasized the importance of the picture, but he asked her '"What would I do with it?" Sort of getting fed up, but then his face broke into a very large grin and he said, "Oh, I thought you meant a puppy," obviously knowing perfectly well all the time.'

Churchill always treated the public with consideration. If he had to turn down an invitation 'he always wanted to say it in a way that wasn't wounding'. He was equally considerate of those making speeches in the process of giving him awards or honorary degrees. Churchill, at eighty, was in relatively good health for his age. However, his hearing loss increased, as it does with age.

As he aged, there were fewer trips abroad, with the exception of many cruises aboard the *Christina*, but Churchill continued to travel between Chartwell and Hyde Park Gate, not changing the work routine of a lifetime. As Pugh explains, 'He was used to it... He thrived on it and I think he would have sunk into a sort of despond if he'd just stayed in one place, because he never had... It was refreshing to go to London to see somebody.' Pugh also realized that 'He did thrive on toing and froing... He thrived on the contrast, being very lackadaisical, then remarkably active. If he came back [to London], he would do ever so much, and go back [to the South of France] refreshed.'[38]

Inevitably, the decline set in and his deafness made matters worse. He became gloomy at times. But he did his best to maintain a cheerful mien in public. 'He was much funnier than most people at mis-hearing... He was always very, very good at putting on the right face as though he could hear... Being given a Freedom, for example, he'd put on the most <u>beautiful</u> face of attention.' His hosts thought him attentive and were pleased. Churchill had honed his skills at making people feel at ease, both in dealing with other politicians and as a host at his numerous dinner parties over a long life – with notable exceptions, of course, such as General de Gaulle. Unlike Churchill's hearing, 'His eyesight was marvellous, [perhaps] because all his typewriters had big type, which was jolly nice, and the speech typewriter had especially big type.'

His beloved wife was perhaps his greatest concern in these later years. Pugh says he thought Lady Churchill not very strong. 'He worried about her and her health... I think that was his great anxiety. He was always so happy when she was all right, so they were together and he was terribly worried when she wasn't [there]. Various troubles with the family were also very distressing. [He was] <u>terribly</u> brought down by his children's [problems].'

Pugh took on more work, drafting letters now instead of just typing what Churchill dictated. But, she emphasizes, there was never any senility or agitation, as can occur in some people in their declining years.

As the work gradually eased off, Churchill played 'endless games of bezique*... and, after he had finished writing *A History of the English-Speaking Peoples* he did a terrific lot of reading.' Books were borrowed from everywhere: 'from the London Library, from Westerham Library... He read <u>all</u> his own books, [and] classics, which he said he had read as a young man and hadn't read since, and he loved them. Things like Dickens, Scott, Stevenson and Kipling.' Late in life Churchill also read *Tom Jones* and *Rob Roy*, and *An Infamous Army*, Georgette Heyer's retelling of the three months before Waterloo. As we will hear from Catherine Snelling (see Chapter 12), he also liked historical novels, such as *Berlin*

---

* Pugh acknowledges that she never played cards with him.

Hotel by Vicki Baum. He read this 'absolutely thrilling' novel in
August 1944, while visiting operations in Italy.[39]

Reading was some consolation, as were some types of music.
As Pugh sadly recalled, 'It was touching how Sir Winston started
having the record player in the afternoons. He played Gilbert and
Sullivan and military marches, and really did his best to get some
pleasure out of them [in spite of his hearing loss]. And, in those
last months, when he could not concentrate so well on reading, he
did a lot of looking at books of pictures.'[40] Pugh says that when he
gave up his seat in the House of Commons 'I think that was the
end, really... I think he just gave up then. I think he absolutely
hated it... He was disconsolate then.'

He decided, after much deliberation, not to stand for re-election
in his ever-loyal constituency, Woodford, in May 1963, shortly
before his eighty-eighth birthday. It was a momentous decision for
him. He had been in the House of Commons almost continuously
for over fifty years. His last appearance in the House was on 28
July 1964.

Lord Beaverbrook died in June 1964 – a bitter blow for Churchill,
as they had been friends for sixty years; indeed, Beaverbrook had
been dubbed by Churchill his 'foul-weather friend'. His other two
closest friends, Lord Cherwell and Brendan Bracken, had died in
1957 and 1958 respectively. Churchill had moments of gloom, as
anyone would at that age, watching his friends die. But Pugh and
Maturin both noticed that the depressions lifted: 'We came to
the same conclusion about how he enjoyed contrasts, and after a
quiet, low time, he would come right up.'[41]

His attention was beginning to wander, his deafness making
friendships difficult to maintain. On his ninetieth birthday, 30
November 1964, she was very busy with 'the endless messages
and presents to be thanked, [but it was] less really enjoyable... an
increasing decline at that stage'. The number of birthday messages
was estimated at around 60,000 from all over the world,[42] most
acknowledged by the 'cyclostyled' machine, but some personally
signed by Churchill. However, some estimates are as high as

70,000. So great was the need that temporary staff were hired to deal with the messages and telegrams, and old secretaries such as Lettice Marston volunteered to return to help out. 'Before the luncheon on the actual day, Clementine had arranged for all his secretarial, nursing and domestic staff, to gather in his bedroom to drink his health in champagne.'[43] Pugh was now senior staff and accustomed to Churchill's ways and needs, so she encouraged Churchill to attend dinner at The Other Club on 10 December 1964, his last, fifty-four years after his first dinner there.[44] All were part of the life of Sir Winston.

Pugh was away when she was called back and 'we were all there in those last few days… and Lady Churchill sat with him sweetly so long. And the cat on the end of the bed.' As his daughter Mary Soames recalls: 'This natural but infinitely sad decline, was slow and uneven. There would be bright clear spells, and then dull rather hazy days… and after the announcement in May 1963 that he would not contest the approaching election, the last stimulus was taken from his life.'[45] Pugh worked with him through these last months, until his death on 24 January 1965, two days before the birth of his great-grandson Randolph.

Pugh contradicts the reports that Churchill himself planned much of his funeral, including picking the hymns. She says 'to the best of my remembrance that was rubbish and he certainly didn't. I think it was done absolutely without his knowing.'

At the time of writing, Doreen Pugh, who was born in 1925, lives outside London. She was awarded an MBE in 1965. In his will, Churchill left her £650 (some £12,000 today).

The Secretaries witness history (*contd.*)

▶ 39 WSC meets Princess Elizabeth arriving in London from Kenya after the death of her father, King George VI, February 1952. Jane Portal, who took down WSC's tribute to the King during the drive to the airport, hid out of sight behind another aircraft to view the arrival.

▼ 40. At the party conference in Margate WSC assures the Tory party of his continued ability to lead, October 1953.

Everyday Chores

◄ 41. A canvas, cases of Pol Roger and a portion of the Churchills' luggage, organized, labelled and shipped by the secretarial staff, January 1953.

► 42. Rufus II returns to Downing Street, primped and pampered, 1954.

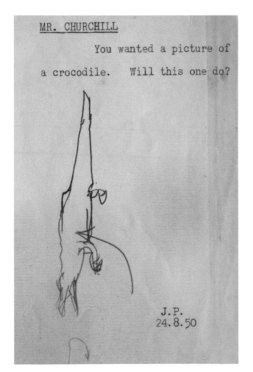

MR. CHURCHILL

You wanted a picture of a crocodile. Will this one do?

J.P.
24.8.50

Precious.
Jane.
NSC

◄▲ 43–4. 'Find me a crocodile!' Jane Portal's sketch in response to a request from WSC, alongside his pleased response, August 1950.

Despatched night of 29.12.50.

For Dispatch.

     16 letters.

Christmas Cards seend. (Sorry it's 3 benedictines!)

Christmas greetings sent direct to Marrakech.

General Public letters sent direct to Marrakech.

Filing.

Third Carbons.

Christmas cards from Lord Brabazon and Mayor and Mayoress of
     Margate to be dealt with as thought best.

Note and account for Ham from Odhams.

Two notes (!) for LA GILLIATT.

Telegram to Cowles to be despatched fm London.

Note to Miss Marston re card from Sir George and Lady Garvie
                                                    Watt.

Cheque fm Houghton Mifflin Co to be paid to bank.

Letter to be regretted from S/Ldr. Cooper re Ilford and
                              Woodford R.A.F.A.

Note to WHOEVER FEELS SAINTLIKE ENOUGH TO COPE WITH IT.

Letter to Mrs. Churchill sent direct to Marrakech .

FPR PRINTER:- Book 12. Cha. XIa AN UNEASY INTERLUDE.
              "   Inserts Section A - Himmler's End.

▲ 45. Note from Jo Sturdee and 'Chips' Gemmell in Marrakesh to 'La Gilliatt'
and staff in London, after three Benedictines, December 1950.

► 46. WSC leaves Downing Street to the applause of his staff, after his resignation as prime minister, April 1955.

▼ 47. Jane Portal, now Lady Williams of Elvel, talks with General David Petraeus at the International Churchill Society Conference, October 2017. The author, centre, looks on.

12

Catherine Snelling

'A very approachable man and lovable.'

Catherine Snelling, oral history

'If he was there, everything was
somehow all right.'

Catherine Snelling, oral history

'He had great courage, an almost inexhaustible energy,
and a generosity of spirit which would disarm all
but the most implacable opponents.'

A. J. P. Taylor[1]

CATHERINE SNELLING CAME to Churchill as a woman with vast experience, a true professional secretary. Described as having 'light brown, shoulder-length hair' by one of Churchill's later valets,[2] she had worked for the Ghana High Commission, the BBC and then in Paris at the OECD. On returning to London, she signed up with Mrs Hoster's employment agency, which, in November 1958, sent her to interview for a job with Churchill – his name was used, it was no secret, she says, as was the case, for example, when Jo Sturdee was interviewed during the war years. Anthony Montague Browne (referred to in these years as AMB), seconded from the Foreign Office to serve as Private Secretary during the last ten years of Churchill's life, interviewed her before taking her to meet Churchill himself in the drawing room at 28 Hyde Park Gate. They 'gazed and gazed at each other', while AMB explained her qualifications. Churchill asked her if she spoke French. She said she did. Churchill said he did, too. He never conceded to critics who claimed his French was of the highly fractured variety, and it is not known whether AMB, who was fluent in French, ever discussed the matter with his boss.

Snelling started work the following Monday and worked for Churchill for five years. It proved to be a unique experience for a well-travelled woman, but one who had never worked 'in a family' before.

AMB had assumed the role of organizing a hiring system he believed to be a bit more formal than the one that had provided Churchill with his secretaries during the war, one that had worked so well for Churchill in the past. In fact, Churchill's method of selecting secretaries hadn't changed: preliminary screening by a trusted aide, a brief meeting to look over the applicant, followed by immediately putting that person to work. In a sense, AMB was performing a function similar to that performed by Jo Sturdee and others. The screeners might change, but Churchill's hiring method did not.

AMB explained to Snelling that her duties were 'to run his private office, work in the house and in London and go to Chartwell at weekends… go abroad with him if needed. Just generally look after him and run his office and other personal things that were needed… organize things, really. Things that weren't totally domestic like the household.'* This job description was not very different in style from the ones that set forth what was expected of secretaries since the very start of his career: broad, vague, no specific limits on what needed to be done. That suited Churchill's habit of moving seamlessly from location to location, and from work to his other interests. It was, of course, different in content, since among other things Churchill no longer bore the burden of the premiership.

Snelling's recollection of her chores is a bit more specific than AMB's description:

> answering letters, keeping his diary up to date, organizing who was coming to stay, who was coming to lunch in London… ringing people up, making arrangements, people ringing us up, wanting to know if they could have this or that… and quite a lot to do with book rights… people wanting to quote… and later the film arrangements.

Snelling also had to manage the switchboard at Hyde Park Gate, 'an old-fashioned thing. It linked up the whole house, Sir Winston and Lady Churchill's bedrooms and others… One of those with the switch up and down.' There was also a switchboard at Chartwell. She spent a considerable amount of time keeping track of the numerous awards and the organizations of which Churchill was a patron: acknowledging the financial reports, thanking organizations, working with veterans, and with the help of AMB preparing Churchill's talks to these organizations. This list of chores, and the volume of correspondence, explain why Snelling was soon overwhelmed and more secretaries were needed. A young woman

---

* The households were run by Grace Hamblin, with Lady Churchill supervising.

named Monica Graham was taken on at the suggestion of Lettice Marston.

Snelling estimated that she spent 'a couple of hours a day altogether' with Churchill, beginning the day by taking up the blotter book for him to sign the letters that she had typed the night before. He was in his four-poster bed,* 'propped up with the budgerigar going round, sitting on his head... and mine... and rolling things off the table like pens.' Like Pugh, she relished going to the library for books he wanted to read; and he could always depend on 'his own copies of Walter Scott'.

Snelling had this to say of one of the books she chose for Churchill to read:

> One of the great successes. I don't know if you've heard of a book called *The Golden Warrior* by Hope Muntz. It came out just after the war and extraordinarily enough it was dedicated to him in the front. I hadn't realized it. It was about William the Conqueror and Harold and she [Muntz] was a history don, and this was the only fiction she ever wrote. And I read it in about 1950 and was absolutely bowled over by it. And so I got it out for him one day and he read it and read it. He wouldn't get up to go to dinner, [saying] I must finish this... So the next morning he was reading it again, [asking] who is this woman? We must have her to lunch. She was a very eminent historian, but she was quite old, and this was fifteen years after she'd written it. But it's a most marvellous book and I knew he'd love it, because it was in a kind of epic style without being boring. Not like *Beowulf* where you can hardly follow. I don't mean boring, but anyway he adored that.

Despite the inevitable effects of the ageing process, Churchill retained his wide-ranging interests (which seem to have included modern novels). Snelling is certain that Lord Beaverbrook gave Churchill a copy of Vladimir Nabokov's *Lolita* (1955) when

---

*   Later changed to a 'regular big bed'.

Churchill was a guest at La Capponcina. She says he 'couldn't be torn away from it'.

And of course, there were still some speeches to be prepared in a manner strictly specified by Churchill. Snelling recalls his habit of composing and dictating: 'quite extraordinary'. He would

> sort of gaze into space and you knew he was going to say something. He'd... say, 'I'll write to him' and then there would be a pause and he'd be reading something else... then he would suddenly say 'My Dear whoever' and just start without warning you – just begin, so you'd have to be quite sort of on the qui vive. He'd sort of try out words without actually saying them and out it would come. So you couldn't take down what he was trying out quietly. I think he's always probably done it like that.

Many others have commented on his practice of trying out words and phrases, sometimes aloud to hear how they sounded, especially if they were meant to be in a speech. Churchill always fretted over his words and phrases. When she typed his speeches, Snelling says that she typed them on cards. She recalled: 'He invented the speech form, which was like a poem. A phrase on each line going down, and you always finished a paragraph at the end of a page, if you could.' It was called the psalm format and was always typed on octavo-sized paper, 5 by 7½ inches. The speech cards were then put together with a tag and handed over to Churchill, who removed the tag when he started his speech.

She also had to make certain he had his 'speech box' with him. She explains this was 'a box with a slot in it which he'd have on the table in front of him when he was making a speech, and as he read a card he'd put it through the letter box.' This way he could be sure that 'he never... got to the end and found himself beginning the speech again... He invented that, really.' None of the other secretaries mentioned this, so perhaps the habit came later. It is another example of a Churchill invention which he used to smooth out his working life, like devising the psalm format, or the 'Bellybandoes' for his cigars, or the sunken Mulberry Harbours used in the Second World War, based on a 1917 sketch by Churchill. 'Churchill,' writes Ferdinand Mount, 'was always a sucker for gadgets.'[3] More precisely, he was a 'soldier-scientist... His appreciation of technical progress, coupled with his powerful but controlled imagination... led him to demand weapons for the war after next, and his energy and his administrative ability have sometimes resulted in his getting them most successfully!'[4]

Because there was less pressure than in earlier years, Snelling recalls, 'I knew it wouldn't be twenty-four hours or eighteen hours a day or anything like that, because it wasn't Number 10 and he was retired [as prime minister], although he was still doing quite a lot of things.' She also undoubtedly noted that his staff now included three nurses, one of whom was Roy Howells, a male nurse and valet, to look after him when he travelled,[5] and – no surprise – he, too, was asked to feed the pets. Churchill was still going to the House of Commons 'pretty well every day', and continued to try to do so until his decision in the spring of 1963 not to stand for his Woodford seat in the 1964 general election. As always, he would work in bed until noon or so and then appear for lunch, which was leisurely, but always ended in time for him to rush off, as Pugh describes it, smartly to the House at half-past two in the 'bullock car', again a Churchill pun on an employee's name. A secretary always travelled with Churchill in his big Daimler, as did Rufus II, Toby the 'chattering budgie', and the Special Branch detective. Snelling had a notepad at the ready should Churchill want to dictate – although she points out that by now that was rare. The Daimler flew the flag of the Cinque Ports as he was still Warden of the Cinque Ports,* so traffic was stopped along the way, allowing for people to wave as they recognized the flag. It was

---

*   Dating from Norman times, an honorary position as defender of five coastal towns in southern England (Hastings, New Romney, Hythe, Dover and Sandwich) – hence its use of the French word for five, *cinque*. Churchill had received this honour in 1946.

quite 'a travelcade... like a royal progress'. There was always a detective with Churchill. As his hearing was slipping away the House had accommodated his regular seat with a built-in hearing aid, which provided some but not unlimited ability to follow the debates. And another hearing device was eventually installed in the Chartwell dining room.

In addition to making certain that the right things ended up in the right place, and were ready for Churchill's use, Snelling had to see to his comfort on the back-and-forth trips. That included making certain that her boss's hand-warmer or 'beaver-skin muff' was available and ready for use. Churchill, who during the war always sought technological solutions to problems, and who at this age wanted to keep his hands warm, had purchased a muff that had a warmer inside. Snelling describes it: 'the muff-warmer is a little thing like a cigarette lighter, but filled with petrol. Highly dangerous... covered in a leather case... It slipped into a pocket in the muff, so that the muff was lovely and warm,' which Churchill needed even though the car was by now heated. Like her predecessors, Snelling reports an act of kindness and consideration: Churchill always asked her if she was warm enough when travelling in his car – even though both were covered with 'a beautiful mohair rug'. As did all the other secretaries, she made sure his black eye band was on hand in case he wanted to nap.

Grace Hamblin, now managing Chartwell, ordered weekend supplies of wine, food and other things from London. On trips from London to Chartwell, Snelling was responsible for sorting and packing the supplies, which would be transported in the convoys of cars that regularly went back and forth between Hyde Park Gate and Chartwell. On return trips to London there would be baskets of flowers and vegetables in season. 'A very cosy outfit, really.' In addition to foodstuffs and flowers, office supplies and correspondence moved back and forth between Churchill's London and Chartwell operations.

When at Chartwell he would play cards, mainly bezique, with Lady Churchill or AMB until his hour-long nap, waking up in time to get ready for dinner at about 8.30. Only occasionally now would Churchill dress for dinner; he usually wore his siren suit if the dinner was 'not smart'. Before he dressed for dinner, Snelling would go in to say goodnight and then go home. If she was working at Chartwell she was expected to work after dinner, which meant 'ring[ing] up the night desk at the *Daily Telegraph* and the *Express* and… they always were ready for us and we'd get the headlines… tomorrow morning's headlines.' She would take the headlines into the drawing room, where dinner guests would be 'sitting around having brandies and things in their evening dress'. Churchill would read out the headlines to his guests, or he might ask Ted Heath or another guest to read out the headlines. Then Churchill would say to Snelling 'Off you go then, my dear.' When working in London, the first editions of the newspapers would be delivered to his home around 11 p.m.

Those guests included many old and some new friends. Churchill was still deeply interested in world events, although he did not discuss those with the secretaries – he never had – but he did have his usual political discussion dinners with well-connected guests such as Harold Macmillan, by then prime minister, and Ted Heath, then a Conservative member of parliament; and, of course, Christopher Soames, his son-in-law. General Montgomery 'came over often, because he was widowed'.

Women guests came, too, primarily Sylvia Henley, a first cousin to Lady Churchill, and a great favourite of Churchill's because of her skill at cards and outspoken lively conversation. She lived another fifteen years after Churchill's death, dying at age ninety-eight. Violet Bonham Carter was a frequent guest as well, as was June Osborne, Randolph's second wife. Snelling reveals that June Osborne had often been invited to dinner, presumably to balance the table. Sarah Churchill, his middle daughter and perhaps his favourite, was often there, 'always in some sort of pickle… she always cheered him up… His most enlivening child, demonstrative. He was very sentimental.'

The working week remained as it always was: Monday to Friday in London, with one of the secretaries off to Chartwell after lunch with Churchill for the weekend. Until a few years before that final retirement from the House, Catherine Snelling and Doreen Pugh alternated weekends at Chartwell. When Snelling went down to Chartwell, she stayed in a cottage on the grounds: 'Terribly comfortable... You just trotted down through the orchard... with your suitcase... sort yourself out a bit... maybe have a drink with Grace [Hamblin].' Snelling admits being 'frightened' walking late at night in the dark down the road to the butler's cottage where she sometimes slept overnight, if the house and maids' rooms were full.

When working, 'Dinner was on a tray brought down to the office ... Whatever they were having... delicious.' The office 'had a lovely big table... a book, magazine and radio. It was very, very comfortable and warm, not electric fire... we usually had dinner there.' Although many of these women noticed that they were generally not included in family and other dinners, Snelling reports, 'Occasionally you were invited up if there were uneven numbers... Very occasionally he had no visitors at all and Lady Churchill wanted to go to bed [and you would] go and have dinner with him just on your own, but that didn't happen very often.'

Snelling recalls vividly how well she was treated. Churchill and Lady Churchill 'had a marvellous, kind way of making you feel comfortable and easy, as if you fitted in because you were part of their outfit... part of the household... absolutely naturally warm and friendly and it was a happy place to work. You never felt condescended to at all.' She gives much of the credit for this atmosphere to Lady Churchill, saying that 'she was very fair-minded and good at picking people to begin with and then sort of running them and making sure they weren't clashing with each other.'

Snelling tells us that her first job after arriving at Chartwell late on Friday afternoon was 'to get him the closing prices of his shares, which involved ringing up the stockbrokers'. Churchill kept his personal accounts in a separate black box that she would bring to him; he would unlock it with a key* that dangled from his key chain, and compare last week's closing prices with the current week. When at the Admiralty, Churchill formed the habit of using his key chain as a place for keeping safe and handy his key to the daily buff-coloured box of intelligence intercepts.[6]

His keen interest in the weekly performance of his shares reflected his long and often difficult relationship with money to satisfy creditors, the taxman and his own tastes and has been related in interesting detail elsewhere.[7] If Snelling is right, those problems arose not from a lack of attention to these matters on Churchill's part, but from a lack of skill in attending to them. Pugh says Churchill was not very good with figures, but his facility with data on shipping tonnage, food requirements and the like suggests that at least when it came to matters other than his personal finances, his statement that he 'quitted' mathematics forever in the year 1894[8] is more amusing than correct.

Churchill's secretaries were on call for late nights at Hyde Park Gate, but there were now fewer calls for them to work after dinner at both Hyde Park Gate and Chartwell. Late nights no longer meant the wee hours of the morning. On most evenings, they could leave for home at 7.30 or 8 p.m., when Churchill dressed for dinner. Of course, a work schedule that begins early in the morning and ends at around 7 or 8 p.m. in the evening and includes working weekends can be considered 'light' only when compared to the work schedule required to meet the unrelenting demands made on Churchill during the war.

---

* This key was kept on his watch chain, which included several 'various lovely things on it like cigar-piercers and his [gold] winkle cuff from the Hastings Winkle Club'. Churchill was the honorary chairman of the Hastings Winkle Club, a charity organization founded in 1900 by Hastings fishermen to aid poor families in the area. In addition to its local members, there were more famous ones such as Churchill, Field Marshal Montgomery and the late Queen Mother, all of whom considered membership an honour. Their motto was 'winkle up'. To Snelling it was 'one of those mad English clubs'. Also on the watch chain was 'a ring that had belonged to somebody'. His father? Intriguing.

At Chartwell, after dinner on Friday nights there might be a film or, if visitors were expected on Saturday, the film would be held over for them and shown on Saturday night, with another one on Sunday. The secretaries bought all the film magazines, listed the choices they knew would be popular with the Churchills and their guests, and then had both Churchills approve the list. Snelling recalls 'he didn't particularly like westerns or war films', a recollection different from that of Doreen Pugh, who was working at the same time as Snelling and says Churchill did like a good western. Memories can vary, of course, after so many years. The selections made, the secretaries had the task of getting the films sent down by train and, after the showing, packed up and returned. Snelling does agree with Pugh that the entire household was invited to watch, and 'as many as were not too tired would come'. There was a ground-floor room, adapted for a cinema, which could accommodate about fifteen to seventeen attendees, armchairs in the front row, with canvas captains' chairs in the back rows. A local man was in charge of running the projector and maintaining all the equipment. Bill Deakin 'later recalled how, after each film show, there would be a sort of silence, then he [Churchill] would give a little verdict on the film, before we all went up to work. After watching *Wuthering Heights* (1939), his only comment was "What terrible weather they have in Yorkshire."'[9]

There was a television set in the Chartwell library, but Churchill watched it only occasionally – he used it most often to watch horse racing, but only if he had a horse running. Snelling confirms that he loved going to the stud and watching the horses, especially if there were foals and colts. He and the stud manager, who came to lunch frequently, would 'go through the lists [of horses and discuss] who was going to be mated with who next year and which colts should be entered... He was very knowledgeable about it. It wasn't just a game.' If his jockey won, Churchill 'of course sent him 10 per cent of the winnings' and Snelling would write the cheque for Churchill's signature. After a win at a French race worth some £10,000 (£250,000 in today's money) in prize money, Churchill said to her, '"Make yourselves out a cheque for £100 [each]", and so we did, and he signed it.' (That £100 cheque would be £2,200 in today's money.) Churchill could sometimes be generous to those who worked such long hours on his behalf.

His birthdays were always big events with much celebratory champagne and late-night work for the secretaries. On one of those nights, 'quite a lot of champagne was sent down and oysters from dinner', as they opened telegrams wishing him well. Snelling opened one and saw it was in Russian, signed by the Soviet premier Nikita Khrushchev. 'What to do?' she thought. 'Was I drunk?' She sent it up for Sir Winston to see and asked for instructions. The message came back: 'Deal with it.' Snelling rang up Number 10 for translation, but, odd to say, the answer came back that no one there late at night could read Russian. So she rang the Russian Embassy, which was only too glad to help out translating Khrushchev's birthday message. The women had to have initiative and they knew that the power of Churchill's name would open many doors when needed.

There were still substantial perks, by way of compensation, foreign travel being the most important. Snelling says she 'only went to Monte Carlo... four or five times... sometimes in the spring, sometimes autumn... three or four weeks in April–May and then, if possible, again in September–October and one of us would go,' taking turns as they all did on foreign trips. There was an important difference, especially towards the end of Snelling's tenure. Late in his life these trips were 'really a holiday... we did some work'. After Churchill became friendly with Aristotle Onassis, the Greek shipowner arranged for Churchill and his entourage to move into the penthouse suite on the top floor of his Hotel de Paris in Monte Carlo. Onassis owned a large share of the Hotel de Paris and the casino.

From then on, whenever Churchill and his party visited the South of France, he stayed there. Rooms on the floor below could be used for staff such as AMB. Snelling (and Pugh) stayed in a little hotel a five-minute walk from Churchill's hotel, which 'was a good thing to get away, really... If you were there for four or five weeks, it was good to get away.' But it wasn't all a holiday: packets arrived from London. Work and messages that could not wait five weeks for a reply were all forwarded to Monte Carlo – presumably by private air courier – after vetting by the private office in London.

By then Churchill's health problems were increasing, as was his deafness. He walked more frequently with a stick and 'had to hold on to a banister more... He was nearly ninety and his mind was OK', as Snelling recalls. But Churchill admitted to Lord Moran that his memory was not what it once was.[10]

In June 1962 he broke his hip while getting out of bed at the Hotel de Paris, and was flown home on an RAF plane, because he 'wanted to die in England', as he put it. For three weeks he was in hospital, brandy and cigars served up to him and his guests after dinner in the hospital room. We can assume, too, that the secretaries were in and out taking down dictation as always. They often found him irritable if he wasn't allowed to get up 'when he thought he should be able to get up to have his birthday, which was very unfortunate... So he was cross with you because – just generally. Not anything you'd done. [He complained]: "You are having my birthday," as he so much wanted to go downstairs to celebrate with the guests.'

Others had slightly differing memories of his anger when work was not done to his satisfaction or on his exacting timetable. But all remember his ability to forgive. He always said to never let the sun go down on your anger. Secretaries who might have been irritated by the impatience or the snappishness of his responses recall that he applied that rule to his own life as well – he never ended the day without an apology of sorts or an endearing smile if he had snapped or lost his temper.

> He'd forget things... You'd think he was having a nice little doze and he'd suddenly turn around and say, 'Well, have you done it?' There was no need for him to talk all the time, chat and be busy.

If he wanted to sit gazing into space for half an hour, why not? He was quite often thinking about – whatever... not sad. I think he regretted not being able to sort of walk. He was much too proud to moan and groan... If he wanted to sit gazing into space for half an hour... he was often thinking about [something].

In 1963 Churchill decided he would not contest the Woodford seat in the 1964 general election. Lady Churchill was relieved, but Churchill was disconsolate. If Pugh is to be believed, he simply gave up. By November 1964 he was pretty much bedridden, although able to enjoy some visits, especially from family. Snelling and other staff would go to his room and sit with him. Doctors came, bulletins were issued, and the crowds built up outside Hyde Park Gate, waiting for news. Lady Churchill spent most of the day in his room, holding his hand.

Snelling recalls that he sort of slipped away, 'just didn't wake up one morning... gradually faded away'. She describes 'a great era ending and a terrific year in my own life... I could not imagine what else I was going to do or what could ever match it.' But then returning to the world of Churchill-work, she says 'we were so busy afterwards'. She stayed on for about six months after Churchill's death, 'clearing up and sorting out... a sad winding down'. All the papers had to be filed and the secretaries had devised the filing system for all the messages and documents that came in after the death, divided sensibly into 'Private' and 'Personal', 'Patronage' and 'Political' and the ever-useful 'Miscellaneous'; not a scrap was thrown out. Snelling's reflections on her long association with Churchill tell us much about the man. She knew he was

the boss... as long as you remembered that. And you made sure everything was as much as possible the way <u>he</u> wanted it, but not being selfish, but why shouldn't he have the things as he wanted? He was the boss. So you spent your life really making everything work as well as possible and make him happy and all the people around him work together.

The unwritten and unspoken rule in Churchill's office was that the women would work out the schedule among themselves, so that Churchill's work would get done, that he would have someone there for him, at all times, should he want to dictate, and to please him, goals they all shared.

Everyone who worked for him seems to have ended up adoring him. When asked why that was so, Snelling said simply:

> He just was extremely adorable. I mean not to the world... There was something likable and more than that, when you were working for him it was partly his aura of what he'd been through all his life. I mean he'd been a pretty great man since 1912... so you had all that plus his extreme humanness. And he didn't act like a great man. He always thought he was pretty great, I think... but he took it for granted without being conceited... But with all that he had quite a lot of humility in a way... normalness, I think, and humanity... still a very approachable man and lovable.

Churchill remembered her in his will with £400, worth about £7,500 today.

Churchill the historian made one last gesture to the benefit of future historians. He directed that all his papers be filed and labelled in an orderly manner, and ready to send on to his son Randolph Churchill, who had been designated to write the biography of his father.

EPILOGUE

MY HOPE IS that by reporting what these extraordinary women – and one man – recall of working with Winston, and consulting related sources, I have added something to our knowledge of this man who preserved our freedoms and way of life. From these women we learned the true extent to which work was his all-consuming passion. As a result, he was often insensitive to the needs of those around him – their need for sleep, for time off to be with their families on holidays, for a simple slowing of the pace of work. But the drive that resulted in such insensitivity was not based solely on a desire for personal recognition and aggrandizement, although those motives were certainly present. The apparent lack of attention to the needs of his secretaries, the over-riding importance of much of his work, was rooted in a deep concern for the welfare of the British people. Were they to live henceforth in a democracy or under the thumb of a brutal dictator? Would they have enough to eat, despite the constraints of war, and was it possible for the burden of shortages to be shared as equitably as any government was capable of arranging? Churchill cared passionately about the circumstances of people's daily lives – indeed, such concerns had led him as a young parliamentarian to become an early advocate of many features of the modern welfare state. Most of all, he wanted to try his utmost to preserve for the British people everything his country stood for. John Keegan says it best 'Churchill reacted to the day-by-day unfolding of the war less by intellect, great though his intellect was, than by force of character. Churchill's moral character determined all he did. [He] was moved by a passion for liberty and moral grandeur, above all the moral grandeur which his own country, first, and then the alliance of the English-speaking democracies epitomized.'[1]

We learned, too, that his absorption in his work did not preclude shows of kindness. When it was full steam ahead on a project, Pugh and Kinna found him 'inconsiderate'. But when he was less pressed, they joined Snelling, Hill and Holmes in recollecting how 'considerate' he could be. A man whose first reaction when seeing a secretary injured was whether she could take down dictation despite her injury, could also notice that a secretary was working in a cold room and build a fire for her, or borrow an extra coat from some sailors for a secretary given too short notice of a trip to wintry Athens to pack a proper coat. A man who seemingly viewed his secretaries as interchangeable parts, to be summoned by the call 'Miss', could also arrange long-term care for a secretary who died while in his service and for the tuition of her daughter. Walter Thompson, a Churchill bodyguard married to one of Churchill's secretaries, spoke of a man 'angry and inconsiderate' one minute and 'full of impish kindness' the next.[2]

In the end, these women who worked so closely with Churchill concluded that his kindnesses outweighed his frequent lack of consideration. Almost all characterize him as 'lovable' (Gemmell, Gilliatt, Snelling); 'kind' (Holmes, Kinna, Pugh, Snelling); 'compassionate' (Holmes, Pearman); and 'sweet' (Gemmell, Pugh, Sturdee).

Looking back over the adjectives used by these women, and by this author to characterize the stories they tell, the most frequently used is 'considerate'. Sharing second place are 'kind' and 'impatient', followed by 'lovable', 'generous', 'curious', 'irritable'. All accurate.

And almost to a woman they stayed with him until outside events required them to leave his service; and then would return, unbidden, at times when they knew the workload would overwhelm their successors. Portal describes his 'temper like lightning and gone quickly', followed by a 'quiet smile... no grudges, no malice'. Holmes characterizes the smile as 'beatific' when he told her, 'When I shout, I'm not shouting at you, I'm thinking of the work.' By and large, the secretaries who worked for him knew and accepted that explanation – that it was work, and important work, that caused his eruptions – and gave little weight to his outbursts in their ultimate appraisals of the man. One appraisal was provided by Holmes to Sir Martin Gilbert in a letter written some four decades after leaving Churchill's service: 'In all his moods – totally absorbed in the serious matter of the moment, agonized over some piece of wartime bad news, suffused with compassion, sentimental and in tears, truculent, bitingly sarcastic, mischievous or hilariously funny – he was at all times entertaining, humane and lovable.'[3]

We learn, too, from the oral histories left us by these women (and one man) and by poring over the observations of diarists and others, that Churchill was quite simply spoiled. He felt no need to abandon the lifelong experience of having his wishes become someone else's command; to Churchill, that was the natural order of things. A friend's observation that 'Mr Churchill is easily satisfied with the best'[4] understates what it took to satisfy him. Yes, the best Cuban cigars and French champagne; food sent at his request by his wife from London's best shops even while he served in the trenches during the Great War, and a bathtub shipped to him from Britain; housing accommodation so costly that his wife often could not cope, unable to see how the family might avoid the financial ruin that befell her mother, who was like Winston an inveterate gambler. This was a man, a fair reading of his secretaries' accounts tells us, who constructed a world around himself and expected others to reproduce it wherever he went. On a train to Scotland, he expected a secretary to arrange to have his bed from home installed. On a dangerous flight to a conference with Roosevelt and Stalin, he expected – without having to ask – that the bedside table in his cabin contain his cigars, ashtray, writing implements and other items precisely as they were laid out on his bedside table at Chartwell, and in Downing Street, and in Chequers – and in any home in which he was a guest.

Obviously, this was the self-indulgent behaviour of the self-styled brightest of all glow-worms. Less obviously, it was the behaviour of a man who was an exquisitely efficient time manager. Churchill productively used the time saved by the fact that no change of venue could interrupt his work routine. The routine that enabled him to manage the Second World War as both prime minister and minister of defence was fixed: there would always be someone available to take down his ideas and instructions. There was a secretary at his bedside when he woke, and another at night until he retired after dinner and a film.

Those who fought fatigue to take down his histories left us with some of the finest volumes ever written about his ancestor and the history of the times in which he himself lived. It might be said, without drifting into sycophancy, that the world benefitted substantially from his insistence that all around him put the meeting of his needs – demands – at the top of their list of priorities. This made him at times 'unreasonable' (Sturdee), and 'exasperating' (Kinna), a view shared more than occasionally by the military commanders whom Churchill often pressed to take actions they deemed unfeasible. But it resulted in a legacy from which the world still benefits.

Time management, conscious or otherwise, was only one of Churchill's management skills. The chaos that seemed to characterize his operations – trips suddenly cancelled, others suddenly scheduled, unrelated projects pursued simultaneously – could be maintained only because of the vetting process that brought to his staff these attractive, clever, talented and self-confident women. Somewhere along the line the people charged with finding applicants, and then sorting those suitable for an interview with Churchill, developed a search method that worked. They used a combination of private contacts and tests of skills at taking dictation to find candidates suitable for presentation to Churchill. They sought the best of what would be to him – a man who disliked dealing with new faces – the best of the new faces available. The cursory nature of the look-over that constituted a final interview by Churchill himself was possible only because of his faith in the prior winnowing process. And in the trial by fire he devised to separate those who could add to his productivity from those who could not.

By today's standard of multiple interviews, psychological testing and other paraphernalia of human resources departments, this was a primitive method indeed. But the results speak for themselves, or in our case speak to us from those who joined the adventure that working for Winston surely was. The process worked, as did Churchill's method of generally allowing the secretaries to decide among themselves how to divide the chores and set individual work schedules.

These women also share with us a man quite different from that seen by British voters. The Victorian gentleman in the three-piece dark suit, walking stick in hand, and with a perfectly folded white pocket handkerchief was much photographed. Slightly different was the man in the one-piece siren suit – odd, but not inappropriate in wartime. But the man who sat in bed, a budgie on his head and a cat chewing on his toes, whisky and cigar in hand early in the morning, as seen in a cartoon by David Wilson, was an image he did not care to project widely. 'Eccentric' says Gemmell, and so he was. Eccentricity on this scale requires a degree of self-confidence that must come in part from being born in Blenheim Palace, in part from a sense of the class to which he belonged, and in part from self-knowledge of his qualities as a statesman, historian, soldier, painter and racehorse owner.

Churchill's secretaries also throw a bit of light on the bouts of what has come to be called his 'black dog', which may be the periods in which Pugh describes him as 'disconsolate' or 'despondent' and Hill as 'moody'. It should come as no surprise that there were times when Churchill suffered the frustration – indeed, the indignity – of seeing clearly what Hitler had in store for his country, a vision to which Britain's political elite steadfastly remained blind. He was not merely ignored but derided for warning that Britain would pay dearly for a lack of military preparation. In short, when the black dog barked it was not without cause. And there were times when the stresses associated with the extraordinary work burdens he bore undoubtedly contributed to his emotional discomfort.

The tales told by his secretaries throw two rays of light on this well picked-over phenomenon. The first, told by Gemmell, relates his eruption at the word 'suicide' and his insistence that discussion of it be stopped. As we know from his letters to Mrs Churchill, he worried about his bouts of depression to the point of considering medical help. The second insight is that none of the secretaries, in their oral histories, mentioned 'black dog', and none reported that there were times when Churchill simply could not work – even when suffering from pneumonia or some other major ailment. This provides some support for the observation that however much he suffered from depression – which must have been considerably when the Tories lost the first post-war election – Churchill maintained his prodigious work schedule. First, he reorganized his staff and turned its direction over to Jo Sturdee, freeing himself from the distraction of a staff reorganization and new faces. Then, Churchill almost immediately resumed work on his history of the Second World War and on the multiple projects to which he was committed. Unless all of these women decided that such a problem was not the sort of thing one discussed with interviewers, creating permanent records to be consulted by future generations, we can conclude that the physical resilience that allowed Churchill to deliver a major speech shortly after his stroke, also characterized any emotional setbacks he might have experienced.

We also learn something about the women themselves. In an age in which women's opportunities were limited, in which they were expected to be more obedient than innovative, these women refused to live down to such expectations. Thrown into contact with Stalin's security thugs, Roosevelt's robust secret service contingent, thousands of homesick and female-deprived soldiers, sailors and airmen, they handled themselves with style and dignity, without adopting frosty exteriors. Faced with problems with which no secretarial school could have prepared them, from shipping Churchill's goldfish to Roosevelt without killing them, to setting up systems that allowed their boss to follow the performance of his shares, to conveying authority when answering correspondence directed at a too-busy Churchill, they retained their aplomb. Yes, they could be rattled on occasion by a boss so intent on his work that he ignored the effect of his impatience on his secretary. But that was rare, and recovery almost instantaneous. It was their work as well as the performance of women in factories during the war that helped persuade Churchill that the roles of women needed re-examination – although backsliding did occur when it came to demobilization, with men given priority so they could find civilian jobs. It was assumed that women would return to home-making.

It is impossible – writing in the second decade of the twenty-first century – to avoid asking whether any of the tasks assigned to these women were demeaning or constituted what today would be call harassment. After all, when he finally retired for the night Gemmell, the last secretary on duty, seeing Churchill's stocking feet protruding from under his bedclothes, removed his socks. She is unclear as to whether she just assumed that chore or was asked to perform it, but in either event 'I never thought anything of it… I just thought it was fun… anything that would let me get to bed.' When he paced the floor of his bedroom in the morning, dictating non-stop, it might be after leaping from bed wearing only a short bed jacket that did not cover all the parts of his anatomy that want covering, at one point giving Holmes 'the best view of his behind that I have ever had'. All unacceptable by the standards of our time, but none, according to their own accounts, upsetting to the women who worked for him and accepted these experiences as just part of the job. Times, and with them job descriptions, change.

Finally, almost all of the secretaries described that great intangible – the electricity when Churchill entered a room, the presence of what we now call 'charisma'. As detective Thompson put it, his boss 'wasn't dull to be around'.[5] There was a 'buzz', a noticeable step up in the pace of activity when he returned to the Admiralty and again when he moved on to Number 10. Neither Chamberlain before him nor Attlee after him had that intangible quality. It had tangible effects, not least motivating those around him to do better, to do more, to cater to his needs and by extension the nation's. That is clear from the historical records left us by the women (and one man) who worked for Churchill, records that constitute a valuable addition to the body of knowledge we have about what working with Winston was really like.

APPENDIX 1

———

Operation Desperate

Collegiality seemed to come naturally to Churchill's secretaries. They worked long hours, made their own decisions as to the division of their many chores, and with no quarrels. Occasionally, they erupted in humour, and a sophisticated, cheeky humour it was. In May 1942, as Churchill and his military staff prepared for a trip to the US, several of the female secretaries wrote a spoof memo, Operation Desperate, to the War Cabinet outlining their needs. Headed *'To Be Burnt Before Reading'*, they asked that 'vital commodities' such as cosmetics, chocolates and silk stockings, preferably in Mist Beige colour, be brought back from the US.

TOP
~~MOST~~ SECRET.   Copy No...........

MOST SECRET – TO BE BURNT BEFORE READING

J.P.(T)(42) 1 (FINAL)

9th May 1942

WAR CABINET

JOINT PLANNING TYPISTS

OPERATION "DESPERATE"

Report by the J.P. Typing Pool

In view of the recent changes in the Government policy
of distribution of coupons,* we have examined the situation,
and the following conclusions have been reached:-

(a) The limitation of supplies in the U.K. has resulted
in the following acute shortages -

(i) silk stockings;
(ii) chocolates;
(iii) cosmetics.

(b) The lack of these vital commodities is regarded as
extremely serious and may, in consequence, become
a source of extreme embarrassment. This must be
avoided at all costs.

(c) It is felt that immediate steps should be taken to
explore the possibilities of U.S. resources.

2.   In the light of the above, it is considered that the most
expedient method of implementing the proposal in (c) would be
the early despatch of a mission to the U.S.A; a Force Commander
has already been appointed, in anticipation of instructions.
Accordingly, we attach a draft directive⌀ to the officer
concerned.

                    (Signed)   NAUSEA D. BAGWASH
                               LIZZI LIGHT-ffOOT
                               MAGGIE DEUCE
                               DEADLY NIGHTSHADE
                               JUNE WINTERBOTTHAM (Mrs)

   ⨯ As from May 31st - only 60 in 14 months!
   ⌀ Annex

DRAFT DIRECTIVE TO FORCE COMMANDER
OPERATION "DESPERATE"

YOU have been selected to command Special Mission to
U.S.A. for the purpose of exploring the rich resources,
believed to exist in the West, of certain vital commodities.
These are:-

      (i) Silk Stockings

     (ii) Chocolates

    (iii) Cosmetics.

You are to assume command as soon as possible, and
in the implementation of this Operation the co-operation of
the acolytes of the Joint Staff Mission will no doubt prove
of great value.

For your guidance we append a Table giving detailed
information of commodities required.

Commodity	Size	Colour
Silk Stockings	10½	Mist Beige
Chocolates	Large	Usual
Cosmetics:-		
Powder	"	Ochre Rosé
Lipstick	"	Garnet
Creams	"	Natural

OPERATION "DESPERATE"

Memorandum by the Force Commander.

        I have examined the directions issued to me with
my usual unremitting attention and wish to bring to the
Chiefs' of Staff attention the following important points: -

      (a) I have so far been allotted only one
           aeroplane. In order to carry out
           my task to the satisfaction of all
           concerned, I shall require a special
           fleet of transport aircraft, suitably
           modified to carry

         (i)   Silk stockings (large).
        (ii) Chocolates ($10\frac{1}{2}$).
      (iii) Cosmetics (Usual).

      (b) If the Chiefs of Staff cannot see their
           way to providing me with this essential
           prerequisite, there will be no alternative
           but to carry out the following modified
           plan.

2.   Before leaving the United States, it is my
intention secretly to remove all my normal clothing and
substitute for it a complete covering of silk stockings. By
this simple ruse de guerre I confidently expect to hoodwink
the immigration authorities, the pilot of the aeroplane, and
the Customs officials. My disguise will be rendered even
more effective by a liberal application of cosmetics.

3.   This will not altogether obviate the difficulty
of providing transport for the chocolates. I anticipate,
however, that I shall be expected to bring back some
unimportant documents, and it should be an easy matter to
substitute chocolates while no one is looking. A detailed
plan will be submitted in due course.

10th May, 1942

APPENDIX 2

The black mollies

Because Churchill's curiosity was boundless, his interests wide-ranging and his contacts extensive, the incoming volume of mail was enormous. Nevertheless, his secretaries knew what letters he would want to see immediately, and which they should keep in mind should he later choose to respond. In November 1950, a five-year-old boy, Andrew Cruikshank, who shared a birth date with Churchill, offered the prime minister twelve black mollies as a birthday present, which Churchill was pleased to accept for his fish tanks at Chequers. More than half a year later, Churchill, who had thanked the boy when the mollies arrived, asked Jane Portal to remind him of the boy's name, so he might write to let the boy know how the mollies were doing. That Churchill thought to do that, and Portal instantly found the boy's letter, testifies to his kindness and her efficiency.

Here are Churchill's letter to the boy and Andrew's response.

10 December, 1950.

Dear Andrew,

I am so very pleased with the little fishes, who
are now safely and happily installed here, and seem to have
settled down in their new home.   Thank you very much for
sending me such a nice birthday present; they have given
me much pleasure already, and I know I shall always enjoy
watching them.   Thank you also for your good wishes, and
those of your family.   I was so sorry to learn that your
Mother had been taken ill, and I hope she will get better
soon.

I hope you had a happy birthday, and that you
will like this book which I am sending you as a present,
and in which I have written your name.

Yours sincerely,
W.S.C.

Master Andrew Cruickshank.

MR. CHURCHILL.

You asked me to find
out the name of the person who gave
you the Black Mollies.   They were
given you on your last birthday
by a little boy called Andrew
Cruickshank.   I attach the correspondence.   Shall I draft a letter
saying they are getting on very
well?

J.P.
25. 6. 51.

W.S.C.

25 June, 1951.

Dear Andrew,

      You might like to know that the Black
Mollies are doing very well and two new ones have been
born, and we are expecting several more. I have now got
several fish tanks, almost an aquarium with Red Platties
and other tropical fish, but the Black Mollies are my
favourites . You started me on this interesting business.

Yours sincerely,
W.S.C.

Master Andrew Cruickshank.

Gift to ~~Parkside~~

PARKSIDE

27 JUNE

DEAR Mr CHURCHILL,

THANK YOU VERY MUCH FOR YOUR LOVELY LETTER. I AM SO GLAD TO HEAR THAT THE MOLLIES ARE QUITE WELL AND HAPPY AND THAT YOU LIKE THEM BEST.

ANDREW CRUICKSHANK

SOURCES

A word about the source on which I have drawn heavily – the oral histories gathered by interviewers from many of the secretaries who worked for Churchill, deposited at the Churchill Archives. I realized that I was dealing with the recollections of events half a century ago, as told by women no longer young. And I was aware of the warning of Churchill biographer Roy Jenkins, 'of the frailty of memory, without will to deceive, which renders unreliable so much personal reminiscence'.[1] Sir Martin Gilbert has also warned us of the 'hazards of oral history'.[2]

Fortunately, the years covered in these interviews overlap substantially, enabling me to check the various recollections, one against the other. I was also able to verify these recollections against unimpeachable sources, such as Sir Martin's biography and other writings, and the diaries of Jock Colville, Joan Bright (later Bright Astley), Elizabeth Layton (later Nel) and Lord Moran, and others; and against the published recollections of the few secretaries who did commit them to print. There were instances in which memories were not precise, others in which more than one secretary claimed to be the central figure in some event. But these were rare and of no consequence to the usefulness of the interviews for the purpose to which I have put them. Working with Winston created lasting and largely accurate memories for these women, for whom those were probably the best years of their lives – their glory days – and as such memorable. All quotes in the text without endnotes are from the oral histories.

The only thing I have been unable to do to my complete

satisfaction is convey to readers the full range of their emotions as they tell tales of Churchill's kindnesses and demanding but forgiving nature, and the depth of their admiration for the man and his accomplishments. It is difficult to convey the accents, the intonation, the emphases, the chuckles that made listening and re-listening to the recorded interviews such a great pleasure. I have underlined words emphasized by these women when their histories were recorded.

I am fortunate to have as a friend Jane Portal (later Lady Williams of Elvel), to whom I was introduced years ago by Gordon Brown. Lady Williams (Jane Portal at the time she worked for Churchill), her memory intact – as is her sense of humour – generously cleared up several ambiguities that the interviewers left unresolved, and supplemented the interviews with details the interviewers may not have had time to elicit.

Given all these factors, I am comfortable relying on the oral histories, duly cross-checked one against the other and against other impeccable sources. All quotations except those identified in the text or endnotes are from the oral histories. Of course, any mistakes are solely my own. Those do not include leaving abbreviated words such as 'cld' where that is how they appear in the source being quoted.

ACKNOWLEDGEMENTS

No one doing research on any aspect of Sir Winston Churchill's life can comment on sources without giving Sir Martin Gilbert and the Archives at Churchill College, Cambridge, pride of place. Thanks to Sir Martin, we have his eight-volume life of Churchill, the three volumes of *The Churchill War Papers* and now the twenty-one Documents volumes from Hilldale College's Churchill Project. All supplemented by numerous books focusing on one or another aspect of that life. In short, researchers start with access to all that Churchill wrote and did. Sir Martin devoted a too-short lifetime to organizing the massive volume of materials generated by Churchill during a very active lifetime, one tenet of which was that everything – everything – must be written down.

Thanks to the ever-helpful and virtually indispensable Allen Packwood, OBE, the Director of the Churchill Archives Centre, scholars have a place to come to gain access to the raw material underlying Sir Martin's work, the memoirs and diaries of Churchill's contemporaries – all now accessible online thanks to the generosity of Laurence Geller, CBE, Chairman of the International Churchill Society.

Thanks, too, to the resourceful and first-rate staff at the Churchill College Archives, whose ability to discover unpublished treasures is legendary. Thanks to them, an 'Aladdin's cave' of treasures, as Sir Martin described the Archives, is kept in perfect order and made easily accessible to historians by the Archives staff.

Patricia Ackerman skilfully interviewed many of the personal secretaries whose oral histories are the basis of this book, asking trenchant questions and letting the women tell their own stories in their own words.

Many people who worked for Churchill have shared their memories with me, and I thank Jane Portal (now Lady Williams) for her long friendship and for sharing her wonderful recall of what it was like to multitask for Churchill, while she 'took down', as he called dictation.

Cecily 'Chips' Gemmell and Delia Morton (Drummond) also shared memories with me, as did Georgina Hill, Kathleen Hill's granddaughter. Sadly, Hugh Lunghi, Anthony Montague Browne and Joan Bright Astley have passed away, but not before sharing with me their experiences of working with Churchill. Hugh was Churchill's Russian interpreter at the major conferences; Anthony was Churchill's Principal Private Secretary and aide during Churchill's final decade; Joan was chief administrator in General Sir Hastings Ismay's office.

Randolph Churchill has generously provided the Foreword and his own recollections, and Andrew Roberts has unselfishly helped in more ways than I can list here.

My researcher at the Churchill Archives, Sue Sutton, and my extremely talented picture editor Cecilia MacKay have added enormously to the value of this book. George Capel, my trusty agent, advised me well, as always.

In my office, Gayle Damiano and Leyre Gonzalez have helped in so many ways, as has Jeff Raben, who defended me when my computer wilfully escalated attacks on my manuscript, and thanks to Diana Obbard for her assistance in sorting out some of the classical references herein.

Professor of History at the University of Colorado at Denver, Dr Myra Rich, called to my attention the literature on the uses of oral histories and I thank her, too, for that, and for her friendship.

With thanks to Edouard Manset for sending me the important special edition of *Paris Match* dedicated entirely to *Churchill: le stratège*.

And I cannot thank Bea Kristol – known also as Gertrude

Himmelfarb – enough for her encouragement, advice and long friendship.

Sadly, the death of my beloved friend, Dr Charles Krauthammer, means I lost the opportunity and pleasure of discussing with him his conclusion that Winston Churchill is 'the indispensable man'.

NOTES

References to *Winston S. Churchill* (Heinemann, 1966–88), the eight-volume official biography, written by Randolph Churchill (Vols I and II) and Sir Martin Gilbert (Vols III to VIII), are shown by volume and page number.

References to the Documents volumes appear as Gilbert, *The Churchill Documents*, followed by volume and page numbers.

References to Churchill's papers in the Churchill Archives Centre at Churchill College, Cambridge, are shown as either **CHAR** (for Chartwell Papers, dated up to July 1945) or **CHUR** (for the Churchill Papers from July 1945 onwards), followed by their series, file and folio numbers: e.g., CHUR 1/25/123.

Epigraphs

1 Martin Gilbert, *In Search of Churchill: A Historian's Journey*, p. 173.
2 Ibid., p. 171.
3 Charles Krauthammer, 'Winston Churchill: The Indispensable Man', in *Things that Matter: Three Decades of Passions, Pastimes and Politics*, p. 22.
4 Martin Gilbert, *Winston S. Churchill: Never Despair*, Vol. VIII, p. 1299.
5 Barry Gough, *Churchill and Fisher: Titans at the Admiralty*, p. 509.

Preface

1 'Churchill used his minutes the way an octopus uses its tentacles – to reach everywhere, to be many places at once.' Barbara Leaming, *Churchill Defiant: Fighting On, 1945–1955*, p. 37.
2 Private communication with the author, with permission.

3   Celia Sandys, *Chasing Churchill: The Travels of Winston Churchill by His Granddaughter*, pp. 240–1.
4   This is not the place to enter the debate about the use of oral histories. Suffice it to say that 'combining them with other historical sources [helps us] to find out what happened in the past', Alistair Thomson, 'Four Paradigm Transformations', *The Oral History Review*, Vol. 34, Issue 1 (2007), p. 54.
5   Virginia Cowles, *Winston Churchill: The Era and the Man*, p. 245.

Chapter 1: Violet Pearman

1   Martin Gilbert, *Winston S. Churchill: The Prophet of Truth 1922–1939*, Vol. V, p. 362.
2   Letter from Pearman to Miss Neal in search of alternative employment (2 April 1934). Churchill Archives Centre, WCHL 1/23. One of Pearman's predecessors, Lettice Fisher, who worked for Churchill when he was chancellor of the exchequer, left her post for what Sir Martin Gilbert describes as a 'rest cure'. Churchill arranged for medical care for her.
3   John Colville, *Footprints in Time*, p. 77.
4   John Colville, *Fringes of Power*, p. 77.
5   Martin Gilbert, *The Churchill Documents: The Coming of War 1936–1939*, Vol. 13, pp. 444–5.
6   Ibid.
7   Joan Bright Astley, *The Inner Circle: A View of War at the Top*, p. 7.
8   Gilbert, *In Search of Churchill*, p. 160–1.
9   Roy Jenkins, *Churchill*, pp. 431, 487.
10   Winston Churchill, 'My New York Misadventure', *Daily Mail* (4/5 January 1932), reprinted *Finest Hour*, No. 136, Autumn, 2007, p. 24.
11   '… a large apartment, No. 11, which spread across the top of two floors' Stefan Buczacki, *Churchill & Chartwell*, p. 175.
12   Samuel H. Howes, 'Recollections', letter dated 20 December 1936 sent to Martin Gilbert (19 November 1981) in Gilbert, *The Churchill Documents: The Coming of War 1936–1939*, Vol. 13, p. 503.
13   David Lough, *No More Champagne: Churchill and His Money*, p. 185.
14   Gilbert, *The Churchill Documents: The Wilderness Years 1929–1935*, Vol. 12, p. 46.
15   Lough, *No More Champagne*, p. 250.
16   Gilbert, *In Search of Churchill*, p, 157.
17   Gilbert, *The Churchill Documents: The Coming of War 1936–1939*, Vol. 13, p. 78.
18   Ibid., pp. 77–8, 84.
19   Pearman was not the only beneficiary of Churchill's generosity. When in Canada for the First Quebec Conference, Layton's mother flew from

Vancouver to see her daughter in Quebec and Churchill offered to pay half her airfare. Layton writes: 'The fact that while pressed upon by matters of international importance, he [Churchill] still never forgot those who worked for him, inspired feelings of real devotion in his staff which will be readily understood.' Elizabeth Layton, *Winston Churchill by His Personal Secretary*, p. 76.

20 Gilbert, *In Search of Churchill*, p. 117. The following narrative is set forth in more detail on pp. 115–17.

21 Ibid., p. 115.

22 Ibid., p. 117.

23 Ibid., p. 124.

24 Gilbert, *Winston S. Churchill: The Prophet of Truth 1922–1939*, Vol. V, p. 874.

25 Gilbert, *The Churchill Documents: The Coming of War 1936–1939*, Vol. 13, p. 422.

26 Gilbert, *In Search of Churchill*, p. 125.

27 Gilbert, *Winston S. Churchill: The Prophet of Truth 1922–1939*, Vol. V, p. 883.

28 Gilbert, *In Search of Churchill*, p. 126.

29 Gilbert, *Winston S. Churchill: Never Despair 1945–1965*, Vol. VIII, p. 632.

30 Gilbert, *The Churchill Documents: The Coming of War 1936–1939*, Vol. 13, p. 300.

31 David Reynolds, *In Command of History: Churchill Fighting and Writing the Second World War*, p. 152.

32 Mary Soames (ed.), *Speaking for Themselves: The Personal Letters of Winston and Clementine Churchill*, p. 351.

33 Ibid., p. xiv.

34 Gilbert, *Winston S. Churchill: The Prophet of Truth 1922–1939*, Vol. V, p. 411.

35 Ibid., p. 319. Churchill was repeatedly distracted by other money-making opportunities.

36 The Churchill Project at Hillsdale College, *Word Counts* (5 September 2015), https://winstonchurchill.hillsdale.edu/word-counts-2/.

37 Gilbert, *Winston S. Churchill: The Prophet of Truth 1922–1939*, Vol. V, p. 559.

38 Mary S. Lovell, *The Riviera Set 1920–1960: The Golden Years of Glamour and Excess*, p. 1. For a video of the Chateau and its famous water slide into the sea, watch: https://www.youtube.com/watch?v=6Oe8GgTCMEU. Also in A&E Home Video's Biography Series *Biography: The Complete Churchill* (VHS), which shows him sliding into the sea head first!

39 Frank Sawyers (1909–72) worked for Churchill throughout the war years and flew to his funeral in Eisenhower's aircraft at the invitation of the American general and former president. In the 1945 Resignation Honours List, he received the new Defence Medal, established in May

1945. 'A little baldish-Cumbrian with a round florid face, piercing blue eyes, and a pronounced lisp... He worshipped [Churchill].' In Gerald Pawle, *The War and Colonel Warden*, p. 166.

40 Leaming, *Churchill Defiant*, p. 40.

41 Gilbert, *Winston S. Churchill: The Prophet of Truth 1922–1939*, Vol. V, p. 559.

42 Gilbert, *In Search of Churchill*, p. 34.

43 Gilbert, *Winston S. Churchill: The Prophet of Truth 1922–1939*, Vol. V, p. 696.

44 Soames (ed.), *Winston and Clementine*, p. 417.

45 Cyril Bainbridge and Roy Stockdill, *The News of the World Story*, pp. 14, 105.

46 Fred Glueckstein, 'Churchill's Sovereigns: King George V (1910–1936)', The Churchill Project, Hillsdale College, 11 December 2017.

47 Jenkins, *Churchill*, p. 487.

48 Bainbridge and Stockdill, *The News of the World Story*, p. 107.

49 Gilbert, *Winston S. Churchill: The Prophet of Truth 1922–1939*, Vol. V, p. 784.

50 Soames (ed.), *Winston and Clementine*, p. 432.

51 Ibid. On 8 January he dined with the Windsors and Lloyd George at the Chateau.

52 Gilbert, *Winston S. Churchill: The Prophet of Truth 1922–1939*, Vol. V, p. 894.

53 Ibid., p. 896.

54 Gilbert, *The Churchill Documents: The Coming of War 1936–1939*, Vol. 13, p. 885.

55 Gilbert, *Winston S. Churchill: The Prophet of Truth 1922–1939*, Vol. 5, p. 897.

56 Gilbert, *The Churchill War Papers*, Vol. 1, p. 820.

57 Gilbert, *In Search of Churchill*, p. 158. It is not clear whether she was first ordered to rest because of her abnormally high blood pressure, or whether the stroke itself forced her to stay at home.

58 Gilbert, *The Churchill Documents: The Coming of War 1936–1939*, Vol. 13, p. 1123.

59 Gilbert, *In Search of Churchill*, p. 159.

60 Ibid.

61 Gilbert, *The Churchill Documents: The Coming of War 1936–1939*, Vol. 13, p. 1033.

62 Gilbert, *In Search of Churchill*, p. 163.

Chapter 2: Grace Hamblin

1   A. L. Rowse, '"There Was Once a Man": A Visit to Chartwell, 1995', The Churchill Project: Hillsdale College, 29 February 2016.

2 Hamblin talk to Inner Wheel Club in Westerham, 1974, Churchill Archives Centre, Churchill College, Cambridge, HAMB 1/1, p. 2.

3 Obituary of Grace Hamblin, *Los Angeles Times* (19 October 2002), http://articles.latimes.com/2002/oct/19/local/me-hamblin19.

4 Gilbert, *The Churchill Documents: The Wilderness Years, 1929–1935*, Vol. 12, p. 477.

5 John Peck, *Dublin from Downing Street*, p. 68. A fuller description of the members of the 'Secret Circle' appears in Allen Packwood's *How Churchill Waged War*, pp. 18–19.

6 Elizabeth Layton Nel, *Winston Churchill by His Personal Secretary*, p. xix.

7 Vanda Salmon, unpublished memoir, Churchill College Archives, SALM 2/1, p. 53 ff.

8 Sir John Wheeler-Bennett, *Action This Day: Working with Churchill*, p. 17.

9 Cowles, *Winston Churchill: The Era and the Man*, p. 214.

10 Lough, *No More Champagne*, passim.

11 Ibid., p. 238.

12 Ibid., p. 202.

13 Hamblin talk to Inner Wheel Club in Westerham, 1974, p. 14.

14 Violet Bonham Carter, *Winston Churchill As I Knew Him*, p. 151.

15 Roy Howells, *Churchill's Last Years*, p. 87.

16 Churchill Archives Centre, CHUR 2/375, image 35.

17 Chartwell Bulletin No. 12, CHAR 1/273/139–45 image 1.

18 *The Churchill Documents: The Ever-Widening War*, Vol. 16, p. 749 and Colville Diary, p. 394.

19 Fred Glueckstein, '"Cats Look Down on You": Churchill's Feline Menagerie', *Finest Hour*, No. 139, Summer 2008, p. 50. A wonderful article on all of Churchill's cats, including especially the favourite, Tango.

20 In the spring of 1959, when Churchill visited President Eisenhower's farm in Gettysburg, Pennsylvania, he complained that he had not been allowed to see the pigs, although all the other animals had been shown to him. Gilbert, Vol. VIII, p. 1296.

21 Hamblin talk to Inner Wheel Club in Westerham, 1974, p. 20.

22 Grace Hamblin, 'Frabjous Days: Chartwell Memories', talk given at the 5th International Churchill Conference, The Adolphus, Dallas, printed in *Finest Hour*, No. 117, Winter 2002–3, p. 24.

23 From DVD: *War Stories with Oliver North: The Life and Times of Winston Churchill*, Fox News Channel (2007).

24 Hamblin talk to Inner Wheel Club in Westerham, 1974, p. 11.

25 Gilbert, *In Search of Churchill*, p. 309.

26 Hamblin talk to Inner Wheel Club in Westerham, 1974, p. 19.

27 In 1930 Churchill had estimated his earnings from his writings in the *Strand Magazine* at £3,000 (about £200,000 in today's money).

28   Lough, *No More Champagne*, p. 225.

29   Vanda Salmon, unpublished memoir, p. 14. Salmon reports that Churchill carried the plant up and down from Chartwell, and that 'during the time it bloomed so he did not miss a day of it'.

30   Winston S. Churchill, *The Second World War: The Gathering Storm*, Vol. 1, p. 365.

31   Gough, *Churchill and Fisher*, p. 507.

32   Gilbert, *Winston S. Churchill: The Prophet of Truth 1922–1939*, Vol. V, p. 1113.

33   Sonia Purnell, *First Lady: The Life and Wars of Clementine Churchill*, p. 164.

34   Mary Soames, *Clementine Churchill: The Revised and Updated Biography*, p. 331.

35   Layton, *Winston Churchill by His Personal Secretary*, pp. 8–9.

36   The Annexe was 'the set of rooms, above ground on the St James's Park side of the old Board of Trade Building at Storeys Gate, which were used by Churchill as his main, sleeping, eating and working accommodations for the rest of the war. Whenever he could, he would hold meetings in Downing Street, but his main base of operation, including his Map Room under Captain Pim, was situated in this Annexe. There was also a bedroom, a small dining room, a study, and a room for the Private Secretaries. Immediately below were the underground Cabinet War Rooms.' In Gilbert, *The Churchill Documents: Never Surrender May 1940–December 1940*, Vol. 15, p. 1107.

37   Purnell, *First Lady*, p. 94.

38   Soames, *Clementine Churchill*, p. 332.

39   Colville, *The Fringes of Power*, p. 278.

40   Hamblin talk to Inner Wheel Club in Westerham, 1974, p. 18.

41   Kim Baldonado, '*Queen Mary* Celebrated on 80th Anniversary', NBC Southern California, 25 May 2016.

42   IWM Document 9858.

43   Purnell, *First Lady*, p. 226.

44   While maintaining her work for the YWCA, in February 1941 she became President of their Wartime Fund. See Soames, *Clementine Churchill*, p. 359.

45   Purnell, *First Lady*, p. 280.

46   Grace in Russia 1945, Churchill Archives Centre, Churchill College, Cambridge, HAMB 1/ 4, p. 3.

47   Ibid., p. 4.

48   Ibid., p. 5.

49   Ibid., p. 6.

50   Soames, *Clementine Churchill*, p. 390.

51   Lord Butler, *The Art of the Possible*, p. 127.

52   Colville, *Footprints in Time*, p. 207.

53   Soames, *Clementine Churchill*, p. 428.

54 Ibid., p. 262.
55 Hamblin talk to Inner Wheel Club in Westerham, 1974, p. 10.
56 Gilbert, *Winston S. Churchill: Never Despair 1945–1965*, Vol. VIII, p. 462.
57 Soames (ed.), *Speaking for Themselves*, p. 580.
58 Rosemary Hill, 'Churchill's Faces', *London Review of Books* (30 March 2017). Vandalism is generally taken to mean 'wilful and malicious' destruction of property. Lady Churchill's was certainly 'wilful' in the sense of 'deliberate'. But an act to preserve the memory of her husband as he was during his greatest years rather than as a 'senile old man who had not done up his fly buttons', as Portal put it, hardly classifies as malicious.
59 Christopher A. Long, 'Chartwell Memories: A Neighbour Looks Back', *Finest Hour*, No. 126, Spring 2005.
60 Hamblin talk to Inner Wheel Club in Westerham, 1974, p. 8.

Chapter 3: Kathleen Hill

1 Martin Gilbert, Vol. V, p. 866.
2 Gilbert, *Winston S. Churchill: The Prophet of Truth 1922–1939*, Vol. V, p. 729.
3 Obituary of Kathleen Hill, *Daily Telegraph* (18 November 1992).
4 Ibid.
5 Private communication to the author, with permission.
6 Gilbert, *In Search of Churchill*, p. 162.
7 Gilbert, *Winston Churchill, The Wilderness Years: Speaking out against Hitler in the Prelude to the War*, p. 254.
8 Lough, *No More Champagne*, pp. 305 ff.
9 Churchill Archives Centre at Churchill College, Cambridge CHAR, 8/639 image 196.
10 Lough, *No More Champagne*, pp. 302, 306, 308.
11 Gilbert, *Winston S. Churchill: Never Despair, 1945–1965*, Vol. VIII, p. 343.
12 Gilbert, *Winston S. Churchill: The Prophet of Truth 1922–1939*, Vol. V, p. 866.
13 Churchill Archives Centre, CHAR, 8/639/99.
14 Max Arthur, *Churchill: The Life: An Authorized Pictorial Biography*, p. 105.
15 Alexander Cadogan, *The Diaries of Sir Alexander Cadogan O.M., 1938–1945*, ed. David Dilks, p. 675.
16 Conversation with the author, 18 February 2018.
17 Pawle, *The War and Colonel Warden*, p. 198.
18 Richard M. Langworth (ed.), *The Definitive Wit of Winston Churchill*, p. 197. As early as aged fourteen, Churchill wrote to his mother asking her to send his Nanny down to Harrow to help him pack 'so I should

not have the anxiety about it'. See Randolph S. Churchill's, *Winston S. Churchill: Youth 1876–1896*, Vol. 1, p. 170.

19   Gilbert, *In Search of Churchill* has a slightly different version, p. 300.

20   Vanda Salmon, unpublished memoir, p. 25.

21   Andrew Roberts, *Churchill: Walking with Destiny*, pp. 609–10.

22   Layton, *Winston Churchill by His Personal Secretary*, p. 26.

23   Roberts, *Churchill: Walking With Destiny*, p. 610.

24   Vanda Salmon, unpublished memoir, pp. 30–1.

25   Peck, *Dublin from Downing Street*, p. 68.

26   Gilbert, *In Search of Churchill*, p. 164.

27   Gilbert, *The Churchill Documents: The Coming of War, 1936–1939*, Vol. 13, p. 1372.

28   Gilbert, *In Search of Churchill*, p. 161.

29   Churchill Archives Centre at Churchill College, Cambridge, CHAR, 1/386.

30   Sir John Martin, *Downing Street: The War Years*, p. 54.

31   Gilbert, *Winston S. Churchill: Finest Hour 1939–1941*, Vol. VI, p. 1102.

32   Purnell, *First Lady*, p. 238.

33   Soames, *Clementine Churchill*, p. 470.

34   Gilbert, *The Churchill Documents: The Coming of War, 1936–1939*, Vol. 13, p. 1346.

35   Lord Moran, *Winston Churchill: The Struggle for Survival*, p. 457.

36   Peter Clarke, *Mr Churchill's Profession: Statesman, Orator, Writer*, pp. 240–1.

37   Gilbert, *In Search of Churchill*, p. 301.

38   Churchill Archives at Churchill College, Cambridge, CHAR 8/639/178.

39   Gilbert, *Winston S. Churchill: The Prophet of Truth 1922–1939*, Vol. V, p. 1113.

40   Gilbert, *In Search of Churchill*, p. 164.

41   Lord Beaverbrook, *Politicians and the War 1914–1916*, p. 127.

42   Gilbert, *Winston S. Churchill: Finest Hour 1939–1941*, Vol. VI, p. 73.

43   W. H. Thompson, *Sixty Minutes with Winston Churchill*, p. 42.

44   Lough, *No More Champagne*, p. 282.

45   Gilbert, *Winston S. Churchill: Finest Hour 1939–1941*, Vol. VI, p. 605.

46   Which 'was really an ice-bucket from the Savoy Hotel'. Ibid., p. 605, n 3.

47   Charles Richardson, *From Churchill's Secret Circle to the BBC: The Biography of Lieutenant General Sir Ian Jacob GBE CB DL*, pp. 97–9.

48   Glueckstein, '"Cats Look Down on You"', p. 51.

49   Gilbert, *Winston S. Churchill: Finest Hour 1939–1941*, Vol. VI, p. 121.

50   Gilbert, *In Search of Churchill*, p. 169.

51   Walter Graebner, *My Dear Mr Churchill*, p. 32.

52   Colville, *The Fringes of Power*, p. 285.

53   Winston Churchill, *The Second World War: The Grand Alliance*, Vol. 3, p. 551.

54 Richard Holmes, *Churchill's Bunker: The Secret Headquarters at the Heart of Britain's Victory*, p. 177.

55 Gilbert, *In Search of Churchill*, p. 169.

56 Gilbert, *Winston S. Churchill: Never Despair 1945–1965*, Vol. VIII, p. 785.

Chapter 4: Patrick Kinna

1   Layton, *Winston Churchill by His Personal Secretary*, p. 18.

2   Virginia Nicholson, *Millions Like Us: Women's Lives in War and Peace, 1939–1949*, pp. 114, 117.

3   Anne de Courcy, *Debs at War: 1939–1945: How Wartime Changed Their Lives*, pp. 60, 211.

4   Robert Meiklejohn, unpublished diary, Harriman Papers, Library of Congress, p. 312.

5   Churchill Archives Centre, CHAR 20/232/10, image 1. Cabinet Papers, 5 July 1945.

6   Meiklejohn, unpublished diary, p. 352.

7   Jean-Paul Flintoff, 'Obituary of Patrick Kinna: Confidential Secretary to Winston Churchill', *Guardian* (6 April 2009).

8   Layton, *Winston Churchill by His Personal Secretary*, p. 58.

9   Martin Gilbert, *The Churchill Documents: Testing Times 1942*, Vol. 17, p. 802, fn 1.

10 Jean-Paul Flintoff, 'Obituary of Patrick Kinna'.

11 Vanda Salmon unpublished memoir, p. 56. She estimated that to be 90 to 100 words per minute.

12 Layton, *Winston Churchill by His Personal Secretary*, p. 18.

13 Bright Astley, *The Inner Circle*, p. 75.

14 https://www.warhistoryonline.com/instant-articles/churchills-favorite-spy.html and Clare Mulley, *The Spy Who Loved: The Secrets and Lives of Christine Granville*.

15 Joanna Moody, *From Churchill's War Rooms: Letters of a Secretary 1943–1945*, p. 63.

16 Ibid., pp. 73–4.

17 Randolph S. Churchill, *The Churchill Documents: Youth 1876–1896*, Vol. 1, p. 192.

18 Brian Lavery, *Churchill Goes to War: Winston's Wartime Journeys*, pp. 22, 24.

19 Peck, *Dublin from Downing Street*, p. 68.

20 Portal in conversation with the author.

21 Martin Gilbert, *The Churchill Documents: The Ever-Widening War 1941*, Vol. 16, p. 1654.

22 Martin Gilbert, *Winston S. Churchill: Road to Victory 1941–1945*, Vol. VII, p. 7. Quoting from Charles Mott-Radclyffe, a long-serving and successful Conservative Party politician.

23 Meiklejohn, unpublished diary, p. 320.

24 Colville, *The Fringes of Power*, p. 633.

25 Pawle, *The War and Colonel Warden*, p. 197.

26 Ibid.

27 Gilbert, *The Churchill Documents: The Ever-Widening War 1941*, Vol. 16, p. 1327, fn 1.

28 Meredith Hindley, *Destination Casablanca: Exile, Espionage, and the Battle for North Africa in World War II*, p. 350.

29 Richardson, *From Churchill's Secret Circle to the BBC*, p. 174.

30 Gilbert, *Winston S. Churchill: Finest Hour 1939–1941*, Vol. VII, p. 308.

31 Gilbert, *Winston S. Churchill: Road to Victory 1941–1945*, Vol. VII, p. 28.

32 Layton, *Winston Churchill by His Personal Secretary*, pp. 65, 69.

33 Gilbert, *Winston S. Churchill: Road to Victory 1941–1945*, Vol. VII, pp. 408–9.

34 Winston S. Churchill, *The Second World War: The Hinge of Fate*, Vol. IV, p. 429.

35 Andrew Roberts, *Hitler and Churchill: Secrets of Leadership*, p. 54.

36 Ben Macintyre, *Rogue Heroes: The History of the SAS, Britain's Secret Special Forces Unit That Sabotaged the Nazis and Changed the Nature of War*, p. 167.

37 Soames, *Clementine Churchill*, pp. 516, 544.

38 The sword is now gathering dust in the Battle of Stalingrad Museum in Volgograd (formerly Stalingrad). See *Independent* (7 November 1993). It is not likely that any of the female shorthand typists would have been entrusted with this honour or of carrying the TA files – in a canoe or elsewhere.

39 Gilbert, *Winston S. Churchill: Road to Victory 1941–1945*, Vol. VII, p. 602.

40 'A little gun-boat patrols up and down in front of the house in case a German submarine should pop up its nose and shoot up the Villa.' In Gilbert, *Winston S. Churchill: Road to Victory 1941–1945*, Vol. VII, p. 615.

41 J. A. Vale and J. W. Scadding, 'In Carthage Ruins: The Illness of Sir Winston Churchill at Carthage, December 1943', *Journal of the Royal College of Physicians*, no page number.

42 Ibid., Abstract 2017.

43 Martin Gilbert, *Churchill: A Life*, p. 762.

44 Layton, *Winston Churchill by His Personal Secretary*, p. 88.

45 When in Rome with Churchill, in August 1944, both Kinna and Sawyers were received by Pope Pius XII. In Pawle, *The War and Colonel Warden*, p. 313.

46 Soames, *Clementine Churchill*, p. 380.

47 Colville, *The Fringes of Power*, p. 459.

48 Moody, *From Churchill's War Rooms*, p. 89.

49 Jason Woodward, 'Eminent Churchillians – Patrick Kinna MBE – "He was sure we would win all along"', *Finest Hour*, No. 115, Summer 2002, p. 38.

50 Gilbert, *Winston S. Churchill: Road to Victory 1941–1945*, Vol. VII, p. 1260.

51 Jean-Paul Flintoff, 'Obituary of Patrick Kinna', *Guardian* (6 April 2009).

52 Gilbert, Winston S. Churchill: Road to Victory 1941–1945, Vol. VII, p. 111.

53 Churchill's tendency to cry at films and emotional events is analysed in Andrew Roberts's article 'Winston Wept: The Extraordinary Lachrymosity and Romantic Imagination of Winston Churchill', *Finest Hour*, Autumn 2016, p. 174.

54 Cowles, *Winston Churchill: The Era and the Man*, pp. 135–6.

55 Emily Russell (ed.), *A Constant Heart: The War Diaries of Maud Russell, 1938–1945*, p. 268.

56 Michael Wardell, 'Churchill's Dagger: A Memoir of Capponcina', *Finest Hour*, No. 87, Summer 1995, p. 4.

57 'Patrick Kinna: Churchill's Wartime Secretary', obituary, *Independent* (17 June 2009).

58 Randolph Churchill, 'Sir Winston Churchill Would Make Mincemeat of Paxman', *Telegraph* (21 January 2015).

59 Woodward, 'Eminent Churchillians – Patrick Kinna MBE', p. 38.

Chapter 5: Jo Sturdee

1 Private communication between the author and Georgina Hill, Kathleen's granddaughter, with permission.

2 Layton, *Winston Churchill by His Personal Secretary*, p. 53.

3 Vanda Salmon, unpublished memoir, p. 9.

4 Bright Astley, *The Inner Circle*, p. 181.

5 Her book is essential reading for all Churchillians. She has been described as 'the organizing genius of the War Cabinet Secretariat'. From Captain Harry Grattidge, *Captain of the Queens: The Autobiography of Captain Harry Grattidge, Former Commodore of the Cunard Line, as told to Richard Collier*, p. 180.

6 Richard Buckle (ed.), *Self Portrait with Friends: The Selected Diaries of Cecil Beaton, 1926–1974*, pp. 170–1.

7 Nicholas Shakespeare, *Six Minutes in May: How Churchill Unexpectedly Became Prime Minister*, p. 168.

8 Richardson, *From Churchill's Secret Circle to the BBC*, pp. 179–80.

9 Ian Kikuchi, 'The Churchill War Room's Remington "Noiseless" Typewriter', IWM website, 18 January 2018.

10 In the Annexe, there was 'a little cubby hole and a machine like a typewriter... called a telex. Anything from the prime minister to the President went in there... you had to lock yourself in or somebody locked you in, and you typed whatever it was, then it went direct to the President. It didn't have to be coded and uncoded.... It went straight there'. Sturdee's oral history.

11 Justin Reash, 'Let It Roll: Churchill's Chartwell Cinema', *Finest Hour*, No. 179, Winter 2018.

12   Colville, *The Fringes of Power*, p. 509.
13   S. M. Plokhy, *Yalta: The Price of Peace*, p. 36.
14   Gilbert, *Winston S. Churchill: Road to Victory 1941–1945*, Vol. VII, p. 1167.
15   Ibid., p. 1167.
16   Marian Holmes, unpublished diary, Churchill Archives Centre, Churchill College, Cambridge, 2 February 1945.
17   Gilbert, *Winston S. Churchill: Road to Victory 1941–1945*, Vol. VII, p. 1223.
18   Bright Astley, *The Inner Circle*, p. 187.
19   David B. Woolner, *The Last 100 Days: FDR at War and Peace*, p. 66.
20   Bright Astley, *The Inner Circle*, p. 192.
21   Martin, *Downing Street: The War Years*, p. 180.
22   Lavery, *Churchill Goes to War*, p. 336.
23   Bright Astley, *The Inner Circle*, p. 192.
24   Gilbert, *Winston S. Churchill: Road to Victory 1941–1945*, Vol. VII, pp. 1210–11.
25   Gilbert, *Winston S. Churchill: Road to Victory 1941–1945*, Vol. VII, p. 1345, quoting Layton.
26   Memorandum of 'Conversation on the Far Eastern War and General Situation' between W. A. Harriman and Stalin, 8 August 1945, Manuscript Division, Library of Congress.
27   Gilbert, *Winston S. Churchill: Never Despair 1945–1965*, Vol. VIII, p. 384.
28   Ibid., pp. 132, 185.
29   Ibid., p. 147.
30   Lough, *No More Champagne*, passim.
31   Max Egremont, *Balfour: A Biography*, p. 321.
32   See also Layton, who describes the cheese as 'a whopper'. In Layton, *Winston Churchill by His Personal Secretary*, p. 127.
33   Lough, *No More Champagne*, p. 357. Despite the warning, Churchill, 'within two months had re-registered his father's racing colours (pink with chocolate sleeves and cap) and assembled a stable of seven fully-fledged racehorses'.
34   Wardell, 'Churchill's Dagger', p. 16.
35   Fred Glueckstein, *Churchill and Colonist II*, p. 17.
36   Colin R. Coote, *Editorial: The Memoirs of Colin R. Coote*, p. 273.
37   Gilbert, *Winston S. Churchill: Road to Victory 1941–1945*, Vol. VII, p. 130.
38   Layton, *Winston Churchill by His Personal Secretary*, p. 8.
39   Philip White, *Our Supreme Task*, pp. 115, 119.
40   Sandys, *Chasing Churchill*, p. 189.
41   White, *Our Supreme Task*, p. 92.
42   Gilbert, *Winston S. Churchill: Never Despair 1945–1965*, Vol. VIII, p. 1012.
43   Sturdee, letter home (8 March 1946), WSC Archives.
44   Ibid.
45   Ibid.
46   Ibid.

47 Ibid.
48 Ibid.
49 Ibid.
50 Andrew Roberts, *The Holy Fox: A Biography of Lord Halifax*, p. 373.
51 Speech in the House of Commons, 17 April 1945, 'The Greatest Champion of Freedom'.
52 Robert H. Pilpel, *Churchill in America 1895–1961*, p. 225.
53 Sturdee, letter home (8 January 1950), WSC Archives.
54 Ibid.
55 Layton, *Winston Churchill by His Personal Secretary*, p. 177.
56 Gilbert, *Winston S. Churchill: Never Despair 1945–1965*, Vol. VIII, p. 631.
57 Ibid., p. 1362.
58 What Andrew Roberts calls 'Churchill's love for unusual words' in *Commentary* (June 2018), p. 55. Unusual and invented ones.
59 Delia Morton in private communications to the author.

Chapter 6: Marian Holmes

1   'Glimpses: Marian Holmes Spicer', *Finest Hour*, No. 118, Spring 2003, p. 20.
2   Gilbert, *Winston S. Churchill: Road to Victory 1941–1945*, Vol. VII, p. 1296.
3   Ibid.
4   Shakespeare, *Six Minutes in May*, p. 41.
5   Colville, *Footprints in Time*, p. 75.
6   Ibid., p. 3.
7   Layton, *Winston Churchill by His Personal Secretary*, p. 12.
8   Sir Ian Jacob in Wheeler-Bennett, *Action This Day*, p. 162.
9   Martin, *Downing Street: The War Years*, p. 4.
10 Ibid.
11 Ibid., p. 93.
12 Ibid.
13 Ibid., p. 4.
14 Holmes, unpublished diary, 21 September 1943, No. 10 Annexe, p. 4.
15 Ibid., 2 August 1943, No. 10.
16 Ibid., 24 March 1943, No. 10 Annexe, p. 1.
17 Ibid.
18 Ibid., 5 April 1943, Annexe, p. 1.
19 Ibid., 19 November 1944, p. 16.
20 Holmes, *Churchill's Bunker*, p. 121.
21 Holmes, unpublished diary, 16 July 1944, Chequers, p. 14.
22 *Finest Hour*, No. 118, Summer 2003, p. 20.
23 Sir John Peck, *The Atlantic Monthly* (March 1965), as cited in Gilbert, *Winston S. Churchill: Finest Hour 1939–1941*, Vol. VI, pp. 891–3.
24 Colville, *The Fringes of Power*, p. 288.

25 Holmes, unpublished diary, 5 June 1943, Chequers, p. 2. Holmes describes Chequers as 'Constables everywhere, wonderful… Furniture is fascinating and all the rooms I've seen have splendid views.'

26 Holmes, unpublished diary, 16 July 1944, Chequers, p. 14.

27 Ibid., 5 June 1943, Chequers, p. 2.

28 Ibid., 6 June 1943, p. 2. 'One of the compensations for the late-night duties here is clearly going to be the excellent "full English" breakfast served to one in bed by the ATS domestic staff'. Ibid. However: 'After he had gone to bed, I remained in the office to type out the statement and got off to bed at 4.15 a.m.'

29 From 1 June 1940, Churchill had the use of Chequers which was run by Grace Lamont, a very efficient Scottish woman. Soames, *Clementine Churchill*, p. 322.

30 Holmes, unpublished diary, 14 July 1944, Chequers, p. 13.

31 Ibid., 25 June 1945, p. 24.

32 Ibid., 21 May 1944, Chequers, p. 11.

33 Ibid., 10 December 1944, Chequers, p. 17.

34 Gilbert, *In Search of Churchill*, p. 169.

35 Holmes, unpublished diary, 26 July 1944, Annexe, p. 14.

36 Ibid., 31 October 1943, Chequers, p. 5.

37 Layton, *Winston Churchill by His Personal Secretary*, p. 21.

38 Holmes, unpublished diary, September 1944, p. 15.

39 Ibid., 31 August 1944, p. 15.

40 Captain Richard Pim (later Captain Sir Richard Pim) had other duties, as all Churchill staff did. He had taken leave from Churchill's staff to help evacuate soldiers at Dunkirk. Later in Casablanca, late January 1943, 'a number of American negro troops sang Spirituals, [including] a solo of the Londonderry Air… an inferior version of Danny Boy [which] touched the prime minister deeply. The following morning while still in bed, Churchill asked Pim to repeat the words of the song so that his typist could record them, and he would send them to Mrs Churchill.' There is no mention of whether or not Churchill hummed the tune. There were no women at Casablanca, so perhaps it was Kinna who took down the lyrics. In Gilbert, *Winston S. Churchill: Road to Victory 1941–1945*, Vol. VII, p. 304.

41 Holmes, unpublished diary, 5 July 1944, p. 13.

42 Gilbert, *Winston S. Churchill: Road to Victory 1941–1945*, Vol. VII, p. 940.

43 *The Montreal Gazette* (11 September 1944), as cited in Moody, *From Churchill's War Rooms*, p. 242.

44 Martin, *Downing Street: The War Years*, p. 160.

45 One of the other women, a secretary to a general, also in Quebec, bought twenty pairs 'for family and friends, and all the girls in the office'. Moody, *From Churchill's War Rooms*, p. 117.

46 Gilbert, *Winston S. Churchill: Road to Victory 1941–1945*, Vol. VII, p. 971, US edn.

47 Ibid.
48 Niall Ferguson, *Kissinger: The Idealist: 1923–1968*, p. 132.
49 Layton, *Winston Churchill by His Personal Secretary*, p. 119.
50 Ibid., p. 15.
51 For more about picnics, see Cita Stelzer, *Dinner with Churchill: Policy Making at the Dinner Table*.
52 Holmes, unpublished diary, p. 20.
53 Layton, *Winston Churchill's Personal Secretary*, p. 70.
54 Holmes, unpublished diary, p. 16.
55 Gilbert, *Churchill: A Life*, p. 794.
56 Holmes, unpublished diary, 25 July 1943, Chequers, p. 3.
57 Gilbert, *Winston S. Churchill: Road to Victory 1941–1945*, Vol. VII, p. 973.
58 Ibid., p. 98.
59 Ibid., p. 1011.
60 Bright Astley, *The Inner Circle*, p. 150.
61 Gilbert, *Winston S. Churchill: Finest Hour 1939–1941*, Vol. VI, p. 1017.
62 Holmes, unpublished diary, 3 November 1944, p. 16.
63 Gilbert, *Winston S. Churchill: Road to Victory 1941–1945*, Vol. VI, p. 1030.
64 Layton, *Winston Churchill by his Personal Secretary*, p. 105.
65 Colville, *The Fringes of Power*, p. 538.
66 Ibid., and Holmes, unpublished diary, Athens, Christmas 1944, p. 1.
67 Gilbert, *Winston S. Churchill: Finest Hour 1939–1941*, Vol. VII, p. 1115.
68 Ibid., p. 1116.
69 *Spectator* (29 December 1944), p. 3.
70 Gilbert, *Winston S. Churchill: Finest Hour 1939–1941*, Vol. VII, p. 1119.
71 Colville, *Fringes of Power*, p. 541.
72 Moody, *From Churchill's War Rooms*, pp. 50–1.
73 Holmes, unpublished diary, Athens, Christmas 1944, p. 2.
74 Gilbert, *Winston S. Churchill: Road to Victory 1941–1945*, Vol. VII, p. 1118.
75 Colville, *Footprints in Time*, pp. 180–1.
76 Ibid., p. 181.
77 Gilbert, *Winston S. Churchill: Road to Victory 1941–1945*, Vol. VII, pp. 1122, 1131.
78 Holmes, unpublished diary, Athens, 28 December 1944, p. 4.
79 Ibid., 13 May 1945, p. 22.
80 Interview with Elizabeth Layton Nel in DVD *War Stories with Oliver North: The Life and Times of Winston Churchill*, Fox News Channel (2007).
81 Holmes, unpublished diary, 7 April 1944, Chequers, p. 9.
82 Ibid., 11 February 1944, Chequers, p. 7.
83 Ibid., 2 January 1945, p. 17.
84 Ibid., 13 January 1945, Chequers, p. 18.
85 Ibid., Argonaut, 2 February 1945, p. 1.
86 Ibid.
87 Gilbert, *Winston S. Churchill: Finest Hour 1939–1941*, Vol. VI, p. 1172.

88　See Cita Stelzer, *Dinner with Churchill*, ch. 7 on the Yalta Conference.

89　Holmes, unpublished diary, Argonaut, 10 February 1945, p. 3.

90　Ibid., Argonaut 13 February 1945, p. 4.

91　Ibid., Argonaut, 18 February 1945, p. 5.

92　Ibid., Argonaut, 19 February 1945, p. 5.

93　Ibid., 29 April 1945, Chequers, p. 21.

94　Ibid., 3 May 1945, No. 10, p. 21.

95　Ibid., 8 May 1945, p. 22.

96　Arthur, *Churchill: The Life*, p. 211.

97　Holmes, unpublished diary, 10 June 1945, p. 23.

98　Ibid., 10 June 1945, p. 23.

99　Ibid., 14 Jun 1945, p. 24.

100　Ibid., 29 Jun 1945, p. 24.

101　Ibid., Potsdam, 15 July 1945, p. 1.

102　Gilbert, *Winston S. Churchill: Never Despair 1945–1965*, Vol. VIII, p. 61.

103　Holmes, unpublished diary, Potsdam, p. 1.

104　Stelzer, *Dinner with Churchill*, p. 292, fn 19.

105　Holmes, unpublished diary, Potsdam, 18 July 1945, p. 1.

106　Ibid., 25 July 1945, p. 2.

107　Ibid., 27 July 1945, p. 25.

108　Ibid., 27 July 1945, p. 25.

109　Ibid., 1 August 1945, no pagination.

110　Ibid., 28 July 1945, p. 25.

111　Ibid., 28 July 1945, p. 25.

112　Obituary of Marian Holmes, *Telegraph* (10 October 2001).

Chapter 7: Elizabeth Gilliatt

1　Rowse, '"There Was Once a Man"'.

2　Gilbert, *Winston S. Churchill: Never Despair 1945–1965*, Vol. VIII, p. 886. At UCL there is now a Gilliatt Lecture Theatre. He was attending obstetrician at the birth of Queen Elizabeth's first two children.

3　Gilbert, *Winston S. Churchill: Finest Hour 1939 –1941*, Vol. VI, p. 384.

4　Gilbert, *Winston S. Churchill: Never Despair 1945–1965*, Vol. VIII, p. 292.

5　See also ibid., p. 179.

6　Ibid., p. 179.

7　Quoted in Bonham Carter, *Winston Churchill As I Knew Him*, p. 151, from *My African Journey*.

8　Moody, *From Churchill's War Rooms*, p. 51.

9　Colville, *The Fringes of Power*, p. 664.

10　Gilbert, *Winston S. Churchill: Never Despair 1945–1965*, Vol. VIII, pp. 534, 629.

11　For a video of his arrival, see https://www.britishpathe.com/video/cap-dail-sir-winston-on-holiday.

12   Gilbert, *Winston S. Churchill: Never Despair 1945–1965*, Vol. VIII, p. 388.
13   During the last decade of his life Churchill owned thirty-six racehorses and twelve brood mares. In 'Winston Churchill and Colonist II', *Finest Hour*, No. 125, Winter 2004–5, p. 28.
14   Gilbert, *Winston S. Churchill: Road to Victory*, Volume VII, p. 997.
15   Gilbert, *Churchill: A Life*, p. 916.
16   Michael Doran, *Ike's Gamble: America's Rise to Dominance in the Middle East*, pp. 60–61.
17   Watch the resignation announcement on https://www.youtube.com/watch?v=m_Uj_01L-e0.
18   Gilbert, *Winston S. Churchill: Never Despair 1945–1965*, Vol. VIII, p. 1135.
19   Ibid., p. 1140.
20   Ibid., p. 1128.

Chapter 8: Lettice Marston

1   Lavery, *Churchill Goes to War*, p. 358.
2   Gilbert, *Winston S. Churchill: Never Despair 1945–1965*, Vol. VIII, p. 221.
3   Ibid., p. 226.
4   However, times do change, although Churchill's work did not. After his retirement, he wrote to his wife laying out in great detail his plan for secretarial help, a rare occurrence when he did not depend entirely on his secretaries to establish the office routine. Churchill Archives Centre, CHUR 1/5. And in Gilbert, *Winston S. Churchill: Never Despair 1945–1965*, Vol. VIII, p. 1132.
5   Gilbert, *Winston S. Churchill: Never Despair 1945–1965*, Vol. VIII, p. 1136.
6   Alan Bullock, *Ernest Bevin: A Biography*, p. 300.
7   Gilbert, *Winston S. Churchill: Never Despair 1945–1965*, Vol. VIII, p. 426.
8   http://www.britishpathe.com/video/churchill-in-oslo.
9   Gilbert, *Winston S. Churchill: Never Despair 1945–1965*, Vol. VIII, p. 486.
10   Ibid., pp. 631–3.
11   Leaming, *Churchill Defiant*, p. 123.
12   Gilbert, *Winston S. Churchill: Never Despair 1945–1965*, Vol. VIII, p. 656.
13   Ibid., p. 1350.

Chapter 9: Cecily 'Chips' Gemmell

1   D. K. R. Crosswell, *Beetle: The Life of General Walter Bedell Smith*, p. 340.
2   Reynolds, *In Command of History*, p. 77.
3   'This archival treasure' contained 'the personal papers of a man who had experienced and shaped the history of the world in the last fifty years – school notebooks from the age of nine, letters and despatches [sic] from the wars in India, the Sudan, Cuba and South Africa; file upon file about

the Dardanelles, the Somme and Czarist Russia, secret telegrams from Roosevelt and Stalin, all entangled with the politics between the two World Wars and private family letters and bank accounts. Everything had been kept and nothing thrown away and all were unique and perishable.' In Gilbert, *Winston S. Churchill: Never Despair 1945–1965*, Vol. VIII, p. 331.

4 Reynolds, *In Command of History*, p. 77.

5 Layton, *Winston Churchill by His Personal Secretary*, p. 13.

6 Paul Bew, *Churchill & Ireland*, p. 164.

7 Layton, *Winston Churchill by His Personal Secretary*, p. 20. Churchill gave a twin (or one quite like it) to a staff member who had forgotten his own. Along with it came the admonition, 'Read before you sign.' That pen, with its gold nib, was recently auctioned off by Humbert & Ellis. Paul Fraser, 'Collectibles', 1 February 2018. https://store.paulfraser-collectibles.com/blogs/most-recent/winston-churchill-s-fountain-pen-valued-at-1-700.

8 Clarke, *Mr Churchill's Profession*, p. 169.

9 Graebner, *My Dear Mr Churchill*, p. 29.

10 Barry Singer, 'Churchill's Smile', *Huffington Post* (11 March 2015), https://www.huffingtonpost.com/barry-singer/churchills-smile_b_6843634.html.

11 Soames (ed.), *Winston and Clementine*, pp. 559, 568.

12 Grace Hamblin OBE, 'Frabjous Days: Chartwell Memories', p. 22.

13 Ibid.

14 Graebner has a similar story of a German POW watching a film with Churchill in Gilbert, *Winston S. Churchill: Never Despair 1945–1965*, Vol. VIII, p. 476.

15 https://www.youtube.com/watch?v=BSz5prkhZng&t=63s.

16 Layton Nel, *Winston Churchill by His Personal Secretary*, 2007, p. 39.

17 Layton, *Winston Churchill by His Personal Secretary*, p. 39. She calls Ismay 'A charming person… one of the gentlest and friendliest among Mr Churchill's circle'.

18 Lavery, *Churchill Goes to War*, p. 361.

19 Lovell, *The Riviera Set*, pp. 101–2.

20 Pilpel, *Churchill in America, 1895–1961*, p. 80.

21 Graebner, *My Dear Mr Churchill*, pp. 272–4.

22 Gilbert, *Winston S. Churchill: Never Despair 1945–1965*, Vol. VIII, p. 479.

23 Ibid., pp. 386–7.

24 Ibid., p. 485.

25 Wardell, 'Churchill's Dagger', p. 21.

26 Gilbert, *Winston S. Churchill: Never Despair 1945–1965*, Vol. VIII, p. 485.

27 Purnell, *First Lady*, p. 17.

28 Celia Sandys' remarks at the opening of the Morgan Library's 'Churchill: The Power of Words', in Gary Shapiro, 'How Churchill Mobilized the English Language', *New York Sun* (12 June 2012).

29   Penman began working for Churchill at Chartwell in August 1938,
     after secretarial training. *The Churchill Documents: The Coming of War
     1936–1939, Vol. 13, p. 1337. She left to get married in June 1939. Penman*
     took down much of the night-time dictation for the early volumes of *A
     History of the English-Speaking Peoples*.

30   Gilbert, *The Churchill Documents: The Coming of War 1936–1939*, Vol. 13,
     p. 1352.

31   Speaking at annual conference of The International Churchill Society,
     11–12 October 2017, New York City.

32   Churchill wrote home: 'Everyone liked shoving their paws into the dish
     and remembered with pleasure that fingers were made before forks.' In
     Soames (ed.), *Winston and Clementine*, p. 558.

33   Gilbert, *Winston S. Churchill: Never Despair 1945–1965*, Vol. VIII, p. 579.

34   Churchill was so taken with the tempera method that he wrote to his
     Swiss paint and brush supplier, ordering 'another outfit of tempera in
     tubes… and let me have the bill as I have a few francs available'. In
     Gilbert, *Winston S. Churchill: Never Despair 1945–1965*, Vol. VIII, p. 588.

35   Ibid., p. 582.

36   Ibid., p. 585.

37   Ibid., p. 576.

38   Ibid., p. 577.

39   Graebner, *My Dear Mr Churchill*, p. 73.

40   Portal, in a conversation with the author, says that Sturdee worked
     only on occasion at Number 10, and then as a volunteer. Gilbert reports
     she was paid an annual salary of £469 (worth about £14,500 in today's
     money), as was Gilliatt. In Gilbert, *Winston S. Churchill: Never Despair
     1945–1965*, Vol. VIII, p. 657, n 1.

41   Moran, *Winston Churchill*, p. xvii.

42   Purnell, *First Lady*, p. 344.

Chapter 10: Jane Portal

1   Speech at Home Park Football Ground, Plymouth, Devon, Churchill
     Archives Centre, CHUR, 5/44 B/215-216.

2   Vanda Salmon, unpublished memoir, p. 35. Salmon added 'Mr Chur-
     chill was a country man at heart.'

3   Hansard House of Commons Debate, 12 May 1949, Vol. 464, cols 2011–
     2131.

4   Vanda Salmon, unpublished memoir, p. 17.

5   Ibid., p. 48. Arnhem was a battle 'which none of us could forget', and
     Browning was 'a delight to know', according to Salmon.

6   In conversations with the author.

7   Walter Graebner, *My Dear Mr Churchill*, p. 49.

8   Churchill partially smoked the four-inch (10 cm) cigar at Le Bourget Airport in Paris on 11 May 1947. BBC, 13 October 2017.

9   Reynolds, *In Command of History*, p. 225.

10   In conversation with the author.

11   Lewis E. Lehrman, *Lincoln & Churchill*, frontispiece.

12   John Maynard Keynes, *Essays in Biography*, p. 54.

13   Lord Chandos, *The Memoirs of Lord Chandos*, p. 168.

14   Interview with Jane Portal, now Lady Williams, as reported by Andrew Lownie, *Stalin's Englishman: Guy Burgess, the Cold War, and the Cambridge Spy Ring*, p. 240.

15   And, on some nights, government or military films. 'One night it was 'Dangerous Moonlight' – about the bombing of Poland… ' In Layton, *Winston Churchill by His Personal Secretary*, p. 37.

16   Charles Drazin, *Korda: Britain's Only Movie Mogul*, p. 215.

17   Lough, *No More Champagne*, p. 231.

18   Michael Korda, *Alone: Britain, Churchill and Dunkirk: Defeat Into Victory*, p. 152.

19   Lough, *No More Champagne*, pp. 231–5.

20   Gilbert, *Winston S. Churchill: Never Despair 1945–1965*, Vol. VIII, p. 485.

21   Richard Brooks, 'Winston Churchill's Secret Love Doris Castlerosse: A Blackmail Risk?', *Sunday Times* (25 February 2018).

22   Andrew Roberts, *The Spectator* Blog, February 2018.

23   John Colville, *The Churchillians*, p. 115.

24   Graebner, *My Dear Mr Churchill*, p. 30.

25   Colville, *The Churchillians*, p. 7.

26   Richard Steyn, *Churchill's Confidant: Jan Smuts, Enemy to Lifelong Friend*, pp. 164–5.

27   Colville, *Fringes of Power*, p. 655.

28   Gilbert, *Winston S. Churchill: Never Despair 1945–1965*, Vol. VIII, p. 631.

29   Leaming, *Churchill Defiant*, p. 120.

30   Norman McGowan, *My Years With Churchill*, p. 101. A former sailor, wearing bell-bottom trousers, he began working for Churchill in 1949. His book is worth reading.

31   In conversation with the author.

32   Gilbert, *Winston S. Churchill: Never Despair 1945–1965*, Vol. VIII, p. 633.

33   McGowan, *My Years With Churchill*, p. 102. And for a wonderful video, watch https://www.youtube.com/watch?v=oPL_LmBxlyc.

34   Orson Welles was in Venice and has a wonderful story to tell on YouTube: https://www.youtube.com/watch?v=TpqwY7QL7r8.

35   Another example of Churchillian humour from Lord Peter Carrington, describing an offer to join the Churchill Cabinet: https://www.youtube.com/watch?v=kjhyNDBLAd4.

36   Anthony Montague Browne, *Long Sunset: Memoirs of Winston Churchill's Last Private Secretary*, p. 118.

37 Sheila Minto, LVO, MBE, was a chief administrator of Number 10 Downing Street through eight prime ministers. Born in 1908, she died in 1999. Nicknamed 'The Queen Bee', she is the great aunt of Sir Christopher Meyer, former British Ambassador to the United States. He called her 'a no-nonsense Scottish woman' in *DC Confidential*, p. 15. She quotes Churchill saying 'with a mischievous grin', 'I shall require two young women tonight,' as he prepared to dictate into the early morning hours. *Finest Hour*, No. 86, Spring 1995, p. 10. On another occasion, John Peck quotes Churchill saying with a twinkle: 'I shall need two young ladies tonight.' In A&E's Biography Series: *Biography – The Complete Churchill*, VHS.

38 Charles Moore, 'Secrets Are Safe With the Garden Room Girls', *Telegraph* (13 July 2009).

39 Peter Hennessy, *The Prime Minister: The Office and Its Holders since 1945*, p. 184.

40 Howells, *Churchill's Last Years*, p. 83.

41 In conversations with the author.

42 Randolph S. Churchill, *The Churchill Documents: Minister of the Crown, 1907–1911*, Vol. 4, p. 753.

43 In conversation with the author. Another favourite ditty: 'He jumped upon his bloody horse, and galloped on the bloody course, the bloody road was muddy, the bloody creek was bloody floody.' One more: 'Whiter than Whitewash on the Wall, Oh, wash me in the dirty water, you washed your dirty daughter in.' A variant last line is 'the colonel's daughter' instead of 'your dirty daughter'. From Don Cusic, *Winston Churchill's Love of Music*, p. 32. Another favourite Churchill tune is at https://www.youtube.com/watch?v=SXmk8dbFv_0.

44 Churchill Archives Centre, WCHL 6/54.

45 Churchill Documents, Volume 14, p. 673.

46 https://www.youtube.com/watch?v=t2gF-jaVuK4.

47 David Cecil, *The Young Melbourne & Lord M*, pp. 289–384.

48 Gilbert, *Winston S. Churchill: Never Despair 1945–1965*, Vol. VIII, p. 836.

49 Colville, *Fringes of Power*, p. 668.

50 Gilbert, *Winston S. Churchill: Never Despair 1945–1965*, Vol. VIII, p. 860.

51 Ibid., p. 886.

52 Ibid., p. 892.

53 Ibid., p. 871.

54 Butler, *The Art of the Possible*, p. 171.

55 Some eight years earlier Churchill had rejected use of 'speech secrecy equipment', because he was told that President Roosevelt said it made the prime minister sound 'like Donald Duck'. He was said to have remarked that 'he would never use that damn thing again'. In Ruth Ive, *The Woman Who Censored Churchill*, pp. 109, 112.

56 Watch to see the audience's reactions to the prime minister's joke:

https://www.britishpathe.com/video/margate-tories-conference. And https://winstonchurchill.org/resources/in-the-media/newsreel-video-archive/margate-tories-conference-1953.

57   Butler, *The Art of the Possible*, p. 171.
58   Glueckstein, "Cats Look Down on You'", p. 50.
59   Sir Evelyn Shuckburgh, *Descent to Suez: Diaries 1951–1956*, p. 117.
60   Colville, *The Fringes of Power*, p. 691.
61   Jenkins, *Churchill*, p. 892.
62   Later recollection. Gilbert, *Winston S. Churchill: Never Despair 1945–1965*, Vol. VIII, p. 1097.

Chapter 11: Doreen Pugh

1   A. J. P. Taylor et al., *Churchill: Four Faces and the Man*, p. 207, fn.
2   Gilbert, *Winston S. Churchill: Never Despair 1945–1965*, Vol. VIII, p. 1128.
3   Roy Howells, *Simply Churchill*, p. 108.
4   Browne, *Long Sunset*, p. 208.
5   Gilbert, *Winston S. Churchill: Never Despair 1945–1965*, Vol. VIII, p. 1140.
6   Ibid., p. 1135.
7   Author's conversation with Jane Portal, now Lady Williams, 9 April 2018.
8   Purnell, *First Lady*, p. 357.
9   Gilbert, The Churchill Documents, *Winston S. Churchill: Wilderness Years 1929–1935*, Vol. 12, p. 874, fn 3.
10   CHUR 2/387/106.
11   Lord Normanbrook, memoir in Wheeler-Bennett, *Action This Day*, p.20.
12   Roberts, *Hitler and Churchill*, p. 117.
13   Hindley, *Destination Casablanca*, p. 157.
14   Stelzer, *Dinner with Churchill*.
15   Ibid., p. 214.
16   Colville, *The Churchillians*, p. 159.
17   https://www.youtube.com/watch?v=wrmR8guKdgU&t=81s.
18   Gill Morton, 'I Was Winston Churchill's Nurse', *The Oldie* (February 2018), p. 16.
19   Ibid.
20   Moore, 'Secrets Are Safe with the Garden Room Girls'.
21   Portal recalls that at one lunch she peeked into the dining room and she saw Churchill 'spellbound by her beauty'. A&E's Biography Series: *Biography – The Complete Churchill*, VHS.
22   Gilbert, *Winston S. Churchill: Never Despair 1945–1965*, Vol. VIII, p. 1267. Churchill also shared the proof of General Ismay's memoirs with his wife. In ibid., p. 1267.
23   Alan Hodge's wife Jane was a favourite of Churchill's and he was amused by the fact that Hodge had named his cat Johnson. Churchill admired

'his use of words' – mighty praise coming from Churchill. In ibid., p. 1148.

24　Wardell, 'Churchill's Dagger', p. 16.

25　Lovell, *The Riviera Set*, p. 120.

26　Ibid., p. 299.

27　Ibid., p. 213.

28　Wardell, 'Churchill's Dagger', pp. 17, 19.

29　Ibid., p. 17.

30　Gilbert, *Winston S. Churchill: Never Despair 1945–1965*, Vol. VIII, p. 1190.

31　Stelzer, *Dinner with Churchill*, p. 76.

32　Grace Hamblin OBE, 'Frabjous Days: Chartwell Memories', p. 24.

33　Glueckstein, '"Cats Look Down on You"', p. 50.

34　Martin, *Downing Street: The War Years*, p. 106.

35　Layton, *Winston Churchill by His Personal Secretary*, p. 44.

36　Ibid., p. 59.

37　Oddly, Hamblin refers to Churchill working 'like a tiger to keep up his literary output', 'Frabjous Days: Chartwell Memories'.

38　Gilbert, *Winston S. Churchill: Never Despair 1945–1965*, Vol. VIII, p. 1285.

39　Soames (ed.), *Winston and Clementine*, p. 500.

40　Gilbert, *Winston S. Churchill: Never Despair 1945–1965*, Vol. VIII, p. 1356.

41　Ibid., p. 1352.

42　Lewis E. Lehrman, 'Toasting Winston Churchill's Birthday', *Putnam County News and Records* (27 November 2013), p. 3.

43　Ibid.

44　Gilbert, *Winston S. Churchill: Never Despair 1945–1965*, Vol. VIII, p. 1358.

45　Soames, *Clementine Churchill*, p. 478, but quoted in Gilbert, *Winston S. Churchill: Never Despair 1945–1965*, Vol. VIII, p. 1345.

Chapter 12: Catherine Snelling

1　Taylor et al., *Churchill: Four Faces and the Man*, p. 51. And W. F. Buckley said of Churchill 'The genius of Churchill was his union of affinities of the heart and of the mind, the total fusion of animal and spiritual energy.' ICS Boston Conference speech by Buckley, 1955.

2　Howells, *Simply Churchill*, p. 108.

3　Ferdinand Mount, *English Voices: Lives, Landscapes, Laments*, p. 70.

4　Professor A. M. Low, 'Churchill and Science', in Charles Eade (ed.), *Churchill by His Contemporaries*, pp. 380–1.

5　Gilbert, *Winston S. Churchill: Never Despair 1945–1965*, Vol. VIII, p. 1269.

6　Sinclair McKay, *The Secret Life of Bletchley Park*, pp. 156–63.

7　Lough, *No More Champagne*, passim.

8　Winston S. Churchill, *My Early Life*, p. 27.

9　Gilbert, *Winston S. Churchill: Never Despair 1945–1965*, Vol. VIII, p. 988.

10　Ibid., p. 1266.

Epilogue

1   John Keegan, *The Battle for History; Re-Fighting World War Two*, pp. 52–3.
2   Tom Hickman, *Churchill's Bodyguard*, p. 95.
3   Gilbert, *Winston S. Churchill: Road to Victory*, 1941–1945, Vol. VII, p. 1148 n. 2.
4   According to Sir John Colville, Churchill's Private Secretary, the remark was made by Churchill's close friend F. E. Smith (Lord Birkenhead). International Churchill Society, winstonchurchill.org.
5   Hickman, *Churchill's Bodyguard*, p. 95.

Sources

1   Jenkins, *Churchill*, p. 552.
2   Gilbert, *In Search of Churchill*, p. 313.

BIBLIOGRAPHY

Anon., Marian Holmes obituary in *Telegraph* (10 October 2001)

Arthur, Max, *Churchill: The Life: An Authorized Pictorial Biography* (London: Cassell Illustrated, 2015)

Associated Press, 'Grace Hamblin, 94; Secretary to the Churchills', obituary in *Los Angeles Times* (19 October 2002)

Astley, Joan Bright, *The Inner Circle: A View of War at the Top* (Stanhope UK: The Memoir Club, 2007)

Bainbridge, Cyril and Roy Stockdill, *The News of the World Story* (London: HarperCollins, 1993)

Baldonado, Kim, '*Queen Mary* Celebrated on 80th Anniversary', NBC Southern California (25 May 2016)

Beaverbrook, Lord, *Politicians and the War 1914–1916* (London: Collins, 1960)

Bew, Paul, *Churchill & Ireland* (Oxford: Oxford University Press, 2016)

Bonham Carter, Violet, *Winston Churchill As I Knew Him* (London: The Reprint Society, 1966)

Brooks, Richard, 'Winston Churchill's Secret Love Doris Castlerosse: A Blackmail Risk?', *Sunday Times* (25 February 2018)

Browne, Anthony Montague, *Long Sunset: Memoirs of Winston Churchill's Last Private Secretary* (London: Cassell, 1995)

Buckle, Richard (ed.), *Self Portrait with Friends: The Selected Diaries of Cecil Beaton, 1926–1974* (New York: Times Books, 1979)

Buczacki, Stefan, *Churchill & Chartwell* (London: Francis Lincoln Publishers, 2007)

Bullock, Alan, *Ernest Bevin: A Biography* (London: Politico's, 2002)

Butler, Richard Austen, *The Art of the Possible: The Memoirs of Lord Butler, K.G., C.H.* (London: Hamish Hamilton, 1971)

Cadogan, Alexander, *The Diaries of Sir Alexander Cadogan O.M., 1938–1945*, ed. David Dilks (London: Cassell, 1971)

Cecil, David, *The Young Melbourne & Lord M* (London: Bello, 2017)

Churchill College Archives Centre at Churchill College, Cambridge

Churchill, Randolph, 'Sir Winston Churchill Would Make Mincemeat of Paxman', *Telegraph* (21 January 2015)

Churchill, Winston S., '"For Valour": King George VI' (In Remembrance of His Late Majesty and to Commemorate the Golden Jubilee of Her Majesty Queen Elizabeth II), printed in *Finest Hour*, No. 114, Spring 2002

——, *My Early Life* (New York: Scribner, 1996)

——, 'My New York Misadventure', *Daily Mail* (4/5 January 1932), reprinted *Finest Hour*, No. 136, Autumn 2007

——, *Secret Sessions Speeches* (London: Cassell & Co., 1946)

——, *The Second World War*, 6 vols (London: Cassell & Co., 1948–54)

The Churchill Project at Hillsdale College, *Word Counts*, 5 September 2015, https://winstonchurchill.hillsdale.edu/word-counts-2/

Clarke, Peter, *Mr Churchill's Profession: Statesman, Orator, Writer* (London: Bloomsbury, 2012)

Colville, John, *Footprints in Time* (London: Collins, 1976)

——, *The Churchillians* (London: Weidenfeld & Nicolson, 1981)

——, *The Fringes of Power: Downing Street Diaries 1939–1955* (London: Hodder & Stoughton, 1985)

Coote, C. R., *Editorial: The Memoirs of Colin R. Coote* (London: Eyre & Spottiswoode, 1965)

Cowles, Virginia, *Winston Churchill: The Era and the Man* (London: Hamish Hamilton, 1953)

Crosswell, D. K. R., *Beetle: The Life of General Walter Bedell Smith* (Lexington, KY: University Press of Kentucky, 2010)

Cusic, Don, *Winston Churchill's Love of Music* (Nashville: Brackish Publishing, 2018)

de Courcy, Anne, *Debs at War: 1939–1945: How Wartime Changed Their Lives* (London: Weidenfeld & Nicolson, 2005)

Doran, Michael, *Ike's Gamble: America's Rise to Dominance in the Middle East* (New York: Simon & Schuster, 2017)

Drazin, Charles, *Korda: Britain's Only Movie Mogul* (London: Sidgwick & Jackson, 2002)

Egremont, Max, *Balfour: A Biography* (London: Weidenfeld & Nicolson, 1998)

Ferguson, Niall, *Kissinger: The Idealist: 1923–1968.* (New York: Penguin Press, 2015)

Giangreco, Patrizio Romano and Martin Garvey, 'In the Land of the Caesars: Churchill and Italy', *Finest Hour*, No. 173, Summer 2016

Gilbert, Martin, *Churchill: A Life* (London: Heinemann, 1991)

——, *In Search of Churchill: A Historian's Journey* (London: HarperCollins, 1994)

——, *The Churchill Documents*, 21 vols, (Hillsdale, MI: Hillsdale College Press)

——, *The Churchill War Papers* (London: Heinemann, 1993)

——, *Winston Churchill, The Wilderness Years: Speaking out against Hitler in the Prelude to the War* (London: Tauris Parke, 2012)

——, *Winston S. Churchill*, 8 vols (London: Heinemann, 1966–88)

'Glimpses: Marian Holmes Spicer', *Finest Hour*, No. 118, Spring 2003

Glueckstein, Fred, '"Cats Look Down on You… " Churchill's Feline Menagerie', *Finest Hour*, No. 139, Summer 2008

——, *Churchill and Colonist II* (Bloomington, IN: iUniverse LLC, 2014)

——, 'Winston Churchill and Colonist II', *Finest Hour*, No. 125, Winter 2004–5

——, 'Churchill's Sovereigns: King George V, 1910–1936' The Churchill Project, Hillsdale College, 11 December 2017

Gough, Barry, *Churchill and Fisher: Titans at the Admiralty* (Barnsley UK: Seaforth Publishing, 2017)

Graebner, Walter, *My Dear Mr Churchill* (London: Michael Joseph, 1965)

Grattidge, Captain Harry, *Captain of the Queens: The Autobiography of Captain Harry Grattidge, Former Commodore of the Cunard Line*, as told to Richard Collier (New York: E. P. Dutton, 1956)

Hamblin, Grace, 'Frabjous Days: Chartwell Memories', talk given at the 5th International Churchill Conference, The Adolphus, Dallas, printed in *Finest Hour*, No. 117, Winter 2002–3

——, Talk to Inner Wheel Club in Westerham, 1974, Churchill Archives Centre, Churchill College, Cambridge

Hansard, *House of Commons Debates*, 12 May 1949, Vol. 464, cols 2011–2131

Hennessy, Peter, *The Prime Minister: The Office and Its Holders since 1945* (London: Penguin, 2000)

Hickman, Tom, *Churchill's Bodyguard* (London: Headline, 2005)

Hill, Rosemary, 'Churchill's Faces', *London Review of Books* (30 March 2017)

Hindley, Meredith, *Destination Casablanca: Exile, Espionage, and the Battle for North Africa in World War II* (New York: Public Affairs, 2017)

Holmes, Marian, unpublished diary, Churchill Archives Centre, Churchill College, Cambridge

Holmes, Richard, *Churchill's Bunker: The Secret Headquarters at the Heart of Britain's Victory* (Profile Books in association with the Imperial War Museum, 2009)

Howells, Roy, *Churchill's Last Years* (New York: David McKay Company, 1966)

——, *Simply Churchill* (London: Robert Hale, 1965)

Ive, Ruth, *The Woman Who Censored Churchill* (Stroud: The History Press, 2008)

Jenkins, Roy, *Churchill* (London: Macmillan, 2001)

Keegan, John, *The Battle for History: Re-Fighting World War Two* (London: Hutchinson, 1995)

Keynes, John Maynard, *Essays in Biography* (New York: W. W. Norton, 1951)

Kikuchi, Ian, 'The Churchill War Room's Remington "Noiseless" Typewriter', Imperial War Museum website, 18 January 2018

Kinna, Martin, 'Patrick Kinna: Churchill's Wartime Secretary', obituary, *Independent* (17 June 2009)

Korda, Michael, *Alone: Britain, Churchill and Dunkirk: Defeat into Victory* (New York: Liveright Publishing, 2017)

Krauthammer, Charles, 'Winston Churchill: The Indispensable Man', in *Things That Matter: Three Decades of Passions, Pastimes and Politics* (New York: Crown Publishing, 2013)

Langworth, Richard M. (ed.), *The Definitive Wit of Winston Churchill* (New York: Public Affairs, 2009)

———, *Churchill by Himself: The Definitive Collection of Quotations* (London: Ebury Press, 2008)

———, *Winston Churchill, Myth and Reality: What He Actually Did and Said* (Jefferson, NC: McFarland & Company, 2017)

———, *A Connoisseur's Guide to the Books of Sir Winston Churchill*, (London: Brassey's, 1998)

Lavery, Brian, *Churchill Goes to War: Winston's Wartime Journeys* (London: Conway, 2007)

Layton Nel, Elizabeth, *Winston Churchill by His Personal Secretary* (New York: iUniverse, 2007)

Leaming, Barbara, *Churchill Defiant: Fighting on, 1945–1955* (New York: HarperCollins, 2010)

Lehrman, Lewis E., *Lincoln & Churchill* (Guilford, CT: Stackpole Books, 2018)

———, *Churchill, Roosevelt & Company: Studies in Character and Statecraft*: (Guilford, CT: Stackpole Books, 2017)

———, 'Toasting Winston Churchill's Birthday', *Putnam County News and Records* (27 November 2013)

Long, Christopher A., 'Chartwell Memories: A Neighbour Looks Back', *Finest Hour*, No. 126, Spring 2005

Lough, David, *No More Champagne: Churchill and His Money* (London: Head of Zeus, 2015)

———, *Darling Winston: Forty Years of Letters Between Winston Churchill and His Mother* (London: Head of Zeus, 2018)

Lovell, Mary S., *The Riviera Set 1920–1960: The Golden Years of Glamour and Excess* (London: Little, Brown, 2016)

Low, A. M., 'Churchill and Science', in Charles Eade (ed.), *Churchill by His Contemporaries* (New York: Simon & Schuster, 1954)

Lownie, Andrew, *Stalin's Englishman: Guy Burgess, the Cold War, and the Cambridge Spy Ring* (New York: St Martin's Press, 2015)

Lyttelton, Oliver (Viscount Chandos), *The Memoirs of Lord Chandos* (London: The Bodley Head, 1962)

Macintyre, Ben, *Rogue Heroes: The History of the SAS, Britain's Secret Special Forces Unit That Sabotaged the Nazis and Changed the Nature of the War* (New York: Crown, 2016)

McGowan, Norman, *My Years with Churchill* (New York: British Book Center, 1958)

McKay, Sinclair, *The Secret Life of Bletchley Park* (London: Aurum Press Ltd; Reprint edition, 2011)

Martin, Sir John, *Downing Street: The War Years* (London: Bloomsbury, 1991)

Meiklejohn, Robert, unpublished diary, Harriman Papers, Library of Congress

Memorandum of 'Conversation on the Far Eastern War and General Situation' between W. A. Harriman and Stalin, 8 August 1945, Manuscript Division, Library of Congress

Meyer, Christopher, *DC Confidential* (London: Phoenix Paperback, 2006)

Milton, Giles, *Churchill's Ministry of Ungentlemanly Warfare: The Mavericks Who Plotted Hitler's Defeat* (London: John Murray, 2016)

Moody, Joanna, *From Churchill's War Rooms: Letters of a Secretary 1943–1945* (Stroud, UK: Tempus, 2008)

Moore, Charles, 'Secrets Are Safe with the Garden Room Girls', *Telegraph* (13 July 2009)

Moran, Lord, *Winston Churchill: The Struggle for Survival* (London: Constable, 1966)

Morton, Gill, 'I Was Winston Churchill's Nurse', *The Oldie* (February 2018)

Mount, Ferdinand, *English Voices: Lives, Landscapes, Laments* (London: Simon & Schuster, 2016)

Mulley, Clare, *The Spy Who Loved: The Secrets and Lives of Christine Granville* (New York: St Martin's/Dunne, 2013)

Murray, Edmund, *I was Churchill's Bodyguard* (London: W. H. Allen, 1987)

Nicholson, Virginia, *Millions Like Us: Women's Lives in War and Peace, 1939–1949* (London: Viking, 2011)

Packwood, Allen, *How Churchill Waged War: The Most Challenging Decisions of the Second World War* (Yorkshire: Frontline Books, 2018)

Pawle, Gerald, *The War and Colonel Warden: Based on the Recollections of Commander C. R. Thompson* (London: George G. Harrap & Co., 1963)

Peck, John, *Dublin from Downing Street* (Dublin: Gill and Macmillan, 1978)

Pilpel, Robert H., *Churchill in America 1895–1961* (New York: Harcourt Brace Jovanovich, 1976)

Plokhy, Serhii, *Yalta: The Price of Peace* (New York: Penguin, 2011)

Purnell, Sonia, *First Lady: The Life and Wars of Clementine Churchill* (London: Aurum Press, 2015)

Reash, Justin, 'Let It Roll: Churchill's Chartwell Cinema', *Finest Hour*, No. 179, Winter 2018

Reynolds, David, *In Command of History: Churchill Fighting and Writing the Second World War* (London: Penguin Books, 2004)

Richardson, Charles, *From Churchill's Secret Circle to the BBC: The Biography of Lieutenant General Sir Ian Jacob GBE CB DL* (Oxford: Brassey's, 1991)

Roberts, Andrew, *Hitler and Churchill: Secrets of Leadership* (London: Phoenix Books, 2004)

——, *The Holy Fox: A Biography of Lord Halifax* (London: Weidenfeld & Nicolson, 1991)

——, *Churchill: Walking with Destiny* (London: Allen Lane, Penguin Books, 2018)

——, 'Winston Churchill and Religion – A Comfortable Relationship with the Almighty', talk delivered at 30th International Churchill Conference, Washington, DC, 1 November 2013, printed in *Finest Hour*, No. 163, Summer 2014

——, Winston Wept: The Extraordinary Lachrymosity and Romantic Imagination of Winston Churchill, *Finest Hour*, Autumn 2016

Rose, Jill, *Nursing Churchill: Wartime Life from the Private Letters of Winston Churchill's Nurse* (Gloucestershire: Amberley Publishing, 2018)

Rowse, A. L., '"There Was Once a Man": A Visit to Chartwell, 1995', The Churchill Project: Hillsdale College, 29 February 2016

Russell, Emily (ed.), *A Constant Heart: The War Diaries of Maud Russell, 1938–1945* (Dorset: The Dovecote Press, 2017)

Salmon, Vanda, unpublished memoir, Churchill College Archives, SALM 2/1

Sandys, Celia, *Chasing Churchill: The Travels of Winston Churchill* (London: HarperCollins, 2003)

Scott, Brough, *Churchill at the Gallop* (London: Racing Post Books, 2017)

Selden, Anthony, *Churchill's Indian Summer: The Conservative Government, 1951–1955* (London: Hodder & Stoughton, 1981)

Shakespeare, Nicholas, *Six Minutes in May: How Churchill Unexpectedly Became Prime Minister* (London: Harvill Secker, 2017)

Shapiro, Gary, 'How Churchill Mobilized the English Language', *New York Sun* (12 June 2012)

Shuckburgh, Evelyn, *Descent to Suez: Diaries 1951–1956* (London: Weidenfeld & Nicolson, 1986)

Singer, Barry, 'Churchill's Smile', *Huffington Post* (11 March 2015)

——, *Churchill Style: The Art of Being Winston Churchill* (New York, Abrams, 2012)

Soames, Mary, *Clementine Churchill: The Revised and Updated Biography* (London: Doubleday, 2002)

—— (ed.), *Speaking for Themselves: The Personal letters of Winston and Clementine Churchill* (London: Black Swan, 1999)

————, *Winston Churchill His Life as Painter* (Boston: Houghton Mifflin Company, 1990)

Stelzer, Cita, *Dinner with Churchill: Policy Making at the Dinner Table* (New York: Pegasus Books, 2012)

Steyn, Richard, *Churchill's Confidant: Jan Smuts, Enemy to Lifelong Friend* (South Africa: Jonathan Ball Publishers, 2017)

Sturdee, Jo, letters, Churchill College Archives Centre at Churchill College, Cambridge

Taylor, A. J. P. et al., *Churchill: Four Faces and the Man* (London: Allen Lane, The Penguin Press, 1969)

Thompson, W. H., *I Was Churchill's Shadow* (London: Christopher Johnson, 1959)

————, *Sixty Minutes with Winston Churchill* (London: Christopher Johnson, 1953)

Thomson, Alistair, 'Four Paradigm Transformations', *The Oral History Review*, Vol. 34, Issue 1 (2007)

Vale, J. A. and J. W. Scadding, *'In Carthage Ruins*: The Illness of Sir Winston Churchill at Carthage, December 1943', *Journal of the Royal College of Physicians of Edinburgh*, Vol. 47, Issue 3, September 2017

Wardell, Michael, 'Churchill's Dagger: A Memoir of La Capponcina', *Finest Hour*, No. 87, Summer 1995

Wheeler-Bennett, Sir John, *Action This Day: Working with Churchill* (London: Macmillan, 1968)

White, Philip, *Our Supreme Task* (New York: Public Affairs, 2012)

Woodward, Jason, 'Eminent Churchillians – Patrick Kinna MBE – "He was sure we would win all along"', *Finest Hour*, No. 115, Summer 2002

Woolner, David B., *The Last 100 Days: FDR at War and Peace* (New York: Basic Books, 2017)

IMAGE CREDITS

Every effort has been made to contact all copyright holders. The publisher will be pleased to correct in future editions any errors or omissions brought to their attention.

1. 'Winston at 9am', cartoon by David Wilson from *Passing* Show, 1920.
2. Advertisement for Mrs Hoster's Secretarial Training College from *The Woman's Leader*, 1922.
3. Churchill at work, photograph by Nat Farbman, 1947. *The LIFE Picture Collection/Getty Images.*
4. Jock VI at Chartwell, 2014. *Keith Larby/Alamy.*
5. Denis Kelly, Gordon Allen, Churchill and Rufus at Chartwell, 1953, photograph by Frank Scherschel. *The LIFE Picture Collection/Getty Images.*
6. Speech notes, annotated by Churchill, 1938. *Churchill Archives Centre, The Papers of Winston S. Churchill [CHAR 9/130D/356]. Reproduced with permission of Curtis Brown, London on behalf of The Estate of Winston S. Churchill and The Sir Winston Churchill Archive Trust. Copyright in the text © The Estate of Winston S. Churchill. Copyright in the reproduction © The Sir Winston Churchill Archive Trust.*
7. Churchill's desk at Chartwell. *National Trust Photographic Library/Andreas von Einsiedel/Bridgeman Images.*
8. Churchill with the 'Sound Scriber', Chartwell, 1946. *Chartwell Booksellers.*
9. Winston S Churchill, portrait by Edwin Arthur Ward, *c.*1900. *Courtesy of Sotheby's.*

10. Grace Hamblin in the 'Factory' at Chartwell, 1966. *PA/TopFoto.*

11. Churchill's office at Chartwell, sketch by Grace Hamblin. *Churchill Archives Centre, The Papers of Grace Hamblin [HAMB 1/6]. © The Estate of Grace Hamblin.*

12. Churchill working on a train, 1941. © IWM [H 10874].

13. Churchill broadcasting from the White House, 1943. *The Print Collector/Getty Images.*

14. The Churchills with John Martin working on a train, 1943. *AP/ Shutterstock.*

15. Marian Holmes in the garden of 10 Downing Street, 1944. *Copyright unknown.*

16. Violet Pearman at the Chateau de l'Horizon, *c.* 1930s. *The Bowyer Collection.*

17. Cecily "Chips" Gemmell, portrait by Winston S. Churchill, *c.* 1952. *Reproduced with permission of Curtis Brown, London. Copyright © Churchill Heritage Ltd.*

18. Jane Portal with Churchill, *c.* 1950s. *Copyright unknown.*

19. Jo Sturdee aboard HMS *Queen Mary*, 1944. © IWM.

20. Kathleen Hill and Churchill on HMS *Prince of Wales*, 1941. © IWM [A 6905].

21. Marian Holmes and Churchill disembarking HMS *Ajax*, 1944. *Fremantle/Alamy.*

22. Lettice Fisher and Churchill, Sussex Square, 1924. © *TopFoto.*

23. Elizabeth Nel at her desk at Chequers, 1940s. From Elizabeth Nel, *Mr Churchill's Secretary*, Hodder & Stoughton, 1958.

24. Kathleen Hill and Churchill, Morpeth Mansions, 1939. *AP/ Shutterstock.*

25. Churchill going down a water slide in the Côte d'Azur. *Churchill Archives Centre, The Papers of Randolph Churchill [RDCH 9/1/28/1]. Reproduced with permission of Curtis Brown, London on behalf of The Estate of Randolph S. Churchill.*

26. Churchill feeding the fish at Chartwell, 1950, photograph by Mark Kauffman. *Time & Life Pictures/Getty Images.*

27. Churchill painting, 1948, photograph by Frank Scherschel. *The LIFE Picture Collection/Getty Images).*

28. Churchill with Colonist II at Newmarket, 1950. *Rex/Shutterstock.*

29. Violet Pearman and Churchill in Rhodes, 1934, photograph by Lady Evelyn Hilda Stuart Moyne. © National Portrait Gallery, London.

30. Elizabeth Gilliat and Jo Sturdee with others at La Mamounia, Marrakesh, 1947. *Churchill Archives Centre, The Papers of Nina, Lady Onslow [ONSL 4A]. Copyright unknown.*

31. Jane Portal in a water taxi with the Churchills, Venice, 1951. *Pictorial Press/Alamy.*

32. "Chips" Gemmell, Lettice Marston Shillingford, Denis Kelly and Evan Davies at Cap d'Ail, France, 1949. *Churchill Archives Centre, The Papers of Evan Davies [EDVS 3/1].*

33. Grace Hamblin riding a camel while on holiday with Patrick Kinna, Tunisia, c. 1964. *Churchill Archives Centre, The Papers of Patrick Kinna [KNNA 3/1].*

34. "Chips" Gemmell with naval escorts aboard a ship at Portsmouth, early 1950s. *Churchill Archives Centre, The Papers of Evan Davies [EDVS 3/2].*

35. Holmes, Sturdee and Layton among Churchill's staff aboard the *Queen Mary*, 1944. © IWM.

36. Marian Holmes, Aboukir RAF base, Egypt, 1945. © IWM [HU 87636].

37 & 38. Identity passes for Lettice Marston while at the Potsdam Conference, 1945. *Churchill Archives Centre, The Papers of Winston S. Churchill [CHUR 3/490E/477a-b]* © Crown copyright.

39. Churchill meets Princess Elizabeth after the death of King George VI, 1952. *TopFoto.*

40. Churchill at the Conservative Party Conference, 1953. *Hulton Archive/Getty Images.*

41. The Churchills' luggage, New York, 1953. *Chartwell Booksellers.*

42. Rufus returning to 10 Downing Street, 1954. *Chartwell Booksellers.*

43. Jane Portal, note to Churchill with her sketch of a crocodile. *Churchill Archives Centre, Other Deposited Collections Relating to Winston Churchill [WCHL 6/54].*

44. Thank-you note from Churchill to Jane Portal. *Churchill Archives Centre, Other Deposited Collections Relating to Winston Churchill [WCHL 6/54]. Reproduced with permission of Curtis Brown, London on behalf of The Estate of Winston S. Churchill.*
45. List made by Jo Sturdee of the contents of a mail bag, 1950. *Churchill Archives Centre [CHUR 1/83].*
46. Churchill leaves 10 Downing Street after his resignation, 1955. *Bettmann Archive/Getty Images.*
47. The author with Jane Portal, now Lady Williams of Elvel, and General David Petraeus at the International Churchill Society Conference, 2017. *Irwin Stelzer.*

Illustrations in the Appendices

p. 312.   Letter from Churchill to Andrew Cruickshank, 10 Dec 1950. *Churchill Archives Centre, The Papers of Winston S. Churchill [CHUR 2/387/23]. Reproduced with permission of Curtis Brown, London on behalf of The Estate of Winston S. Churchill.*

p. 313.   Memorandum from Jane Portal to Churchill, 25 June 1951. *Churchill Archives Centre, The Papers of Winston S. Churchill [CHUR 2/387/22].*

p. 314.   Letter from Churchill to Andrew Cruickshank, 25 June 1951. *Churchill Archives Centre, The Papers of Winston S. Churchill [CHUR 2/387/20]. Reproduced with permission of Curtis Brown, London on behalf of The Estate of Winston S. Churchill.*

p. 315.   Letter from Andrew Cruickshank to Churchill, 27 June 1951. *Churchill Archives Centre, The Papers of Winston S. Churchill [CHUR 2/387/19].*

p. 308–310. Memorandum and draft directive drawn up by the staff of the War Cabinet Joint Typing Pool relating to Operation "Desperate", 9 May 1942. © Imperial War Museum *[Documents.9858, 1–3].*

INDEX

4th Hussars 111
49th Parallel (film, 1941) 206
ABC-1 meetings (1941) 69
Abdication Crisis (1936) 19, 34
Aitken, Max *see* Beaverbrook, Max
   Aitken, 1st Baron
Alanbrooke, Field Marshal Alan
   Brooke, 1st Viscount 158, 278
Alexander, Field Marshal Harold,
   1st Earl of Tunis 87, 90, 110–11,
   157, 160
Allen, Commodore G. R. G. 202
AMB *see* Montague Browne,
   Anthony
American Secret Service 147
Amery, Leo 187
Anderson, Torr 7, 8, 9
Anglo-Iranian Oil Company 182
Annecy 238
Anzio 87
Armistice Day 279
Arnhem 225
Athens 92, 134, 152–6, 159,
   160–1, 300
   Acropolis 155
   Mount Lycabettus 155
Atlas Mountains 153, 214, 276
ATS *see* Auxiliary Territorial Service
Attlee, Clement XV, 83, 127, 134, 163
   and note, 166, 192, 238, 245, 306
Auxiliary Territorial Service (ATS)
   182

Bad Gastein, Austria 57
Balaclava, Battle of 160
Balfour, Arthur 113
Balmoral 251
Bangalore 14n
Baruch, Bernard 5, 218, 225, 255,
   263
Baum, Vicki 280–1
BBC 247, 284
Beaton, Cecil 98
Beaverbrook, Max Aitken, 1st Baron
   19, 56, 59, 115, 172, 188, 190, 212,
   251, 256, 269, 272, 275, 273, 274,
   281, 286
Belted Galloway cattle 24
Berlin 162, 182
   Cumberland House 182n
Berlin Hotel (Baum) 280–1
Berlin, Irving 171
Berlin, Isaiah 171
Bermuda 172, 177, 178, 253, 254–5
Berry, William *see* Camrose,
   William Berry, 1st Viscount
Bevan, Aneurin 43, 256
Bevin, Ernest 66, 93, 164, 224, 245
bezique (card game) 148 and note,
   187, 280, 289
Birley, Mark 204
Birley, Sir Oswald 173, 204
black mollies 204, 311
Black Move (Government
   Evacuation Scheme) (1940) 61

Blenheim Palace 20, 27, 53, 158, 271, 303
Boer War 63, 69, 71n
Bolshoi Ballet 38, 150, 174
Bombay 48
Bonar, Lorraine 118, 119
Bonham Carter, Violet *see* Carter, Violet Bonham
Boulogne 60
Bracken, Brendan 54, 59, 60, 76, 115, 176, 187, 269, 281
Brain, Dr Russell 176, 191, 249–50
Bright, Joan XVII, 97, 105–6, 149, 150, 317, 320
Brighton 85, 93, 203
British Red Cross Aid to Russia Fund 36–7, 40
Broadstairs, Kent 10
Browne, Anthony Montague *see* Montague Browne, Anthony
Browning, Lieutenant General Sir Frederick 'Boy' 225
Bullock (chauffeur) 246, 288
Burgess, Guy 232
Burton, Richard 206
Butler, Josephine 70
Butler, R. A. 'Rab' 222, 223, 241, 243, 250, 253
Butler, Sydney Elizabeth Courtauld 222
Butterfly House (Chartwell) 21

Cabinet Office 100, 101
Cadogan, Alexander 50, 157n
Cairo 37, 77, 86, 92, 158
    Mena House Hotel 161
Cairo Conference (1943) 70, 78, 91
Calcutta 48
Camrose, William Berry, 1st Viscount 115, 117
Canada 5, 206
Canadian Pacific Railway 5
Cancer Research 193

Cap-d'Ail, South of France 172, 188
Carezza 210–11
Carter, Violet Bonham 58, 187, 269, 290
Carthage 36, 86
Casablanca Conference (1943) 11, 79–80, 153, 267, 278
Cassell & Co. (publishers) 57, 239, 265
Castlerosse, Doris 234
Castro, Fidel 120
Chamberlain, Anne 33
Chamberlain, Neville 59, 99, 134, 135, 306
Chandos, Lord 231
Chartwell 4, 5, 6, 7n, 9, 13, 16, 18, 21 and note, 24, 27, 29, 34, 41–2, 44–5, 49, 50, 53, 58, 60, 63, 67, 110, 111, 114, 116, 125, 134, 167, 169, 170, 177, 182, 183, 184, 185, 186, 187, 190, 196, 197, 201, 202, 204, 205, 206, 215, 219, 225, 229, 230, 232, 235, 241, 243, 246 and note, 250, 261, 263, 268, 270, 279, 285, 289, 291, 292–4, 302
Château de l'Horizon, French Riviera 10, 12–13, 52, 208
Cheltenham Ladies College 135
Chequers 18, 57, 61, 62, 72, 92, 99–100, 140, 141, 147, 150, 159, 167, 174, 192, 204, 230, 232, 235, 236, 243, 245, 264, 277–8
Cherwell, Frederick Lindemann, 1st Viscount 11, 179, 187, 191, 215, 230, 261, 268–9, 281
Chief of the Imperial General Staff (CIGS) 99, 158, 278
Christ Church, Oxford 208
Christ, George 240
Christina (yacht) 275, 279
Churchill, Clementine XII, XIII, 100, 172, 219
    Aid to Russia fund 36–41

appoints Hill as early morning
secretary 49
arranges staff toast to Churchill
on his ninetieth birthday 282
at Chartwell 18, 41
attends the Coronation 249
character and description 236,
237, 291
comment on Churchill 267
concerned with intra-staff
differences 209
correspondence with Winston 5,
12, 42, 157–8, 204, 213
fear of gambling 212
health of 280
hires domestic staff 31–2
intervenes on behalf of the
secretaries 169, 170
London flats 29–30, 45, 111
organises present-buying at
Christmas 266
overseas visits 10, 34–40, 42, 86,
102, 103–5, 108, 117, 126, 179,
188, 191–2, 240
protects Churchill from unwanted
visitors 269
reaction to Sutherland portrait
43–4, 256
secretaries to 29–35, 42, 97, 101,
103–4, 140, 216
surrenders lease on Chartwell
21n
takes an interest in the
secretaries 18, 265, 267–8
'tearing-up sessions' 58n
war work 32, 35–40, 109
Churchill College Archives,
Cambridge XI, XVI, 2, 16, 20n,
40, 67, 121, 134, 138, 166, 178,
268n, 317, 319, 320
Churchill College, Cambridge 261
Churchill, Diana see Sandys, Diana
Churchill

The Churchill Documents (Gilbert)
157n
Churchill, Gwendoline 11
Churchill, John see Marlborough,
John Churchill, 1st Duke of
Churchill, John Strange Spencer
'Jack' 31, 76
Churchill, Mary see Soames, Lady
Mary Churchill
Churchill, Randolph (great-
grandson) 282
Churchill, Randolph (son) 10, 86,
91, 93, 162, 208, 269, 275, 290, 297
Churchill, Sarah see Oliver, Sarah
Churchill
Churchill, Winston
'Action This Day' policy 28, 135,
148
becomes Leader of the
Opposition 40–1, 92, 108–9,
111, 163, 166, 167, 191, 224
becomes prime minister again at
age seventy-seven 128–9, 192,
216, 240–1
becomes prime minister in 1940
30, 40, 135–6
as bricklayer 24, 53
buzzing atmosphere surrounding
59, 305–6
celebrates his eightieth birthday
42–3, 192–3, 244n
celebrates his golden wedding
anniversary 193
chaos surrounding his
movements 3, 188–9, 279, 302
character and description 27,
51–2, 60, 73, 77, 78, 92–3,
121–2, 138, 142–3, 156, 204, 220,
223, 224–5, 226, 230–2, 254,
299–300–1, 302–3
comment on bathroom in
Moscow 82–3
comments on Stalin 83–4

continuous shuttling between residences 5, 50, 54, 56–7, 67, 167–8, 185–6, 289

daily routine 227–8, 289–90, 292

death and funeral 164, 193, 282

delivers last major speech in the Commons 257–8

dictating style and locations 26–7, 52, 57, 61, 71, 73–4, 78–9, 80–1, 98–100, 108, 129, 138–9, 139, 142, 146–7, 148, 162, 169–70, 193, 198, 199, 200–1, 216–17, 229, 247, 263–4

dislikes Sutherland's portrait 43–4, 256–7

dislikes talk of suicide 141, 206–7, 304

enjoys company of visitors and friends 44–5, 56, 58–9, 140–1, 186, 187, 269, 271, 274, 290

exchanges his cigar butt for a newspaper 228

finance and commerce 6, 19, 24, 24–5, 51, 58, 115, 211, 236, 239, 291–2

fondness for family 235

Fulton speech 123

has badger skinned and stuffed after road accident 245

hates 'Lili Marlene' tune 214

hates noise when concentrating on work 148, 210–11

health of 13, 16, 44, 54, 80, 86, 88, 144–5, 176–7, 190, 249–51, 253, 279, 279–80, 281, 290, 295–6

impish humour 151, 278–9

interview style 16, 48, 98, 137–8, 166, 183, 196, 222–3, 261, 284

learns of the death of George V 11–12

likes to play card games 148 and note, 187, 280, 289

liking for food and drink 186–7, 217–18, 268, 272, 275–6, 294

lively and imaginative use of vocabulary and punctuation 53, 72, 79, 80, 159, 203 and note, 279, 287–8

love for Chartwell 41–2, 229

love of music and books 63, 145, 150, 280–1, 286–7

love of painting 11, 34, 126, 170, 173, 187, 189, 204, 211, 212, 215, 225–6, 246–7, 272, 275

meets the new queen 129–30, 247

menagerie of 21–4, 61, 67, 170 and note, 203, 204, 205, 229–30, 276–8, 311

near-fatal train accident near Venice 238–9

nude episode with Roosevelt 81

overseas visits 5, 9–13, 25, 27, 34–6, 42, 60, 63, 69–72, 73–5, 80–8, 101–7, 108, 110–11, 116–28, 143–4, 146–8, 149–61, 159, 163–4, 172–5, 178, 179–80, 183, 187–92, 209–16, 238–40, 251, 254–5, 272–6, 294–5

Pol Roger as his favourite drink 177n, 187

problems of moving his bed and bathtub when necessary 171

reads every regional and national newspaper 98

receives many awards and honours 125, 187, 218, 253, 264

regularly watches films 206, 232–4, 246, 270–1, 293

relationship with and expectations of his secretaries 2–4, 6–7, 16–17, 51–2, 55, 58, 62–3, 78, 91–3, 126–7, 141–2, 156, 178, 198–200, 201–2, 218–19, 230–1, 251–2, 262–3, 264–5, 291, 300–1

resigns as prime minister 130–1,
178–9, 204, 257
response to death of George VI
247–8
Secret Session speeches 112 and
note
shares details of his work with
Clementine 32
siren suit worn by 84, 198, 312
suffers from 'Black Dog' depression 18–19, 179–80, 207, 303–4
supplied with clandestine
information 6–9
susceptible to good looks and
wit 234–5
takes an interest in horse-racing
115, 175, 184–5, 185, 293–4
unremitting workload 3, 5, 11,
12, 28, 53–4, 77–8, 79–81, 84,
99–102, 113–14, 116, 118–19,
121–2, 126–8, 139–40, 142–3,
149–50, 152–5, 160, 161, 162,
169–70, 173, 201–2, 215–16,
236–8, 243, 252–3, 266, 273
use of nicknames 18, 178
uses hand muff to keep warm
289
visits casinos in Monte Carlo
212–13
visits FDR's grave 125
Wilderness Years 2, 19, 28
'Great Events of Our Time' 12
A History of the English-Speaking
Peoples 9, 14, 41, 49, 52, 57, 113,
119n, 180, 234, 252, 257, 263,
265, 271, 272, 275, 280
Marlborough: His Life and Times
9, 10, 11, 13, 25–6, 52, 202
The Second World War 9, 169,
230, 239, 304
Story of the Malakand Field
Force 54
'A Testing Time for France' 12

Triumph and Tragedy 252
The World Crisis 1916–1918 10, 58,
113, 251
Churchill, Winston Jnr 93, 235, 237
CIGS see Chief of the Imperial
General Staff
Cinque Ports 288 and note
Clark, Kenneth 256
Clark Kerr, Archibald 83
Clarke, Colonel Frank 116, 117–18
Cold War 131
Colonist II (racehorse) 115, 175, 185
Colville, Jock 3, 23, 61, 62, 75, 86,
102, 135, 138, 145, 148, 154, 155, 156,
172, 179, 234, 238, 241, 248, 249,
250, 251, 254, 255, 275, 278
Coningsby (Disraeli) 251
Conservative Central Office 114,
128, 240
Conservative Party Conferences
176, 203n, 226, 252–3
Control Commission for Germany
182 and note
Copenhagen 127
Fredensborg Palace 127
Frederiksberg Palace 127
Courtauld, Sydney Elizabeth see
Butler, Sydney Elizabeth
Courtauld
Cowles, Virginia 93
Crin Blanc (film, 1953) 233, 246
Crockham Hill Church of England
School 16
Cruikshank, Andrew 311
Cuba 120–1
Cunard, Emerald 20
Cunningham, Admiral John 157
Cyanide in My Shoe (Butler) 70

Daily Express 290
Daily Mail 50
Daily Telegraph 98, 115, 211, 290
Daily Worker 50

Daladier, Édouard 60
D-Day XX, 84, 86, 142, 144
Dam Square Royal Palace,
    Amsterdam 126
Damaskinos Papandreou,
    Archbishop 155
Danish Navy 127
Darlan, Admiral François 60
Davies, Evan 'Bish' 111, 119, 207, 210,
    211
Davis, Godfrey 215
de Gaulle, Charles XV, 200n, 280
Deakin, Mrs 174
Deakin, William 'Bill' 57, 202, 230, 293
Delhi 48
Der Fall des Hauses Stuart und die
    Succession des Hauses Hannover
    (Klopp) 53
Derby, Lord 207
Dickens, Charles 280
Disraeli, Benjamin 251
Ditchley Park, Oxfordshire 56–7
Dixon, Pierson 152
Dodo (bulldog) 22
Dolomites 210
Drummond, Delia Morton 130–1
    and note
Duff, Lady Juliet 269
The Duke's Children (Trollope) 145
Dulles, John Foster 177

Eade, Charles 112n
East Africa 247
Eden, Anthony 44, 76–7, 130, 139,
    151, 152, 179, 197n, 225, 239, 243,
    248, 249, 250, 253, 254, 264,
    269, 276
Eisenhower, Dwight D. 70, 86, 122,
    144, 172, 177, 179, 218, 253–4
Eisenhower, Mamie 122
El Glaoui, Thami 213
Elizabeth II 115, 129–30, 131, 180, 247,
    248

Elizabeth, the Queen Mother 261,
    292n
Elliott, Maxine 10, 13, 52, 208
Epsom Derby 207
Evening Standard 12, 228

Fellowes, Daisy 212
Ferdinand Magellan (train) 122
Ferrari 210
Fielding, Henry 280
First World War 4, 10, 32, 171, 187,
    277, 301
Fish, Mr 21, 54
Fisher, Admiral Sir John 'Jackie' 28
    and note
Florida 121, 117, 228
Floris, Madame 43
Flynn, Errol 240
Foreign Office 40, 50, 93, 182n, 232,
    284
French Foreign Legion 214 and note
Fulton, Missouri 117, 122, 123, 124,
    172

Garden Room Girls 113, 136 and
    note, 166, 216, 241–2, 244, 254,
    269, 276
Gemmell, Cecily 'Chips' 78, 169,
    171n
    archival work at Chartwell 197–8
    birth and background 196
    Churchill's attitude towards
        199–200
    cleans Churchill's paintbrushes
        187, 204, 225
    comment on Hamblin 45
    comments on Churchill 98, 203,
        212–14, 217–20, 300, 304
    hates looking after the tropical
        fish 204
    joins Churchill's secretaries
        196–7
    looks after Rufus II 203, 205

made aware of class barriers 207,
208–9
moves to New York 218
overseas visits 127, 209–16
portrait painted by Churchill
204, 226
recollections of Lord Ismay 207
relationship with Mrs Churchill
237
retains friendship with the
Churchills 218–19
selects films for the Churchills to
watch 206
visits the races 207
working conditions 185, 198–203,
204–5, 215–17
Geneva 238
George V 11, 171, 234
George VI 73, 85, 129, 143, 240, 247
German POWs 206, 233
German-Jewish Aid Committee 57
Germany 6, 7, 19
Ghana High Commission 284
Gibraltar 66
Gilbert, Sir Martin XVI, 2, 6, 7, 14,
25, 79, 152, 157n, 188n, 266, 301
Gilbert, W. S. 150, 281
Gilliatt, Elizabeth 93, 200, 216, 300
appointed secretary to Churchill
166–7, 175–6
arranges for forgotten teddy bear
to be returned 173
arranges shipment of worms 170
birth and background 166
comment on Churchill's eightieth
birthday 176–7
comment on Edith Watson 135
comment on Sutherland portrait
43
comments on Churchill's health
176, 190, 250
as godmother to Portal's son
244n

leaves Churchill's employment
175, 180, 261
mix-ups in arrangements 170–1
notes arrival of crocus bulbs 22–3
overseas visits 126, 172–5, 178,
179–80, 187, 190
perks working for Churchill
171–2, 174–5
provides Churchill with hot
water bottle 168
rides one of Churchill's horses
185
working conditions and
locations 112, 113, 115, 125,
128–9, 130, 167–70, 183, 244
Gilliatt, Sir William 166, 175, 223
Giraudier, Antonio 120
Girl Guides 48
Giselle (ballet) 150
goats 23
golden orfe (fish) 170 and note,
203
The Golden Warrior (Muntz) 286
Graebner, Walter 201, 215–16
Graham, Monica 265, 286
Graham-Dixon, Leslie 115
Granville, Christine 70
Great Depression 2
Greece 134, 152–6, 159, 160–1
Greenock, Scotland 143, 148
Grigg, Sir Edward 37

Haakon VII 190
Halifax, Lady 'Aunt Dorothy' 124–5
Halifax, Lord 124, 125
Halifax, Nova Scotia 146
Hamblin, Grace 2, 6, 169, 285n
awarded the OBE 45
becomes Clementine's secretary
29–35, 42, 101, 110, 111, 237
becomes godmother to Hill's
granddaughter 30n
birth and family background 16

in charge of financial management and brick supply 24–5,
198
comment on Holmes 139
comment on Sutherland portrait
43–4, 257
description of Churchill's eightieth
birthday party 42–3, 44
dictation as main job 25–6
final years and death 45
given responsibility for
Churchill's menagerie 21–4
helps with moves into and out of
London 28–31, 40–1, 42, 111
helps to look after Rufus II 230,
277
helps to organise dinner at
Chartwell 268
hires domestic staff 31–2
lack of knowledge and
experience 20–1
manages Chartwell 289, 291
nicknamed 'Hambone' 18
overseas visits 34–40, 42, 63, 86
relationship with the Churchills
32–4, 45
working conditions 16–20, 25–8,
29–33, 41–2, 54, 63
Hamilton, Emma 157
Hamlet (Shakespeare) 206
Hansard 244
Hardy, Robert 244n
Harriman, Averell 66, 109
Harris, Dr Robert 122, 123
Harrow School 71
Harvey, Mr (valet) 215
Hastings Winkle Club 292n
Havana 120
Hotel Nacional 120
Hawkey, Sir James 3, 4
Heath, Edward 'Ted' 269, 290
Henley, Sylvia 58, 290
Henry V (film, 1944) 145n

Hepburn, Katherine 206
Heyer, Georgette 280
Hill, Georgina XVI, 48, 30, 320
Hill, Kathleen 21, 30 and note, 38,
71, 72, 99, 100
becomes permanent secretary to
Churchill 4, 48–9
birth, marriage and divorce 48
briefs Kinna on work
expectations 72
Churchill's treatment of 51–2, 62,
122, 300, 303
close friendship with Hamblin 30
and note
death of 63
discretion of 55–6, 62–3
health of 68, 78
helps hire domestic staff 31, 50
ingenuity and forethought 54–5,
57–8
interviews prospective secretaries
96, 97, 166, 167, 182
joins the Chequers Trust 63, 110,
111, 183, 244–5
night train adventure 60–1
overseas visits 60, 63, 102, 118–19,
144
receives the MBE 56, 63
variety of jobs done by 50–1,
53–5, 56, 58
working conditions and hours
49–54, 59–60, 61, 109–10, 113,
126, 140
Hill, Richard 63
Hitler, Adolf 36, 147, 247, 252, 303
HMS *Ajax* 153–4, 155–7, 161
HMS *Codrington* 62
HMS *Orion* 159
HMS *Prince of Wales* 62, 72–3, 157n
HMS *Repulse* 62
Hoare, Oliver 157n
Hodge, Alan 186, 273
Hollis, General Sir Leslie 70

Holmes, Marion 92
  appointed secretary to Churchill
    137 0
  attends Churchill's funeral 164
  birth and background 134
  Churchill's attitude towards 138–9,
    141–2, 156, 157–8, 300, 301
  comment on Mrs Churchill 140
  comments on security
    arrangements 147–8, 150–1
  comments on Truman 162–3
  description of 139
  experiences of Churchill in his
    bedroom and bathroom 146,
    148, 150, 153
  joins Downing Street typists
    134–5, 137
  marriages and death 164
  memories of Christmas en route
    to Athens 152–4
  nicknamed 'Miss Sherlock' 142,
    178
  overseas visits 35, 102, 105, 143–4,
    146–8, 149–61, 163–4, 174
  private moments with Churchill
    158–9
  working conditions 139–43,
    151–2, 161–2
  works for Attlee 163–4
Home Office 108
Hotel Berlin (novel) 280, 281
Hopkins, Harry 79, 141n, 147
Hoster, Mrs 96, 196, 260, 284
House of Commons 43, 44, 48, 52,
  79, 108, 116, 128, 129, 137, 148–9,
  168, 176, 183, 185, 193, 200, 224,
  226, 238, 244, 253, 255–6, 257, 266,
  270, 281, 288, 289, 291
House of Lords 43
Howells, Roy 22, 288
Hozier, Lady Blanche 212
Hughes, Detective Inspector Bill 151
  and note

Hyde Park house, New York 38, 85,
  89, 104–5, 122, 125, 134, 146, 147,
  160

Independence (aeroplane) 173
India 19, 21
An Infamous Army (Heyer) 280
İnönü, İsmet 71
Intelligence Corps 69
Ismay, Hastings, 1st Baron 52, 83, 90,
  93, 97, 104, 113, 163, 169, 182, 187,
  207, 230, 269

Jacob, General Sir Ian 62n, 83
Jamaica 130, 172–3
James Woodward & Sons
  (gunmaker) 55
Jenkins, Roy 4
Jinnah, Mohammed Ali 167
Jock I (cat) 23, 278
Jock VI (cat) 23 and note
Jockey Club 207
Johnson, Mabel 37n
Jutland, Battle of (1916) 145n

Keegan, John 299
Kelly, Denis 50, 114, 191, 197, 273
Kenya 129
Keynes, John Maynard 231
Khrushchev, Nikita 249, 294
Kinematograph Rental Society 271
King George V (battleship) 69
Kinna, Patrick 157n, 166, 167, 199, 300
  agrees to work for Churchill 75–6
  assigned to the Intelligence
    Corps 60
  birth and family background 67,
    68–9
  character and description 67–8
  as Churchill's only male short-
    hand typist 66–7, 75–6
  comments on American food
    74, 81

death of 94
health of 77
impressions of Churchill 73–4,
    77, 91–3
meets many famous politicians
    and military men 88–91
overseas visits 69–72, 73–5, 80–8,
    105, 106, 143
recommended for an MBE 94
working conditions 78–81
works as secretary to Bevin 93
Kinna, Captain Thomas 68–9
Kipling, Rudyard 280
Kirkwood (valet) 268
Kissinger, Henry 147
Klop (paper fastener) 72, 152, 227
Klopp, Onno 53
Korda, Alexander 101, 157n, 206,
    212, 232, 233–4, 271

La Capponcina, South of France
    172, 173, 190, 211, 212, 234, 251,
    272, 273–5, 287
La Pausa, South of France 275
Labour Party 40, 191, 224, 238, 240
Lac des Neiges, Laurentian
    Mountains 85
The Lady 31
Ladysmith 68–9
Lake Garda 210
    Grand Hotel Gardone Riviera 210
Lake Geneva 173, 187
Lamb, William *see* Melbourne,
    William Lamb, 2nd Viscount
Lamont, Miss 100
Land Girls 32
Landemare, Mrs (cook) 50, 88, 101,
    111, 186, 268
Lascelles, Sir Alan 171, 250
Lawrence of Arabia (film, 1962) 234
    and note
Layton, Elizabeth *see* Nel, Elizabeth
    Layton

Lean, David 234n
Lee, Jennie 43, 256
Lehrman, Lewis 231
Leigh, Vivien 270
Lena (maid) 110, 111, 120
Life magazine 212, 218
'Lili Marlene' (song) 214
Lincoln, Abraham 231
Lindemann, Sir Frederick *see*
    Cherwell, Frederick Lindemann,
    1st Viscount
Liverpool 66
Lloyd George, David 49n
Lloyds Bank 49
'Locksley Hall' (Tennyson) 159
Lolita (Nabokov) 286–7
London 12, 27
    Admiralty House 29, 40, 55, 59,
        60, 135, 292
    The Annexe 86, 101, 102, 110
    Buckingham Palace 107–8, 240
    Cabinet War Rooms 94
    Claridge's 93, 109–10
    Downing Street 30, 31, 40–1, 42,
        86, 96, 99, 100, 102, 108, 129,
        134, 135–7, 143, 159, 175–6, 192,
        216, 240, 241–4, 248, 253, 302
    Fortnum & Mason 120
    Harrods 61, 170n
    Hyde Park Gate 41, 44, 111–12,
        114, 116, 125, 129, 166, 167, 183,
        185, 186, 187, 192, 196, 215, 216,
        222, 223–5, 226, 227–8, 232,
        240–1, 260, 270, 279, 284–5,
        289, 292, 296
    Hyde Park Hotel 260
    Knightsbridge Barracks 185
    Middlesex Hospital 269
    Morpeth Mansions 5, 7n, 13, 27,
        49–50, 51
    Pimlico 30
    St James's Park 162
    St Paul's Cathedral 164

Turnbull & Asser, Jermyn Street 25
Westminster Gardens 110
London Library 280
London Zoo 204, 277
Lord Kitchener (film project) 234
Love, Judy *see* Rowan, Judy Love
Luce, Clare Boothe 234–5
Luce, Henry 212, 219
Lullenden 277
Lumberjills 32
Lytton, Lady Pamela Plowden 187, 269

McGowan, Norman 215, 238–9
Macintyre, Ben 84
Macmillan, Harold 153, 290
Madeira 126–7
  Reid's Hotel 126
Malenkov, Georgy 177
Malta 159
Margaret, Princess 250
Margate 176
Margate (cat) 253
Marina, Princess, Duchess of Kent 27
Marlborough, Charles Spencer-
  Churchill, 9th Duke of 16, 54
Marlborough, Gladys Spencer-
  Churchill, Duchess of 56
Marlborough, John Churchill, 1st
  Duke of 25–6, 202
Marrakesh 36, 63, 86–7, 127, 172, 174,
  186, 209, 211, 213, 214, 215, 246,
  275
  La Mamounia 11–12, 87, 174, 213,
  275
  Villa Taylor 88
Marseilles 161
Marsh, Sir Edward 9, 50
Marston, Lettice 113, 211, 265, 286
  appointed secretary to Churchill
  182, 183
  birth and background 182
  Churchill's attitude towards
  184–5

comment on Churchill's health
  190
comment on Churchill's
  paintings 187
comment on food and drink
  186–7
comment on Ismay 207
helps out on Churchill's ninetieth
  birthday 282
marriage and death 193
overseas visits 128, 173, 187–92,
  210, 238
rides one of Churchill's horses
  185
working conditions and locations
  115, 125, 183–6, 188–9, 192–3
Martin, John 70, 74, 75, 136–7, 142,
  146, 261, 277–8
Massachusetts Institute of
  Technology (MIT) 172
Maturin, Gillian 180, 261, 262, 267,
  281
Mayfair Secretarial College 96
Medina 213
Meiklejohn, Robert 66, 67
Melbourne, William Lamb, 2nd
  Viscount 248
Menelaus, King 255n
Miami 82, 116, 117–20
Middle East 10, 23
The Mikado (Gilbert & Sullivan) 150
Milbanke, Sir John 71 and note
Ministry of Health 108
Ministry of Information 232
Minto, Sheila 241–2
MIT *see* Massachusetts Institute of
  Technology
Moir, Mr (solicitor) 115
Molotov, Vyacheslav 84, 106, 149
Molotov–Ribbentrop Pact (1941) 36
Moltrasio 110–11
Molyneux, Edward 251, 273
Monet, Claude 205

Montagu, Venetia Stanley 58, 187
Montague Browne, Anthony 45,
    260, 269, 275, 284–5, 289, 294,
    320
Monte Carlo 208, 212, 294–5
    Hotel de Paris 211, 294, 295
Montgomery, Field Marshal
    Bernard, 1st Viscount
    Montgomery of Alamein 90–1,
    222, 269, 290, 292n
Moore, Charles 136n
Moran, Charles Wilson, 1st Baron
    58–9, 80n, 86, 111, 144, 190, 212,
    249, 253, 254, 269, 295, 317
Morning Post 69
Morocco 11–12, 36, 63, 86–7, 88, 127,
    172, 174, 211, 213, 215, 246, 275
Morton, Delia *see* Drummond,
    Delia Morton
Morton, Desmond 58
Moscow 38, 82, 149–51, 174
    Kremlin 38, 83–4
    Red Square 39
    State Villa No.7 82
Mott-Radclyffe, Charles 74, 75
Mount, Ferdinand 288
Mountbatten, Louis, Earl 236–7
Mulberry Harbours 288
Muntz, Hope 286
Munuswamy (servant) 14n
Murray, Edmund 26n
Murray, Sergeant 215

Nabokov, Vladimir 286–7
Naples 87, 152, 156, 157, 158
    Villa Emma 157
    Villa Rivalta 157
National Health Service (NHS) 43
National Liberal Party 240
National Service (No.2) Act (1941)
    66
National Trust 21 and note, 45
Neal, Miss 2, 10

Nel, Elizabeth Layton 161
    comment on how to dress 97
    comments on Churchill 24, 141,
        143, 151
    engagement and move to South
        Africa 110, 111
    overseas visits 63, 101, 102, 105,
        106, 111, 147, 149, 151, 152, 154,
        159–60, 174, 175
    working conditions 17, 68, 99,
        100, 110, 141
    worries about Churchill's health
        155
    *Winston Churchill by His
        Personal Secretary* 17
Nelson (cat) 61, 277–8
Nelson, Horatio 157
New York 117, 172, 218, 255
Newmarket 272n
News of the World 11–12
Niagara Falls 146
Normandy Campaign 144
North Atlantic Treaty (1949) 224
Northolt, Middlesex 152
Notre Dame School, Cobham 134

Oberon, Merle 212, 234
OECD *see* Organisation for
    Economic Cooperation and
    Development
Official Secrets Act 69, 138, 197
Oliver, Sarah Churchill 10, 23, 86,
    91, 106, 111, 159, 174, 209, 235, 290
Oliver, Vic 174
Olympic Airways 275
Onassis, Aristotle 272 and note, 275,
    278, 294
Onslow, (William) Arthur, 6th Earl
    of 124, 131
'Operation Desperate' 35, 307
Operation Overlord (1944) *see*
    D-Day
Operation Torch (1942) 82

Organisation for Economic
    Cooperation and Development
    (OECD) 284
Orkney Islands 60
Osborne, June 290
Oslo, University of 190
The Other Club, London 44, 193,
    245, 258, 272, 277, 282
O'Toole, Peter 269

Palliser novels (Trollope) 251n
Paris 12, 60, 69, 188, 200n
    Ritz Hotel 60
Parliamentary Private Secretary
    (PPS) 54 and note, 55
Parmiter, H. F. 22, 23
Parsons, Jane 276
Pearl Harbor 80
Pearman, Violet
    character and description 7–9
    death of 2, 14
    difficulties in coping with
        workload 3–4
    health of 6–7, 13–14, 17, 51
    interviews Grace Hamblin 16
    length of service 2
    'miraculous' filing system 58
    overseas visits 9–13, 27
    relationship with Churchill 2–3,
        300
    seeks new post away from
        Churchill 3
    variety of chores performed by
        5–6, 52
Peck, John 164
Penman, Mary 14, 212
Phineas Finn (Trollope) 145
pigs 24, 203, 277
Pim, Captain 144
Piraeus Harbour 153
Pitblado, David 248, 254
Placentia Bay, Newfoundland
    69–70, 74, 80, 246

Plowden, Pamela see Lytton, Lady
    Pamela Plowden
Plummer, Major General William
    120
Pol-Roger, Madame Odette 177 and
    note
Poland 107
Port Lympne, Kent 56, 126
Portal, Air Chief Marshal Charles
    'Peter' 222, 223, 230
Portal, Jane 169, 199, 200, 216, 311
    appointed secretary to Churchill
        222–3
    comment on Giraudier 120
    comment on Sutherland portrait
        43, 256–7
    comments on Churchill 51–2,
        223, 224–5, 227–8, 230–2, 234,
        235, 247–52, 254, 300–1
    family background 135, 222
    finds picture of crocodile for
        Churchill to paint 246–7
    fondness for Mrs Churchill 236,
        237
    helps to look after Rufus II
        229–30
    helps to select films for Saturday
        night showings 232–3
    listens in on Churchill's
        telephone conversations
        232
    marriage to Baron Williams of
        Elvel 258, 261
    nicknamed 'The Portal' 178
    overseas visits 128, 191, 238–40,
        251, 254–5
    witnesses Churchill's meeting
        with Princess Elizabeth
        247–8
    working conditions and
        responsibilities 128–9, 223–4,
        225–6, 228–9, 237–8, 241–2,
        243–5, 246, 247–8, 257–8

Potsdam Conference (1945) 109, 134, 162–4, 182, 207
Pound, Ezra 131
Pownall, General Sir Henry 202, 206, 215, 219–20
PPS *see* Parliamentary Private Secretary
Principal Private Secretaries 36, 45, 70, 74, 99, 124, 136, 141, 145, 146, 152, 171, 175, 177, 203, 241, 245, 248, 250, 254, 277, 320
Private Secretaries 3, 55, 66, 68, 69–70, 75–7, 79, 84, 90, 92, 99, 100, 106, 110, 113, 137, 139, 140, 142, 162, 166, 176, 216, 265, 284
Pugh, Doreen
   appointed secretary to Churchill 180, 260–2
   awarded an MBE 282
   comments on Churchill 98, 262, 278–82, 300, 303
   comments on Churchill's menagerie 276–8
   comments on meals 268, 269–70
   helps choose films for the Churchills to watch 270–1, 293
   overseas visits 272–6, 294
   recalls loyalty of secretaries 262–3
   recollections of friends and visitors 269, 271
   requests three-week holiday 267–8
   witnesses Churchill's decline 279–82
   working conditions and responsibilities 130n, 262, 263–7, 268, 280, 291
Pugh, Mrs (nurse) 144, 145

Quebec 34–5, 63, 101–4, 116–17, 134, 143–6, 160
   The Citadel 103, 146
   Hotel Chateau Frontenac 103, 146

Quebec Conference (codename QUADRANT) (1943) 34, 84, 85, 101, 117
Quebec Conference (Octagon meeting) (1944) 63, 101, 143, 148–9

RAF *see* Royal Air Force
Red Army 38, 82, 150
Red Cross 36–7
REME *see* Royal Electrical and Mechanical Engineers
Reuters 260, 263
Reves, Emery 115, 117, 205, 275
Richmond, Virginia 122
RMS *Queen Elizabeth* 117, 211n, 218, 255
RMS *Queen Mary* 34–5, 68, 84, 102–3, 144–6, 147–8, 156, 172, 211n
Rob Roy (Scott) 280
Robbie (dog) 277
Roberts, Andrew 135, 213, 234
Roosevelt, Anna 106
Roosevelt, Eleanor 33, 80, 81, 89, 105, 146, 147, 236
Roosevelt, Franklin D. XV, 11, 38, 69, 70, 73, 75, 79, 80, 81, 84, 85, 89, 101, 104, 105, 107, 122, 123, 125, 134, 143, 145, 146, 147, 152, 153, 156, 157, 159, 163, 170, 196, 232, 246, 267, 301, 304, 305
Rose (butler) 268
Rostov-on-Don 40
Rota (lion) 277
Rowan, Judy Love 84–5
Rowan, Sir Leslie 84, 90, 137, 159
Royal Air Force (RAF) 8, 34, 163, 188, 192, 295
Royal Electrical and Mechanical Engineers (REME) 37
Royal Navy 70, 154
Rufus I (poodle) 22, 203n, 277
Rufus II (poodle) 22, 203, 205, 215, 229–30, 246, 253, 277, 288

St Benedict's School, Ealing 164
St Martin's Church, Bladon 45
Saki Field, Crimean Peninsula 105
Salmon, Vanda 18, 97, 175, 223, 225
Saltwood Castle, Kent 256
Samothrace 160
Sandys, Diana Churchill 10, 110, 208–9, 276
Sandys, Duncan 110, 208–9
Sargent, John Singer 225
Sassoon, Sir Philip 56, 126
Sawyers, Frank (valet) 11, 50, 51, 74, 77, 79, 87–8, 106, 110, 111, 116, 118, 121, 123, 127, 141, 148, 150, 151, 158, 187
Scadding, Dr John Guyett 86
Schwab, Charles 5
Scobie, General Ronald 153
Scotland Yard 214n
Scott, Dr 16
Scott, Sir Walter 280, 286
Seal, Eric 142
Second World War 20, 69, 107, 127, 182, 199, 214, 233, 277–8, 288, 302, 304
Secret Circle 16, 99, 205, 238, 278
Secret Session Speeches 112 and note, 168
Shakespeare, William 206
Shearburn, Mary 60 and note
Shillingford, Robert 193
Shuckburgh, Evelyn 248
Simpson, Mrs Wallis see Windsor, Wallis Simpson, Duchess of
Skymaster aircraft 152, 153, 156, 163
Smokey (Persian cat) 277–8
Smuts, Field Marshal Jan 89, 225, 236–7
Snelling, Catherine 280
   appointed secretary to Churchill 284
   chooses books for Churchill to read 286
   comments on Churchill 235, 291–2, 295–7, 300
   comments on friends and visitors 290
   helps to select films for the Churchills to watch 271, 293
   makes sure Churchill is warm enough 289
   overseas visits 294–5
   receives prize money from a horse race 293–4
   stays on after Churchill's death 296
   working conditions and responsibilities 284–6, 287–9, 290–2
Soames, Christopher 115, 175, 187, 205, 249, 251, 290
Soames, Lady Mary Churchill XIII, 29, 44, 57, 84, 162, 187, 235, 238, 249, 251, 282
Soames, Rupert 235
Sophocles, Ajax 156
South of France 7, 25, 34, 52, 172, 174, 188, 208, 234, 253, 272–5, 279, 294–5
Southampton 144
Southwick Manor, Hampshire 144
Soviet Union 36–9, 85
Spears, General Sir Edward 267
Special Branch 119, 188, 288
The Spectator 153
Spencer-Churchill, Charles see Marlborough, Charles Spencer-Churchill, 9th Duke of
Spencer-Churchill, Gladys see Marlborough, Gladys Spencer-Churchill, Duchess of
Spetchley Park, Worcestershire 61
Spicer, James 164
SS Aguila 66
SS Franconia 160
Stalin, Joseph XVII, 38, 70, 77, 82, 83, 84, 85, 89, 106, 109, 134, 138, 143, 149, 150, 151, 154, 159, 174, 221, 249, 301, 304

Stalingrad, Battle of (1942) 82, 85
Stanley, Venetia *see* Montagu, Venetia Stanley
State of the Union (film, 1948) 205–6
Stenhouse, Margaret 'Mags' 96, 135, 246
Stevenson, Frances 49n
Stevenson, Robert Louis 280
Strand Magazine 25
Stratocruiser (aeroplane) 255
Sturdee, Nina Edith 'Jo' 38, 169, 174, 197, 199, 200, 201, 216, 238, 284
    accompanies Churchill on his British campaign trips 128
    administrative competence and responsibilities 111–12, 114–15, 116, 117, 182, 224, 225
    appointed secretary to Churchill 96–7
    awarded the MBE 131
    bets on Churchill's horse 115
    birth and background 96
    celebrates twenty-first birthday in Quebec 103
    comment on Fulton 123
    comment on Gemmell 204
    comment on ironing clothes 104
    comment on Roosevelt's health 105
    comment on Truman 122, 163
    comments on Lady Halifax 124–5
    death of 131
    description of Kinna 67–8
    impressions and memories of Churchill 98, 100, 108, 119, 121–2, 129–30, 300
    interviews secretaries 196, 222, 260
    marriage to Earl of Onslow 131
    memories of VE Day 107–8
    overseas visits 101–7, 110–11, 116–28, 159, 183, 189, 215
    refuses to use early electric typewriter 101
    resigns but continues to help when needed 130–1
    sprains her ankle 219–20
    working conditions 97–101, 108–10, 113–14, 118–19, 121–2, 129
Suez 264
Sullivan, Sir Arthur 150, 281
Sunday Express 3
Surf Club, Miami 119 and note
Sutherland, Graham 43, 177, 256
Swan Lake 38
Switzerland 172
Syracuse, Sicily 179, 180, 257, 260, 261
    Grand Hotel Villa Politi 179

Tangier 12
Tango (cat) 23
Taylor, A. J. P. 257
Teheran 149
Teheran Conference (1943) 70, 85
Tennyson, Alfred, Lord 159
That Hamilton Woman (film, 1941) 157 and note
Thompson, Commander 'Tommy' 66, 99, 106, 146, 160
Thompson, Walter 26 and note, 60n, 61, 300, 305–6
Time magazine 212
Time-Life 211 and note, 239
The Times 50, 98
Tinehir 214
Toby (budgie) 243, 276–7, 288
Tom Jones (Fielding) 280
Townsend, Peter 250
Tracy, Spencer 205–6
the Treasury 134
Tree, Nancy 57
Tree, Ronald 57
Trollope, Anthony 145, 251n
Truman, Bess XV, 121n
Truman, Harry S. 38, 113, 117, 120, 121n, 123, 162–3, 172, 172–3

Tube Alloys (code for atom bomb) 85

Tunisia 86

Turf Club, London 238

Uganda 21

United Nations 107

United States 5, 172, 183, 206

USS *Augusta* 157n

USS *Quincy* 159

Vale, Dr J. A. 86

VE Day (8 May, 1945) 39, 107

Vedel, Admiral 127

Venice 128, 191–2, 238–40
    Excelsior Hotel 191, 239

Victoria, Queen 248

Viking Ships Museum, Oslo 190

Villa Choisi, Lake Geneva 187

Villa delle Rose, Lake Como 11

WAFS *see* Women's Auxiliary
    Ferrying Squadron

Walker, Steve 164

Walter (butler) 209, 218

War Cabinet Secretariat 267

Washington DC 69, 72, 80, 81, 82,
    117, 120, 122, 124, 126, 172, 255
    British Embassy 118, 124, 125,
        126, 232
    White House 80, 86, 121n, 232,
        255, 267

Watson, Edith 135, 136, 143, 166, 167

Welby, Justin, Archbishop of
    Canterbury 244n

Wells, Somerset 192

Westerham 170, 200
    Kings Arms Hotel 183
    Over the Way (cottage) 196
    Pitts Cottage 183

Westerham Library 280

Westminster College, Fulton
    (Missouri) 117, 122, 123

Whitby, Brigadier Lionel 144–5

Whyte, Miss 29

Wilhelmina, Queen 125

Williams, Charles, Baron Williams
    of Elvel 258

Williams, George 118, 119

Wilson, Charles *see* Moran, Charles
    Wilson, 1st Baron

Wilson, David 303

Winant, John 140

Windsor, Edward, Duke of 69, 147,
    188

Windsor, Wallis Simpson, Duchess
    of 69, 188

Women's Auxiliary Ferrying
    Squadron (WAFS) 244

Women's Royal Naval Service
    (WRNS) 66, 74, 84, 244

Wood, Charles C. 'Mr Literary
    Wood' 9, 24n, 239

Wood, Mr 'Accounts' 24 and note

Woodford, Essex 185, 263, 288, 296

WRNS *see* Women's Royal Naval
    Service

Wuthering Heights (film, 1939) 293

Yalta
    Sanatorium A Corpus I 107
    Sanatorium B Corpus I 106 and
        note
    Vorontsov Palace 106, 160

Yalta Conference (1945) 105–7, 134,
    147, 159

Young Women's Christian
    Association (YWCA) 37

YWCA *see* Young Women's
    Christian Association

Zurich 173, 187